1968, JAN 21: Failed North Korean attempt to assassinate South Korean president in Blue House Raid; JAN 23: North Korean navy seizes U.S.S. *Pueblo;* OCT–DEC: Over 100 N. Korean commandos land to incite guerrilla warfare along the coast between the cities of Samcheok and Uljin, South Korea.

1969, MARCH: N. Korean infiltration in Jumunjin, S. Korea; JUNE: North Korean infiltration at Daeheuksando, South Korea.

1974, NOV: Discovery of first North Korean tunnel under the DMZ.

1975: Discovery of second North Korean tunnel under the DMZ; SEPT: North Korean infiltration in Gochang, South Korea.

1978: Discovery of third North Korean tunnel under the DMZ.

1979, OCT: Pro-democracy movements in the cities of Pusan and Masan, South Korea.

1980, MAY: South Korean troops' crackdown on pro-democracy civilian uprising in Kwangju leads to a massacre.

1987: South Korea establishes a democracy with vigorously contested elections.

1990: Discovery of fourth North Korean tunnel under the DMZ.

1994: N. Korea pledges to abandon its nuclear program in exchange for energy assistance and oil.

1996, SEPT: N. Korean infiltration in Gangneung, S. Korea.

1999, JUNE 15: North and South Korea clash in maritime battle west of the DMZ.

2000, JUNE 13–15: Inter-Korean summit.

2002, JUNE 29: North and South Korea clash in maritime battle west of the DMZ; OCT: U.S. uncovers evidence that N. Korea has program to enrich uranium (used in nuclear weapons) and U.S. halts oil shipments to N. Korea; N. Korea expels UN weapons inspectors and reopens its key nuclear facility at Yongbyon.

2003, JAN: N. Korea withdraws from the nuclear nonproliferation treaty; FEB: Pyongyang reactivates its nuclear program and North Korean leader Kim Jong Il verbally threatens the United States; APRIL: N. Korea claims possession of nuclear weapons; AUG 27: Six-nation meeting begins in Beijing, China, to discuss ending standoff about N. Korea nuclear weapons program; SEPT 30: N. Korea's vice foreign minister, Choe Su Hon, states that in order to de-nuclearize the Korean Peninsula there must be a fundamental change in U.S. policy toward his nation.

MAY 12: General Matthew Ridgway accepts appointment in European Command and General Mark Clark succeeds him as United Nations Commander.

MARCH 5: Soviet Union dictator Josef Stalin dies.

NOV 4: United States elects President Dwight D. Eisenhower.

APRIL: Savage battle at Pork Chop Hill.

JULY 27: Armistice Agreement signed by United Nations Command (UNC), the Democratic People's Republic of Korea (DPRK), and China—South Korea never signed.

SEPT–OCT: Brutal battles at Heartbreak Ridge.

| 1952 | 1953 | 1954 | 1955 | 1956–2003 |

APRIL: LDS member, Merlo Pusey, awarded Pulitzer Prize.

Less than 900 full-time missionaries set apart.

Sponsor Corps unit established at BYU.

JAN: Ezra Taft Benson begins service as Secretary of Agriculture under Pres. Eisenhower.

OCT: Pres. Hilton Robertson installed as Far East Mission President.

Pres. Hilton Robertson released as Far East Mission President.

AUG: Elder Joseph Fielding Smith, President of the Quorum of the Twelve Apostles, dedicates Korea for the preaching of the gospel.

AUG: Elder Harold B. Lee, Committee Chairman for the LDS Servicemen's Committee, visits the servicemen and reports the progress of the Church in Korea.

1956: First full-time missionaries begin work in Korea.

1960: Elder Gordon B. Hinckley visits South Korea for the first time.

196?: Korean Mission founded.

1967: Book of Mormon published in the Korean language.

1973: Seoul Korea Stake organized by Pres. Spencer W. Kimball.

1985, DEC: Seoul Korea Temple dedicated by Pres. Gordon B. Hinckley.

...st of fire ...ng.

...EPT: LDS ...ember, ...olleen ...utchins, ...rowned Miss ...merica.

D1443650

SAINTS

AT WAR

KOREA AND VIETNAM

Published by Covenant Communications, Inc.
American Fork, Utah

Printed in Canada
First Printing: November 2003

10 09 08 07 06 05 04 03   10 9 8 7 6 5 4 3 2 1

ISBN 1-59156-340-2

SAINTS

AT WAR

KOREA AND VIETNAM

ROBERT C. FREEMAN AND DENNIS A. WRIGHT

DEDICATION

As we approach publication of *Saints at War: Korea and Vietnam,* our nation is embroiled in yet another conflict in the world. Once again American lives are being placed at risk in distant lands. As these vigilant ambassadors of freedom stand guard over the liberties we all enjoy, we pay tribute to them and to their predecessors.

This book is specifically dedicated to Latter-day Saints who served in either the Korean or Vietnam Wars. In a general way, it is also dedicated to Church members who have served in the military at any time, be it in times of war or peace. Each of our fathers have worn the uniform of their nation proudly—one in a time of relative peace and the other during World War II. We are justly proud of them, and honor tens of thousands of other Latter-day Saints like them.

Recently, a veteran of the Korean War, Don A. George, wrote to us regarding his life since his wartime service. "Now it is fifty years down the road and my Korean War experiences are still very much a part of my life. I have been ruled 100% disabled by the Veteran's Administration doctors because of my Meniers' disease and my deafness. I have less than 10% hearing left in my right ear and my left ear has been deaf for twenty years or more. The tinnitus has never left me for a single day and my attacks of vertigo have subsided some in recent years. My head still has the pressure and unpleasantness that I've had for most of my life since the Korean incident. Headaches and pressure are my constant companions. My stability is nonexistent; I sometimes stagger like a drunken sailor. I walk with my arm around my wife to keep from staggering too much, but even then she thinks that I am trying to knock her down. Would I do it again? In a heartbeat! I love my country, and I will always be a patriotic citizen. May God bless this country with a never-ending supply of patriotic young men to come to her aid in times of need."

Of those who sacrifice in times of war it can truly be said, "All gave some, some gave all." A signpost outside a World War II military cemetery in Kohima, India, echoes the sacrificing soldier's plea, "When you go back, tell them for your tomorrow we gave our today." Our sincere hope is that as we live our "tomorrows," we will hold the sacrifice of the faithful Latter-day Saint servicemen and women in sacred remembrance.

ACKNOWLEDGMENTS

The success of the first *Saints at War* volume encouraged us to expand the project by inviting the LDS veterans of the Korean and Vietnam Wars to participate. The Korean and Vietnam veterans were enthusiastic in their response. What a great experience it was to interview these wonderful Latter-day Saints, read their accounts, and review their photographs. As with the first project that focused on the LDS World War II veterans, we soon found that we could not succeed without a great deal of help. Veterans Virgil Kovalenko, Roan McClure, and many others stepped forward to provide excellent help with gathering and organizing material. These veterans also read the manuscript drafts and provided excellent suggestions and insights that improved the accuracy and clarity of the accounts.

Don Norton, our mentor in collecting LDS veteran accounts, and Paul Kelly, a valued colleague who has also researched and published in this area were also of great help as consultants. We further recognize that Joseph Boone's groundbreaking dissertation provided an invaluable foundation for our work.

The Saints at War Project could not have succeeded without wonderful student interns. Included among this group are the following: Joy Adams, Matt Gardner, Ryan Alldredge, Lauren Campbell, Michael Deardeuff, Lindsay Payne Halgren, Anita Harker, Brian Jackson, Shelly Baugh Jones, Nicole Likes, Tammi Rae Olsen, Ashley West, Barret Runyon, and Chris Winters. A special thanks to Kimberly Lovejoy and Jenny Layton for organizing the photographic collection that proved so important to our effort. These bright and capable students brought their youthful energy and enthusiasm to the project, making so many things possible.

We are also grateful for the specialists at Covenant Communications for their assistance. It was most enjoyable to work with the editors, graphic designers, and so many others necessary for a successful publication.

Another important person in our efforts is Dr. Brad Westwood, chairman of the Special Collections Department in the Harold B. Lee Library. With his patient help, the Saints at War Archive is now a reality. Others who have contributed to the success of this archive include the directors of the Veterans' History Project at the Library of Congress, the Charles Redd Center for Western Studies, the Brigham Young University Religious Studies Center, and the Joseph Fielding Smith Institute for Church History.

Of course, we wish to express our appreciation for our talented and patient wives, Ja Neal and Kaye, whose encouragement and assistance proved to be an invaluable asset.

Finally, we express our gratitude to all the veterans who served our country during the Korean and Vietnam Wars. We all owe a great debt of gratitude for their courageous service. All of our efforts have been our way of thanking them for the sacrifices they made for us all.

Val Lyman Ball (on the right) served in the Korean War.

TABLE OF CONTENTS

THE KOREAN WAR

Perhaps the most tragic fact of the twentieth century is that its wars cost more lives and imposed greater devastation upon the world than all wars of the previous nineteen centuries combined. In World War II alone, more than fifty million lives were lost as whole nations lay in ruin—a testimony of man's inhumanity toward man. Still reeling from the devastation of World War II, few people would have predicted that the world would be taken to the brink of World War III within just five years of the close of the most awful war in history.

Ink on the surrender documents of World War II had scarcely dried before the clouds of war were again been looming on the Korean Peninsula of Southeast Asia. Characterized by great mountains and many rivers, the land itself made a poor battleground. Nevertheless, war was certainly a familiar thing for the people of Korea as its neighbors—Japan, China, and Russia—had spent centuries vying for control over the strategically important peninsula.

In 1910, Japan took control of Korea and established itself as a colonial dictator. In the ensuing decades leading up to World War II, Japan ruled Korea with an iron fist. Everything from its natural resources to its human workforce was exploited in order to fuel and build up the Japanese Empire prior to World War II. In 1931, Japan invaded neighboring Manchuria.

REPUBLIC OF KOREA
KOREAN WAR SERVICE MEDAL
Criteria for this award (ROK-KWSM) have been established by the government of the Republic of Korea. To qualify for the medal, the veteran must have:
1) Served between the outbreak of hostilities, June 25, 1950, and the date the armistice was signed, July 27, 1953.
2) Been on permanent assignment or on temporary duty for 30 consecutive days or 60 non-consecutive days.
3) Performed his/her duty within the territorial limits of Korea, in the waters immediately adjacent thereto or in aerial flight over Korea participating in actual combat operations or in support of combat operations.

A Korean man sits in the rubble of a destroyed building in Seoul, 1951.

THE KOREAN WAR

Those Americans who fought in the Korean War from 1950–1953 returned home to a country that was less than eager to memorialize either that war or those who served. However, those men and women who were involved in that conflict could never view the Korean War as a forgotten war, nor could they dismiss the impact it had on their lives, on the lives of their families, and the difference it made on the stage of both United States and world history.

As is so often the case, time has changed the perspective with which the world and particularly the American people view this conflict and its aftermath. On July 27, 1995, a memorial was dedicated to honor and remember those who served, some of whom made the ultimate sacrifice.

Located in Washington, D.C., the memorial depicts all phases of combat and pays tribute to the 22 countries of the United Nations who sent troops or gave support in any way in defense of South Korea. The memorial is a circle intersected by a triangle. Stainless steel statues depict all phases of battle and those who participated, bringing together a collage of Air Force, Army, Marines, and Navy from a variety of ethnic backgrounds. A polished black granite wall mirrors these statues and intermingles them with faces that are etched into the granite. The faces are based on actual photographs of unidentified American soldiers.

An adjacent Pool of Remembrance, encircled by a grove of trees, provides a quiet setting. Numbers of those killed, wounded, missing in action, and held prisoner-of-war are etched in stone nearby. Opposite this counting of the war's toll another granite wall bears a message inlaid in silver: Freedom Is Not Free.

On the occasion of the dedication of the Korean War Veterans Memorial, President Kim of South Korea spoke these stirring words: The free world's participation in the Korean War, its first resolute and effective action to stem the expansion of communism, changed the course of history. . . . [It] was the war that heralded the collapse of the Berlin Wall . . . Let all succeeding generations remember the truism engraved in this great memorial—freedom is not free."

On this same occasion, President Clinton referred to the memorial as "a magnificent reminder of what is best about the United States. . . . [T]he creators of this memorial have brought to life the courage and sacrifice of those who served in all branches of the Armed Forces from every racial and ethnic group and background in America. They represent, once more, the enduring American truth: from many we are one. . . . Now we know with the benefit of histo-

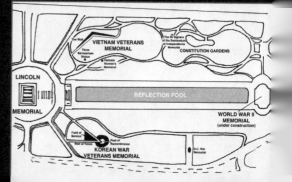

This was followed by the invasion of China in 1937 as the Japanese war machine began its carefully orchestrated sweep through the nations of Southeast Asia and the Pacific. Japan's aggression and wars to increase its power became part of World War II in the Pacific

As World War II engulfed the world in conflict, a 1943 conference of allied nations was held in Cairo during which an agreement was reached to provide for the liberation of Korea before the war was over. The actual liberation of Korea itself was achieved in the late summer of August 1945 as the Pacific War concluded. Russian forces swept into Korea from the north, and American forces invaded from the south. In the face of the Allied invasion, the Japanese quickly retreated; their 35-year occupation had ended.

The Division of North & South Korea

As a result of the defeat of Japan by Allied Forces in World War II, Koreans were liberated from nearly forty years of occupation by Japan. In November of 1947, the United Nations General Assembly adopted a resolution that called for the establishment of elections so that both North and South Korea could vote for their own leaders and possible reunification. Unfortunately, neither was allowed to proceed toward elections without substantial interference from outside political interests. Finally, in the summer of 1948, elections were held in which the South Korean "Republic of Korea" (ROK) was formed under the leadership of Cr. Syngman Rhee. Later that same year, Kim Il Sun organized a communist regime to lead the North Korean "Democratic People's Republic of Korea" (DPRK).

A COUNTRY DIVIDED

In an effort to avoid a more complicated confrontation with the Soviet Union, United States president Harry Truman issued an order calling for the 38th parallel to be the line separating U.S. and Soviet interests. Stalin agreed and overnight the Korean Peninsula, an area approximately the size of the state of Utah, became a symbol of the opposing ideologies of communism and democracy. Korea became a chessboard upon which the emerging superpowers would jockey for position in the new, post-World War II environment.

The formal creation of North and South Korea came after several years of political wrangling between the United States and the Soviet Union during the last half of the 1940s. Various attempts to reach agreement on a means by which Korea could avoid division met with failure—largely owing to the political squabbling of the two emerging superpowers. Finally, in the summer of 1948, free elections were conducted in South Korea, and Syngman Rhee was elected president of the newly founded Republic of Korea (ROK). Later that same year the Democratic People's Republic of Korea (DPRK) was established in North Korea under the leadership of Kim Il Sung. Any hopes for a reunification in the "land of the morning calm" had vanished.

Over the next two years, frictions between the North and South steadily increased as the militarily superior North Koreans sought advantage over their neighbor to the south. Unbeknownst to either South Korea or the United States, North Korean officials initiated several secret meetings with Russian leadership, including meetings with Josef Stalin himself, to organize a strategy for reuniting the two Koreas under communist rule. In addition, Chinese leader Mao Zedong (Mao Tse-Tung) participated in the conspiracy. Though not personally enamored by Stalin himself, Mao saw the goal of spreading communism as an important objective and so supported the plan. The strategy and timeline for the invasion was complete.

U.S. troops capture Chinese Communists on the central Korean front, 1951.

Without the involvement of the U.S.S.R. and . . . China . . . the duration of the Korean War would have been measured in terms of months rather than years.

The U.S.S.R., under Josef Stalin, guaranteed North Korea both the technology and air power it needed to wage war. And China guaranteed troops. Although beset by economic challenges resulting from World War II and the 1949 revolution led by Mao Zedong, China was able to supply a seemingly inexhaustible stream of men to the war effort. Without the involvement of the U.S.S.R., and especially China, in the conflict, the duration of the Korean War would have been measured in terms of months rather than years. Emboldened by the three-way relationship, North Korea was confident of its eventual success.

THE ELEMENT OF SURPRISE

House in Korea countryside September 1953 after armies had battled through area four times.

The stage for military action was set by the summer of 1950. In the early hours of Sunday, June 25, North Korean forces crossed the 38th parallel and began the invasion of South Korea in an unprovoked attack. Finding the ROK troops largely unprepared, DPRK forces were able to sweep into South Korea with lightning speed. Within hours, the South Korean government leaders were in full retreat as ROK forces collapsed and civilians fled for their lives. Within days, the capital of Seoul was under enemy occupation, and the very survival of South Korea was seriously threatened. North Korean military strategists envisioned a campaign in which the total occupation of the peninsula would be achieved within two weeks of the invasion.

Alarmed at the rapid success of the DPRK, an emergency session of the United Nations Security Council was convened to respond to the crisis just two days after the invasion commenced. United States representatives declared that the developments on the Korean landscape were a brazen attempt to expand communism throughout all of Asia. The United States resolved to lead a military response to such naked aggression.

United States president Harry S. Truman knew the price of such involvement would be high for American soldiers. In his presidential memoirs, the president defended his determination to deploy United States forces to Korea:

> In my generation, this was not the first occasion when the strong had attacked the weak. I recalled some earlier instances: Manchuria, Ethiopia, Austria. I remembered how each time that the democracies failed to act

The "Truman Doctrine"

President Harry S. Truman knew only too well the horrors of war, as he was Vice President and later President of the United States during World War II. Truman was convinced that communist aggression must be checked or Asia would be completely controlled by non-democratic governments. In 1947, President Truman announced the "Truman Doctrine," which asserted that the United States would oppose aggressors who sought to invade or otherwise influence the governments of democratic countries. This doctrine became pivotal not only in the context of the Korean War, but also in connection with the Cold War which continued for decades after the cessation of hostilities on the Korean peninsula.

President Harry S. Truman declaring a national emergency, 16 December, 1950.

> it had encouraged the aggressors to keep going ahead. Communism was acting in Korea just as Hitler, Mussolini, and the Japanese had acted then, fifteen, and twenty years earlier. I felt certain that if South Korea was allowed to fall, Communist leaders would be emboldened to override nations closer to our own shores. If the Communists were permitted to force their way into the Republic of Korea without opposition from the free world, no small nation would have the courage to resist threats and aggression by stronger Communist neighbors. If this was allowed to go unchallenged it would mean a third world war, just as similar incidents had brought on the second world war. It was also clear to me that the foundations and the principles of the United Nations were at stake unless this unprovoked attack on Korea could be stopped.

The Korean War was an unpopular war in the United States almost from the beginning. Americans were just beginning to recover from World War II, and they wanted to enjoy the peace and prosperity that accompanied victory. Furthermore, many citizens of the United States perceived no national interest in such a remote region. Finally, many became disillusioned by the war, perhaps in part because of the complicated nature of the conflict and because it was characterized by "limited war" strategies. Progress in the conflict was impossible to gauge since it was not an "all or nothing" military campaign. Many voiced the sentiment, "Why die for a tie." Those Americans not directly opposed to the war were generally apathetic to the eventual outcome.

A POLICE ACTION

The Korean War provided the first real test of the United Nations' ability to marshal forces against an aggressor nation. United Nations involvement in Korea was designated as a "police action" and the purpose of the United Nations was to simply bring peace again to the troubled region. United Nations forces were unified under the command of the seasoned American general, Douglas MacArthur. MacArthur's reputation in Southeast Asia and in the Pacific was legendary. During World War II, he had served as commander of Allied Forces in the Pacific.

MacArthur's first priority was to stabilize the retreat of ROK forces which had been on the run

The Korean War was an unpopular war in the United States almost from the beginning.

United Nations "Police Action"

Established in 1945, the United Nations was created as a means for nations to resolve differences in ways that avoided military confrontation. At the center of the power of this organization was the establishment of a permanent Security Council composed of five nations—the United States, the Soviet Union, Germany, and France. China was added later. The Korean War provided the first great test to see if the United Nations could make a difference in such open acts of aggression as North Korea's unprovoked invasion of South Korea. In what was officially labeled a "police action," fifteen nations (Australia, Belgium, Canada, Columbia, Ethiopia, France, Great Britain, Greece, Holland, Luxembourg, New Zealand, Philippines, South Africa, Thailand, and Turkey) combined under American leadership to stop the sweep of North Korea across the peninsula. The stated objective of the United Nations was to return the parties of the conflict to their respective positions before the war ignited.

Having completed a combat mission over North Korea, these navy planes are coming in for a landing on the U.S.S. Boxer.

since the first hours of the conflict. As Commander in Chief of the United Nations Command (CICUNC), MacArthur quickly implemented a strategy to turn back the progress of North Korea toward the Pusan Perimeter, the last major barrier to the DPRK troops. Americans were the first to arrive in Korea. Undermanned and ill-equipped, members of the 8th Army provided the primary resistance to the invading force during the month of July. By mid-August 1950, other nations began to join in the fight as, one by one, U.N. member-nations deployed troops to the troubled region. In all, a coalition of fifteen United Nations countries actively took part in the conflict; however, United States participation in the war far exceeded the involvement of all other U.N. nations combined.

North Korean forces knew that their hopes for a true advantage in the war could only be realized if they built on their early successes during the first month of the conflict. In

August 1950, DPRK forces mounted offensives on several different fronts. But by this time American troops had been strengthened by reinforcements. Under the watchful leadership of seasoned soldier General Walton Walker, the 8th Army bravely fought first to maintain the Pusan Perimeter and then to force a retreat of the North Korean Army. Positive reports of the 8th Army's progress was just what MacArthur needed to solidify preparations for his plan to invade the occupied South Korean coastal port city of Inchon. As history would record, the Invasion of Inchon was to be MacArthur's last brilliant military scheme.

The plan to invade Inchon called for a huge amphibious landing. The plan was controversial, but succeeded brilliantly. In addition, the successful placement of thousands of members of the 1st Marine Division and the 7th Infantry Division was crucial for the success of the operation. At the time of the invasion, September 15, 1950, U.N. forces enjoyed a five to one advantage over the unsuspecting enemy, whom they quickly overwhelmed. By the end of September, North Korean forces released their hold on Seoul and the surrounding areas. Soon a full retreat was ordered north across the 38th parallel. Greatly bolstered by the remarkable success of the landing at Inchon, MacArthur ordered the offensive northward. He

An American tank endeavors to cross the Naktong River in a northern advance.

The USS Missouri *at Chong Jin, Korea.*

immediately issued a call for the surrender of North Korea, and insisted the DPRK leaders agree to the creation of a democratic government in Korea. The demand was ignored, and MacArthur ordered an invasion of the North Korean capital of Pyongyang.

By October, American forces had advanced to the Yalu River, which defined the border between China and North Korea. By this time, MacArthur was predicting that the war would be over by Thanksgiving and that the troops would be home by Christmas of 1950. Unfortunately, the general's predictions were not realized. MacArthur believed that the Chinese would not enter the war—a mistake which cost his forces dearly. In late November 1950, Chinese troops entered the conflict and immediately pushed the U.N. offensive back across the 38th parallel in a matter of weeks. Still reeling from the sudden change in momentum in the conflict, MacArthur watched as United Nations forces retreated south across the 38th parallel.

A soldier raising the American flag at the U.S. consulate in Seoul, South Korea.

At the same time that MacArthur's miscalculations regarding China left the 70-year-old general in a state of shock, U.S. General Matthew B. Ridgway began planning a set of counteroffensives. In early 1951, Operations "Killer" and "Ripper" were launched, and while success was limited, Seoul became once again a part of South Korea.

In January 1951, the United Nations proposed a ceasefire. One week later China rejected the offer. On February 1, China was chastised by the world body as an "aggressor state." Many believe that China's entrance into the war was actually welcomed in some regards by General MacArthur. In early 1951, he began advocating bringing the war to China. He believed that bombing Manchuria, blockading the Chinese coastline, and bringing Nationalist Chinese from Taiwan into the fray would eventually lead to the demise of communism altogether.

MacArthur's larger-than-life reputation commanded instant respect, but ultimately his uncompromising style set him on a collision course with his commander in chief. As the war dragged on, MacArthur and Truman became hopelessly deadlocked in mutual distrust and dislike for each other. In addition to their private spats, differences between the two men were noted in public. Finally, in April 1951, MacArthur was relieved of his command for what was officially deemed as public insubordination. The general returned home a popular, but frustrated soldier.

When MacArthur returned to the United States, General Matthew Ridgway became the commander of the United Nations forces as the war raged on. Over the next two years, essentially no progress was made, and peace talks were stalled repeatedly. Meanwhile, more soldiers and civilians died in a war in which the only possible outcome was a stalemate. Occasional calls for a cease-fire and POW exchanges provided the only highlights to the otherwise hopeless war. During this period of intransigence, in places like Pork Chop Hill, Sniper's Ridge, Old Baldy, T-Bone, White Horse Hill, and the Punchbowl, the awful work of killing continued. Such sites came to characterize the kind of fighting for which the Korean War was to become famous.

General Douglas MacArthur, Commander in Chief of U.N. Forces, in Korea with other military personnel.

Occasional calls for a cease-fire and POW exchanges provided the only highlights to the otherwise hopeless war.

In the winter of 1952–1953, two events occurred that were pivotal in bringing an end to the war. In November, the legendary World War II General Dwight D. Eisenhower became the United States president. He brought a new tough-

Chronology of the Korean War

1950   JUNE 25   North Korea commences an unprovoked attack across the 38th parallel and sweeps into South Korea.

1950   JULY 7   The United Nations creates the United Nations Command under the leadership of American General Douglas MacArthur.

1950   SEPT 15   Inchon landing commences. American-led forces successfully strike back against the North Koreans and retake Seoul and other key positions along the 38th parallel.

1950   OCT   China enters the war, joining the North Koreans.

1950   NOV 27–DEC 25
                   The month-long Battle of Chosin Reservoir results in the loss of thousands of American servicemen and the greatest retreat in U.S. military history.

1951   APRIL 11   President Truman dismisses General Douglas MacArthur, and General Matthew Ridgway is chosen as successor.

1951   JULY 10   The first of numerous cease-fire negotiations commences at Kaesong. Most of these efforts will result in fruitless outcomes.

1952   MAY 12   General Matthew Ridgway accepts appointment in European Command and General Mark Clark succeeds him as United Nations Commander.

1952   NOV 4   United States elects President Dwight D. Eisenhower.

1953   MARCH 5   Soviet Union dictator Josef Stalin dies.

1953   JULY 27   The Armistice Agreement is signed by representatives of the United Nations Command (UNC) and of the Democratic People's Republic of Korea (DPRK).

✳✳✳ ness to the negotiation table. Then in March 1953, Josef Stalin's death opened the way for renewed efforts to negotiate peace. Armistice talks resumed on April 26, 1953, in the remote city of Panmunjom. Two months later, the goal that for so long had eluded the warring nations was reached. On July 27, 1953, the Armistice Agreement was signed and a cease-fire was invoked.

Right: Syngman Rhee presenting Presidential Unit Citation to the 4th Fighter Interceptor Wing, 4th Communications Squadron, of which Ruel E. Anderson (a Latter-day Saint) was a member. Rhee was President of South Korea at the time. 1953.

Below: General W. K. Harrison and his North Korean counterpart sign the armistice ending the Korean conflict. July 23, 1953.

THE FORGOTTEN WAR

In the years following the cease-fire, the world largely forgot the conflict in Korea. But for those many Americans and others whose loved ones fought and died in this remote peninsula, their memories of the horrible conflict could never be erased. Truly, the Korean War epitomized the notion that in war there is no true victor. In the three years during which the war was waged, over 50,000 Americans died—nearly as many as would be lost in the decade-long Vietnam conflict. In addition, over four million Koreans (one-tenth of the Korean population) and well over a million Chinese lost their lives.

Ironically, the forgotten war posed the first real threat to world stability during the nuclear age. Indeed, the Korean War was the only conflict to bring the world to the brink of World War III, as it was the only conflict in which the superpowers were engaged in a military showdown against each other. It was a dangerous first chapter in the Cold War, which dominated the landscape of world politics for the next forty years.

The Forgotten War

The Korean War is often referred to as the "Forgotten War" for several reasons. First, the war was substantially overshadowed by its predecessor. It lacked the dramatic and pivotal battles that had, in many ways, defined World War II. It was fought in a land even less well-kown than places in which World War II was fought. It was also a limited war with few decisive moments, and those reading about the conflict found it a confusing war to follow. In many ways, most Americans simply didn't want to deal with another conflict. For those not directly affected by the war, it was too easy to ignore the awful event.

For Korea, there was no Invasion of Normandy and no Iwo Jima to provide a decisive advantage to one side or the other. Although violent battles such as the Inchon Invasion, Battle of Chosin Reservoir, and the Fifth Phase Offensive imposed great destruction and widespread death, victory eluded both sides. In the end, the Korean War was characterized by three years of seesaw battles and no lasting military success. The Korean conflict was unique in that it carried with it no declaration of war to mark its beginning and no peace treaty to mark its end. When a cease-fire was finally negotiated to still the violence, it seemed more a reflection of the cumulative fatigue experienced by both sides than a

A Korean girl lays a wreath on an American soldier's grave at the United Nations cemetery, 1951.

representation of skilled negotiation. Truly, it was a war that redefined the nature of military conflict.

The uniqueness of the conflict in Korea continues today. In some sense, the parties to the war never went home. Fifty years after the conflict, the armies of both North and South Korea stand watch over the 38th parallel. In addition, the United States maintains a substantial military presence in South Korea, and the world community maintains a watchful eye over the region. In the fifty years since the cessation of hostilities in Korea, numerous skirmishes have provided regular and painful reminders that the peace in Korea is fragile. In addition, decades of struggle in North Korea under communism have imposed great economic hardships upon its people. By contrast, South Korea's market economy and self-styled democracy have thrived.

Recently, international attention toward this relatively small peninsula has been renewed in response to North Korea's progress toward the goal of manufacturing nuclear weapons, thus creating a renewed threat to military stability on the peninsula. The United Nations is again at the center of the effort to broker a peaceful solution to the complicated situation.

Reflecting upon the price paid for the preservation of South Korea, one may ask if the sacrifice was worth it. In the decades since the cease-fire was achieved in Korea, military historians have debated the wisdom and impact of the conflict within the broader context of human

While many questions about the fate of the two Koreas still loom ahead, one thing is certain: too many have fought and died in this place ironically known as the "land of the morning calm."

events. Still, it was a war in which the United States and her United Nations allies served notice to the world that unprovoked aggression could be countered by international resolve.

Though the cost was great, the dividend of the Korean conflict has been reaped by many people in diverse nations throughout the world. One can only wonder about the future of the two Koreas. Of course, the hope of most Koreans is for reunification. Substantial obstacles stand in the way, however, making the realization of such hope still seemingly many years away. While many questions about the fate of the two Koreas still loom, one thing is certain: too many have fought and died in this place ironically known as the "land of the morning calm."

BIBLIOGRAPHY

Catchpole, Brian. *The Korean War.* New York: Carroll and Graf Publishers, 2000.

Chambers, John Whiteclay II, ed. *The Oxford Companion to American Military History.* New York: Oxford University Press, 1999.

Malkasian, Carter. *The Korean War: 1950–1953.* Botley, Oxford England: Osprey Publishing, 2001.

Harry S. Truman. *Memoirs: Years of Trial and Hope,* 2 vols. (Garden City, NY: Doubleday and Company, 1956), as cited in Joseph F. Boone, "The Roles of The Church of Jesus Christ of Latter-day Saints in Relation to the United States Military, 1900–1975," 2 vols. (Ph.D. diss., Brigham Young University, 1975), 430–31.

THE CHURCH AND THE KOREAN WAR

Prophets have warned us that one of the signs of the latter days is that the world will be filled with "wars and rumors of war." Military conflicts of the twentieth century offer ample evidence that the prophecies are being fulfilled. Few intervals of time provide greater evidence of this truth than the period between the outbreak of World War II and the close of the Korean War, a period of approximately fourteen years. World War II, the most devastating war in history, saw a death toll of approximately fifty million people. A short time period and a long war later, the Korean War added perhaps three million more, a staggering statistic for a war fought in such a small region.

ARTICLES FROM THE CHURCH NEWS
Throughout the Korean Conflict the Church News *served as a means by which news of Latter-day Saints' involvement in the conflict could be shared with Church members on the homefront. Much of the content and pictures of the scenes of the war in Korea were provided by the LDS servicemen in letters and reports they sent home. Besides reporting on the progress of the War, the Church News focused much of its attention on the humanitarian efforts of the servicemen and of Church members at home in relieving the suffering of Korean civilians, especially women and children. Such reports also provided insight into the early development and growth of the Church in that part of Asia.*

A NEW ERA DAWNS FOR THE CHURCH

The outbreak of the Korean War in 1950 came just as the Church was beginning to emerge as a worldwide body. By then, Church membership had surpassed the one million member mark with much of the growth occurring abroad. Increasingly, converts who joined the Church in international settings remained in their homelands to build up the Church beyond the borders of the United States. And as the Church grew, so did its influence, both in the United States and elsewhere.

In 1947, the Church was the subject of a cover story in *Time* magazine. The article recounted the pioneers' arrival in the Rocky Mountains. It was the first time the Church had received such attention from a national periodical. Other "firsts" followed as the decade of the 1950s opened. In

30 LDS Servicemen Hold Services In War-Worn Seoul

By G. L. FOWLES

"Verily, verily, I say unto you *gathered together in my name* *the midst of them. . . ." (D.*

Mormon Soldiers In Korea Worship Under Army Tent

By Pfc. JAY NORBERG

SOMEWHERE IN KOREA —

"We Thank Thee Oh God For a Prophet" echoed through the hills of North Korea late in December as the Church of Jesus Christ of Latter-day Saints opened its conference for members of the Ninth Corps of Eighth Army, in Korea.

om the hills in all dire

LDS Bomber Crewmen May Worship in Cloud

RANDOLPH AIR FORCE BASE — Latter-day Saint crewmen aboard a B-29 bomber can hold priesthood meeting above clouds if occasion requires g to Chaplain Grant lv Church chap

Ei also Th A

The crewmen can be attending the San A Branch on Sunday, along scores of their fellow se men.

During the past 41 nearly 2000 servicemen (containing a servicemen tion of the Book of M little book entitle Gospel) ha tter-da

Mormon Boys, Girls Gather Of Clothing To Send to Kore

TO THE RESCUE—When the Blazer class of the Smith Ward heard of the need for children's clothing, they assigned out with their wagons and gathered 75 pounds which helped them package in eight boxes. Shown with Mrs. glas Wixom, Steven Farr, Larry Latimer, Gerald Fra er, Brent Gudgell, Thomas R. Slater, Veon G. Smith, Not present were, Allen Schmidt, Albert Abrams,

Special Tags Available For LDS Soldiers

SPECIAL IDENTIFICATION tags—known to all G. I.s as "dog tags"—are now available for all Latter-day Saint service-men.

They will be distributed to members now in the armed services through stake and mis-sion presidents in whose areas they are stationed. Servicemen aboard ships or in areas outside the various stakes and missions may receive their "dog tags" from LDS chaplains and group leaders or by writing the Gen LDS Servicemen's Com-47 East South Temple Lake City, Utah.

IN CASE OF NEED NOTIFY L.D.S. CHAPLAIN OR MEMBER

MORMON TEMPLE

I AM A MEMBER OF THE CHURCH OF JESUS CHRIST OF LATTER-DAY SAINTS "MORMON"

DOG TAGS—New identification tags now issued servicemen by Church Servicemen's Committee.

In some instances special sion has been gained in

ns Attract Record Number

emen and Investigator Friends

TIME

THE WEEKLY NEWSMAGAZINE

AGRICULTURE SECRETARY BENSON
"No real American wants to be subsidized."

1951 Latter-day Saint Colleen Hutchins was crowned Miss America, and in 1952 Church member, Merlo Pusey, was awarded the Pulitzer Prize. But perhaps the most public achievement of a Latter-day Saint in the early 1950s came in 1953 when Ezra Taft Benson began his service as secretary of agriculture under President Dwight D. Eisenhower.

In some ways, attention to the Korean War was overshadowed by the forward momentum of the Church as members enjoyed newfound acceptance. Throughout the thirty-seven months of the conflict, very little was said about it by General Authorities, although the position of the Church on war was reiterated. Church leaders taught that war was the result of unrighteousness in the world, and that peace would come only if mankind would embrace the Savior's teachings. One of the few public remarks came from Church Patriarch Eldred G. Smith, himself a veteran of World War II, who commented in general conference, "After reading the Book of Mormon, ask yourselves how long would this Korean conflict last if ten percent of the United Nations armed forces were living righteous lives? Then go another step in your imagination, say, if ten percent were Latter-day Saint men living the gospel, and about fifty percent of all the servicemen were living righteous lives, the power of God would touch the hearts of men and bring peace into the world. And I do not know how we can have real peace any other way."[1]

WAR EFFORTS OF THE CHURCH

The impact of the Korean War upon Church programs was less dramatic than during World War II, but some challenges did emerge. Missionary work, in particular, suffered when the national draft was reinstated. In 1950, the year in which the war began, over three thousand missionaries were set apart for full-time missions. In January 1951, the First Presidency issued a statement to Church leaders instructing them to recommend

> **Missionary work ... suffered when the national draft was reinstated.**

for missions only those young men who were not eligible for the draft. In 1952, the last full year of the war, the number of missionaries set apart was under nine hundred.[2] To fill the void created by the national draft,[3] the First Presidency sent Seventies and married men on full-time missions.[4]

Institutionally, the Church endeavored to support those in uniform through various means. Perhaps the greatest vehicle of support was the LDS Servicemen's Committee. Organized during World War II, the LDS Servicemen's Committee was active throughout the duration of the Korean conflict. Elder Harold B. Lee continued to serve as committee chairman. A memorable moment of his service during the Korean War era came when he actually visited many of the Latter-day servicemen in Korea. It provided great support to the servicemen and became the catalyst for heightened awareness of Korea in the Church at home.

Elder Harold B. Lee served as Committee Chairman for the LDS Servicemen's Committee. He was given a uniform and made "Brigadeer General" for the day. This photo of him standing with Mission President Hilton Robertson (in glasses) was taken on Elder Lee's visit to Korea. His presence there provided a support to the servicemen, as well as a heightened awareness of the Church in Korea in 1954. One chaplain, Richard H. Henstrom, wrote of Elder Lee's visit: "We've been able to sit with him for hours and have him explain the gospel and to answer our questions. We've listened to his excellent advice to the servicemen and we've knelt down with him in private prayer. I didn't think it possible to learn to love a man in such a short time. My three years in the Army are worth this one week that I had with him."

Under Elder Lee's leadership, the LDS Servicemen's Committee met regularly to organize support for the servicemen and women deployed to the conflict. The committee produced and distributed materials to Church members in the military, including a pocket-sized Servicemen's Directory which helped servicemen find the missions and stakes of the Church.[5] In addition, the servicemen's edition of the Book of Mormon and Principles of the Gospel were also made available to those entering the military. These volumes became the backbone of portable doctrine for those in the service.[6] The committee also endeavored to get dog tags stamped "LDS" issued to members in uniform whenever possible.[7]

Local priesthood leaders were encouraged to write letters and implement other outreach programs where possible. The Washington D.C. Stake, under the direction of President J. Willard Marriott, reported great success in such efforts. Not only did most of their seventy-two servicemen sent abroad

Special Tags Available For LDS Soldiers

SPECIAL IDENTIFICATION tags—known to all G. I.s as "dog tags"—are now available for all Latter-day Saint servicemen.

They will be distributed to members now in the armed services through stake and mission presidents in whose areas they are stationed. Servicemen aboard ships or in areas outside the various stakes and missions may receive their "dog tags" from LDS chaplains and group leaders or by writing the General LDS Servicemen's Committee at 47 East South Temple Street in Salt Lake City, Utah. There is no charge.

The new tags, oval in shape, are about one inch wide and an inch and a half long. On one side, in capital letters, is the declaration:

"I AM A MEMBER OF THE CHURCH OF JESUS CHRIST OF LATTER-DAY SAINTS" followed by the word "MORMON" in quotation marks.

On the other side is stamped a small picture of the Salt Lake Temple with the words "Mormon Temple" printed underneath. Above the temple are the words: "In case of need notify an LDS Chaplain or member."

THESE DOG TAGS are being distributed free to Church servicemen under the provisions of a new military regulation which permits members of the armed forces to wear a "third" identification tag supplied to him by the church of his choice.

Those in the armed services are required to wear two identification tags on a chain or string around their necks. These tags are duplicates of each other, and each has stamped on it the name, serial number, blood type, and other pertinent data pertaining to the man involved. The tag also carries a symbol showing church affiliation. Regulations of the armed services permit the following symbols: H for Hebrew, P for Protestant, C for Catholic, and X for No Preference.

Individual LDS servicemen have frequently resisted the feeling that the Church of Jesus Christ of Latter-day Saints is a Restored Church, distinct and separate from all of recognized categories.

In some instances special permission has been gained to have the letters LDS stamped on the regular military dog tags, but more frequently this permission has been denied.

FINALLY, RATHER than change their formal regulations so as to permit the use of other church identification symbols, the armed services adopted the regulation permitting the "third" dog tag to be supplied to servicemen by their respective churches. It is under this new regulation that the Church is sending out these new identification tags.

One of the chief values of the new tags will be to identify Latter-day Saints members in hospitals or otherwise

Continued on Page 13

DOG TAGS—New identification tags now issued for LDS servicemen by Church Servicemen's Committee.

SPECIAL DOG TAGS

Continued from Page 10

wounded on the battlefield. The Church symbols on the standard tags are used to summon a chaplain of the Catholic, Protestant, or Hebrew faith. The specific identification as a Latter-day Saint will now permit the summoning of an LDS chaplain or other Church member so that the person in need may receive administration and other help from bearers.

The new dog tags, made of aluminum, are of such appropriate wording and design that they will also have a considerable souvenir value among servicemen.

Brethren going in the service in the future will receive them at the same time they get their free set of the servicemen's books, that is the servicemen's edition of the Book of Mormon and the little book Principles of the Gospel.

These sets are sent out by the General LDS Servicemen's Committee after receipt from the various Bishops of the names and military addresses of the servicemen from their wards. Bishops are urged by the General Committee to see that none of their servicemen are overlooked.

The above article announcing that LDS soldiers would finally receive dog tags that specified their religion appeared in the CHURCH NEWS, *Wednesday, May 9, 1951, p. 10. Prior to this time, LDS servicemen had been issued dog tags with "P" for Protestant.*

hear monthly from their bishops, but priesthood leaders in the area went to great lengths in reaching out to LDS servicemen stationed in the Washington D.C. area. One member of the bishopric from the Capitol Ward would travel 120 miles each Sunday to hold services at a naval air base.

Understanding an effective motivating factor, this same bishopric organized a group that had the purpose of getting servicemen from a large base in their boundaries to the Washington Ward. The *Church News* reported: "That ward is both closer and more heavily endowed with LDS girls—an incentive that somehow never fails to attract a man in uniform. Part of the Washington Ward's program includes dinners for servicemen and all young people. One friendship begun there has ended in temple marriage."[8]

The Church on the home front also organized itself in humanitarian efforts. Often these efforts were in response to letters sent by servicemen stationed in Korea. These letters spoke of cold winters and a war-ravaged people. They spoke of the particular needs of war orphans. A letter sent home by Captain Jack H. Adamson soliciting clothes for the Korean people was published in Utah's *Deseret News*. It generated such support that Utah's governor, J. Bracken Lee, officially declared a "Clothes for Korea Week." Primary children, seminary students, Boy Scouts, Sunday School leaders, and others responded to the call and collected hundreds of pounds of clothes for the cause.[9]

Another example of Latter-day Saints responding to the difficult circumstances in Korea came when a chaplain by the name of Lawrence R. Rast asked local ward leaders in Utah to help provide much-needed winter clothing to the poor in Korea. Soon, approximately 1,500 pounds of warmth were sent to many victims of the war.[10]

Brigham Young University responded to the war as well. In 1951, with the approval of the Church Board of Education, an Air Force Reserve Officers Training Corps (ROTC) unit was established at the university. Students enrolled by the

Mormon Boys, Girls Gather Stack Of Clothing To Send to Korea Tot

By HAROLD LUNDSTROM

SEVERAL THOUSAND packages of warm children's clothing are now on their way to Korea all because hundreds of persons believe that "he gives twice who gives quickly."

Only three weeks ago Deseret News learned of . . .

BOY SCOUTS . . . as well as Church seminary students have been doing their bit, too, in donating and gathering items from generous friends and neighbors.

With Bishop Alonzo Olsen directing their campaign, the entire Emery Ward in Emery Stake cleaned, repaired, and mended every article of clothing before sending them. And a . . . Builders boys of . . .

eret News learned indirectly the appeal and published story.

Immediately hundreds of inquiries were received from sons as to how they could their clothing donations an began the campaign which resulted in stacks of cloth being sent to alleviate the fering of thousands of Koreans.

Any person desiring to donations to the . . . Cay . . .

PRIMARY BOYS TO THE RESCUE—When the Blazer class of the Smith Ward Primary, Grant Stake, heard of the need for children's clothing, they assigned two boys for each district and went out with their wagons and gathered 75 pounds which their teacher, Mrs. Wayne R. Embley, helped them package in eight boxes. Shown with Mrs. Embley are, Emmet Miller, Douglas Wixom, Steven Farr, Larry Latimer, Gerald Francis Brent Figgins, Frank Spiker, Brent Gudgell, Thomas R. Slater, Veon G. Smith, Burton Arrington, and Kurt Mons. Not present were, Allen Schmidt, Albert Abrams, and Gary Pepper.

This clothing drive organized in a Salt Lake City area ward was typical of the many efforts of members of the Church to relieve the suffering of children in the distant land of Korea.

hundreds. The unit grew from a hundred to nearly two thousand cadets by February 1953, making it one of the largest units in the nation.[11] The ROTC organized annual blood drives on the BYU campus to support U.S. servicemen in Korea and elsewhere. And not to be outdone by the men, the Sponsor Corps—the female complement to the all-male ROTC—was established in 1952.[12]

The Brigham Young University ROTC was established in 1951 in response to the Korean War and grew to nearly two thousand members by 1953. The ROTC Band (shown above) was one of the best bands in the state of Utah and performed at both ROTC and other events. (Photo from the CHURCH NEWS, *February 28, 1953.)*

LDS SERVICEMEN ON THE BATTLEFIELD

Of course, the most direct contribution of the Church toward the war effort came from the Latter-day Saint servicemen themselves. Actual records of Latter-day Saint involvement in the war were not maintained by the Church until approximately one year into the war. At that time, the LDS Servicemen's Committee solicited statistics from the stakes of the Church, but some stakes did not respond. Thus, estimates were made from the responses that were received. The years of 1953 and 1954 provided the highest statistics indicating that there were approximately 18,000 to 19,000 Latter-day Saint servicemen.[13] Of course, many of these men did not see action in Korea but were only trained for the conflict.[14]

The Latter-day Saint Chaplain

The history of Latter-day Saint Chaplains dates back to the Spanish-American War when Elias S. Kimball was commissioned as the first LDS chaplain in the United States military. During World War I three more chaplains were commissioned, and by World War II the number of active service LDS chaplains rose to forty-five. At the height of the Korean War, twenty-seven LDS chaplains served in active duty service. Five were commissioned in the Navy, five in the Air Force, and seventeen in the Army. The duties of the LDS chaplains were not dissimilar from the responsibilities given to other chaplains in the military in that they conducted church services, counseled the injured and downtrodden, and dedicated the graves of fallen soldiers and sailors. LDS Chaplains were, however, a key means by which the General Authority leadership in Salt Lake City maintained contact with Church members in uniform and often assisted in the organization of servicemen's conferences and other worship services. (Joseph Boone, *The Roles of the Church of Jesus Christ of Latter-day Saints in Relation to the United States Military: 1900-1975*, vol. I & II)

1954 GROUP MEETING WITH PRESIDENT HILTON ROBERTSON (President of the Japanese Mission) Chaplains present: (front row L-R) Harlan Y. Hammond, Leland Campbell, Mark L. Money, President Hilton Robertson, Earl Beecher, Lell O. Bagley, Spencer D. Madsen. Other servicemen in attendance not identified.

LDS Chaplain Irons Commended for His 'Devotion, Ability'

HIGH PRAISE from his superior in the chaplain's corps was forthcoming this week for one of the Church's ten chaplains now on active duty with the armed services.

Chaplain Timothy J. Irons, only Latter-day Saint chaplain presently serving in Korea, was commended for his zeal, devotion, and ability under Korean battle conditions by his division chaplain, Lt. Col. Maurice E. Powers.

"Chaplain Irons came to us a few weeks ago. Immediately he assumed his responsibilities as head of the all important Seventh Medical Battalion," Chaplain Powers wrote the General LDS Servicemen's committee.

"His zeal, energy, devotion to duty, his performance of religious works has stamped him as one gifted with bringing the message of Christ into the hearts of men," Chaplain Powers continued

NOTING THAT he has had many of his chaplains wounded, that two are missing in action, "probably killed," and that several have received silver and bronze stars for heroism, the Division Chaplain also wrote of Chaplain Irons: "The soldiers love him because he understands them. His past experience, his present zeal, his kindliness, his informality and pleasant sense of humor blended with deep spiritual qualities make him one of our finest chaplains."

"You have reason for righteous pride in his work," he continued, "and we in the division consider him as a friend and a wonderful chaplain. He carries out the mandates required of a chaplain in the highest sense of religious service and according to the highest traditions of the military service and the chaplain's corps. May God continue to bless his work."

Chaplains received a certificate like the one shown here for completion of chaplain school.

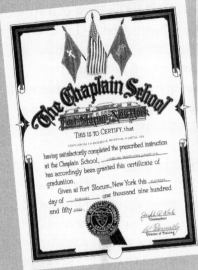

This photo appeared in the Church News *along with an article written by Chaplain Lawrence R. Rast detailing a conference in Seoul, Korea, in which approx. 300 LDS soldiers on the front lines were able to attend.*

GROUP LEADERS' CHAPLAINS—Im charge of the many contingents of L D S men who attended special conference meetings in the Korea battle area were these chaplains and group leaders. Chaplains Rast, Parsons and Covington may be recognized on the front row.

LDS Chaplains Who Served During the Korean War

NAME	BRANCH	NAME	BRANCH
Bagley, Lell O.	Army	Mann, Grant E.	Air Force
Beecher, Earl S.	Army	Marsh, Herbert J.	Navy
Benson, Reed A.	Air Force	Money, Mark L.	Army
Bowers-Irons, Timothy H.	Army	Mortensen, Benjamin F.	Army
Campbell, Leland H.	Army	Nielsen, Cornelius W.	Navy
Cheesman, Paul R.	Navy	Palmer, James R.	Air Force
Coats, Leo W.	Air Force	Palmer, Spencer J.	Army
Connell, John R. Jr.	Army	Parker, Morris W.	Air Force
Cook, Calvin C.	Air Force	Parsons, Robert E.	Army
Covington, Ross L.	Army	Pearson, Jack R.	Air Force
Garrett, Joel R.	Air Force	Pearson, Raynal	Air Force
Green, Marvin R.	Army	Rast, Lawrence R.	Army
Green, William H. Jr.	Army	Robertson, Russell C.	Army
Gwilliam, Robert F.	Navy	Romney, Keith B.	Air Force
Gwynn, Edward R.	Navy	Schwendimen, Kay A.	Army
Hammond, Harlan Y.	Army	Seastrand, James K.	Air Force
Harper, Darrel A.	Air Force/Army	Sirles, James W.	Air Force
Hatch, Howard F.	Air Force	Smith, Robert W.	Air Force
Henstrom, Richard H.	Army	Tanner, William C. Jr.	Army
Madsen, Spencer D.	Army	Wahlstrom, Elmer W.	Army

Some of the largest groups of Latter-day Saints to serve in Korea came from National Guard units from Utah. Many accounts tell of the valor and courage of the men in these units. One involves the famed 213th Field Artillery Battalion based in Cedar City, Utah (later renamed the 222nd), whose roots dated back to the Nauvoo Legion. In the Korean War, members of the 213th were activated for service shortly after the violence began. Led by Lt. Col. J. Frank Dalley, over 600 men were involved in the deployment. According to the accounts of members of the unit, none of the soldiers in the group originally deployed died while there.

Members of this unit were revered by many as a modern example of the 2,000 Stripling Warriors described in the Book of Mormon.[15] Although regularly exposed to danger, they maintained a deep commitment to God, prayed together often, and, as a result, felt divine protection throughout their experience.[16]

During the war, the Church directed that LDS servicemen should be organized in much the same way as they were during World War II. Group leaders were set apart to organize and hold meetings for Latter-day Saint servicemen wherever they could be found. Even without a group leader, however, Latter-day Saints would often find each other and worship together. The absence of formal leadership did not stand in their way. Most often, one or more soldiers would recognize an opportunity and lead out in organizing a group of fellow Latter-day Saints into a worship service of some kind. The need for brotherhood with a fellow member of the Church, and the even greater need for communion with God resulted in some very powerful moments of war-time worship.

Church meetings were held in a variety of settings. Everywhere from rice paddies to vacant mess-hall tents, and from foxholes to corps chapels found Latter-day Saints in worship.[17] In the fall of 1951, three separate LDS servicemen's groups learned of each other's presence in the Yanggu Valley. They quickly organized a "Conference at the Front." Sixty-four men were able to attend and were grateful for the opportunity to bear testimony and strengthen one another. Within a few short hours the men were back to the work of war.[18]

LDS chaplains, while commissioned by the military to serve military personnel of all religious persuasions, kept LDS servicemen abreast of the Church's progress at home and conveyed messages from Church leaders to the men on the front lines. When North Korean forces crossed the 38th parallel, Grant E. Mann (Air Force) and Theodore E. Curtis, Jr. (Army) were the only active-duty LDS chaplains in the United States military. They were soon joined by four former World War II chaplains—another from the Air Force and three from the Army. When the three former LDS army chaplains were reappointed at the end of 1950, the Church began the practice of setting apart Latter-day Saint chaplains. The inauguration of this practice occurred when Elder John A. Widtsoe set apart Warren Richard Nelson.[19]

Statistics for the years of 1953 and 1954 . . . indicat[ed] that there were approximately . . . 19,000 Latter-day Saint servicemen.

The maximum number of active-duty LDS chaplains serving during the Korean War reached a high of twenty-seven in the spring of 1953. Of course, many of these chaplains were never stationed in Korea. The LDS Servicemen's Committee reported, "We now have 27 brethren serving on active duty as chaplains which is one chaplain for about every 700 of our brethren in the service. We also have a set apart group leader for about every 30 of our brethren in the service."[20] The highest number of LDS chaplains actually stationed in Korea at one time was nine in 1954.[21]

Latter-day Saint chaplains served as an important catalyst in bringing LDS servicemen together—especially in servicemen's conferences, which were most often organized by the chaplains themselves. An example of the LDS chaplain's commitment to his men is illustrated by the dedication of Chaplain Lawerence R. Rast. Over a period of three days, Chaplain Lawrence R. Rast covered the entire front line in order to spread word to unit chaplains and group leaders of an LDS servicemen's conference in Kunsan.[22]

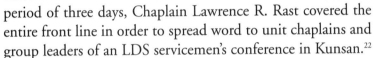

LDS Servicemen's Conference. 8th Army Chapel, 1953.

Furthermore, in an effort to help servicemen find the Church in Korea, LDS chaplain and group leader lists were periodically published in the Church section of the *Deseret News.* The newspaper also printed upcoming servicemen's conferences and asked members at home to help get the word out to friends and family stationed in Korea.[24] It was reported that at one LDS servicemen's conference, soldiers came representing almost every state in the Union as well as The Netherlands, New Zealand, and Canada.[25]

Servicemen's conferences were convened in places such as Seoul, Chunchon, Kunsan, Pusan, and Munsan. LDS soldiers used almost every form of transportation to attend these conferences. They walked and hitchhiked, they came by plane, they traveled in jeeps and trucks, and they came by weapon carrier. Such travels were often made over rugged terrain and bumpy roads and often through rain and stormy weather.[26]

Col. Vasco Laub, Coordinator of LDS Military Activities, Far East Command.

These conferences were highly successful and well attended. One conference in particular witnessed attendance in excess of six hundred men at twelve sessions.[27] Between April 20 and May 5, 1954, seven servicemen's conferences were held in Korea with a total of 976 in attendance. One of the facilities that was used in this particular conference was the 2nd Division chapel. This chapel was designed by an LDS officer, Major LeRoy J. Walker. It was a wonderful experience for him to see the building filled with 273 fellow Latter-day Saints.[28] Included among those who addressed such gatherings were President Vinol G. Mauss of the Japanese mission and counselor Peter Nelson Hansen.[29] Many of the servicemen's conferences were also graced by the presence of Korean members and investigators. These pioneers did much to bring the spirit of the gospel into the meetings.[30]

The growing international Church was also present at these meetings in another way. Chaplain Robert E. Parsons, a former missionary in New Zealand, made it a priority to look up the United Nations soldiers from New Zealand. An LDS meeting was organized and several Maori Saints came to worship. Before long, the men were officially organized and group leaders were set apart. The Maori group provided special musical numbers at a servicemen's conference held in Seoul, Korea on December 29, 1952.[31]

SERVICE AWAY FROM THE BATTLEFRONT

The light of the gospel was not felt exclusively in formal gatherings. LDS servicemen sought out ways to be ambassadors of goodwill. These expressions of kindness did much to alleviate the suffering of others. In Taegu, a group of LDS servicemen adopted a care center that served approximately 120 orphans and 45 elderly patients. They gathered donations of food and clothing and collected money to assist in the construction of a new building to house the elderly.[32] In other areas LDS servicemen found ways to serve suffering Koreans as well. The plight of orphans was often the focus of their efforts. LDS servicemen provided food and clothing and found shelter whenever they could. They often asked for help from their home wards.

The goodwill efforts of the Latter-day Saint servicemen did not go unnoticed by their superiors. Chaplain Lell O. Bagley received a letter of commendation from his commanding officer that not only praised his efforts in his assignments, but also noted his concern for those beyond his charge. It read: "You are to be further commended for your interest in the work toward the betterment of the Korean orphans, which not only makes you a practitioner of the Christian doctrine that you so ably represent, but further increases your value to the service and to our country as an ambassador of good will and a proponent of our American way of life."[33] Through such service, Latter-day Saints had the opportunity to bless the lives of others even amidst the violence of a war they were waging.

MISSIONARY ACTIVITIES

Perhaps the lives that the servicemen touched the most were those of the early Korean converts. It was to this group that the servicemen brought the gospel of peace. Because Korea was not dedicated for the preaching of the gospel until well after the war concluded, regular missionaries were not sent into Korea. LDS servicemen in Korea were often called "soldier

Left: School children singing to Chaplain Mark L. Money, Chunchon, Korea, October 1953. The 8189th Signal Battalion, Hg. Co. contributed school supplies and clothing for the children.

Below: Lell O. Bagley received a letter of commendation noting his concern for those beyond his charge.

Far Below: An art class in the Chunchon School, September 1953. The artistic talents of these children were truly remarkable according to Chaplain Mark L. Money.

Dr. Ho Jik Kim, the first Korean member of the Church, speaks to a congregation. As a pioneer in the early missionary efforts in South Korea, Dr. Kim was greatly admired for his organization and speaking skills.

The Church in Korea

Dr. Kim Leads LDS Group in Worship

By H. GRANT HEATON

PUSAN, Korea—Out of the chaos and destruction of this war-torn country has grown a stirring story of a small band of converts to the Church, stemming from the faith and courage of one man, Dr. Ho Jik Kim.

Dr. Kim was born in Korea into the religion of Confucius but after many years of searching for a fuller expression of spiritual needs, he embraced the principles of Christianity.

A year after war broke out in Korea, Dr. Kim was sent to Cornell University for further studies in the field of nutrition. While in New York, Dr. Kim visited many local churches and was invited to attend an LDS meeting. He became interested in the doctrines of the Church, and a series of cottage meetings was arranged for his benefit. In a short while, Dr. Kim was baptized into the Church.

Returning to Korea in September, 1951, he was appointed president of the National Fisheries College in Pusan, which since the outbreak of the war had been completely disrupted. In a few short months, the college was again on an efficient working basis.

While given the responsibilities of guiding the youth of Korea, Elder Kim was spreading the principles of the Gospel to his own family. His two sons, Tai Whan and Shin Whan, and their young sister also were baptized into the Church.

In the months that followed, the faith of this Korean family spread to others. Regular meetings were started with LDS servicemen based in Pusan and its vicinity. The use of the base chapel was procured, and meetings expanded from Sunday services to include Tuesday and Saturday study gatherings. The number of investigators, both Korean and servicemen, steadily grew.

By April, 1953, a regular Church Group had been organized in Pusan. A new presidency was sustained at that time, under the direction of Chaplain Spencer D. Madsen, of Provo. Sustained as Group Leader was Elder (Lt.) Howard G. Hall, of Kamas, with Elder (Pvt.) H. Grant Heaton, Salt Lake City, and Elder (Lt.) Junius Gibbons, Phoenix, as his counselors.

On Easter Sunday one of several baptismal services was held, in which seven Koreans and one serviceman were baptized into the Church. In June, a conference was held in Pusan. Five LDS chaplains were present and the meeting was largely arranged and conducted by the Korean converts.

missionaries," and they did all they could to foster relationships with the local citizens. Some of the servicemen taught at local schools for the children, and in the process instructed young people about gospel principles such as the plan of salvation.[34] The missionary zeal of LDS servicemen resulted in the baptism of several Koreans during the war years and even after the cease-fire in July 1953.

LDS servicemen were not alone in their efforts to teach the gospel by word and deed. A well-respected and beloved Korean, Dr. Ho Jik Kim, was a true pioneer in his own land. A native of Korea, Dr. Kim was raised in the religion of Confucius. As a young man, he looked for greater understanding, and his search led him to the doctrines of Christianity. While studying at Cornell University he found The Church of Jesus Christ of Latter-day Saints and recognized its truths. He was soon baptized and became the first Korean member of the Church. Upon his return to his homeland, he became instrumental in converting several members of his own family and many other Koreans.[35]

In the summer of 1953 the *Church News* reported: "During the past 18 months L.D.S. servicemen and Dr. Ho Jik Kim, who was converted to the Church while attending Cornell University in 1951, have baptized sixteen Korean converts. There are an additional fifty investigators who attend services regularly. Dr. Kim has recently been ordained an elder and three young Korean members have been given the Aaronic Priesthood."[36] By April 1955, another *Church News* article

KOREAN TESTIMONY MEETING—Elder Ho Jik Kim addresses Korean members of the Church and L D S servicemen during a recent testimony meeting in Pusan, Korea. Elder Kim was largely responsible for the starting of a Church Group in the area.

reported that through the efforts of these early "missionaries" in Korea, over sixty Koreans had been brought into the Church.[37]

In September 1954, approximately one year after the hostilities in Korea had ceased, Elder Harold B. Lee made an historic nine-day visit to South Korea. He returned home to Salt Lake City, Utah, only one day ahead of October general conference.[38] Greatly impressed with the people and with the pioneer efforts of LDS servicemen in Korea, Elder Lee was convinced that the time had come to move the work of the gospel forward in South Korea.

The LDS Servicemen who labored among the Korean Saints knew that their time in Korea would come to an end. Therefore, they did all that they could to teach and train the new converts. Sharing testimonies was a frequent and important source of strength. The servicemen also gave the new members opportunities for service and leadership within the Church. Furthermore, investigators were encouraged to take part in Church functions. One report that reached Salt Lake City said of the investigators, "They are almost as enthusiastic as the members themselves."[39]

In Pusan, each Saturday was termed "Welfare Day" by the LDS servicemen. Property and materials were secured, and the Korean Saints and the servicemen worked side by side to build a home for one of the members. This home also served as a meeting place for the Korean Saints.[40]

A significant effort was undertaken to compile a book of fifty favorite hymns. Chaplain Spencer J. Palmer was appointed as the chairman of the committee. Key to the committee was a group of Korean Saints. It was determined that the hymnal would be printed and bound with the finest materials available in Korea. Korean members and servicemen alike financed the undertaking, which turned out to be a great blessing to the local congregations.

The early successes of these soldier missionaries and Korean pioneers paved the way for the dedication of Korea for the preaching of the gospel in August 1955. It was at this time that Elder Joseph Fielding Smith came to Seoul, South Korea, and offered the dedicatory prayer. Although it would be seven years more before the first Korean mission was to be organized, already the field was white in Korea.

Pictured is a group of converts baptized around the time of an LDS Servicemen's Conference which both Robert Parsons and Howard Bradshaw attended in Pusan, South Korea, in 1952 or 1953. L–R: Tai Whan Kim (Dr. Kim's son), Young Sook Kim (Dr. Kim's daughter), Sung Ja Lee (behind Young Sook Kim), Yung Hee Han, and LeRoy Uncles (a serviceman from Montana).

Above Inset: Elder Joseph Fielding Smith dedicating the land of Korea for the preaching of the gospel. From Left to Right: President H. Grant Heaton, President Hilton Robertson, Rodney Fye, Elder Joseph Fielding Smith, and Dr. Kim Ho Jik. Seoul, Korea, August 2, 1955.

Above: Elder Joseph Fielding Smith looking into North Korea from Hill Block Charley, 24th Division Area. August 3, 1955.

THE MIRACLE IN KOREA

If the story of the beginnings of the Church in Korea is unusual, the progress of the gospel in that land is nothing short of a miracle. In the fifty years since the Armistice Agreement, the Church has taken great strides. From the dedication of Korea for the preaching of the gospel in 1955 until the turn of the twenty-first century, over 70,000 members joined the Church in South Korea.

In 1973, the first stake in Korea was organized in Seoul. In 1985, President Gordon B. Hinckley dedicated the beautiful Seoul Korea Temple. Today the Seoul temple along with nearly twenty stakes and several missions stand as a witness of the strength of the gospel in Korea.

In the several decades since the Korean War, many Church leaders, missionaries, and others have served in South Korea and have come to know of the goodness of the Korean Saints. Few, if any, have had a greater love for the people than President Gordon B. Hinckley who is regarded by many as the father of the Church in Asia. His first of many visits to South Korea came in 1960.

Speaking of his feelings for the Korean Saints, President Hinckley has said, "I have loved those people, I have come to know them. Now all up and down South Korea we have branches, we have buildings. We have that beautiful structure, the temple, in Seoul. We have missions with many missionaries. What a glorious thing it is to see the work there and to know the people there. I just love the people and love the place."[41]

Although once deeply scarred by war, the place known as the "land of the morning calm" has become a glistening gem touched by the gospel of peace as Zion has once again stretched its borders to all the earth.

Seoul Temple: Built on a five-acre site in Seoul, South Korea, the Seoul Temple is the first in Asia. This picture was taken at the time of its dedication in December of 1985. (Photo from the CHURCH NEWS, *December 14, 1985.)*

ENDNOTES

1. Joseph Boone, *The Roles of the Church of Jesus Christ of Latter-day Saints in Relation to the United States Military: 1900-1975,* Vol. II, 433. The authors are deeply indebted to Joseph Boone whose dissertation is the foremost authority on the subject of Latter-day Saint involvement in the military during the twentieth century. Joseph's own service as an Air Force chaplain was exemplary and earned him admiration the world over. Following his retirement from the military he and his wife presided over the Singapore Mission.

2. *Deseret News Church Almanac, 2001-2002* (Salt Lake City, *Deseret News,* 2000), 586.

3. Sheri L. Dew, *Go Forward with Faith* (Salt Lake City, Deseret Book Co.,1996), 145.

4. *Deseret News Church Almanac, 1999-2000* (Salt Lake City, *Deseret News,* 1998), 139.

5. *Deseret News: Church News Edition,* May 16, 1951, 12.

6. "Directory Published for LDS Men,"*Deseret News: Church News Edition,* 16 May 1951, 10.

7. "Pres. Mauss Reports Visits to Servicemen," *Deseret News: Church News Edition,* 16 January 1952, 10. See also "Chaplain Flint Briefs Neophytes," *Deseret News: Church News Edition,* 24 January 1953, 6.

8. "Washington Stake Leaders Help Soldiers Get to Church," *Deseret News: Church News Edition,* July 18, 1953, 13.

9. *Deseret News: Church News Edition,* January 30, 1954, 12.

10. "Valley View's Supplies Reach Korea," *Deseret News: Church News Edition,* 21 March 1953, 2.

11. *Deseret News: Church News Edition,* February 28, 1953, 3, 8. See also Brigham Young University, *The First One-Hundred Years,* (Provo: Brigham Young University Press, 1975), Vol. 2, 630.

12. Ibid.

13. Boone, 434–36.

14. Boone, 434–36

15. See Alma chapters 53, 56–58.

16. Thomas Christensen, "Activation into the Korean War," April 10, 2002, Supplement to *The Richfield Reaper/Rooster Valley Shopper.*

17. "Mormon MP Forms Classes in Korea," *Deseret News: Church News Edition,* 8 August 1951, 11.

18. "LDS Servicemen in Korea Hold Services," *Deseret News: Church News Edition,* 26 September 1951, 10.

19. *Deseret News: Church News Edition,* December 27, 1950, 11–12.

20. Boone, 556, Servicemen's committee to "The General Authorities," June 5, 1953, Historical Department, The Church of Jesus Christ of Latter-day Saints

21. *Improvement Era,* October 1954, 727, as cited in Boone, 440.

22. Lawrence R. Rast , "LDS Boys in Korea Attend Conference," *Deseret News: Church News Edition,* 22 November 1952, 11.

23. "Group Leaders, Chaplains in Korea Listed," *Deseret News: Church News Edition,* 24 January 1953, 10. See also "Chaplains Confer in War Area," *Deseret News: Church News Edition,* 25 April 1953, 7.

24. "LDS Servicemen in Korea Area Set Conference," *Deseret News: Church News Edition,* 22 November 1952, 11.

25. "Six Chaplains, 180 Servicemen Hold 2-Day Conference in Korea," *Deseret News: Church News Edition,* 14 November 1953, 14.

26. "LDS Servicemen Hold Conference in Korea," *Deseret News: Church News Edition,* 24, October 1951, 10. See also "Church Members Hold Conference in Korea," *Deseret News: Church News Edition,* 18 July 1953, 13. One group of individuals travel 150 miles (by air) to attend such a conference. See *Deseret News: Church News Edition,* 27 June 1953, 10.

27. "625 LDS Servicemen Attend 12 Sessions,"*Deseret News: Church News Edition,* 27 June 1953, 10.

28. "Defense-line Conferences . . . Strengthen Testimonies of G.I.s," *Deseret News: Church News Edition,* 29 May 1954, 8–10.

LDS Servicemen in Korea.

29. "Pres. Mauss Reports Visits to Servicemen," *Deseret News: Church News Edition*, 16 January 1952, 10. See also "Native Members Bear Testimonies," *Deseret News: Church News Edition*, 31 January 1953, 13.

30. "LDS Boys in Korea Attend Conference," *Deseret News: Church News Edition*, 22 November 1952, 11.

31. "LDS Maoris in Korea Hold Meetings," *Deseret News: Church News Edition*, 29 November 1952, 13. See also "Native Members Bear Testimonies," *Deseret News: Church News Edition*, 31 January 1953, 13.

32. "LDS Soldiers in Korea Take Project," *Deseret News: Church News Edition*, 30 January 1954, 12.

33. "C.O. Praises Korea Work of LDS Chaplain," *Deseret News: Church News Edition*, 31 July 1954, 4.

34. Howard Bradshaw, personal papers, Saints at War Archive, L. Tom Perry Special Collections, Harold B. Library, Brigham Young University, Provo, Utah, n.p.

35. *Deseret News: Church News Edition*, August 29, 1953, 5. Dr. Kim is often referred to as the father of the Church in Korea.

36. "625 LDS Servicemen Attend 12 Sessions," *Deseret News: Church News Edition*, 27 June 1953, 10.

37. Gary M. Van Wagoner, "Army Missionaries in Korea," *Deseret News: Church News Edition*, 16 April 1955, 8–10.

38. "Elder Lee Praises Work of Chaplains in Japan and Korea," *Deseret News: Church News Edition*, 25 September 1954, 5.

39. *Deseret News: Church News Edition*, 16 April 1955, 8–10.

40. *Deseret News: Church News Edition*, 16 April 1955, 8–10.

41. Gordon B. Hinckley, *Korean Saints*, documentary (KBYU, Provo, Utah), 1999.

DEAN S. ALLAN

Dean served in the U.S. Air Force from January 1951 to October 1953 during the Korean War. He served with the 345th Squadron, 98th Bomb Wing as a gunner, and was involved in twenty-five combat missions. Dean achieved the rank of staff sergeant, and has served in both Church and public service, including serving as mayor of Mapleton, Utah.

Dean S. Allan and several friends joined the United States Air Force in January, 1951. As left gunner, Allan's crew flew many missions over enemy territory. Their main targets were bridges, airfields, and hydroelectric plants.

I graduated from Springville High School in 1950 just as the Korean War started. On January 5, 1951, some of my classmates and I joined the U.S. Air Force.

We went through basic training at Lackland Air Force Base in San Antonio, Texas. After basic training we were sent to Lowry Air Force Base in Denver, Colorado, for gunnery training on B-29s. After gunnery training we were sent to Randolph Air Force Base [Texas] for crew training. But I took a slight detour in getting to Randolph. I went home on leave to put a diamond on my girlfriend's finger.

When I arrived at Randolph Air Force Base, Captain Donald Funk came to me and asked if I would like to be on a Mormon crew. I was delighted to say the least. He asked me if I knew any other gunners who were LDS. I told him about my classmate from high school, Kenneth Russell. We (Ken and I) were assigned to the Mormon crew as left and right gunners. The crew consisted of eleven members: the pilot, Donald Funk, Ferron, UT; the copilot, Robert Sorensen, Logan, UT; the bombardier, Horace Crandall, ID; the navigator, Lee Reason, KY; the radio operator, Gerald Gerber, Salt Lake City, UT; the engineer, Art Grim, TX; the left gunner, Dean S. Allan, Mapleton, UT; the right gunner, Kenneth F. Russell, Springville UT; the central fire control gunner, Joe English, NC; the tail gunner, J. Lynn Lundell, Benjamin, UT; and the radar operator, Donald Robb, Boulder, CO.

After our crew training at Randolph, we were sent to Forbes Air Force Base in Topeka, Kansas, for combat crew training. While there, our crew was sent to Colorado Springs for survival training. This was a week spent without food and hiking many miles through Pikes Peak, while "enemy soldiers" were looking for us. All of this took place in January with a lot of snow in the mountains.

The crew was then given orders to pick up a new B-29 at Travis Air Force Base in California and fly it to Yokota Air Force Base, thirty miles west of Tokyo, Japan.

Our first combat mission was to drop forty 500-pound bombs on the enemy's front lines. Our airplane was an old

B-29 named *Trouble Brewer.* (The new airplane we had flown over was given to one of the older crews.) We flew missions every three to five days against bridges, airfields, and hydro-electric plants. Most all of our missions were flown at night so the enemy's MiG-15 could not see us. Ground fire was intense. The communists were using German 88s which were radar-controlled flak guns and very accurate.

We flew our missions in a bomber stream, one airplane at a time over the target every three minutes at different altitudes for each airplane (33,000 feet then 31,000 feet, then 32,000 feet). These staggered altitudes helped us avoid their antiair-craft guns.

On our ninth mission we were unable to land at our home base because of dense fog. They sent us to a fighter aircraft base in southern Japan (Ashiya). When we got there we were nearly out of fuel, and we landed on a short runway causing

Mormon B-29 Crew, 345th Bomb Squadron, 98th Wing, Crew 46L.
Pictured (L to R):
Pilot–Captain Don Funk
Co-pilot–Lt. Bob Sorensen
Navigator–Lt. Lee Reasor
Bombadier–Lt. Horace Crandall
Radar Operator–Pvt. Gerald Gerber
CFC Gunner–Pvt. Joe English
Left Gunner–Cpl. Dean Allan
Right Gunner–Cpl. Kenneth Russell
Tail Gunner–J. Lynn Lundell.
Photo taken in December, 1951.

us to go over the end of the runway into a road dugway. This stopped our airplane abruptly, breaking it in half. The bombardier put his feet through the Plexiglass in the nose of the airplane, shattering both of his ankles. Needless to say this was the end of *Trouble Brewer,* our old airplane.

The Air Force grounded our pilot, Captain Funk, for causing the accident. Our crew was then assigned a new pilot, Lieutenant Max Kinnard, who really knew how to fly B-29s. Several times on our missions over North Korea, we would have two or three 500-pound bombs hang up in the bomb bay, and we would have to go out in the bomb bay with the doors open and trip the bomb shackles so they would drop. You don't want to land with live bombs on board your airplane.

We flew the remainder of our missions under his command and were recommended for the Distinguished Flying Cross because of our accuracy on targets and our leadership as the "Wing Lead Crew."

While we were in Japan we attended church at the Tachikawa ward, and Ken Russell and I were ordained elders there by Captain Donald Funk, in preparation for our temple marriages when we got home in October.

Many prayers were offered in our behalf by family and ward members. I personally prayed each mission for our collective safety as a crew and my own [safety]. I promised the Lord that I would do everything He asked of me if I could return home safely.

Charles V. Anderson

CHARLES V. ANDERSON

Charles served in the U.S. Marine Corps from June 1949 to April 1952 during the Korean War. He served with the Charlie Company, 1st Battalion, 7th Regiment, 1st Marine Division as a Browning automatic rifleman, and achieved the rank of sergeant. The following account describes a situation in which only a fraction of the soldiers on both sides of the conflict survived.

It was 1949, and I was an Eagle Scout enjoying the good life as a member of the third ward of Springville, Utah. School had just let out and I had no prospects for a job. The international situation was fairly stable, and there was no apparent threat of war, and it seemed like a good time to join the Marine Corps.

One year later, on June 25, 1950, North Korea invaded South Korea. The United States was immediately involved, and sent troops to South Korea.

Battle of the Chosin Reservoir

Chosin Reservoir was the scene of some of the most mournful fighting of the Korean War. During this two-week battle, approximately 50,000 died in the conflict. Soldiers endured terrible cold, supplies were greatly lacking, and eventually a retreat was ordered back below the 38th parallel.

By early November, my unit, the 1st Marine Division was approaching the Chosin Reservoir power complex, which supplied electricity to North Korea and parts of Manchuria. There was a rumor circulating that we would reach the Manchurian border by Thanksgiving, and be home for Christmas. China had threatened to enter the war if U.N. forces went into North Korea, but that threat was ignored.

The Chosin Reservoir lies on the high Taebek Plateau, some

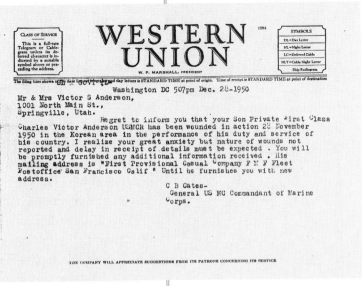

Charles V. Anderson was wounded at the Battle of the Chosin Reservoir.

seventy miles from the nearest seaport along a primitive single lane dirt road. When we reached Chosin we encountered sub-zero weather and Manchurian winds that were almost unbearable. The daytime temperature was below freezing, and at night it reached twenty to forty below zero. With a chill factor of up to seventy degrees below zero, blowing drifting snow, no water, and very little edible food, it was difficult just to survive.

The 5th and 7th Regiments of the 1st Marine Division were spread out around the south and west shores of the reservoir. The 1st Regiment had its base of operations at Koto-ri, about ten miles south of Hagaru-ri and twenty-five miles south of Yudam-ni along the main supply route. A 3,200-man army unit known as "Task Force Faith" was moving north on the easterly side of the reservoir. The army unit suffered 90 percent casualties during the next few days.

During the night of November 27 more than 100,000 Chinese attacked the marine and army units in the vicinity of the reservoir. By December 1, my 240-man company was reduced to 50 and was no longer a fighting force. Many of the 50 had been wounded, but could still carry a rifle. We were combined with the remnants of three other companies, making up a force of near 500 and were told to rescue a company several miles away who had been surrounded by the Chinese for five days. We started our attack after dark.

The terrain was mountainous; it was snowing, and we kept losing our way even though a star shell would burst every three minutes, fired from a faraway howitzer to lead us to the site. Miraculously there was a short break in the snowstorm and a small clearing in the sky that helped us to find our way. After fighting throughout the night and into the next day, we contacted the trapped company. The snow field leading to their position was covered with hundreds of dead Chinese soldiers. The snow was covered with blood and close by were piles of bodies frozen together resembling haystacks covered with snow. Tears and nausea overcame many of us after witnessing this horrendous scene. The enemy had fought a heroic battle and suffered terrible losses. Many of my comrades were emotionally drained and bowed their heads in prayer. The battle continued for about two weeks, but I was evacuated after ten days and flown to a hospital in Japan.

One redeeming feature of the 78-mile breakout fight to the sea was that the troops were followed by almost 100,000 North Korean refugees. They all suffered the effects of extreme cold and hunger and many died as others were born along the road. All who reached the Fort of Hungnam were rescued by the U.S. Navy. The Navy had assembled a flotilla made up of every type of ship that could be brought to the port, and transported everyone to safety.

It was truly a Christmas miracle.

(Below) Winter of 1952. Airman Ruel Anderson standing at the rear of his tent (quarters) at Kimpo AFB just outside of the city of Seoul, Korea.

RUEL E. ANDERSON

From 1949–1951 Ruel served as a missionary in the Southern States Mission. During the Korean War, he was a ground radio operator in the 4th Fighter Interceptor Wing of the United States Air Force. His responsibility was to send radio messages to Japan in Morse code requesting military supplies. After the Korean War he was an officer for 35 years with the Utah Highway Patrol.

Ruel Anderson is receiving a message in Morse code. Sergeant Gordon is answering on a telegraph key known as a "bug." Anderson was stationed at Kimpo Air Force Base, outside of Seoul, Korea, in 1951.

The communications center at Kimpo Air Force Base, 1952. 55-gallon barrels filled with sand surrounded the building for protection.

(Left) 1952 Kimpo Air Force Base, Korea. A/3C Ruel E. Anderson in front of an armored vehicle.

(Below) 1952. F-86 Sabre jets parked on the air strip. They are protected by sandbags that are stacked as high as the aircraft themselves.

VAL LYMAN BALL

Corporal Val Lyman Ball served in both World War II and in the Korean Conflict. Between the two wars he continued his high school education which had been interrupted by his service in World War II. He also served a full-time mission for the Church in the Southern States mission. During the Korean Conflict he served in the Medical Company of the 350th Infantry. Val's unit was involved in providing supplies to the armed forces in Japan.

Val Lyman Ball, Corporal 350th Medical Company

Vall Lyman Ball made friends with four or five other soldiers, and they were good friends with the missionaries: Elders Blauser and Pasoni. Shown in this photo is a group of LDS members after church. Elder Blauser, second from the left and Elder Pasoni fifth from the left. Val is in civilian clothes on the far right. 1952 was the first year that soldiers did not have to wear their uniforms off base.

Photo taken after a parade at Camp Truscot, Austria. Val Lyman Ball is on the far right.

David B. Bleak
Medal of Honor Recipient

Perhaps the only Latter-day Saint recipient of the Award during the Korean War was David B. Bleak, whose heroic story of courage is well-documented in military histories. The official description given relative to the experiences of Bleak reads as follows:

Rank and organization: Sergeant, U.S. Army, Medical Company 223d Infantry Regiment, 40th Infantry Division.
Place and date: Vicinity of Minari-gol, Korea, 14 June 1952.
Entered service at: Shelley, Idaho.
Born: 27 February 1932, Idaho Falls, Idaho. G.O. No.: 83, 2 November 1953.

CITATION: Sgt. Bleak, a member of the medical company, distinguished himself by conspicuous gallantry and indomitable courage above and beyond the call of duty in action against the enemy. As a medical aidman, he volunteered to accompany a reconnaissance patrol committed to engage the enemy and capture a prisoner interrogation. Forging up the rugged slope of the key terrain, the group was subjected to intense automatic weapons and small arms fire and suffered several casualties. After administering to the wounded, he continued to advance with the patrol. Nearing the military crest of the hill, while attempting to cross the fire-swept area to attend the wounded, he came under hostile fire from a small group of the enemy concealed in a trench. Entering the trench, he closed with the enemy, killed two with bare hands, and a third with his trench knife. Moving from the enplacement, he saw a concussion grenade fall in front of a companion and, quickly shifting his position, shielded the man from the impact of the blast. Later, while ministering to the wounded, he was struck by a hostile bullet but, despite the wound, he undertook to evacuate a wounded comrade. As he moved down the hill with his heavy burden, he was attacked by two enemy soldiers with fixed bayonets. Closing with the aggressors, he grabbed them and smacked their heads together, then carried his helpless comrade down the hill to safety. Sgt. Bleak's dauntless courage and intrepid actions reflect utmost credit upon himself and are in keeping with the honored traditions of the military service.

TIMOTHY HOYT BOWERS-IRONS

Timothy served with distinction as an Army Chaplain during World War II and then affiliated with a National Guard Unit from Salt Lake City during the Korean Conflict. He was one of the first LDS Chaplains to arrive in Korea and was of great assistance in organizing LDS groups and servicemen's conferences.

When I came out of World War II, I thought within ten years we would be at war some place again with communists. At one time, when I was a kid, I was quite interested in Communism. I read some books on it and finally came to the conclusion that that wasn't the way to live although they have a right to their viewpoint I understand. Anyway in view of the experience, especially after World War II, I thought that the Soviets would force their way into every place they could and take over and set up their puppet governments. I assumed that would continue until someone called their bluff. It was only four years from the spring of 1945 until the spring of 1950. I had kept my commission with the expectation that we would probably be at war again. Then there was the fact that they needed a chaplain to go with this group out of Salt Lake [Utah] which had some appeal. Maybe I just like the smell of gunpowder.

I was the first LDS chaplain in Korea and, except for isolated instances, I don't think that

This article from the CHURCH NEWS details an LDS servicemen's conference in which Chaplain Irons was the opening speaker.

LDS Servicemen Hold Conference in Korea

SOMEWHERE IN KOREA a "Korean Conference" for LDS servicemen fighting with U. S. Army units on the central front was conducted recently by Chaplain (Captain) Timothy H. Irons, formerly of Nephi, the only Mormon chaplain on duty in this war-torn country.

The Sunday afternoon conference meeting at the headquarters of the 17th Infantry (Buffalo) Regiment attracted 76 Latter-day Saint men representing 10 states and the Island of Samoa.

Some of the men traveled as far as 40 miles in army trucks to attend the conference. Other men from units unable to furnish transportation walked and hitch-hiked over the dusty roads to the meeting site.

The conference was the first effort by Chaplain Irons to gather the Mormon servicemen from various sections of Korea to a general meeting. It was made possible following extensive checking by the chaplain into the location of Church members in the combat units near where he is assigned — the 7th Division Medical Battalion.

A CIRCULAR LETTER announcing the service was mailed to all Mormons, Chaplain Irons had noted in his directory search. He had hoped for an attendance of 50 and as the group surpassed all expectations it overflowed the big pyramidal tent that was reserved for the meeting.

For many men it was a real effort to make the necessary arrangements with unit commanders along with securing transportation. Not one of the 76 young servicemen regretted the trip, however. Without exception they praised the conference and expressed their gratitude for the opportunity to meet in worship service, to partake of the sacrament, and to testify to their personal knowledge of the truthfulness and goodness of the Gospel.

The major portion of the conference following the sacramental service was devoted to testimony bearing. It gave members an opportunity to become acquainted, to relate their experiences under the trying conditions of the Korean campaign, and most of all to acknowledge the blessings of the Lord.

CHAPLAIN IRONS in opening the conference called on the men to live their religion, to set an example within their units, and to remember the counsel of Church authorities in their daily activities.

"The conditions imposed by war and the new and strange environment of combat units places new and greater difficulties on us all in our attempts to live our religion," the chaplain pointed out.

Along with it, however, he explained, comes the opportunity to make contacts that may lead to conversions within the Church.

"By clean living, by exemplary conduct, we have a real opportunity to further the work of the Lord," he said.

Other speakers were Lt. Leland H. Tuft, Murray, and Corporal Robert H. Lee, Beaver, group leaders from units represented at the conference.

Lieutenant Tuft urged members to make every effort to avail themselves of the chance to study and improve their knowledge of the Gospel and to take every opportunity to tell others of the fundamental precepts of the Church.

CORPORAL LEE urged those present to attend the unit meetings whenever possible and to contact other LDS men in their companies who are coming into Korea as replacements.

Corporal Lloyd Sharp, Richfield, chorister, led the group in four familiar LDS hymns, "Come, Come Ye Saints," "Jesus Once of Humble Birth," "For the Strength of the Hills," and "We Thank Thee O God for a Prophet." Sergeant Max Tomkinson of Fillmore was accompanist at the portable field organ.

The 76 men in attendance at the meeting were drawn from every one of the combat arms — infantry, artillery, engineers, quartermaster, signal corps, and armored forces. States represented were Alabama, Arizona, California, Colorado, Georgia, North Carolina, New Mexico, Oregon, Utah and Wyoming.

Two brothers, Sergeant Vine S. Edwards Teo and Corporal Eliga A. Teo Tuilesu of Samoa, missionary converts, also were in attendance. Both indicated a desire to serve on missions, as soon as they are released from Army service, as a means of furthering the Gospel among their people.

The meeting place and surroundings of the meeting were a far cry from those in the wards and stakes of the States but the spirit was as strong and contagious as ever. Chaplain Irons is making plans for an extension of the conference to other areas of Korea.

there was as much done there as there was in World War II. I guess it took a little while to crank up. There are always a few LDS boys that will get organized. Once I was there, of course, I helped wherever I could, and wherever I would hear of LDS men I would try to go there.

In World War II, you could take off almost any place, if you dared, and go where you wanted to go. But in Korea, it was a little different. You had to go back down through those rough canyon roads and way back across to get from one corps area to the other. I was pretty busy also.

I know I had a group I visited within the 1st Marine Division part of the time. Were they hooked on to us or were we hooked on to them? I had better be careful. The Marines wouldn't like us if I put it wrong. Anyway, we had adjoining units and that gave me an opportunity to visit with them. Whenever I would hear of a group, I would try to get to them. Here again, though, the hilly terrain and the danger of moving made it a near impossibility for visiting the LDS groups.

We had these three battalions which were largely Mormon and they all had services. I know our 7th Division Forward held a service every Sunday. So did some of the others, and some of the air bases did too. My chances for the kind of movement I had had before and the freedom I had before were not the same.

I think possibly one of the best things we did in Korea was to hold this series of conferences. It developed a lot of our LDS men over there that we hadn't had contact with. Before I left, we had one or two other chaplains, and I think finally there were five Mormon chaplains in Korea before the thing finally closed down. Of course, that meant we had a lot better coverage than we had when I got there.

I came home from Korea expecting to be treated like a hero, I guess. With my help, we had distributed something like 800,000 pounds of clothing to Koreans. In Utah, they had had a clothing drive or whatever they call it. They sent us thousands of pounds of clothing. Major Jack Adamson from the Air Force was in on it. We had written home to our families telling them of the situation, and I think it sort of fired the imagination of a writer on the *Deseret News*.

I couldn't get out [of the military] right then. I was still committed for some time. But by the end of my first period of obligation, I had decided that it was a good enough life. The war was over and I liked doing what I was doing so I stayed in.

HOWARD W. BRADSHAW

Howard served in the U.S. Army during the Korean War, from 1951 to 1953, achieving the rank of sergeant. As a soldier and as a missionary, he has shared the gospel with those around him throughout his entire lifetime. He has also served as a stake patriarch.

As I landed in Korea I was sent to Inchon, then south on a train to Pusan, arriving approximately December 15, 1951.

My first Sunday in Korea I found the Latter-day Saints meeting in an old building in a small room in downtown Pusan. There were present that day seven American servicemen (GIs) and Dr. Ho Jik Kim. During the holidays Dr. Kim said he had a student he would like to bring to the services. We invited him to bring his friend. As the time passed, many more Koreans began to come to our meetings. At that time Elder Ralph Erickson from Delta,

Utah, was the group leader. He chose me and Elder Kay Buchanan from San Jose, California, as his assistants. Later Brother Erickson went home and I became the group leader. Beginning in early 1952, I suggested there was a good friend in my company, Edward Solle from Grand Rapids, Michigan, (not a member of the Church) who could teach the Koreans English. He was a college graduate.

L–R: Franklin Kay Buchanan, Ralph D. Erickson, and Howard W. Bradshaw standing outside a hospital in Seoul, Korea.

Edward did agree to teach English to the Koreans that would come to the meetings each Tuesday night for our Mutual. After teaching English lessons we taught them the gospel. With the teaching of English and the gospel we had many join the Church. The Spirit of our Heavenly Father was really strong in these meetings.

The attendance of the Mormon servicemen increased also at this time. We soon had to have a larger room and then we corresponded with the Japanese mission president, President Hansen. We were sent supplies and literature at that time.

Some of the Americans questioned whether we should be teaching the Koreans the gospel, but as the Spirit and the success of the work bore witness to them, they all knew it was to be so. Not only did we have success among the Koreans, but several servicemen were baptized and became great Latter-day Saints. My friend Edward Solle never joined the Church, but he really loved the Church and was a strong Christian, and he did a wonderful job teaching English to those Koreans.

Dr. Kim was our interpreter for the gospel, and as we taught the Spirit bore testimony of the truth of this great work. Teaching English to the Koreans was really a great tool in teaching the gospel.

Dr. Kim's two children did join the Church early but I do not recall the day or when Mrs. Kim joined the Church or if she ever did while I was in Korea.

It is recorded on my pictures that August 3, 1952, was the date of the first Korean baptisms in Pusan, Korea. Each baptism service was really special as we would go to the China Sea for the baptisms. We were so grateful when the chaplains would come to our area and we would have special meetings; also when President Hansen came to visit we had him the center of attraction.

Easter Sunday, April 5, 1953, was a most glorious day when many were baptized in the China Sea. This was the last baptismal day for me in Korea as I was to leave for home on April 26. With these many baptisms, it was a very happy time to be together on such a beautiful day. We did rejoice in the pouring out of the Spirit of the Lord as we sang, "The Spirit of God."

In the words that are on the back of my pictures, I recorded that I was able to baptize thirty Koreans with the help of the Lord. Many others were also baptized during this time.

Before leaving for home, Dr. Kim and his wife took me out to dinner, to one of the best cafés in Pusan. He paid tribute to me for the great work accomplished. We talked of the future and wondered if someday there would be a temple in Korea. He seemed to know of a place in Seoul that would be

Below: Official US Army Photograph: Photo celebrating the first baptism of the Latter-day Saints in Pusan, Korea. 1st row L-R: Chaplain L. Covington (Base Chaplain), Sgt Ralph Erickson, Cpl. Howard W. Bradshaw. 2nd row: Cpl. Jessard L. Ellis. Dr. Ho Jik Kim, the first Korean Latter-day Saint member, is on the back row first one on the right. Sister Han is the tallest Korean on the front row.

Right: Official US Army Photograph: Cpl. Franklin K. Buchanan baptizes Young Sook Kim at the first baptism of the Latter-day Saints in Pusan, Korea.

a great place. His family had fled into Pusan during the war, and he knew they had been blessed. His wife was so sweet; I had a difficulty with chopsticks so she had the waitress bring

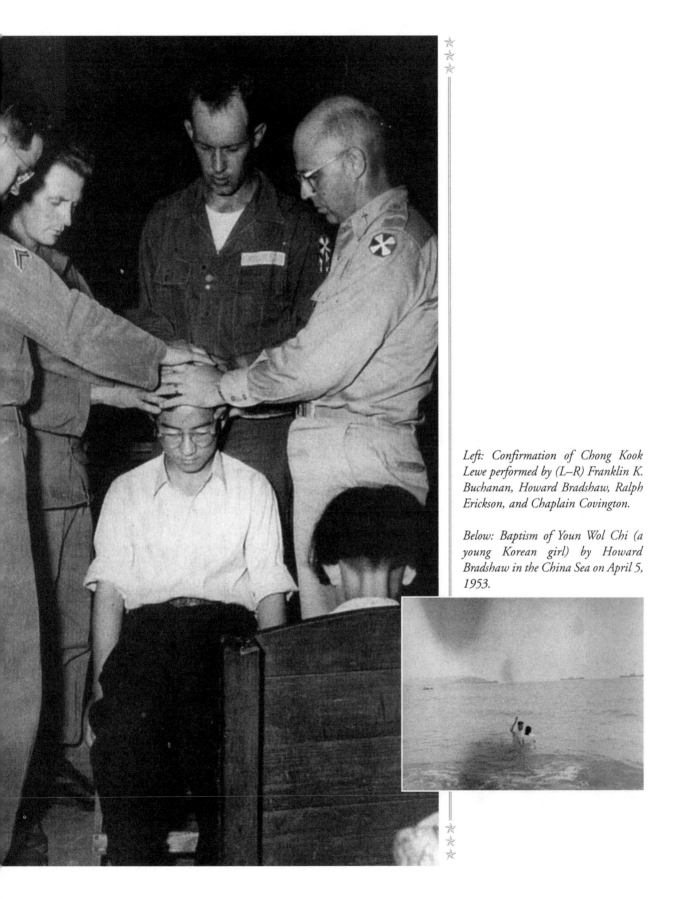

Left: Confirmation of Chong Kook Lewe performed by (L–R) Franklin K. Buchanan, Howard Bradshaw, Ralph Erickson, and Chaplain Covington.

Below: Baptism of Youn Wol Chi (a young Korean girl) by Howard Bradshaw in the China Sea on April 5, 1953.

me a spoon. They said they had never taken an American to dinner until then. I left approximately April 26, 1953, for home and my family.

Later my wife and I sponsored a Korean girl, Yoon Chung Kim, to come to the United States for schooling in Salt Lake City, Utah. Later on, one of Dr. Kim's sons came and visited with us here in Beaver, Utah.

We love the Korean Saints, and I am so grateful for the opportunity I had in playing a small part in the Church being established in Korea. I thank the Lord for that opportunity and consider my stay in Korea my second mission. It was sad to be away from my wife, son, and family, but the work of the Lord helped me with happiness in the Korean work.

Pontoon bridge crossing the Imjin River, Korea, 1952.

DON S. BRIMHALL

Don served in the U.S. Army during the Korean War. He served in Company C, 6th Tank Battalion, 24th Infantry Division, and achieved the rank of lieutenant in this service. Don also served in World War II and as a Green Beret for ten years following the Korean War. He is a former school teacher and counselor and has dedicated his life to helping youth.

Our first mission was to cross the 38th parallel and go north up the Imjin River into enemy territory to destroy a bridge. This would not be an easy task. Our column of twenty-one tanks zigzagged back and forth for about five miles before we ran into enemy fire. The fireworks then began. Enemy artillery and mortar fire exploded everywhere. Later, nearby enemy machine-gun fire and grenades ricocheted off our tanks. We had difficulty seeing the well-camouflaged enemy troops. Therefore, we retaliated with searching and grazing .30- and .50-caliber machine-gun fire. We also threw hand grenades from our tanks at any suspected target.

Breaking through the enemy front lines and destroying bridges, supply lines, and ammunition dumps were our main objectives. Our tanks were very effective in this type of warfare; however, we were vulnerable to antitank mines and enemy bazooka teams. On two different occasions my tank was disabled because of land mines. Due to staggering losses of tanks and sometimes men, we had to make our patrols up and down the river bottoms to avoid the minefields. The powerful bilge pumps in the lower part of the engine compartments would pump the water out of our tanks whenever necessary.

Don S. Brimhall served in the Korean War from 1950–1952.

On one occasion while our company was on patrol, we had a very emotional experience. The Chinese had entered the war to help the North Koreans. Our objective was to blow a railroad tunnel deep inside the enemy front lines. We calculated that one volley of high explosive, 90-millimeter rounds would blow the whole face of the mountain apart. We didn't realize the resistance that we might encounter. During our movement up the river, in water three and four feet deep, we encountered some resistance. Artillery shells were exploding all around us and enemy machine-gun rounds were ricocheting off our tanks. Finally we recognized our target about a thousand yards away. We quickly maneuvered our tanks in a line formation so that all twenty-two tanks could fire at the same time. We were given the signal to fire by the command tank's radio. It appeared that the whole mountain was moving. Then it erupted like a volcano.

But that was just the beginning. Shortly after, a bonsai charge of Chinese and North Koreans came screaming off the mountains from every direction. They were firing their rifles and machine guns and throwing hand grenades. In my entire life I have never felt so confused and insecure. They even tried to crawl on our tanks to deposit large satchel charges over the grill work of the tank engines. In desperation we kept our tanks moving, running over the enemy and firing in all directions. We even fired our machine guns at each other's tanks in an effort to keep the crawling and reckless enemy from climbing aboard.

Finally, we received a message from the command tank to head for the river. It was about time. We were almost out of ammunition. The enemy losses were staggering. Mangled dead bodies were everywhere. This could have been called an Oriental graveyard. After getting into the deeper water of the river, we were relatively safe from enemy action. Two of our tanks were lost from enemy satchel charges. Ten of our men lost their lives. I suppose this is the price we have to pay when we fight a war.

The subzero winter months of 1950–1951 were extremely miserable. The bone-chilling winds from icy Siberia and the deep blanket of snow created real problems. We lived in bunkers dug into the hillside, and used a small oil heater as a source of heat for each of the 5-man tank crews. For food, we had the improved C-rations. They were tiresome, but nutritious. The greatest day of each week was our weekly mail call. Dawnie my wife was extremely attentive in writing letters and keeping me informed of news back home.

The American and North Korean leaders established a truce line at the 38th parallel, and negotiations began. However, the war continued. It was extremely difficult to maneuver our tanks up and down the frozen rivers with a foot of ice to penetrate. Whenever we would get stuck, we would use our long tow cable and hook up to another tank. This was a common occurrence. Churning through the thick ice was like riding a roller coaster. It was fun. With all the maneuvering of my tank up and down the Korean rivers, I am surprised that I didn't wind up with webbed feet.

As we were moving our tank column to the rear, a wounded infantryman flagged down my tank. Part of his lower leg had been shot off. He was desperately in need of medical treatment. I stopped my tank and asked for volunteers to help him into our tank so that we could take him to a nearby field hospital for medical treatment. Due to the sporadic enemy rifle and machine-gun fire on my tank, no one volunteered. Therefore, I dove headfirst out of the turret to the ground. As I was lifting the wounded young man up the side of my tank, an enemy motor shell hit the tank and mortally wounded the already wounded infantryman. With my arms around his legs lifting, the tank crew pulled him into the tank. I was stunned from the concussion, and my face and neck were marked with particles of shrapnel. (In fact, I am still carrying a piece of that shrapnel in my cervical vertebrae.) As we were on our way to the field hospital, our wounded infantryman passed away.

The crew members of my tank wrote me a citation for a Silver Star. They were furious when the battalion commander changed the citation to a Bronze Star.

"Fighting a war and surviving the frigid winter weather in Korea was almost unbearable. The Army [tried] to provide protective winter clothing, but it was not always effective."

Below: During the Korean War, Brimhall spent sixteen months in a 50-ton General Patton Tank. Brimhall was promoted to Captain and became commanding officer of a tank company. Brimhall, standing 2nd from left, is pictured with his tank company (22 tanks).

THOMAS MERLIN BUNKALL

Thomas served in the U.S. Army Infantry from October 1950 to September 1952 during the Korean War. He served with the 40th Infantry Division, 223rd, Regiment E Company as a platoon squad leader; he achieved the rank of sergeant. The following is a collection of stories, both good and bad, from his time spent overseas.

The first night in the barracks, I met Jim, who was in a bunk next to mine. He asked if I was Mormon. I said, "Yes, are you also?"

He said, "Well, sort of." He explained his parents were inactive members and that he had never been baptized. He had attended Primary and Sunday School once in a while. He had a girlfriend, Ila, who he attended church with. We became very best friends. Jim asked many questions about the Church, and a pocket-sized Book of Mormon became used very much. We spent many hours talking about the Church.

We went from Fort Douglas, Utah, to Fort Riley, Kansas, and then for basic training at Camp Cook near Santa Maria, California. For five months, Jim and I attended church in Santa Maria. We were welcomed and invited to dinner nearly every Sunday by the members there. After five months, Jim asked me to baptize him. Bishop Maughn called Jim's bishop in Midvale, Utah, who interviewed Jim, and I baptized him. About three weeks later, Jim broke his ankle while on bivouac training and spent two days in the hospital after which they allowed him to go home for three weeks. When Jim returned he said, "Tom, Ila and I got married while I was home."

"No you didn't."

"Oh, yes I did. See my ring."

I was taken by surprise!

* * * * *

Before arriving at the assigned position, my scout came across the body of a North Korean soldier. We were to retrieve all bodies if possible, but the North Koreans would often booby-trap a soldier with a wooden hand grenade. We had been instructed to carefully tie a rope around one leg and then from a rock or tree, pull the body three to five feet. We tried this, but his body was frozen to the ground, and we were not able to recover any information from the body.

Thomas Bunkall received much recognition for his service during the Korean War. He received the Korean Service Medal, Bronze Service Star, United Nations Service Medal, Army of Occupation Medal (Japan), and the Combat Infantry Badge.

We were to stay out for six hours when a replacement squad of fourteen men and a K9 dog and trainer would relieve us. That night we saw below us in a clearing two shadows, then a third [shadow] in the clearing. They were in white uniforms to blend in with the snow. Three of us simultaneously opened fire when the fourth shadow appeared. He dropped down and didn't move. We then could not return to our bunkers for fear of running into an ambush by the other soldiers—ten or fifteen of them. We stayed until it was light enough to go and retrieve the body. A medic and two of our men came with a stretcher. The soldier was in his thirties. In the pocket search, we found information as to the group he was with. He had a picture of his wife, a four-year-old daughter, and six-year-old son.

* * * * *

A week before Christmas, we went on a well-earned R&R (rest and recuperation) to a Quonset hut. It was so nice since we could get a hot shower, clean clothes, and a delicious meal. It was a welcome change from the K-rations left over from World War II which had been our meals since arriving at the post. As I was leaving the mess hall, I emptied the leftovers into a barrel. Near the barrel was a little, raggedly dressed Korean girl (about seven years old). She begged for the food in exchange for a paper flower she had made. I thought she was gathering food for piglets her family was raising. One container had coffee, tea, milk, hot chocolate, and a cigarette floating on the top. The other had a mixture of beans, potatoes, meat, and bread. In the morning, the little girl was accepting the breakfast leftovers. I overheard a GI say, "Good morning, Blossom!" Inquiring who she was, I learned they allowed her to come into the camp to collect food for her family. I thought about our K-rations, which seemed like a Thanksgiving dinner in comparison. After learning of her situation, the GIs were much more particular about sorting the food and liquids. We always had an extra slice of bread, cookies, or apples to give her. The R&R personnel said the new group coming in would learn her routine without their instructions. She never missed a meal—three times a day, seven days a week. I was impressed. In the summer, she replaced the paper flowers with wild flowers at every evening meal. Always a smile, always a bow or curtsy, always very happy. Hence, the name "Blossom."

While on our R&R, Jim and I were sitting in the recreation hall at a table. Bill from our unit and another fellow came over. Bill said, "This is my friend, Andy, and Andy wanted to ask you to do something for him."

Jim asked, "What's that?"

Andy offered each of us a can of beer which we both refused. He coaxed, "Oh, come on. Just take a swallow."

Jim said, "Not for me; I simply don't drink."

Andy then turned to me, and after I refused he asked, "Just lick the foam off of the top of the can," he said, shaking it so the foam came up, then forcing it into my hand. I took it and sat it on the table. "Guess you're not going to lick it."

"Nope," I said.

"I just can't believe you two guys. Well this just cost me seventy-five dollars on a bet with Bill." By then there were ten or twelve other soldiers watching. Bill knew us and knew for sure we would never touch a beer, as he had lived among the Mormons in Salt Lake City, Utah.

On Christmas Eve, Jim and I got on a truck to return to our bunkers (our home on the front lines for nine months). Inside the ceiling of logs we saw huge rats nesting for warmth. To distance ourselves from them and their odor, we used small electrical field wire and nailed it to the logs, crisscrossed to hold the pine bows on the ceiling. This hid the rats from sight and caught their droppings. The pine bows also masked the horrible stench.

We found a two-foot-high pine tree for a Christmas tree. We had saved silver tin foil from chewing gum, which we rolled into tiny balls for decorations. I bedded down in my bunker on Christmas Eve thinking about Blossom, where she was planted, and how happy she was. She had little; I had little. She was happy, and I was happy because of her.

I was told a 24-hour period of silence was declared by the United Nations Command. No small arms, artillery, or air strikes of any kind on Christmas day were allowed. Because of this, it was a silent night and all was calm. I closed my eyes and said a prayer for all the GIs in Korea and for Blossom and her family. I was happy where I was planted because of a 7-year-old Korean girl. That night, I slept in heavenly peace and awoke to a beautiful Christmas day. The sun was shining and everything was covered with glistening snow. The great quiet and peaceful feeling were wonderful!

B. ALLEN BUNKER

Allen Bunker served in the U.S. Army Air Force during the Korean War and in World War II, between the years 1943 and 1954. He served in the U.S. Army Air Corps Training Command, 4th Air Force, 3995th Flying Training Wing. Allen achieved the rank of first lieutenant. He is a witness that the Lord keeps His promises, as described below.

This is not an experience of heroics or bravery during combat in World War II or the Korean conflict. This experience began prior to my enlisting in the U.S. Army Air Corps Reserve after receiving an alternate appointment to the U.S. Military Academy (West Point). My appointment was from a U.S. senator from Nevada while I was attending Utah State Agricultural School in Logan, Utah, during 1942.

The appointment was for the first alternate position, which was in case the principal appointee became ineligible by reason of health or other disqualification [I would] be admitted at West Point. The principal appointee was accepted to West Point so I was released June 1, 1943, to be drafted unless I enlisted in a branch of the military prior to a draft board call to duty.

Knowing I was nineteen years old and swift action by my draft board was imminent, I chose the branch of the military I wanted. It was my desire to fly instead of being on the ground or on the sea; therefore my enlistment in the U.S. Army Air Corps.

I had never received a patriarchal blessing prior to this time, so I contacted my bishop and asked for a recommend for this purpose. It was granted and my paternal grandfather, Martin Allen Bunker, the Moapa stake patriarch, gave me a blessing which included a promise that I would never have to take a life while in the service of my country:

> I bless you to the end that in your labors as a soldier you will be a defender of right-
> eousness, and though your work might take you into the fields of adversity, I bless you
> to the extent that you will never be called to take the life of your fellow men unnec-

essarily, but that all your actions might be tempered with mercy and that you might be enabled to set such an example before those with whom you associate that they will see your good works and place upon you many, many responsibilities.

My assignments in chronological order were: basic training (Lowry Field, Denver, Colorado); aviation student Washington State College (Pullman, Washington); aviation cadet classification (Santa Ana, California); Aviation Cadet Aerial Navigation School (Hondo, Texas), graduating as a second lieutenant in the top 5 percent of my class and assigned as an instructor; Hanford AAFB, California, for B-24 Crew assignment; Mt. Home AAFB, Idaho, as a B-24 aerial navigator for phase training prior to combat assignment; reassignment to Gowen Field AAFB, Idaho, to finish phase training with original crew. (Here we were graded and rated the "Top Crew" out of the entire squadron class BE 7-9.) This caused a new assignment to March AFB, California, where we were assigned to B-24 "Ferret" training to eventually be assigned to Headquarters Far East Command in the Pacific Theater of [World War II].

While in ferret training Word War II ended, and I was released from active duty and mustered out of the service. I stayed in reserve status with a mobilization assignment at Nellis Air Force Base, Nevada. Meanwhile I married my wife in the Salt Lake Temple. We both returned to school earning our bachelors degrees from the University of Utah. After graduation we returned to Las Vegas, Nevada. Then I decided to enter the mortuary business with my father and moved to the Los Angeles, California area to attend the California College of Mortuary Science. While at that school I was recalled to active duty for the Korean conflict. I was permitted to graduate and take my Nevada State License examinations for Funeral Directors and Embalmers Licensures. Passing these, I returned to active military service at Nellis Air Force Base near Las Vegas, Nevada (my birthplace and hometown). I was assigned as a purchasing officer, clothing sales officer, with an additional duty as the base mortuary officer. Released from active duty in June 1953, I refused active duty status when my commission expired in 1958 after six months of active duty and nine years of reserve time during World War II and the Korean conflict (1943–1958).

Throughout my military career, I was never assigned to combat where I might have been responsible for taking a life, which was a fulfillment of my patriarchal blessing.

DOUGLAS P. BUSH

Douglas served in the U.S. Army during the Korean War from January 1951 to December 1952. Douglas achieved the rank of sergeant. This account describes the fulfillment of Douglas's patriarchal blessing and how that has "been an anchor to [his] faith in times of trial and doubt."

I come from what used to be called a "split-member family." My mother was a member of the Church, but my father was not a member of any church and was not religious.

Just before I went to Korea, my mother prevailed upon me to get a special blessing from the stake patriarch. He told me in the blessing that if I was prayerful and kept myself clean and pure so that I could receive the promptings of the Holy Ghost, I would be led and directed while in Korea. He blessed me that the destroyer would pass me by, that my life would be preserved, and that I would be able to return home to my family.

A few months after arriving in Korea, and after a couple of combat experiences . . . I was finally wounded . . . and sent back to the U.S . . . and spent seven months in a military hospital . . . and then was discharged.

One of the first things I did after being discharged was to pay a visit to the patriarch. As we talked, he told me that as he was giving me the blessing . . . he had a vision . . . in which he saw me and my fellow squad members surrounded by a force of Chinese soldiers. He said he saw death and injury in my squad, but he knew that, even though I would be injured, I would not be killed. He told me he did not mention these things in my blessing because he did not want to disturb my mother.

His remarks were confirmed to me about a year later, as I was walking across the campus at Brigham Young University. I was stopped by a friend of mine from my home stake in California, who had recently heard the patriarch talk to a group of young adults at a fireside. The patriarch had mentioned my blessing and his vision as an indication of what can take place during a blessing.

RALPH J. CARLSON

Ralph served in the U.S. Army Infantry during the Korean War from February 1951 to January 1953. He served in the 1st Battalion, 19th Regiment, 24th Division as a sniper, jeep driver, and company commander. Ralph achieved the rank of private first class. Since the war, he has worked in broadcasting and has run in and completed thirty-seven marathons.

Ralph J. Carlson—Jeep driver for the Company Commander, December 8, 1952.

The Korean War had been going on since June 25, 1950, when I was drafted into the United States Army. The date was February 4, 1951. Reporting to Fort Douglas in Salt Lake City, Utah, I was immediately sent by train to Fort Lewis, Washington. I was fortunate to meet up with returned missionaries Bob Isaacson and George Jeppson. They would

play a big part in my church activities. After two weeks at Fort Lewis, we were transferred, by train, to Camp Rucker, Alabama. The trip took thirteen days, and we were glad to reach our destination.

We joined the 47th Infantry Division, which had just been activated as part of the Minnesota/North Dakota National Guard. I was assigned to Headquarters Company, 2nd Battalion, 164th Regiment, Company F. There I went through basic training several times with a two-week bivouac

Carlson spent fourteen days aboard the troopship USS General J. C. Breckenridge *(shown below).*

training at Fort Hood, Texas. Long marches activated an old knee injury from skiing, and I had an operation at the base hospital. After recovering, I was assigned to be the company commander's jeep driver to Captain John Cain.

Home on furlough, I married Catheryn Kallas on August 25, 1951, and she came to live with me, off base, in Ozark, Alabama. In July 1952, I received orders to report to Fort Lewis, Washington, to embark to the Far East. A week after arrival, we boarded the troopship USS *General J.C. Breckinridge.* After fourteen days, we arrived in Yokohama Harbor and were transferred to Camp Drake [Japan].

At the time, the Battle of Bloody Ridge was taking place in Korea. Our troops had suffered

Camp McNair–Ralph J. Carlson was stationed here after an amphibious landing. Mt. Fuji is in the background.

many casualties. One morning, we fell out and the sergeant called out numbers one through forty, and said those men would catch the train to Sasebo, Japan, to go to Korea. I was number forty-one; the sergeant said those from forty-one on would go to Sendai, Japan, to join the 24th Division. The 24th Division had just come back from Korea where it had suffered heavy casualties.

Arriving in Sendai, I was assigned to go to Hachinohe to join Headquarters Company, 1st Battalion, 19th Regiment,

24th Division, Camp Haugen. One of our maneuvers involved a landing in Yokohama off an LST [landing ship, tank]. The flat-bottomed ship caused a lot of seasickness from its rocking in rough seas. I finished out my tour of duty and was discharged January 30, 1953. The war ended June 27, 1953.

Today I count the experience at Camp Drake as a blessing and for providence saving my life. Others were not so fortunate and lost their lives or were wounded. Everywhere that I was stationed, we LDS soldiers formed our own group for services. With help from the Servicemen's Church Committee, we received materials and guidance. We held testimony meetings, sacrament meetings, and while in Japan we attended a servicemen's conference in Tokyo. My home ward sent letters regularly.

L–R: Duane Midgley, Wayne Johnson, Phil Leigh, Leonard Patchen, Ralph Carlson, and Wayne Adams on their way to the Tokyo Serviceman's Conference on October 18, 1952.

Some of the men in our group were: Roy Faucett, Wayne Carrol, George Jeppson, Bob Isaacson, Leonard Dutson, Roy and Ray Dunn, Phil Leigh, Leonard Patchen, Ross Johnson, Duane Midgley, Delores Erickson, and Wayne Adams. Today, I count my blessings for the Lord allowing me to raise a family of six children, serve in many callings in the Church from elders quorum, bishopric, high council, and presently as an usher on Temple Square. I was also blessed with a wonderful wife who passed away April 20, 2000.

CARL H. CARPENTER

Carl served in the U.S. Army during the Korean War from June 1952 to May 1954. He served in the Intelligence and Reconnaissance Platoon headquarters and Headquarters Company, 19th Infantry Regiment, 24th Infantry Division as a reconnaissance specialist and rifleman. Carl achieved the rank of staff sergeant. Carl worked as a civil engineer for forty-five years and has filled several positions of responsibility in the Church.

On July 9, 1953, our unit boarded a ship in Hachinohe Harbor bound for Korea. We first boarded an LCM [landing craft, mechanized] to go out to the ship. We then had to climb aboard by "landing nets" hanging over the ship's side. The

Carl H. Carpenter was inducted into the U.S. Army in June 1952.

water in the harbor was somewhat rough that day, and it was difficult to climb from the barge to the net with a full field pack. I got onto the net all right, but as I climbed upward the barge banged against the ship and my foot became wedged between the barge and the ship. Someone must have been praying for me at that moment because just as the barge came up toward the ship on a wave, that same wave backed away and my foot was only lightly squeezed instead of being crushed. I almost became a casualty before I even got to Korea!

We thought we were on our way to the combat zone when the ship changed course to a more southerly direction. On July 17, 1953, we dropped anchor off shore from an island that reminded me of "Bali Hai" in the movie South Pacific. It had a high mountain covered by clouds in its middle, and the sea was very calm. The name of the island was Cheju, and it contained a POW camp for about 20,000 Chinese POWs. (We would be there for the next three months until the end of the war!)

We clambered down the landing nets into landing barges and headed for shore. My thoughts were with those of my predecessors in moving toward the beach, although there was no danger for us. We hit the beach, and loaded onto trucks and headed for camp.

The Chinese POWs had been guarded by Republic of Korea (ROK) troops; but, when the South Korean president, Syngman Rhee, thought a truce was about to be declared, he had his troops start to release North Korean POWs held on Koje Island. They thought he was going to do the same thing on Cheju, and that was the reason for our change in course on the ship.

Cheju was a barren, volcanic rock off the southern tip of Korea. The mountain in the middle of the island was called Sambangsan, and there were two main villages on the island called Mosul-po and Cheju City. In former times the island had been a resort for Korean nobility in the winter. In addition to being a POW Camp, it was also used by the ROK Army as a training base. In the summer it was a hot, humid, and sultry place.

I will never forget our first night on the island. The ROKs were having night maneuvers, and tracer ammunition was flying all over the mountain. In addition, there was a terrific thunderstorm on top of the mountain. It looked like the Fourth of July fireworks! We didn't know whether or not the ROKs were going to turn on our small battalion! I was glad when morning came!

The POW camp consisted of a large rectangular enclosure with two barbed-wire fences surrounding it on all sides. The fences were about ten feet high; there were guard towers at each corner, and sand-bagged bunkers at each corner manned by machine-gun crews. Inside, the enclosure was divided into twelve compounds; six on each side of a wide runway which ran down the middle of the enclosure. In the middle of the enclosure was another tower that overlooked the entire facility. Each compound had a gate that opened to the runway, and one GI guard tended each gate. It was our job to stand guard, either in a tower, a bunker, or as a gatekeeper. We would be on duty for four hours, and then off for eight hours. Sometimes I was a gatekeeper and sometimes I was in a tower. Being in a tower was boring. It was all I could do to stay awake! All there was to do was to watch the POWs do exercises and march around the compound, or watch the navy destroyer circle the island on patrol.

Being a gatekeeper was more interesting because I could talk to the POWs , although we were not supposed to. As gatekeeper, we were not allowed to have any weapons—only a gas mask and a steel helmet. We were told that if the prisoners were to riot, we were to try and make it to the center watch tower. Fat chance of that!

The Chinese were friendly, and most of them wanted to go to Taiwan when the war ended. Once in a while though, a dead one would be discovered. It seemed that all of them did not want to go to Taiwan. They had their own internal organization, and would march and drill around the compound every day. At about 4:00 A.M. each morning they would awaken to the sound of a bugle. The bugler would point to the four directions of the compass and blow like crazy. It was a weird sound, and the first time I heard it I didn't know what to think.

The first few weeks we were there I thought the Army had forgotten us. We didn't get any mail, and every meal was the same—pancakes and wieners. Then everybody got dysentery. It was awful! There we were—sick, hungry, and lonesome!

This picture was taken after an LDS Servicemen's Church service on the island of Cheju-do, Korea. L–R: Carl Carpenter, Richard Elyinga, Phil Leigh, Al Potter, Duane Midgley, Claude Parkinson, Gordon Leavitt, and Kenneth Hedin.

They had only two movies to show us in our time off. I saw the *I Don't Care Girl* with Mitzi Gaynor and *The Hangman's Tree* with Joel McRay about fifty times.

But there was some humor. There had been rumors of guards falling asleep on duty. We heard that some officer was going to be sneaking around after dark to check on us. I was

in a tower above a bunker one night when I noticed a shadow sneaking along the fence. I passed the word below. When the officer got about ten feet from the bunker they slammed the bolt on a machine gun. He jumped up and shouted, "Don't Shoot! Don't Shoot!"

One time the tail end of a typhoon hit the island. I have never experienced such wind! I was in a watch tower, and was fascinated by the huge waves pounding against the vertical cliffs south of the camp. The navy destroyer (Tin Can) would roll and pitch in the heavy sea, and would almost go out of

Carl on Jeep patrol in the Yangu Valley north of the 38th parallel, Korea. April 1954.

sight. I was very happy to be on dry land!

It was while I was on Cheju that Keith Chapman of Manti [Utah] and Richard Elzinga of Salt Lake City [Utah] joined our unit. It was great to see familiar faces, and especially one from my hometown. They added two more men to our little LDS Church group. They also helped me to clean up my language. We had our own services on Sunday, and used mess kits for the sacrament service.

On July 27, 1953, the Korean War ended and a truce was declared. We had heard rumors for several days. There was no celebration—just a big sigh of relief.

JOE J. CHRISTENSEN

Joe was admitted into the first class of advanced Air Force ROTC students at Brigham Young University, and thereafter served in the U.S. Air Force during the Korean War from July 1953 to July 1955. He served in the Tactical Air Command at Charleston Air Force Base as a personnel officer and a base exchange officer. Joe achieved the rank of captain in the Air Force, and later became a General Authority in the Church.

Joe J. Christensen.

Howard [Carroll] was the young, single, clean-cut, newly commissioned lieutenant who was assigned to succeed me as BX [base exchange] officer. To learn the job, he came to work with me about two months before I was to be released from active duty. Barbara and I invited him to our home for a get-acquainted dinner and after we had taken him back to the BOQ (bachelor officers' quarters) we almost simultaneously commented, "Howard would make a great member of the Church!"

Howard was a graduate in engineering from Clemson University. He came from a devout Protestant home. He was intelligent with an engaging smile and sense of humor. He didn't smoke, swear, and if he drank at all, it was only occasionally and socially while he was at college. As we worked, attended temporary duty assignments, and played golf together, we became very well acquainted. We had the chance to have several long conversations about life and the gospel.

As I look back on it now, one of the defining experiences in Howard's process of conversion occurred early on. We were assigned to a brief training session for base exchange officers at the air force base in Biloxi, Mississippi. We flew from Charleston about 4:00 A.M. in a C-47. We were in meetings throughout the entire day from morning until about 10:00 P.M. that evening. When the class was dismissed, several said they wanted to go to some bar and "relax." Not wanting to do that, I said, "Howard, I'm really tired. I think I will go back to our room and write a note to Barbara."

He said, "Joe, I'm bushed too. I think I'll join you."

[A few weeks later] we [Howard Carroll and I] were billeted in the same room, and so when we were ready to go to bed, it was a bit awkward for me. What should I do about my personal prayer? Maybe to be less intrusive, I should just slip into bed and say a silent prayer. Then, for whatever reason, I said, "Howard, in my faith I have a custom of kneeling and praying at night and morning and if it is all right with you, I'll do that now." He nodded and I knelt down next to my cot and offered what probably was a much shorter prayer than usual because I felt like there were two eyes staring at the back of my head.

When I finished and was getting into bed, Howard said, "Joe, uh, uh . . . spiritually, I am in bad shape. Would you mind kneeling down again and saying another prayer—only this time out loud?" And so we did.

The prayer experience Howard and I had that night in our room in Biloxi, Mississippi, opened the door to having several conversations about religion, our belief in God and the nature of God, the purpose of life, etc. We had a lot more time to visit during the last month of my active duty since Barbara [my wife] had gone home for our daughter Susan's birth. We had moved out of our house and for the final few weeks, I was temporarily rooming in the BOQ [bachelor officers' quarters] just down the hall from where Howard was living. The night before my being released from active duty and beginning the long trip west to home, Howard and I had another conversation. By this time we had become good friends, having shared a lot of experiences at work, on the golf course, eating at the officers' club mess hall, etc.

As we visited about a variety of things, Howard said, "Joe, you know, everything you have told me about your religion is better than mine. The only problem is, I don't know that it is true. If the time ever comes that I do, I'd like to come out to Idaho, and you could baptize me." Even that made me feel good. We continued our conversation about a wide variety of things, including religion. Then he stopped, hesitated for a few moments, put his clenched fist over his heart and said, "Joe, I don't know how or why, but for some reason, I know that

Joe J. Christensen.

LDS services were held in this building in Tokyo, Japan. Christensen was able to visit here while on R&R in June 1951.

it is true. Would there be a chance that arrangements could be made for me to be baptized?"

Arrangements were made with Bishop Royall and the next evening in the Charleston ward chapel, I had the privilege of baptizing Howard. He subsequently was instrumental in the baptism of his fiancée and mother-in-law and later became bishop of the Charleston ward. For Barbara and me, it was a great thrill to welcome two of his sons as missionaries while we presided over the Provo Missionary Training Center.

THOMAS R. CHRISTENSEN

Thomas served in the Army National Guard during the Korean War. He served in the 1866 EAB-857 EAD, 213th AFA Battalion as an executive officer, and he achieved the rank of first lieutenant. Thomas had also served in the Pacific during World War II, and after his service he returned to Utah to work the land and serve in the state legislature.

We hit the beach at Inchon, Korea (the city of Seoul had just been won back from the Chinese just a few days before), and the loading doors at the front of the LST [landing ship, tank] opened. Men and equipment were going out one by one to the beach. In the normal delay of the events and with a little trouble unloading, the interior of the LST filled up with carbon monoxide gas. Several from our battery were taken off the ship unconscious and some others unable to move. All were taken to an army hospital where they all recovered and returned to action with their units. No casualties occurred in this behind-the-line action.

One night during some night fire exercises, one of the howitzers exploded, sending parts of the howitzer and shell fragments all over that particular area. The gunner on the gun was wounded, but nobody else was touched. It was incredible that no one was hit by those explosive parts. No wonder we felt protected.

One day as we moved to a new battle line and during a bit of a lull in the fighting, three of our men went forward, on their own, to see what actions were taking place on the line. Battle lines are not always too definitive and these three walked through a swale and past the defended line and on into no-man's-land (between the battle lines). They did not realize their predicament until the opposing forces fired on them, and they then took cover. Our side (the U.N. Forces) soon became

The Able Battery Officers in Yansan, Korea, March 1951. Front L–R: Lt. Tom Christensen, Cpt. Ray E. Cox, Lt. Lynn Barnes. Rear L–R: Lt. Logan Carr, Lt. Leland Tuft, Lt. Arthur Chaffee.

aware of the situation, and sent a couple of squads to neutralize the situation and bring them back to the friendly side of the battle lines. Again, no casualties.

Apostle Harold B. Lee came to the front the fall of 1951 and those who were able to get away went back and shook his hand and received his counsel and blessing. He went to other Utah units as well.

JOSEPH W. DAILEY

Born in the Ozark Mountains of Arkansas, Joseph joined the Church in 1940. He served in the Marine Corps for over thirty years, rising to the position of sergeant major. In addition to his service during the Korean War, Joe also served in World War II and in the Vietnam War. During the Korean conflict Joseph received several awards, including the Purple Heart and the Navy Cross. The following are excerpts from several letters he wrote during his service in Korea.

October 16, 1952.

I am on the front lines now. We do most of our work at night. The enemy is about two or three hundred yards in front of us. We are on one hill and they on another across from us. If we move around in the daytime, they start shooting at us.

Christensen's 213th Battalion served 893 days of combat before the cease-fire. During that time they fired four different major weapons: the 105-mm, 155-mm, and 240-mm howitzer, as well as a 90-mm anti-tank gun. This photo shows parts of an exploded howitzer.

After dark, patrols are sent out from our lines to try to find out about them. They have a lot of land mines in the area, so you have to watch out where you step, and that is hard to do in the dark. We had four boys get wounded about two nights ago from one that blew up.

October 23.

I'm so glad when morning comes, and I can get into my warm sleeping bag. We have a place dug into the ground and covered over with sandbags—it is about six feet deep with room for four people to sleep in. At night we stay in the trenches, which are about six feet deep. A patrol was out the other night and made contact with the enemy. Three boys were injured and one killed. They couldn't bring in the one that was killed, and when they went back the next night to get him, the enemy was waiting with guns set up all around.

November 1.

I go out on patrol every fourth night. There is one officer and one platoon sergeant to each platoon, and there are three rifle platoons in a company. We take fifteen men on a patrol with a radio and telephone with a roll of wire. We roll the telephone wire as we go out, and have the phone hook on the wire so we can talk with the company commander about what goes on around us. If the enemy gets in behind and cuts a wire, we always have the radio to fall back on. We never start a fight with them. We have good medical care. We have a hospital corpsman along with us. If a person is wounded really bad, they call a hospital plane and they can have him back in the division hospital within an hour. We have been on the front lines one month and will stay about another six weeks, and then go back for a month. We had another boy killed last night and one the night before.

The following is the citation for the Navy Cross, which Technical Sergeant Dailey received during his service in the Korean War.

Joseph W. Dailey, Sgt. Major of US Marine Corps. Headquarters USMC, Washington D.C., 1973.

Navy Cross

Authorized February 4, 1919, the Navy Cross was the Navy's 3rd highest award for combat heroism and other distinguished services. On August 7, 1942, Congress made the Navy Cross a combat only decoration with precedence over the Distinguished Service Medal, making it the Navy's 2nd highest award ranking below only the Medal of Honor. It shares this position with the Army's Distinguished Service Cross and the Air Force Cross.

Navy Cross Citation:

For extraordinary heroism while serving as a platoon leader of Company F, 2d Battalion, 5th Marines, 1st Marine Division (Reinforced), in action against enemy aggressor forces in Korea on 25 February, 1953. While participating in a company raid on an enemy outpost, Technical Sergeant Dailey unhesitatingly volunteered to lead a rescue squad in an attempt to recover four Marine casualties who were discovered lying a few feet from a strongly fortified enemy-held trench.

Moving quickly to his objective, he skillfully maneuvered his squad into a position from which he was able to rescue the casualties and, despite an intense hail of enemy machine gun, grenade, and automatic weapons fire, carried out a further search of the surrounding terrain until he located and recovered two other wounded Marines.

As an enemy force advanced toward his position, he skillfully withdrew his men and all the recovered casualties to friendly lines. By his exceptional courage, outstanding leadership, and daring initiative in the face of continuous hostile fire, Technical Sergeant Dailey was directly instrumental in saving the lives of six wounded Marines and upheld the highest traditions of the United States Naval Service.

WILLIAM J. DUMAS

William joined the Marine Corps at age seventeen, in July 1948, and served during the Korean War until July 1952. Months before the war officially started, William was the platoon leader for a group in the Criminal Investigation Department of the Marine Corps responsible for parachuting into Seoul to get civilians out. William achieved the rank of gunner sergeant.

Opposite: This article appeared in THE DAILY HERALD, *Provo, Utah, Wednesday, November 29, 2000.*

Below: Louis Edward Weber sits atop his tank. Louis trained as a paratrooper at Fort Benning, GA and also certified as a tank gunner. He served in the U.S. Army until Jan. 1954.

A BAR is a Browning automatic rifle. It's a heavy duty rifle. Anyway, I opted to carry one. I also carried a 40 aught. My 32, that I had, sure, but that was my private weapon. Then I had my BAR. And ironically enough, we always had problems with BARs freezing. They would freeze up because they fired so fast and so hard that the barrel would become white hot and a lot of times if you didn't continue, and you let it set for 30 seconds or a minute, it would freeze up and it wouldn't work. We had four BARs that did not work. All we

Weather

Historically, the impact of weather on the progress of war campaigns has been pivotal. Entire battles have owed their success or failure to weather conditions which set the stage for victory or defeat. The Korean War was no different. One of the consistent reflections of veterans who served in the conflict is that the weather was generally terrible. During the winter the thermostat often dipped to 30 degrees below zero. Summer weather was generally hot and sultry. In the rough terrain and with meager rations and water, such miserable conditions often made fighting virtually impossible. In particular, the winter of 1950–51 was one of the worst in the memories of most Koreans, and many servicemen reported frozen conditions at the battlefront.

had were M1 rifles; no machine guns, nothing. We were laying on this ridge, and these Koreans were—I don't know if they were Koreans or Chinese, but one of the two—they were dug in on the side of this whole hill. So I called the tank commander, and he brought up four tanks and they parked the tanks right behind us. Then they started firing with their machine guns, and their howitzers, and we fired our rifles and stuff. All of a sudden one Korean guy broke and ran. He came down the valley and yelled, "Surrenda! Surrenda! Surrenda!" We called a cease-fire, and two of my guys got up, stripped him down to his underwear, gave him a cigarette, and walked him behind the line. And that was the key to the

Orem veteran teaches of war

By CONSTANCE GLENCO
Special to Our Towns

Originally I didn't want to watch "Saving Private Ryan." I didn't feel comfortable viewing a "typical" war movie — all blood, guts and gore. But after my husband and dear friend, **Sandy Home**, insisted, I rented it. It moved me to learn more about the war and the Americans who served in it.

William J. Dumas

Not long after seeing this movie, I needed to do a research paper on history for a college class. I chose the Korean War. I didn't know much about it and I had a great source, Sandy's father, Orem resident, **William J. Dumas**.

Bill served in the Korean War from '50-'52 as a Gunny Sergeant in Fox Company, 2nd Battalion, 1st Marine Division. Along with his division, Bill experienced one of the bloodiest and most horrific events in American History — the battle of the Chosin Reservoir.

On Nov. 30, 1950, the Marines were commanded to withdraw their position. So began the 13-day retreat of 20,000 troops down a narrow, mountainous, one-lane supply road. They were surrounded by 120,000 Chinese. In the bitter sub-zero weather of the Chosin, the Marines fought valiantly. The men had to keep their hands moving or their fingers would turn black and fall off. The enemy suffered as well. "They studded the mountains of Chosin, squatting with rifles slung on their shoulders, packs on their backs, sheathed in snow, frozen to death," Dumas recalled.

The Marines not only

Courtesy photo

Staying alive: This photo of Orem resident William J. Dumas, then a Marine sergeant, was taken after the Marines' 13-day retreat from the Chosin Reservoir. The photo, taken by David Douglas Duncan, appeared in the Dec. 25, 1950 issue of "Life."

fought their way out of the valley, but they heroically brought out their wounded and most of their dead. They would be known throughout history for their courageous victory overcoming the Chinese in the battle of the Chosin Reservoir.

Dumas received two Pur-

ple Hearts during the Korean War. The first he received after marching toward the crest of a hill about 10 paces behind his best friend. An incoming shell exploded just in front of his friend blowing the man's head off and peppering Dumas's body with shrapnel.

whole division. The division of Koreans was not anywhere near our division; there was basically maybe about 2000 men. All came over the top of the bench. All surrendered. And the commander came across, and he spoke very good English. He looked at me and said, "This is why I surrender? Fifty men and five tanks?"

We had our dinner of C-rations, and everybody fell in and we headed back. Now we figured we had already secured the whole area. So we were perfectly safe. Full moon. Gorgeous night, not a cloud in the sky. We're walking down the middle of this road, and I knew they were there. I could smell them. The Koreans and the Chinese eat so much kimchi that is just laced with garlic that we could smell them before we could see them. And I knew that they were there. Why they didn't open fire on us . . . I mean, we were just walking down the road, like we were out for a nice stroll . . . I'll never know.

* * * * *

One of the guys in my company shimmied up the flagpole to the capital and pulled down the Seoul flag and put up the American flag. And that was the securing of Seoul.

We got up just about to the point, and an artillery shell landed about 4 feet in front of Mel. The only thing I remember was seeing his head fly by me, and from that point on, I was out. I came to in the MASH [mobile army surgical hospital] unit, but as I woke up, the doctor had a saw in his hand, and I looked up at him and I said, "What are you doing?" He said, "Well, I have to amputate your leg above the knee because we have no way of fixing your leg."

"Well, what are my options?"

"Well, we could try to get you back to Japan."

"Okay, try to get me back to Japan. That's fine by me." And so I passed out, and I guess three or four days later I came to, and I still had my leg. They were able to put a plate in the cartilage area that was blown out and a plate up in the top over my eye which was the part that was really bad because they couldn't stop it from bleeding. They got that stopped and so I'm still here.

* * * * *

My platoon was pinned down on a street in Seoul. We could not raise our heads more than six inches off the ground. I observed the following: papa-san/mama-san and three children carrying all their worldly possessions, walking down the middle of that street. Two blocks down we had a tank escort, and were again pinned by several snipers in an apartment building. The tank commander pulled his tank up to the building and swung the turret around to point the howitzer to blow the building down. He spotted an elderly man sitting in the doorway waving an American flag and yelling "Americans, Americans." At the risk of his own life the tank commander lifted the hatch and waved the man out of the doorway. The man just sat there and would not move. So rather than blowing the building from the bottom, he started at the top and after the second or third shell blew up, the man got the message and left.

* * * * *

The one thing that is prevalent, or stands out in my mind with all of this is that the military does make mistakes. My mother received a "Killed in Action" telegram when I was wounded the second time. I got back to Hawaii, and at the hospital I received my second Purple Heart. The colonel was surprised that my mother had been sent a "Killed in Action" telegram. He put a phone on my bed, and he said, "You call your mother and you tell her you're alive and everything's okay." And so I did, and at that point she had not received the Killed in Action telegram, so that when she did receive it she knew that it was a mistake. Of course, the newspapers at that time were monitoring all the telegrams, telegraph offices, and stuff like that. So they picked up on it, and there's an obituary for me somewhere in the *Minneapolis Star Tribune*.

BEN C. FULLMER

Ben served in the U.S. Army during the Korean War until October 1953. Having received basic training and intelligence training while in the Navy, he was assigned to work with the Intelligence Department getting POWs out of North Korea. Ben achieved the rank of corporal and returned home to work in business and to serve in various positions in the Church, including serving three missions.

One morning, when I landed at the main air base in Taegu, Korea, there were about two feet of snow on the ground. As I drove my jeep to the auxiliary air base twelve miles west of Taegu, I noticed some small children gathered around a small fire on the ground trying to keep warm. I asked a Korean adult about the children, and he said they were children of parents who had been killed by the North Korean soldiers and bombs. It broke my heart to see those small children alone, cold, and hungry.

When I arrived at the auxiliary base, I went directly to the commander and asked him if he was still using the vacant ammunition shed just inside the compound. He said no. I

Corporal Ben C. Fullmer.

explained that experience I encountered with the children after landing at the main air base in Taegu. I asked if we could use the shed as an orphanage, feed the children from the PX

Ben Fullmer set up a makeshift "orphanage" in a vacant ammunition shed for young Korean children like the two girls shown in this photo who had been orphaned when their parents were killed by North Korean soldiers and bombs.

Bottom Left: Orphaned young Korean boys playing a game that involved tops, a stick, and string.

[post exchange] and furnish them bunk beds and blankets from the supply center. I explained we could get some "mama-sans" to care for the children. He said that would be fine. We began making the necessary arrangements and brought a number of the small children to the shed along with some women to care for them. The children didn't have much clothing so I sent a letter to my Primary teacher from the Hillcrest ward and asked her if she could have our ward send some clothes for the children. The ward sent me thirty-two boxes of clothing.

* * * * *

Chung Ill Lee was a young North Korean soldier we captured. The commander said I could keep him as a houseboy to clean our weapons, tents, and make our beds rather than sending him to the POW camp at Pusan. The commander said, "Fullmer, you don't drink do you?"

I said, "No."

Then he said, "Rather than sending him down to the POW camp, you can use Chung Ill Lee as a houseboy if you will be the bartender in the officers' club." I became a bartender.

When I left Korea, Chung Ill Lee had a Book of Mormon in his possession. I have often wondered if he is now a member of the Church.

FERREL S. GAILEY

Ferrel served in the U.S. Army from April 1951 to January 1953 during the Korean War. He served with the 8th Army 558th Military Police Company Palace Guard, 3rd Division Military Police Company, maintaining equipment. Ferrel achieved the rank of corporal. The following account describes how he was protected from having to participate in any combat situations.

Ferrel Gailey in winter dress at Base Camp in Panmunjom, Korea, 1951.

I had just completed a mission for the LDS Church in the Northern States Mission. I was drafted in March or April 1951. I was sent to Fort Lewis, Washington, to be outfitted, then to Camp Roberts, California, for basic training. When my training was completed, I was sent to Korea on a troopship. It took seventeen days.

While being unloaded, I could hear what I thought were artillery shots, and to say the least—I really didn't want to leave the ship. I said a silent prayer, and as I walked down the gangplank and arrived at the bottom, there were fifteen of us who were pulled out of line for some reason or another and loaded onto a truck. When we arrived at our destination, I found that we had been selected to serve in the palace guard in Taegu. It was a spit and shine outfit called the 558 Military Police Company. I had been trained to be a combat infantryman so I knew that my prayer had been answered.

I walked the perimeter of the 8th Army headquarters under the leadership of General Van Fleet. As time passed, there was another assembly of MPs [military police]. I, along with another fourteen, was assigned to go to Panmunjom as one of the honor guard to protect the peace tent and its contents, usually at night. I along with a North Korean would stand or sit together through the tour of duty. Three hours on

Right: Ferrel Gailey standing next to the helicopter that flew delegates and other honor guard personnel to the peace talks at Panmunjom, Korea.

Top: A balloon being filled with gas at the peace talks in Panmunjom, Korea, December, 1951.

Center: Four of Ferrel's buddies standing guard at the site where the peace talks were being held in Panmunjom. L–R: Cpl. Richard Walters, PFC Delmore McAboy, PFC Patsy Montemurino, PFC Bill Scott.

Bottom: Honor Guard stationed at Panmunjom, Korea, 1952. Front L–R: PFC Howard Miller (Chicago, IL), PFC Joseph Nash (Monroe, NY), Lt. Henderson (Dallas, TX), Sgt Bill Pearce (Plant City, FL), Pvt. Merl Perves (Vista, CA). Back L–R: PFC Bill Scott (Froid, MT), Pvt. Ferrel Gaily (Syracuse, UT), Pvt. Loll Germadio, PFC Delmore McAboy (Pontiac, MI), Cpl. Vernon Scroggins (Rollins, WY).

and three hours off duty. To say the least, this was a great experience for me to be side by side with the enemy. I couldn't speak or understand the language although I felt comfortable with him. I may have been the only Latter-day Saint to serve at the peace talks in Panmunjom.

I also stood guard at the Bridge of No Return many times. It may be interesting to know that there was a neutral zone between the enemy and us. It was a circle with a radius of about a thousand feet as I recall. Neither the enemy nor us were to fly or shoot over it. Big gas-filled balloons marked it during the day and a huge light shone heavenward at night. The North Koreans had a base camp on the north perimeter and the allied forces had a base camp on the south.

The schedule for the peace talks would usually begin by our delegates flying in by helicopter to our base camp anytime from about 10:00 A.M. to 1:00 or 2:00 P.M. They would be driven to the tents where the talks would be held. The session would last anywhere from a few minutes to two or three hours, depending upon what was taking place. It was not unusual to see delegates come out and leave in a huff. We knew by their actions that things hadn't gone too well.

I served there several months and then I was transferred to the 3rd Infantry Division and was once again assigned to the MPs where I served for a month until they learned of my mechanical ability. I was then assigned to the motor pool where I helped keep the jeeps and trucks moving, made and installed road signs, etc. It was while I was there that I learned how precious life is and how quickly a man can be changed from being healthy to becoming a vegetable in a second.

My commanding officer had ordered me to take a truck and go to a certain fuel depot to get a load of gasoline for company use. Usually, it was kept in 50-gallon drums. I picked up my load of about twelve drums of gasoline and returned to my company. I had just turned off the truck and stepped on the running board when I heard an explosion. I looked in the direction of the sound and saw a young man tumbling through the sky like a rag doll, approximately fifty feet in the air. He had been standing in the back of [another] truck when it had struck a land mine. A helicopter medical team arrived shortly and took him to one of the medical units. I don't know whether he lived or not. When I got my wits about me I wondered why it had been him and not me. A truck with a load of gasoline had missed the land mine while an empty truck with a soldier in the back was not so lucky.

While serving in the 3rd Division I took the opportunity of visiting a buddy I had met in basic training who was serving in the 45th Division as a medic. When I found him, he was working on some GIs who had been brought in off the front lines. I had never seen in my lifetime such a scene of blood and dismemberment. After a short visit, I returned to my outfit and gave thanks for the blessings that were mine.

Late in November 1952, I had earned enough points to return home along with five or six others from the company. The night before we left to come home, two of the group came to my tent and invited me outside. I went with them. One of them being spokesman said as near as I can remember, "Corporal, we've been watching you from the day we met. We know there is a chaplain nearby but we feel you are closer to God than he. Would you kneel with us and give thanks for the protection we have received while we have been here?" The three of us knelt in a foot of snow beside a jeep. I prayed and gave thanks while we wept unashamedly. These were nonmembers of the Church. I was humbled. My testimony of the Word of Wisdom, chastity, the taking of the Lord's name in vain, and the keeping of covenants I had made in holy places, etc., had all been for my benefit. Others had recognized that there is something more valuable than self-gratification and immoral acts. I think perhaps I was the only LDS serviceman in our company.

I have seen the destruction and the misery that comes from war and the pain that is inflicted upon the innocent and homeless children. I have seen the ravages of hunger. No one really knows until they have been there. You can hear and read about it, but seeing it firsthand makes a guy more appreciative of America. It was a privilege to serve our country, and I would do it again if called upon to do so. I am so grateful to be an American. I don't feel this would be complete without saying that when we arrived on these shores (America) just three or four days before Christmas in 1952 that it was an emotional homecoming. We arrived in the evening and anchored in Puget Sound in the state of Washington and waited to disembark the following morning.

This is a land choice above all the lands.

DON A. GEORGE

Don served in the U.S. Navy during the Korean War from July 1950 to May 1954. He served aboard the USS Hector *AR 7 as well as the USS* Elkhorn *AOG 7 as a diesel engineman. Don achieved the rank of engineer 2 petty officer second class. He has since worked as a salesman and a nuclear technician.*

It was to be my first Christmas away from home and admittedly I was looking for anything from home. On Christmas day I remember standing at the handrail waiting for the mail plane to come in. Our mail was flown in by navy PBYs (seaplanes that landed in the harbor). We watched with eagerness as the plane made the approach and began to settle down next to the water when a Japanese boat crossed the landing path. In order to miss the boat the pilot dipped one wing and it hit the water. It kind of cartwheeled into the water with all hands watching. They made a real attempt to keep her afloat but it was to no avail. We watched all our Christmas mail go down with the plane. It left a lump in my throat to witness such a crash and to be without any mail from home at Christmas time. Later I did get a card from a neighbor but that was all.

* * * * *

We were in dry dock in Yokosuka to have the bottom of the ship sandblasted and painted before going home. We had no work to do and there was a missionary conference at Karazawa that lasted for five days that Sam and I plus two friends that were investigating the Church wanted to go to. During that time there was just no overnight liberty for any of the United Nations forces in Korea. I knew that, but I thought it was worth a try anyway. We all put in requests for the time off. The request had to go up the chain of command through the division and on to the executive officer. Of course, each in turn was denied the requests as expected.

That was when we went to request mast before the executive officer. The four of us were standing at attention in his office and he said, "This is the most unusual request. Why would I even consider it?" Then he leaned back in his chair and closed his eyes. All was quiet for a long time and then he said, "I know what kind of people you Mormons are, I knew a little Mormon girl in Pearl once some time ago." Then from out of the blue he said, "I don't know when they are going to be finished with the ship, but I do know that as soon as they are, we are going home. Can you be back in four days?"

I said, "Yes sir, we will be here when you say to be here."

Then he turned to the investigators and said, "You two be back in two days. Kelsey and George, be back in four days." I was shocked; we were going to conference. I know that the Lord inspired that decision.

We went and had just a wonderful time with the missionaries and on our own playtime that we took. We rented motorcycles and went into the mountains and toured the country. It was so special, that time together with special people. Sam and I had become real close friends since I had baptized him in Tokyo. We had always been friends, but now it was a real special relationship. We both enjoyed the conference and I still think to this day that the Lord was looking after us. We sat in a missionary testimony meeting from 6:00 A.M. to

George was able to attend an LDS missionary conference in July 1952. Vinol G. Mauss, President of the Tokyo Mission, presided at the conference. Pictured from left to right are: President Hansen, President Mauss, and President Anderson.

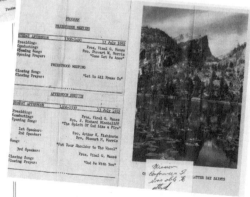

Program from an LDS missionary conference, Sunday September 13-17, 1952 in Kanazawa, Japan. The testimony meeting was in Japanese, and lasted 12 hours (6 A.M.–6 P.M.).

Program for the Tokyo Mission's quarterly conference held in Sasebo, Japan, July 12, 1952. Don was able to attend this conference just before setting sail for home.

6:00 P.M. Yes, for twelve hours we sat in a testimony meeting, listening to the Japanese converts bear their testimonies. Most of the testimonies were in Japanese but some were in English. You could feel what they were saying, and we were mesmerized as we took it all in. I was the last to stand and when I finished, President Maus got to his feet and said, "Brother George, I have been waiting all day for you to speak." My own testimony grew a thousandfold that day. When it was time to leave, we knew that we had had a special treat to remember for the rest of our lives. We arrived back at Yokosuka and out to the ship just as she was pulling out of the dry dock. In two hours we were at sea on our way home. The time was exactly right and we were on time.

Don completed a 12-week diesel course in 1952 at San Diego, California. He is pictured in the third row, third from the right. During most of his instruction Don maintained third in his class rankings. However, two weeks before graduation he met his future wife and dropped to thirteen by graduation. Upon graduation George's ship set sail for Japan.

* * * * *

It didn't take us long to know that Ruth and I were meant for each other, and we decided to get married while I was on

leave if I could get a recommend to the temple in Salt Lake City, Utah. I had been away for a long while, and I would have to go see a General Authority of the Church to see if I was worthy before they would let me go to the temple. I was able to talk to President Kimball, and for two days he questioned me and we fasted and prayed together. Finally, he invited Ruth into the office and wrapped his arms around me and said, "The Lord is pleased with you, Brother George, and He has forgiven you your sins."

We went through the temple on December 5, 1952 and were sealed together for time and all eternity. In my interview with President Kimball, he promised me that I would always be able to wear my temple garments as long as I was faithful and had a desire to wear them. I had no idea how that could be when I was stationed on a ship with no privacy at all and no way to care for my sacred garments.

That didn't set well with the chief and the first thing he said to me was, "George, you and I aren't going to get along."

My remark to him was, "That's okay by me, Chief; I am a short-timer." He had seen my records and found out that I was a Mormon, and he didn't like Mormons. He did everything in his power to mess me up, but it always backfired, and he came out looking bad. He reorganized my section and put all the guys with problems in my section. Every guy who had ever screwed up was now my responsibility to get them to perform. I got the crew together and told them that if they worked for me that I would protect them from anything that the chief could do to them.

* * * * *

Don served on the USS Hector, *a repair ship weighing 16,000 tons and carrying 800 crew members.*

HAPPY FAMILIES GREET RETURNED NAVY VESSEL

The Navy repair ship Hector returned from Korean waters yesterday to be greeted with an enthusiastic ovation from hundreds of families at the San Pedro Navy Supply Depot.

The 16,000-ton vessel returned with 800 crew members and 250 service passengers after 14 months in the Far East.

Her captain, S. F. Oden of Macon, Ga., said they had repaired 790 ships during the trip, many of them while under fire during the Inchon landing and during other crucial periods.

The Hector is a virtual scientific laboratory with 31 shops ranging from refrigerator-repair units to optical and lens-grinding departments.

"This picture was taken at the Hollywood Palladium on the occasion of honoring the United States servicemen from Korea. We pulled into port that day and were lucky enough to hear of the party in time to go and have a ball. This was before the dance started. The band was Les Brown." Don is pictured in the middle.

Now it is fifty years down the road and my Korean War experiences are still very much a part of my life. I have been ruled 100 percent disabled by the Veterans Administration doctors because of my Ménière's disease and my deafness. I have less than 10 percent hearing left in my right ear, and my left ear has been deaf for twenty years or more. The tinnitus has never left me for a single day, though my attacks of vertigo have subsided some in recent years. My head still has the pressure and unpleasantness that I've had for most of my life since the Korean War. Headaches and pressure are my constant companions. I sometimes stagger like a drunken sailor. I walk with my arm around my wife to keep from staggering too much. Would I do it again? In a heartbeat! I love my country, and I will always be a patriotic citizen. May God bless this country with a never-ending supply of patriotic young men to come to her aid in times of need.

BERT GIVIDEN

Bert served in the U.S. Army during the Korean War from January 1953 to December 1954. He served with A Company, 2nd Battalion, 38th Regiment, 2nd Division. During the war, Bert served as a machine gunner on the front line, and after the war as a TI&E NCO for his battalion, achieving the rank of sergeant first class. Bert has worked in school administration in Utah and is now retired.

Bert Gividen, basic training, 1953.

It is impossible to describe everything that goes on during a battle. It becomes very intense, adrenalin runs high and thick through your bloodstream, muscles tighten as though they were wired, your mind races to find solutions, eyes diligently watch the front . . . the side . . . you concentrate on sweeping with machine-gun fire, concerned about bullets hitting near your position or sailing through the front opening. You hunker down around the machine gun, fire away, holding to the cross-fire pattern, but tempted to sweep in front of your position at what you can see coming; trusting that the cross-fire pattern will catch the enemy, stop the enemy advance. You shout at the top of your lungs. Noise during a battle is one of the best weapons available: chilling sounds send shivers up and down your back, the enemy's back; your skin tightens. The hair on the back of your neck feels like it is standing straight out under your pith helmet and steel pot.

Enough said! This is the first time I have actually walked back through these experiences since that time. So far, I have been successful in pushing them to the back of my subconscious and learning to live with what happened. It was a nightmare. How did I ever get into that mess? How did I ever get through it in one piece? Why me in one piece and here today when others were not so fortunate. Why?

Bert Gividen on a troop train to Pusan, Korea, for Riot Duty.

Over the years it has become very obvious why young men are called (drafted) into the military. Older men are more cautious because of their experience and responsibilities. Younger men want to prove something to themselves and everyone else. Younger men are invincible and without responsibilities. Battles are exciting, but when it is all over . . . so what happened? What really happened? Did anything really happen? What was the cost? Who really cares—especially forty years later?

* * * * *

Sometime in the spring, I remember that Elder Harold B. Lee came to Korea. I suppose rumors had hit Salt Lake City, Utah, and the General Authorities regarding what was happening in Korea now that the fighting was over. Moral issues were rampant, and I am sure that is why Elder Lee came to hold this conference. It took quite a lot of preparation. The chaplains took most of the responsibility. Getting the men notified, free of mundane duties to attend, and then the logistics of travel were a challenge. However, we did it, and the conference was held. I had recently purchased a reel-to-reel tape recorder so I took it with me to the conference and set up right on the right side of the Quonset hut where the conference was held. Elder Lee stood right in front of me, and I recorded the first session. I was not the only one recording Elder Lee's remarks.

Elder Harold B. Lee at LDS Korean Conference.

Right: Bert Gividen planting flag on our side of the DMZ (Demilitarized Zone) in Korea.

Top: Bert Gividen in front of a sand bag bunker with eight-foot-thick walls. Korea.

Bottom: Bert Gividen in a helicopter used for patrol.

Then Elder Lee quit speaking and indicated that we would take a little break and return shortly. However, when we returned the power to the Quonset hut was not working. There were not even any lights. Wow, it was quickly apparent why. Elder Lee then got very specific regarding what he wanted to say to the men stationed in Korea. The reason the power had shut off is that he did not want his remarks recorded.

I had the opportunity to meet with Elder Lee. His wife had passed away and my Aunt Irene (my mother's sister) had been hired to take care of his cooking and household needs, so we had a good visit together.

Later, when Val and I were married in the Salt Lake Temple, I sent a letter to Elder Lee to see if his busy schedule would permit him time to marry Val and me. I never heard from him so just before our marriage, I called to see what I could find out. His remark was very interesting: "You asked me, didn't you? So, I'll be there." And he was.

Because of the contact with Elder Lee in Korea and because he married Val and me, I have always considered him a special man in my life. I was stunned when he died after only a short tenure as President of the Church.

* * * * *

There were no missionaries in Korea during the war or while I was there. Part of Elder Lee's message was that each of us should be living examples to others—be representatives of the Lord and take the gospel to those who do not have the gospel. His words sunk in. Many men had been on missions and knew how to effectively spread the gospel. I was timid about pressing my beliefs onto others, but found that through example, lots of questions were asked.

Through efforts of LDS men in Korea, the gospel began to spread. I do not know when the Korean mission was opened (sometime after I left), but when the missionaries arrived there were a lot of members. This is one of the strongest missions in the Church due to the effective work of military men who had been on missions and went to work in their spare time.

While I was the TI&E NCO, I would try to get members of the Church assigned to my unit to work for me. So, I would go to the back of a Duece truck delivering replacement soldiers, lift the back of the flap, and holler, "Is there anyone in there from Utah?" and if so, I would invite them to get off the truck and come with me. I would take them to the battalion commander and ask him to assign this man to my unit. Before I left TI&E, I found seventeen men to work with me who were all LDS.

I will never forget the one day that I flipped open the back of a truck and hollered, "Is there anyone in there from Utah?" and out bounded Jim Baird from Provo, Utah. He was so glad to see someone who was LDS that he jumped off that truck and said, "You just saved my life. I was headed to a rifle company." I knew how Jim felt because I was all by myself for so much of the time. Well, Jim was great to work with. He wrote home to his mother, who was a widow, and told her about me and my family. She then contacted my mother and they became very good friends. Jim was dependable and a hard worker. After he returned home from Korea he brought his mother to meet Val and me. Jim finished his college career at Brigham Young University and stayed on in the Department of Elementary Education. When I eventually came to BYU, Jim was the department chairman. My assignment was to work with the College of Education so Jim paved the way through the college by telling everyone how I saved his life in Korea by getting him off that truck headed to a rifle company. Well, over the years this has made a great story, and we have continued to be great friends.

HOMER K. HANSEN

Homer served in the U.S. Air Force from 1941 to 1974, participating in World War II, the Korean War, and the Vietnam War. He served as a fighter pilot and achieved the rank of major general. Promoted to captain in 1950, Homer was the first Air Force pilot to complete one hundred combat missions in the Korean War. He flew thirty-two different planes and saw twenty-eight countries during his military career.

Homer Hansen.

Colonel Samways called me and three wingmen one evening for a briefing. Our mission was to hit the airfield where North Korean aircraft were located. They had very few and most were concentrated at Pyonggang, an airfield east of the capital. Photoreconnaissance planes had taken pictures of the airfield that day and we reviewed them carefully that evening. The takeoff was scheduled at dawn on July 19—the first approved air strike north of the 38th parallel! The next morning we took off in fair weather from Itazuk, Japan, to fly our mission. It was the greatest distance from Itazuke that the F-80s had ever flown. Arriving in North Korea at 35,000 feet, we sighted the air base, let down, and attacked the airfield. Photos had shown there were twenty-three airplanes on the tarmac the day before. Well, they were all there, and we destroyed seventeen of them and damaged the other six. I am quite sure none were reparable to fly again, as our .50-caliber machine guns either set all the aircraft on fire or cut them in half.

I flew some good missions in Korea, but the following one was tops in the F-80. Not long after the Pyongyang strike in North Korea, I was asked by Colonel Samways to fly David Douglas Duncan, a *Life Magazine* photographer and reporter, on a combat mission. Colonel Samways didn't tell me to have David sit in the rear cockpit where anyone riding in an F-80 was always placed. Well, I thought much better photos could be taken from the front cockpit. After returning from our 300-mile, two-hour flight of rocketing tanks and strafing vehicles, David was perspiring profusely and looked beat; he stayed in the front cockpit for at least twenty or thirty minutes saying he couldn't get out for a while until he recovered from the flight. To follow another jet on strafing passes and to be trailing on his wing to get the photos of his aircraft, the target and the smoke from his rockets and guns all at one time requires you to rock the aircraft a bit. So this is what happened to David, but his photo coverage later shown in *Life Magazine* was great. By the way, when I came back to help him out he took the picture of me with my helmet on which was on the cover of *Newsweek* in November 1950.

The hairiest mission in a P-51 was when we moved and flew out of Sawaki, Japan, on the Inland Sea. I took off leading a flight of four P-51s with bombs, about 6:30 P.M. My P-51 was equipped with an eight-channel VHF radio, whereas many of our P-51s still had an old four channel set that really didn't handle range and clarity needed in combat. After takeoff we received the radio code word, "Fat Girl" which meant return to base. Rather than jettison our eight 500-pound bombs over the water and knowing my radio could relay the "Fat Girl" message to all that were on one of the eight channels, I proceeded on. Mistake? Yes! We hit the target about 9:30 P.M. and started home. I thought that the recall was due to threatening bad weather, but didn't realize until later that it was a serious typhoon. Well, I've flown in bad weather before and since, but never like that. Heavy rain and high winds buffeted our flight of four in close formation. It was now after 10:30 P.M., and it was dark! I elected to descend to enable the other three in my flight to have better visual contact with me as I knew our navigation lights on the wing tips and tail were often inoperative on these old P-51s. My wingmen later told me they were flying off my exhaust flames emitting from my 12-cylinder Merlin engine, six "flame throwers" on each side of the fuselage. Our heading, due to the extreme winds, was almost 90 degrees off.

Newsweek

NOVEMBER 20, 1950   20c

U. S. Air Power: The Long Arm of Retaliation

Captain Homer Hansen was asked to take LIFE MAGAZINE *photographer David Douglas Duncan on a combat mission in his F-80 fighter plane. It was a memorable experience for both men, and the resulting photographs were exceptional. Duncan took this photo of Homer, and it later appeared on the cover of* NEWSWEEK *magazine, November 20, 1950.*

I was trying to see lights on Hakata Peninsula but saw none and then Fukuoka came into view and that was the first indication to me that we would make it back to Itazuki. I chose to return to Itazuki rather than Sawaki due to the lack of mountains and a better radar control. Itazuki was only a few miles from Fukuoka so we had it made after seemingly hours of driving rain and turbulence. I take my hat off to the three guys on my wing. To remain in formation without losing sight of me was truly remarkable.

At Itazuki I dropped one off at a time circling at low altitude, three hundred feet, to keep the runway in sight. In fact, there was five inches of water or more on the runway and it was difficult to see the lights indicating where to turn off after the landing. We were glad to shut down and get out of our aircraft and into the vehicle that met us. Even though the water was over our shoes and our flight suits were soaking wet! We made it safely! Thank the Lord!

Phil C. Harrington is a veteran of both World War II and the Korean War. Harrington received the Air Medal for his service while in the 67th Tactical Reconnaissance Wing (called the "Fireflies.").

PHIL C. HARRINGTON

Phil served as a pilot in the U.S. Armed Forces in both World War II and the Korean War, starting his service in January 1942, and retiring from active duty as a lieutenant colonel in July 1964. He attended Brigham Young University and earned a degree in industrial education at the age of fifty, then he worked as a junior-high teacher for thirteen years.

On February 7, 1951, I was assigned to the 67th Tactical Reconnaissance Wing in Korea, flying unarmed C-47 aircraft to light up the sky and land by dropping flares. We were called the "Fireflies." I was the assistant commander of our unit. Two special flights come to mind. The first, on a cold wintry night, over a bend in the Yalu River, we dropped our flares, lighting up the enemy attempting to cross the frozen river. Each time they attempted to cross, our friendly units mowed them down. For this and other flights I was awarded the Air Medal.

The other [special flight] was when I piloted my C-47 over the Red supply center of Sibyon-ni, dropping flares to aid marine night fighters. It was a very clear night. As we dropped our flares and circled for another pass, we could see the Marines dropping their bombs and the enemy shooting back at them. Then there was a terrific explosion when the enemy's fuel dump was destroyed. Helping to destroy the dump as well as thirty-two enemy supply vehicles was the reason I received the Distinguished Flying Cross. Here is what the award says:

DISTINGUISHED FLYING CROSS

1. It is recommended that the following individual be awarded the Distinguished Flying Cross: Harrington, Phil "C", Captain AC1049872 45th Tactical Reconnaissance Sqaudron, 67th Tactical Reconnaissance Group APO970, United States Air Force Post Office Box 23, American Fork, Utah.

The Distinguished Flying Cross medal is a bronze cross patee on which is superimposed a four-bladed propeller, 1–11/16 inches in width. Five rays extended from the reentrant angles, forming a one-inch square. The medal is suspended from a rectangular shaped bar. The ribbon is 1–3/8 inches wide and consists of nine stripes: two outside stripes are Ultramarine Blue; the next stripes in from the outside are white; then two thick stripes of Ultramarine Blue; and the center stripe in Old Glory Red with narrow white stripes on either side.

Distinguished Flying Cross

The Distinguished Flying Cross was established in the Air Corps Act (Act of Congress, 2 July 1926, Public Law No. 446, 69th Congress). Various designs from the U.S. Mint, commercial artists, and the Office of the Quartermaster General, were submitted to the Commission of Fine Arts and on 31 May 1927, the Commission approved a design submitted by Mr. Arthur E. Dubois and Miss Elizabeth Will. Initial awards of the Distinguished Flying Cross were made to persons who made record-breaking long distance and endurance flights and who set altitude records. The Secretary of War authorized the first Distinguished Flying Cross to Captain Charles A. Lindbergh in a letter dated 31 May 1927. With the support of the Secretary of War, the Wright Brothers retroactively received the Distinguished Flying Cross. This award required a special Act of Congress, since the law precluded award to civilians.

The criteria for receipt of this award is to any person who, while serving in any capacity with the Armed Forces of the United States, distinguishes himself by heroism or extraordinary achievement while participating in aerial flight. The performance of the act of heroism must be evidenced by voluntary action above and beyond the call of duty. The extraordinary achievement must have resulted in an accomplishment so exceptional and outstanding as to clearly set the individual apart from his comrades or from other persons in similar circumstances. Awards will be made only to recognize single acts of heroism or extraordinary achievement and will not be made in recognition of sustained operational activities against an armed enemy.

(The Distinguished Flying Cross Society, 2003, www.dfcsociety.org)

Harrington received the Distinguished Flying Cross for his "extraordinary achievement" on an April 1951 mission. Shown above is Harrington receiving this award from Maj. Gen. Everest on January 6, 1952.

2. On 13 April 1951, Captain (then first Lieutenant) Phil C. Harrington displayed extraordinary achievement while participating in aerial flight. As Aircraft Commander of an unarmed C-47 flare launching aircraft, Captain Harrington displayed exceptional airmanship by piloting his aircraft over targets of opportunity for a continuous four-hour period, despite heavy intermittent ground to air automatic weapons fire encountered. During this trying period, Captain Harrington, supporting five fighter type aircraft, directly aided in destroy-ing one (1) fuel dump and thirty-two (32) supply-laden vehicles, by successfully illuminating the sighted targets during the periods of time when such illumina-tion was critically needed to insure the outstanding success of this mission. As a result of this mission, direly needed fuel, lubricants, and ammunition were destroyed, seriously hampering the enemy's potential. As of the date of this recom-mendation, Captain Harrington has flown seventeen (17) combat sorties.

3. a. At the time of this deed, offi-cer held the rank of First Lieutenant, and was assigned duty as pilot (1051), Base Flight Tactical Section, 3d Air Base Group, APO 954, flying combat missions. On 21 May 1951, officer was promoted to his present grade of Captain with no change in assignment or duty.

HARRY P. HEAD

Harry P. Head served in the U.S. Navy during the Korean War. While aboard the USS Philippine Sea, he joined a group of LDS sailors who helped to reactivate him and strengthen his testimony. Aboard another ship, the USS Kearsarge, he was set apart as an LDS Group Leader (1953–1954) and was able to have many experiences fellowshipping fellow sailors joining the church and coming into the war.

Above: Harry P. Head.

Above Left: April 19, 1952, Tokyo, Japan. "Philippine Sea *Brothers.*" L–R: Donald Johnson, Donald Cornwall, Harry P. Head, James D. Martin, Keith Gygi, Adam C. Cartwright, Fred Peterson, (Hartman Rector Jr. photographer).

Left: Homeward Bound! Harry P. Head and members of the LDS Serviceman's group he was a part of. They are relaxing on the island of Oahu, Hawaii, 1952. L–R: Donald Johnson, Hartman Rector Jr., Harry P. Head, Keith Gygi, Fred Peterson.

H. GRANT HEATON

Grant served in the U.S. Army during the Korean War from July 1952 to May 1954. He served with the 511th Military Intelligence Service Company as an interpreter and translator, and with POW exchange. Grant achieved the rank of corporal. He had the rare skill of being able to speak Chinese, and so was able to interact directly and become friends with many of the Chinese POWs.

One of the first things I did was to locate where the LDS meetings were held. I found Lieutenant Howard Hall, an engineer at one of the POW compounds. He actually did some work on our annex. Also a young man from Santa Clara, Utah, named Kimball, was stationed at a radar station not too far from the annex.

The beginning of 1953 saw the LDS Pusan Group well organized and working effectively as a missionary unit. Under the leadership of Elder Howard W. Bradshaw as group leader, and Elder Leon Ballard as assistant, the LDS men in the Pusan area were encouraged to take advantage of the opportunity afforded them of teaching the gospel to the Koreans.

Three meetings were held each week in the KBS Base chapel. The Sunday meeting was conducted as a testimony meeting. A special investigators' class was organized under the direction of Elder (Major) Glen Gillette, and Brother Ho Jik Kim. Meetings were held Tuesday and Saturday nights. These meetings were Bible discussion meetings and English classes. At the beginning of 1953, a group of Koreans were baptized into the Church. These were Mr. Johng, Sun-Chu, Mr. Kim, Jae-Hyung, Mr. Kim, Shin-Whan, and Miss Kim, Jung-Sook. In March, Chaplain Spencer D. Madsen was assigned to the Pusan area and added much to the leadership of the Pusan group. On April 5, the group was reorganized, due to the prior departure of Brothers Bradshaw and Ballard. Elder Howard G. Hall was appointed as group leader with Elder H. Grant Heaton and Elder Junius W. Gibbons as assistants.

One day, near Pusan, I was stopped by an MP [military police] for speeding. I was on my way to an evening Bible class at the Pusan Base chapel. Because so many Koreans had been killed or injured in automobile accidents, the military was very strict on speeding. It usually brought at least a one-month suspension of driving privileges for enlisted men. When the MP saw the trip ticket, he apologized and told me he would give me a "red light and siren escort" to my destination, which he did. I had him stop across from the base chapel, but my Korean students were all there waiting for me to open the door. They were really impressed that I had a police escort to attend their classes.

The base chapel was a wonderful facility for us. Not too many other denominations used it because they never had enough people out to church to warrant such a building. Chaplain Madsen was very helpful in getting use of this facility on days other than Sunday. Before it burned down in late November 1953, we had more than four hundred Korean students attending classes, both gospel and English during any week. When President Robertson (of the Japanese mission) came to a conference just before the chapel was destroyed, he saw the large group of Korean students there and said we were teaching more people in Korea than the entire Japanese mission force in Japan.

Because of the notice given to this conference, the chief of chaplains, Colonel Darky, informed us that we could no longer use the building for Korean civilians. A week later the chapel was destroyed by fire. Most of the LDS men in Pusan saw this as God's vengeance.

RICHARD H. HENSTROM

Richard served in the U.S. Army during the Korean War from December 1952 to December 1955, and remained in the Army Reserve until September 1961. He served as a chaplain, achieving the rank of first lieutenant in active duty, and a captain in the Reserves. Following his military service, Richard worked as a radio-TV newscaster and as an administrator for Brigham Young University Continuing Education.

The Korean War started during the time I was on my mission in Sweden. It was obvious that I would be drafted into the armed services when I returned from my mission. While in the mission field, I read in the *Church News* an article about how the Church was able to have members serve as chaplains. The process for requesting consideration was included. I wrote a letter of inquiry, receiving a response providing additional explanations, but indicating that I would need to wait until returning from my mission before beginning the process.

I was released from my mission in December 1951. After my return, I was required to report to the draft board to register my being available for service since I had been granted a deferment during the mission period. When I reported at Fort Douglas [Utah] the woman handling my papers indicated that I had never had a deferment for schooling, and I was allowed one year. Since I had been gone for two and one-half years, I decided it would be nice to be home with my family for awhile so I made the decision to return to the University of Utah and work on my master's degree.

This one-year's delay in military service basically kept me from being drafted immediately. (I would probably have been sent into active duty in Korea during the difficult time of 1952.) During the year I was studying, I worked with the Church on the chaplaincy appointment, which required that I volunteer before being drafted. I checked on volunteering as

Henstrom graduated from chaplaincy school in February, 1953. He was able to attend with two other LDS chaplains. L–R: Richard H. Henstrom (Army), Calvin C. Cook (Air Force), and Harlan Y. Hammond (Army). Richard H. Henstrom finished chaplaincy school fourth in his class, and with a rating of "Excellent." Upon graduation he was assigned to Fort Lewis, Washington. He was able to stop, "unofficially," in Salt Lake City and be set apart by Elder Harold B. Lee for this Army assignment.

As an LDS Chaplain, Richard Henstrom was able to organize and be a part of several LDS Servicemen's Conferences. The one shown above was particularly memorable because Elder Harold B. Lee was in attendance (seated on front bench in the center of the group).

an enlisted man if I could be placed in a military assignment related to my college study in radio/television communications. I would have liked some experience with the Armed Service Radio Network, but there would be no guarantee in this respect. Part of the chaplain processing required a meeting with Elder Harold B. Lee of the Council of the Twelve who was chairman of the Church's Military Services Committee. The following is an excerpt from my accounting of associations with President Harold B. Lee:

As a part of the application process to become a chaplain in the Army, the Church needed to make a formal recommendation to the army chief of chaplains. I was interviewed in the fall of 1952 by Elder Harold B. Lee in his office. He created a very friendly atmosphere, asking me about my background, my mission, schooling, and then about my not being married since I was twenty-four years of age at the time. He made no direct emphasis on my needing to give immediate consideration on this important step; however, he did make a few humorous comments: "Remember, two can live cheaper than one. It's when it becomes three and four that it becomes somewhat of a challenge," and "Remember, love is blind, but the neighbors aren't." There was a folder on his desk. It must have been an inch or more thick. At the conclusion of the interview he slapped his hand down on the folder and remarked: "Well, Richard, there is nothing in here that would prevent the Church from recommending you for the Chaplain's Corps." This is all I can recall about this first meeting.

* * * * *

The Protestant ministers did everything in their meetings—they did the prayers, read the scriptures, and gave the sermons. They got help from other serviceman for the music. I didn't have to do anything against my basic beliefs such as wearing robes and passing the plate. They usually had collection boxes or plates at the back of the chapels or tents. I did have to keep track of this money and turn it in to the division offices each month. This first meeting took place on Sunday, November 22, 1953. It was held in the large mass tent. It had been raining hard all night and continued up to the meeting time. I thought everything had been prepared, but I was nervous. How would they accept a Mormon giving a talk in a Protestant service? Everything went as planned, except that right in the middle of the service the tent split open and poured water on the congregation. It had collected water from the rain into a sagging portion of the canvas tent. Of course, this meeting didn't last very long. Later, a number of the men humorously accused me of trying to baptize them. After this experience there wasn't much that bothered me when it came to conducting services in these surroundings.

Directly below: Each chaplain serving in Korea was allowed to visit the Holy Land during his tour of duty. Henstrom made this trip, but due to the political unrest there were many areas closed to the public. Before his return to the United States, he was also able to visit Cairo, Egypt.

Below left two photos: The servicemen put on a Christmas celebration for the Korean children in 1953.

DON RUE HICKMAN

Don served for over thirty years in the U.S. Army during World War II, the Korean War, and the Vietnam War. Don was drafted into the Army in July 1941 and eventually retired from the armed services as a brigadier general in September 1972. He served in the 27th Infantry Regiment during the Korean War. During World War II, Don was a captain in General Patton's 3rd Army.

Above: Don Rue Hickman served in World War II, the Korean War, and the Vietnam War.

Below: "I spent six to eight hours a day over the battlefield in my chopper!" says Hickman of his experience in Vietnam, 1968.

Below Right: Maj.Gen. Ray Peers with Brig. Gen. Hickman in firebase, 1968.

That afternoon, Lieutenant Colonel Gilbert J. Check, the 1st Battalion commander, and I talked to the principal of the school where our battalion was housed. The school principal spoke good English, and we asked him his views on the Korean "police action." We had noticed that no cheering crowds were at the port to greet us, and as we moved the battalion through town toward the school, we noticed that the Korean people were very indifferent to our actions. Some gazed as though seeing a miracle, but others just looked away and continued about their normal business of the day. We asked the Korean schoolmaster what he thought about the communist invasion, and who he thought would win. His answer then seemed to explain the attitude of most Koreans toward the war. He said, "We hope you win, but in any event, we hope someone wins because we do not want our country to be divided. If we can be united in a democracy, that is fine; our next choice would be to be united in a communist state; it would be no choice at all to be a divided state." The schoolmaster offered his services to us as an interpreter, but we declined his offer, as we felt he was not very sympathetic to our cause.

Later, I was reminded of this teacher's words when I read in the *Stars and Stripes*, the service newspaper, that when an old Korean statesman had been asked who he wanted to win, he replied, "If you are a blade of grass, does it matter if you are eaten by a sheep or a cow?"

JAMES K. HILL

James served in the U.S. Army from October 1951 to September 1953 during the Korean War. He served with the Howe Company, 27th Infantry Regiment "Wolfhounds," 25th Division, as an administrative sergeant. James is an alumnus of Brigham Young University, and has worked as a banker and in various assignments dealing with youth in the Church.

I was drafted shortly after my graduation from Brigham Young University. I took basic training at Camp Roberts, California. I was in a 16-week infantry training group, and it was about the toughest experience of my life, to that date. I was in excellent physical condition due largely to my years on the BYU track team under Clarence Rovison. I was a pole-vaulter and that probably was an advantage for me because so much of army training is physical. After the training cycle was completed, I was awarded the "Outstanding Trainee" plaque. I still have it hanging in my office at home.

Before going to Korea, I was selected to train further at the Leader's Course at Camp Roberts. This was even stiffer training because the competitive atmosphere was so evident. These were selected participants from around the base and everyone was trying to outdo each other. I enjoyed this part of my training and made some worthwhile friends there.

I was then placed on orders for Korea. Several thousand troops were shipped out of Camp Stoneman in California for a two-week sea voyage to Japan. We were sent to Camp Drake, Japan, for a few days of added training and then left for Pusan, Korea, on another troopship. At Pusan we were packed into a small train headed for the front lines which at that time (November 1952) were above the 38th Parallel in North Korea. Two or three days later, we arrived at a military base in Chunchon and then separated out to various infantry outfits. I was lucky enough to be assigned to H Company of the 27th Infantry Regiment (25th Division). This was one of the elite units in Korea at the time with an outstanding reputation for military excellence. I was originally assigned to the machine-gun platoon which is a difficult place to be on the front lines.

We fought against the Chinese in most of our battles, but occasionally we'd encounter the North Koreans. We had forty ROK (Republic of Korea) soldiers attached to our company, ten in each platoon. They were, by far, the best soldiers in our company because they were all professional soldiers. The ROK leader was one of the finest men I have ever met, a man by the name of Kim Tu Chuel. He and I became good friends after I was called off the line to serve with a new company commander by the name of Albert E. Teller, Jr. Teller was a first lieutenant, a veteran of the World War II in the South Pacific, and he turned out to be the finest example of leadership I had ever seen. I've yet to meet another man who could inspire others as well as Lieutenant Teller.

*27th Infantry Regiment
Distinctive Unit Insignia crest.*

Our regiment was involved in a number of important military engagements while I was in Korea, and we lost a number of extraordinary men. I was one of the very fortunate ones who came out of the war with nothing more than frostbite on both feet.

The most important story of my military tour of duty, however, centers around a young Korean boy whose parents had been killed in the bombing of Seoul. He was with Howe Company when I arrived there, having been picked up by a previous first sergeant while he was on a trip down to the city of Seoul. This little boy, twelve or thirteen years old, was being evacuated from the city along with thousands of other homeless people. Our sergeant was looking for someone to act as a houseboy while we were off the line. He picked up this boy, whose name was Kim Hyun Gun, and stuffed him in a duffel bag so he could get past the MPs [military police] on the road to the front. Little Kim and I became the best of friends. He could speak English well and even acted as an interpreter when we picked up a prisoner, etc. He could speak English even better than the much older ROK soldiers.

38th Parallel

In consequence of the swift movement into Korea by Russian forces at the end of World War II, President Harry S. Truman issued General Order No. 1, which designated the 38th parallel as the dividing line of U.S. and Soviet interests in the Korean peninsula. Over the ensuing years, efforts by the United Nations and the U.S. to reunify Korea met with little success. With the formal division of North and South Korea in 1948, any hopes for erasing the importance of this imaginary line in the sand evaporated. Today, the 38th parallel continues

United Nations troops crossing the 38th parallel.

to provide the fragile line separating the two Koreas. Even since the official cessation of hostilities in July of 1953, many skirmishes have taken place along this border, and hundreds of soldiers and civilians have died on both sides of the border.

After accumulating enough points (thirty-six) to rotate home from Korea, I made a promise to my little Korean friend. I promised that I would find a way to bring him to this country so he could go to school here and start a new life for himself. We corresponded regularly for nearly twelve years after the war ended, and I finally got clearance to bring him to the United States as an exchange student. He had, by then, served his military time in the Korean Air Force. My family and I were living in San Jose, California, when he arrived in San Francisco. The local newspapers got wind of this story and were at the airport when he got off the plane. It was a wonderful reunion for Kim and me, and my family fell in love with him instantly. He was eventually enrolled in Pasadena City College and had a part-time job with the Burroughs Corporation. My family and I moved back to Utah shortly afterwards while Kim was going to school and working.

A tragedy struck us all when my wonderful friend, Kim Hyun Gun, contracted cancer of the stomach which spread to his spine. In a very short time, he passed away in California, but before he died, I promised to bring his younger brother, Kim Hyun Chull to America. He lived with us for nearly three years while attending BYU. He received his master's degree from BYU and then departed for Korea where he became an officer for a major steel company in that country. He subsequently married and had three beautiful little girls. They have visited with us in this country on three different occasions with their charming family. We always visit the gravesite of his brother when he is here.

The above story is, to me, more important than any other military activities that I was involved in.

National Guard 116th Engineer Combat Battalion

No story of Saints at war in Korea would be complete without mention of the National Guard 116th Engineer Combat Battalion and the LDS men who were a part of it. The 116th was composed of members of the Idaho National Guard, with Battalion headquarters at Idaho Falls: Company A, Rigby; Company B, St. Anthony; and Company C, Ashton. Many of the men were veterans of World War II, having served in the Army, Navy, Marine Corps, and the Air Force. Most of this group were married with children at the time we were activated for federal service during the Korean War. The 116th was one of the first, if not the first, National Guard unit activated for federal service during the Korean War. The 116th was the first National Guard unit to land in Korea. This battalion was also activated, along with many of the same men, for service during the Berlin Airlift and for the Vietnam War. *(Provided by Eldon D. Hinkley. Eldon served in the U.S. Army from August 1950 to July 1952 during the Korean War. He served with the 116th Engineer Combat Battalion, Company A and Headquarters Company as a commander and supply officer. Eldon achieved the rank of captain, receiving commendations for an outstanding job of simply doing his duty and doing it well. He also served in the Marine Corps in World War II.)*

ALBERTA JEAN OWENS HULEN

Alberta Jean Owens Hulen.

Alberta Jean Owens (Hulen) served in the U.S. Navy as a WAVE (Women Accepted for Volunteer Emergency Service). She served as a Hospital Corpsman from February 1952–April 1954. She was trained at the Hospital Corps School in San Diego. She was stationed both in Seattle, Washington, and also at the Camp Pendleton Naval Hospital in Southern California, where she worked in obstetrics. Her first husband was also a Corpsman in the Fleet Marines.

(quoting Alberta)—"Worked mainly in camp Pendleton, California, hospital there on base. I loved my job working in the hospital. My first husband was also a Corpsman in the fleet marines. Served in a variety of Church callings, including: Primary presidency, and Relief Society presidency."

CLIFTON W. JENKINS

Clifton served in the U.S. Navy from October 1948 to April 1969, during both the Korean and Vietnam Wars. He served with numerous ships and stations in his eleven years as an enlisted man and ten as an officer. Clifton achieved the rank of lieutenant. His civilian career has included being a school teacher and a justice of the peace.

We were at general quarters for gunnery exercises. At this time I was assigned to the port 20-millimeter. When it was my turn to shoot, my right barrel jammed with the breach open.

I called "silence" and we checked it out. We found that an empty brass hadn't come all the way out and was blocking the breach from going forward. We recocked the gun and the brass fell out.

I got ready to fire next time and got in my harness. I ordered the magazines loaded. As I looked into the breach of the gun I saw something where I shouldn't have seen anything. Something told me it was bad.

I ordered unload and had the gun crew run a ramrod through the right barrel. Out fell a live round. Each round contained four ounces of propellant powder and two ounces of explosives. If I had pulled the trigger, the round in the barrel would have been exploded by the round rammed forward by the breach. This would have caused the explosion of twelve ounces of explosives with nothing between the blast and my body but a canvas bag.

No one, gunnersmates or others, was able to explain how the round in the barrel got past the empty brass. This is one of several times I can honestly say the Holy Ghost saved my life.

Thank God.

KEITH A. JENSEN

Keith served in the armored cavalry during the Korean War from 1950 to 1953. He served in the Officer 6th Tank Battalion, 24th Infantry Division as platoon leader. Keith achieved the rank of first lieutenant. Since the war, he has worked in construction and real estate, and has served in several positions in the Church, including being stake patriarch in four different stakes.

In June 1951, Keith A. Jensen received his commission as 2nd Lieutenant and was attached to the 6th Tank Battalion of the 24th Infantry Division. As commanding officer of the reconnaissance platoon, Jensen had thirty-two men under his direction.

During my tour of duty with the 24th Infantry Division, several battles were fought, in which waves of North Koreans attempted to penetrate the U.S. battle lines. They were thrown back with many losses. As the year 1951 ended, temporary peace was made effective when a conference was held at Panmunjon, in the demilitarized zone.

* * * * *

While in Korea, I wrote many letters and poems. Most of the verse was for Mildred, but a few were about other subjects including the conditions which we faced daily. Two of these were "Night on the Battlefield" and "Cowboy of the Road." While in Korea, I sent one of my poems entitled, "An Anchor is Needed," to the *Improvement Era* (a magazine published in Salt Lake City, Utah). I received a letter of acceptance dated January 31, 1952 with a check for $4.20, which I still have in my files. These poems, together with over six hundred and fifty others, will one day be found in my new book of poetry, yet to be published.

It was about this time [that my poem was accepted] that my interpreter, a Korean, by the name of Lew Yong He, was baptized in the icy waters of the Kumsong River. A few of us waited on the snowy bank for a large ice floe to pass. When it had gone by, Lew and I quickly entered the fast-moving water where I performed the baptism. After getting dressed, we met in my tent, where he was confirmed a member of the Church. Lew loved the Church and wanted to be fully involved. We learned of Sunday services being held in an adjacent battalion and joined with them each week when not on active duty. I had occasion to use the powers of the priesthood on several occasions with good results.

On or about January 15, 1952, another officer and I were allowed to fly to Tokyo, Japan, for a week of R&R (rest and recuperation.) He immediately found himself a Japanese lady of the night, while I did some sightseeing and stayed in my hotel room. I kept my standards of morality during that war as well!

By February 1952, I had been promoted to the rank of first lieutenant and was asked to stay with my battalion by signing up for another tour of duty. By that time, I had almost enough points for eligibility to return to the United States. I decided that I had been in Korea long enough and elected to return home. On April 3, 1952, orders were issued, which released me from the 6th Tank Battalion and attached me to the 82nd Airborne Division, then located at Fort Bragg, North Carolina. My trip home was much shorter in length than it was when en route to Korea (twelve days) on the troopship, USS *America.* My first flight was on a four-engine, propeller-driven military airplane, which carried me to Tokyo, Japan. I hurriedly called Mildred and informed her of my expected time of arrival in the U.S. She, together with our little daughter "Cookie" were then at my parent's home in Pocatello, Idaho. Several days later, I was on my way to the United States of America in another four-engine, troop carrier propeller airplane. We stopped at Wake Island and Honolulu, Hawaii, after which we finally landed at the United States Air Force base in San Francisco, California. There I learned that another army airplane was leaving shortly for the airbase at Mountain Home, Idaho, and I decided to become a passenger.

BLAINE H. JOHNSON

Blaine Johnson served during the Korean war in the 213th as a captain and a gunnery officer for his battalion. He was involved in Korea from 1950-1951, and was given a medical discharge in 1952. After WWII Johnson finished his masters degree at Columbia in vocal music and choral conducting and took a teaching job at Dixie College in Saint George, UT. After his service in Korea he taught at what eventually became Southern Utah University for 30 years. He was Bishop of the Cedar City 8th Ward and later served a mission with his wife in Florida. He is currently a sealer in the Saint George, Utah Temple.

The Korean experience was a strange disoriented episode in the flow of my life as well as in the lives of all my friends and comrades. Many who were called to active duty during that fateful month of 1950 had to change radically the direction of their lives.

Korea was a place that came close to being that which every GI at some time called "the place God forgot." Other sayings were less complimentary and inappropriate to quote here.

We landed at Pusan Harbor after a voyage of about twelve days. The sun was shining when we stood on solid ground, but the temperature was three degrees below zero. There was no snow. Kids were running around dressed only in a gunny sack with arm and head holes cut into it. No shoes. No underwear. I was dressed with thermal underwear and two pair of trousers (one pair was heavy wool). I was freezing. I'm sure there are miserable people everywhere in the world perhaps worse off than those Koreans. They had suffered deprivation of homes, food, clothing, bedding, garden space—everything. They had run up and down the peninsula as the fortunes of the war changed.

We had arrived at the time General Richardson had consolidated the allied lines and had begun the gradual push back to the north. So successful was the drive that by the time we had passed the combat-ready tests and been assigned to a unit, we had to travel northward to the

Hwachon Dam in what is now North Korea. We were in support of the U.S. 1st Marine Division.

On the night of our first twenty-four hours of position occupation, the Republic of Korea (ROK) lines broke. The Chinese troops poured through and we were forced to evacuate, pull south about twenty-five miles, and go back north into another valley. This valley narrowed down to a narrow defile with high cliffs on either side. A stream ran down the canyon by the side of a very narrow road.

We occupied a firing position where the canyon widened enough to accommodate the battalion. We hadn't occupied our spot more than a few hours when our forward observer, Lieutenant Stafford Snow, returned saying that Chinese were pouring down the canyon toward us. Every effort was made to communicate with X Corps headquarters, but because of the high cliffs about us, the radios couldn't reach them.

It was getting on toward evening, and every minute we expected to see the Chinese pouring over the low hills in the bottom of the canyon immediately to our front. Thousands of refugees had been pouring down the narrow road. It was a scene of absolute chaos. Frank Dalley, our CO [commanding officer], ordered all units to pack up and be ready to move. Still no radio communication. We were really in a tight spot.

Suddenly a radio message came through—just one fragment, "Move south to vicinity of Blue Star Airstrip." No authentication. That was all we heard. No other radio message came for the next several hours. The message was taken as official, and we began to move with the refugees down the road. Darkness came quickly. We couldn't show lights at all. I rode on the hood of the half-track armored vehicle in order to direct the driver, Arthur Dustin.

213th Armored Artillery Battallion

One of the most celebrated units of the Korean War was the 213th Field Artillery Unit from Southern Utah, which was activated in August of 1950. The original composition of the unit was made up of 600 men, almost all of whom were LDS. The participants came from battallions in Cedar City, Richfield, Fillmore, and St. George. Remarkably, of those sent in the original deployment, all returned home safely. Under the capable leadership of Col. Frank Dalley, a faithful Latter-day Saint, the men of this unit were commended on multiple occasions for their valor—even in the midsts of some harrowing battlefield experiences. Headquarters Battery and A Battery were given the Distinguished Unit Citation. Truly, the men of the 213th performed impressively as a band of modern stripling warriors. (The above description was inspired by an article on the history of the Unit by Don Ray Alger, Command Sargent Major. It was published in the *Richfield Reaper* in commemoration of the 40th Reunion of their activation which was held in August, 1990. The photograph is from the *Church News*.)

KOREA CHORUS—Seated on the ground among the trees on a hill-top, Mormon boys of the 213th Armored Artillery batallion are led by Sgt. Norman W. Gates in singing a familiar L. D. S. hymn as a part of their Sunday service.

The move down the canyon was tedious and terrifying. We occupied a position about ten miles south and set up a firing position and began firing back up the canyon from informa-

tion received from adjacent units. Sniper fire was everywhere. Lieutenant Sullivan, commander of Battery B, phoned in to the Fire Direction Center, which I was in charge of. He informed me that he had six Chinese troops bottled up in a culvert. What should he do with them? I told him under the circumstances we couldn't handle prisoners and to use his own judgment. Well, Mac solved it somehow. I never did find out for sure what happened. I do know that he could not have harmed a soul, enemy or not.

We survived that night and the next day, the next night, and several days and nights after that with no sleep day or night. It was a weird, awful experience. Although it was still cold and wintry, I went down to the Pukhan River, stripped off my clothes, and bathed. What a great feeling to be clean again. We had a chance to sleep for the first time in over four days. I will not soon forget the feeling of ecstatic repose as I lay down to sleep. It seemed I had slept for many hours. I looked at my watch and ten minutes had elapsed. This went on for the next twelve hours.

As we moved south and arrived at a safe distance below the Pukhan River, we set up tents and tried to get our operations back to normal. Since we had lost one half-track loaded with parts of tents and other equipment, we found we needed a ridgepole for one of the large squad tents that was to house the battalion headquarters. The tent had to be raised between two trees. This was difficult and required every available man to raise the four to five hundred pounds of weight. I called [Arthur] Dustin to come help, but he was busy polishing his vehicle. I called again with the response, "Just a minute." When I called the third time with a dozen men trying hard to raise the tent, I lost my temper and, with an ax in my hand, I walked swiftly in his direction, the ax raised above my head. I guess I had "lost it." However, Dustin came running, and the tent was raised. We were awfully tired.

* * * * *

I had spent a pleasant day with the LDS chaplain touring some spots of interest around the city. The greatest impression of our afternoon was to stand at the foot of Mount Fujiyama. What an awesome sight. When I returned to the hospital, the door to my room was closed. Usually it was always open. As I entered, a cloud of cigarette smoke filled my eyes and nose. A Japanese girl, a nurse, was smoking a cigarette which she had taken from the nightstand by my bed. We all were given a carton of cigarettes each week, which I used for trading. Anyway, the girl was very embarrassed and frightened. I gave her the carton and forgot about it until after I had gone to bed.

A knock on my door was rather strange. Nurses and attendants never knock. There stood the Japanese nurse. She came to give back the cigarettes because she couldn't leave the hospital with them. She would be arrested for stealing military supplies. This was five hours after she was supposed to go home. She offered to sleep with me if I would give her written authorization to carry the cigarettes home! I was astounded. Of course I gave her a note so she could pass through the gate. I scolded her for waiting so long. Her simple answer was, "I was afraid." In return for my note, she promised she would look up the LDS chaplain and tell him what had happened. I knew he would tell her to receive the missionaries. I perhaps will never know how that all turned out.

By July, 1951, I was home in Cedar City, Utah, after stopping at the hospital for a few weeks near Santa Barbara, California. In fact, while at that hospital, Loa, Nancy Claire, Fella, and Grandma Johnson came down to see me. I was poor company even though I was glad to see them again.

So ended my military years. I have to attest that I was preserved through several incidents that could easily have been disastrous. I thank God for that deliverance and for the deliverance of so many of my dear friends, but especially that my brothers survived even more hazardous duty than I experienced.

JACK R. JONES

Jack served in the U.S. Navy from 1945 to 1962. During the Korean War, he served in Company C, 1st Battalion, 5th Marines, 1st Marine Division as a commanding officer. Jack achieved the rank of captain and was awarded the Navy Cross for combat heroism, along with several other medals and awards. He currently serves as a stake patriarch and temple worker in southern California.

The President of the United States takes pleasure in presenting the

NAVY CROSS

to

CAPTAIN JACK R. JONES, UNITED STATES MARINE CORPS,

for service as set forth in the following CITATION:

For extraordinary heroism as Commanding Officer of Company C, First Battalion, Fifth Marines, First Marine Division (Reinforced), in action against enemy aggressor forces in Korea, from 27 November to 7 December 1950. Assigned to reinforce friendly troops pinned down on a reverse slope by direct automatic weapons fire when driven from commanding high ground near Yudam-ni by a numerically superior hostile force estimated at two regiment strength, Captain Jones boldly led his company over unfamiliar terrain under cover of darkness and, reaching his objective to find that all other officers in the immediate area were casualties, unhesitatingly assumed over all command to launch an attack, killing approximately 65 of the enemy and driving the remainder from the ridge line. In the early morning of 29 November, he bravely exposed himself to direct enemy small-arms, mortar and machine-gun fire to reconnoiter hostile positions well in front of his own lines and, although painfully wounded in the right leg, continued to observe the opposition and direct his troops in beating off heavy attacks. Throughout the day, he continually moved among his men, supervising and personally assisting in the removal of more than 200 casualties while refusing aid for himself. When a regiment of the enemy employing small-arms, machine-guns, mortars and hand grenades attacked his defensive position in sub-zero weather on the night of 30 November, Captain Jones daringly moved back and forth along his sector in the face of intense hostile fire, encouraging his men, supervising the evacuation of casualties and directing the defense. By the following morning, the enemy were repelled with losses of approximately 200 killed, with but 16 casualties to our forces. Again attacked by an enemy regiment on the night of 6 December at Hagaru-ri, he continually exposed himself to heavy mortar barrages while maneuvering his men to fill gaps in the defensive perimeter. During the heaviest period of fighting, he gallantly led a tank into position to place effective fire on the enemy and, although again wounded in the right leg by mortar shell fragments, continued to direct his forces throughout the long, bitterly cold night until the opposition retired, leaving 241 of their dead within 200 yards of the company front lines. Later, despite his wounds and frostbite in the hands and feet, he led his company into Majon-Dong as a well organized and fighting unit. By his outstanding courage, skilled leadership and valiant devotion to his duty, Captain Jones served to inspire all who observed him and upheld the highest traditions of the United States Naval Service.

For the President,

(signed) Secretary of the Navy.

JOHN MILTON JONES ✬✬✬

John served in the U.S. Navy during both World War II and the Korean War. He had joined the Navy in 1933, and continued reenlisting until he retired from the Navy in 1959. His last few years were spent training the new sailors. John achieved the rank of chief boatswain's mate.

I reenlisted in 1952 and was stationed aboard the APA George Clymer #27 (attack transport flagship). After I was on board I found out that the ship was going to South Korea to be in the Korean conflict. We went into South Korea as China was with North Korea. I was master at arms, in charge of making sure that the South Koreans had something to eat, and somewhere to sleep. We sometimes fed them on board ship and let them sleep aboard. When the fighting ended we helped them clean up the different places and build or put up tents on shore so they could return to land. It was during this time General Macarthur wanted to cross over the Yellow River and go on to North Korea.

In Tokyo in 1953, President Robertson of the Far East Mission set me apart as a group leader for the ships and bases in our flag group. There were three of us LDS members aboard the flagship to begin with, a Lieutenant Richardson, a third class electrician's mate (Brother Roberts) and myself. We started holding services on board ship and attended services at the ports we stopped at. Our services aboard ship were soon attended by a nice-sized group of servicemen. Many of them

After serving in the Pacific Theater during World War II, Jones re-enlisted in 1952 and served through the remainder of the Korean War.

General Douglas MacArthur

Few soldiers in the history of military engagements have cast a longer shadow than General Douglas MacArthur. Over his career, General MacArthur was both revered and despised. A graduate of the United States Military Academy and a seasoned veteran from prior conflicts, MacArthur served as Commander of the United Nations forces in the early months of the Korean Conflict. Ironically, he viewed Korea as an incidental player in terms of American interests in the Pacific. It was during the Korean War that MacArthur celebrated some of his greatest victories, including the landing at Inchon. It was also during the Korean War that he endured some of his costliest defeats. Although his command over U.S. and U.N. troops lasted only nine months, his impact upon the conflict was key. Following a series of well-publicized spats with his commander and chief, President Harry S. Truman, General MacArthur was relieved of his post. Shortly afterwards, he arrived home to a hero's welcome.

were from the troops that we carried for amphibious landing.

In Hong Kong, with the help of a Sister Nora Ko and others, we were able to conduct an all-Chinese meeting in the back of Chuck Pak Lun's clothing store. I read in the Church News that Elder Harold B. Lee and President Robertson, mission president of the Far East Mission, were speaking at a meeting with the Saints in Hong Kong. Nora Ko walked up to President Robertson and asked "When is the Church coming back to Hong Kong?"

President Robertson put his hand on her shoulder and said, "Nora, as long as there are loyal Saints like you in Hong Kong, the Church is always here." We entered Hong Kong for R&R [rest and recuperation]. I met a Catholic priest on the dock. He asked if I was LDS. When I told him I was he told me of Louise Wood, a mother of two—a girl of fourteen and a boy of twelve. Her husband was chief engineer of American Airlines. She wished to meet me. I contacted her and we made arrangements to hold a meeting in her home. We were able to hold several meetings there before my ship pulled out to sea.

I kept reenlisting and in 1956 I started pushing Boots or shall we say, I started giving the sailors the kind of training they need to be a success in the Navy. I stayed at the Navy Training Center in San Diego, California, until I retired from the Navy in 1959.

RAY D. LLOYD

Ray served in the U.S. Army from September 1950 to May 1952 during the Korean War. He served with the 555th Field Artillery, 24th Infantry Division, as battalion operations chief, as well as with the 1st Field Artillery Observation Battalion as chief forward observer. Ray achieved the rank of master sergeant. His work since the war has been in the area of biomedical research. The following are excerpts from several letters he wrote during his service in Korea.

December 23, 1951.

Well, today was Sunday and I believe it was one of the most outstanding days of my life. I went over to the 6th Tank Battalion to church. We had about ten guys there, and I led the singing. The lesson was about Christmas. It occurred to me that I am real lucky to be here for Christmas, because over here, Christmas means just what it is supposed to—not a commercialized drinking day. The lesson, given by a major, who is division artillery surgeon and from Salt Lake City, Utah, was about Christ's First and Second coming and was really fine. (The man's name is Dr. Newton.) But the best part of all was after Sunday School we went out and witnessed the baptism of Loo, one of our Korean brothers. Lieutenant Jensen of the 6th Tank Battalion has been working with him for months now, and he finally decided to be baptized. Lieutenant Jensen wanted to wait until it was warmer, but Loo wanted to have it done now. So we broke holes in the ice, and they went out into the river. It was really a beautiful thing to see. Then after they got into some dry clothes we went into the lieutenant's quarters and confirmed Loo.

My experiences here today have really made me realize how wonderful the whole thing really is. It made us all feel humble and renewed our faith and strengthened our testimonies. In the confirmation blessing the lieutenant told him that the thing that he had expressed a desire to do (genealogy for his people) was a number one thing, and he prayed for health and strength for him and for help to complete his work. I know the Spirit of the Lord was with us today and that it was a mighty thing in which we were allowed to take part. Now Loo will go to Seoul and start teaching school again and will try to do some missionary work along with his genealogy. He is really humble and I know he is a good man. He has much, much faith, because it took a lot to wade out in that ice-cold water.

It is quite odd, that over here the LDS soldiers are not looked upon as they are anywhere else in the world. The other troops accept us more here and don't think that we are weird except for two things: we don't need a chaplain to hold services, and our officer-enlisted man system does not operate during the period when we meet. We are all "Brother So and So" and not Major, Sergeant, Private, etc.

Ray D. Lloyd served as as chief forward observer in the 1st Field Artillery Observation Battalion. The above photo shows U.S. troops adjusting fire from the observation post in Hwachon, Korea. September 1951.

December 26, 1951.

On Christmas Eve, the battery put on a show which was #1 (the best) and we went to see it. After the show we sang carols, and then we were given presents, which were sent to the Triple Nickel by various organizations in Port Gibson, Mississippi. Christmas morning it started to snow and has been ever since. At noon, the section chiefs (mostly master sergeants and other top-grade enlisted men) served chow again. (we also had done it on Thanksgiving to give the KPs [kitchen patrol] the holiday off; it was a long-standing tradition in the battalion.) We had turkey, dressing, potatoes, yams, rolls, pie, fruitcake, etc, etc, etc, and it was sure good. Every serviceman in Korea was supposed to get a full Thanksgiving dinner and a full Christmas dinner—troops were pulled off the front lines to be fed, even if it wasn't right on the very day. It has been the most Christian Christmas I have ever had. We had a mess tent, so we didn't have to eat in the snow—also a latrine tent so we didn't freeze.

This is the funniest war in history. The other night, Item Company heard some noise out in front and when it got light, there was a fully decorated Christmas tree that the Chinese had put there the night before with stockings full of presents. Then the Chinese got Koreans to bring presents to the GIs—silk handkerchiefs, combs, shoe laces, etc.—and a few propaganda leaflets. Then the Chinese set up loudspeakers and played Christmas carols. On Christmas Eve, the Chinese sent two squads out and they got up close to Fox Company and started firing at them. Well, Fox opened up with everything it had, but the Chinese started hollering, "Hey, Fox Company—stop firing that BAR (Browning automatic rifle)." Then on Christmas day they sent out invitations to come to a Christmas party at Kumsong. Really funny war.

April 5, 1952.

Got some more combat time yesterday. As usual, it was funny after it happened, except not quite so funny this time, because one of the boys got hurt, but not too bad. There we were, nine of us, up on the hill building a bunker. Then here come the artillery rounds. No bunker or anything to get into, but there is an old, abandoned foxhole once used by the Chinese about ten feet away. I was the second one into it, until there were all nine of us in it. We sat there and laughed and talked and said, "I wonder if the Chinese laugh when we shoot at them?" About an hour later, we went out and started building the bunker again. I guess that the Chinese forgot about us because their artillery worked on another hill then. The good part about being shot at is that it feels so good when they quit.

JAMES D. MARTIN

James served in the U.S. Navy during the Korean War from June 1948 to May 1952. He served with the Fighter Squadron 112 (VF-112) Carrier Air Group 11 as an aircraft mechanic. James achieved the rank of Aviation Machinist Mate Third Class. After his military service, James served a mission and attended Brigham Young University, where he earned a bachelor's degree and later a master's degree in education.

It was during this time at sea that one of the greatest spiritual experiences of my life occurred. Because the men of the squadron did not keep the standards, which I was striving diligently to keep, I often spent much of my time either working on my plane or sitting in it when it wasn't flying. When it was up in the air I walked about the ship or went down to our quarters, but there was usually nothing to do there because they had the bunks up for cleaning. I did everything I could to stay away from the line shack where the other plane captains gathered when the planes were flying. The room had no windows and was used to store all of the equipment we used to take care of the planes. It was located just under the flight deck and had only one entrance. It did have a small vent fan to blow out all the cigarette smoke, but sometimes the smoke was so thick I could not see from one end to the other. Besides all they did was sit there and tell dirty stories and use vulgar language. It was a very difficult situation for me. There were few places I could go to get away from this kind of environment.

I often wished that I could find the companionship of other LDS men. I wondered if there were any Mormons aboard the ship at all and contemplated how I might find out. There were three thousand men on the ship, and I knew that I couldn't just go about asking everyone if he was a Mormon! I was invited to attend other church services. I went to one Protestant meeting and to a Catholic mass, but I didn't feel satisfied. I knew that I needed the Lord's help. Thus, one night after everyone had gone to bed, I went to the squadron line shack. I knew that no one would be there at that time of night, and I would not be bothered. There, I poured out my heart to God as I had never done before. I pleaded with Him to help me find the companionship I felt so desperately in need of. I begged His forgiveness of my sins and weaknesses. Tears freely flowed. As I left the room I felt a peace and calm I had never felt before. I knew that somehow the Lord would help me. I felt that I had left it in His hands and that it was up to Him now, but I didn't know how it could happen.

What took place the next few days happened so naturally that I hardly took notice of it until I reflected upon it later. The very next day a note came out in the "Plan of the Day" requesting all Mormon men to turn in their names to the chaplain's yeoman at the ship's library. When I went there that evening there were only two names on the list. I recognized neither.

A day or two later the leading chief told me that I was to report to an Ensign Farnsworth of Squadron VF-113. At first I was frightened and wondered if I had done something wrong. In those days enlisted men walked in fear of officers. When I arrived at the squadron flight quarters there were only two or three pilots standing in the center of the room talking to each other. I told the duty officer at the desk why I was there, and he directed me to the men in the middle of the room. I went up to them and asked for Ensign Glen Farnsworth. A tall, good-looking fellow with sandy hair responded and said that he was the man I was looking for. I told him who I was and that I had been told that he wanted to see me. His face lit up and he grabbed my hand. He told me that he was a Latter-day Saint and asked if I would like to start holding some group meetings. I was relieved and overjoyed. We had our first meeting in the ship's library, but there were only three who came. After that we met in a small room near the mess hall. We often took turns reading the Book of Mormon aloud and discussing it. Ensign Farnsworth was the most knowledgeable and was able to answer many of our questions. I also spent a lot of time reading it by myself. I was deeply moved, often to tears, as the Holy Ghost manifested the truth of its message to me. I had never read anything that had such a profound effect upon me.

By Sunday, January 27, we had returned to sea off the coast of Korea. Toward the end of our evening service, a pilot came into the meeting and sat at the back. After the meeting was over he introduced himself to us and told us that he was interested in learning about the Mormon faith. His name was Hartman Rector, Jr. We were thrilled at the prospects of having an investigator, especially an officer since all of us were enlisted men. This was the beginning of a great friendship and many happy experiences.

Top: Ward is pictured standing at one of the GCA operation sites to which he was assigned during the war. Bottom: Ward Middleton wearing the headgear of a GCA (Ground Control Approach) operator in connection with his assignment to direct aircraft to safe landings, often in bad weather.

WARD T. MIDDLETON

Ward served in the United States Air Force during the Korean War from 1951 to 1955. His duties as a GCA (ground control approach) operator were to guide Marine pilots to safe landings through the use of radar scope. After the war, Ward Middleton became a full-time educator.

I was an Air Force GCA (ground control approach) operator whose duties included directing aircraft, by the use of radar, to safe landings in bad weather. I was sent to Korea in 1953 and assigned to the base K-6. It was a Marine base, and the USAF operated the communications, control tower, and the GCA facilities. K-6 was a rather small base with a PSP (pierced steel plank) runway, very minimal lights, and several squadrons of Marine aircraft. The planes were vintage WWII F4U Corsair and AD-1 ground support planes. With their blue paint fading, they looked old and shabby, particularly when compared to the clean, brightly painted Navy jets that occasionally used the base; however, it was truly amazing how much ordnance those older planes could carry.

When I arrived in Korea, I reported to the CO of the AACS (Airways and Air Communication Stations) detachment. He greeted me in this manner, "Welcome to Korea. Should we have an air attack on this base, your life expectancy as a GCA operator is 12.5 seconds." He said tower operators had a life expectancy of 10 seconds during an air attack; I felt lucky to be one of the guys who was safe.

My job was to assist the Marine pilots to safe landings when the weather conditions required it. One day we were making practice GCA runs with one Marine pilot while other planes were out on missions, when we suddenly got an excited telephone call from the tower. We couldn't understand a word he said. About this time one of our maintenance men ran in and said, "You've got to see this!" We followed him outside, and there, less than 50 feet from our GCA unit, sat an AD-1 with the dust still rising as it was being surrounded by emergency equipment. The plane's right gear had collapsed as it returned from a mission and attempted to land; the plane had slid off the runway headed right for our unit. No wonder the tower operator was so excited. Another 50 feet or so could have been fatal for all of us in the GCA.

Another time, there was a big battle going on up north—Pork Chop Hill, Bloody Ridge, or some other important battle. Our Marines were really getting clobbered and needed help. The weather at this time at K-6 was zero/zero. You could hardly see your hand in front of your face.

That was a minor concern. The planes were loaded with all the bombs they could carry and led to the end of the runway by a "follow-me" jeep. There the pilots set their compasses on the runway heading and took off. As soon as they were off the ground, GCA vectored them away from any obstructions (we had some hills only a few miles from the runway) until they were above the fog. The pilots were not worrying about the fog at K-6 because there were other bases in South Korea where they could land after their missions.

K-6 had a fence around the base, with barbed wire running from the top all the way to the bottom. My Quonset hut was located right next to the perimeter fence, and one night we were awaked by shouts of "Halt! Halt! Halt!" followed by the firing of some shots: Bang! Bang! Bang! I guessed someone hadn't halted.

Our Quonset hut was about 50 feet long. Suddenly one door flew open and in the dark you could hear someone running—stomp, stomp, stomp—in one door and out the other. Then there was a batch of confused noise as some Marines came storming though with their weapons on the ready, looking all around to make sure nothing was amiss.

The next morning a hole was found under the fence, right next to our Quonset hut. That's where the intruder got away. Prior to this time we hadn't had to carry a weapon on base, but after this we had to carry our carbines everywhere we went. This change made it seem more like there was a war going on.

As far as I knew there were only five Latter-day-Saints at our base—two enlisted men (myself and a Marine Sgt.) and three Marine pilots. The pilots, being officers, were in charge of our church meetings, but we got along just fine. We got together as a group and held very basic meetings. Many times all five of us weren't able to attend as duty called. We'd have the sacrament. As I recall, we didn't sing—we tried it once and it didn't sound too good.

We talked about how things were going for each of us in Korea and how things were going back home. Usually someone gave a lesson of some sort, always short. When you entered the service, the Church gave you some small books. Mine were blue, because I was in the Air Force. The GCA unit was attached to a large 6x6, a large truck that that had a huge generator in the back to power the unit in case the power went out. Part of my time I sat in the 6x6 and read the Book of Mormon. I still have that Book of Mormon, with dates noted in the margin—the dates when I was reading certain parts as an airman in Korea.

MARK L. MONEY

Mark served in the Chaplain Corps from February 1952 to September 1955 during the Korean War, and remained in the military for thirty-three years in the active reserve. He served with the 8189th Signal Battalion, 8th Army as a chaplain and achieved the rank of Colonel. Since the war, Mark has worked in university administrative positions.

Chaplain Mark L. Money 1953.

Chaplain Mark L. Money conducting worship service 8189th Signal Battalion, Korea 1953.

Corporal Samuel J. Hughes–Chaplain assistant with Chaplain Mark L. Money. Korea 1953.

After attending the chaplain school at Fort Slocum in New York, I was assigned to the 6th Division Reception Center at Fort Ord, California. It was a beehive of activity. Following the old army saying with regards to problems, "Take it to the Chaplain," many did. I spent long hours helping soldiers with a large variety of personal problems. It was most demanding, but I thoroughly enjoyed the assignment because of the opportunity to help young men adapt to the military, solve some serious problems, and in some cases redirect their lives. While this was my principal duty, the post chaplain assigned me to be responsible for the LDS personnel of the post. There was a large contingent of young Church members from the western part of the United States. Our church services were held on Sunday afternoons at the post chapel and a large percentage of the more than four hundred who were stationed there attended. They were encouraged to invite the Church members in their units and also to extend invitations to those who showed an interest in the gospel and the Church.

Early in 1953, I received orders to report to Camp Stoneman, California, on April 23 for processing to go to Korea. It was my good fortune that LDS chaplain Tim Irons was at that processing center. His reputation was widespread because his military career spanned World War II and Korea. He was with the 7th Infantry Division northeast of Seoul where some of the most fierce action of the war took place. He later continued to serve on active duty into the Vietnam era.

My departure to Korea was delayed because the army transportation was required for the exchange of prisoners during that time. Doris Irons, Tim's wife, suggested that my wife and infant son fly to California because there was no telling how long the delay would last. I eagerly accepted the invitation and the Irons' shared their post housing with us and their family of four children for over a week. Their kindness is illustrative of what chaplains will do for each other and for others in the military.

* * * * *

Above: 7th Division Area Servicemen's Conference, Autumn 1953.

Left: (Back Row L–R) Chaplains: Herbert J. Marsh, Mark L. Money, Spencer D. Madsen, Leland Campbell, Richard H. Henstrom, John R. Connell, Lell O. Bagley, Harlan Y. Hammond. (Front Row) LDS Group Leaders: Not identified. The words on the building behind them read, "In memory of our honored dead. 7th US Infantry Division."

Post Chapel, Fort Ord, CA, 1952. Where the LDS Sunday Services were held.

It is acknowledged that the LDS members in the military by their examples of faith and devotion sowed the seeds of the dramatic growth of the Church in Korea. I remember that during the time of these servicemen conferences, there were fewer than fifty Koreans who were members of the Church. Through the efforts of the LDS members in the significant military force which has remained there, and the subsequent missions established in the 1950s, there are now seventeen stakes, six districts, four missions, and a temple, serving approximately 75,000 members.

* * * * *

After six months in Korea, I returned to my final active duty assignment in Fort Bliss, Texas. In September 1955 I was discharged from active duty and remained in the reserve program for a total of over thirty-six years of military experience. Being involved in counseling, ministering to the sick, visiting those in disciplinary confinement, performing marriages, conducting funerals, and teaching core values, I have developed a perspective of what is important and what is not. I will always be grateful for the opportunity of serving as a military chaplain.

Glen D. Morgan

The family of John and Catherine Morgan included eight sons. They worked together on their farm in Malad, Idaho, until the beginning of World War II. Then one by one the sons accepted the call to serve their country. From World War II through the Korean War seven of the Morgan boys served in the military. Glen, the last son to enter military service joined the Navy in 1952. After the end of the Korean War, Glen remained in the Navy until 1956. After leaving the Navy, Glen became a schoolteacher and later the superintendent of schools in Lewiston, Idaho.

LLOYD R. MULLICAN

Lloyd served in the U.S. Army during the Korean War from 1950 to 1954. He achieved the rank of sergeant first class. Lloyd grew up in central Texas and joined the Church after the war. He served in the Headquarters Company, 3rd Battalion, 32nd Infantry Regiment (the "Queen's Own") of the 7th Division (the "Hourglass Division").

Lloyd R. Mullican

I landed in the invasion of Inchon, Korea, on September 15, 1950. It was cold, wet, and it was a state of confusion and fairly light resistance. From the invasion on it was almost constant combat. Korea is largely mountains, and we were so tired, we actually slept while marching. I received total support from my family and fiancé. We had no time or place for religious services, but I can tell you there are no agnostics in a firefight or foxhole. I was not LDS at that time, but I certainly called on God for help many times. I can remember one night on Hill #902. We were dug in a circular perimeter and had heard we were going to be hit that night, so we were in full alert. When the moon went down, we heard bugles and whistles and the Chinese hit us hard. We fought from hole to hole, hand-to-hand combat all night long. We played what we called "Chinese Baseball," that night. We would throw a grenade or the Chinese would, and the opposing side would pick it up and throw it back. I received shrapnel in my hands that night and a cut in my field jacket where a Chinese bayonet barely grazed me.

I was also involved in the Battle of Chosin Reservoir. It was probably a big mistake going out ahead like that, but the Marines went ahead and got trapped up north just south of the Yalu River. We were sent up to reinforce, really to rescue them as they were cut off. They were very thin in numbers. We got up there and sort of got trapped ourselves. We had moved real rapidly and had sort of outrun ourselves. Our supply depot was back at Hamhung. When I say way back, as a matter of miles it wasn't so far back, maybe thirty-five to forty-five miles, but when you fight for every square inch, it's a long ways. It was also in December and the weather was bitterly cold (maybe forty below) and we were just not equipped for it. When we finally reached the Marines to start evacuating them we had to hold the road and allow for other units going back and forth. We just sort of played leapfrog as best we could. The retreat lasted five or six days and six-bys (trucks) were stacked completely full of dead bodies. Some of the trucks would hit a mine or an ambush and turn over and be on fire. I was also in a couple of places "fighting southward" where no more trucks could be found so engineers dug mass graves with bulldozers and placed multiple corpses in unmarked graves as we didn't want to leave them for the enemy. I came home in the later part of 1951. During the conflict I had received small-arms fire and was the recipient of the Purple Heart.

ELDER RUSSELL M. NELSON

This future Apostle served in the Army during the Korean Conflict. For much of the war, Elder Nelson was assigned to Walter Reed Army Medical Center. He also made a tour of all MASH Units in South Korea during the summer of 1951. In addition, he made recommendations for improved medical care for injured soldiers. His tour of MASH units took him right to the battlefront.

At the time of the Korean War in 1951, Sister Nelson and I lived in Minneapolis, Minnesota. We had one nice little girl and were expecting our second daughter when it was evident that I was needed in the Korean War. I had finished medical school four years before and was now in surgical training and advanced training in Minneapolis. So I was asked by the Army to come and help them in their surgical research efforts during the Korean War. I received a commission as a First Lieutenant in the Army Medical Corps. We moved to Washington, D. C., where I was headquartered at Walter Reed Army Medical Center. Our second baby arrived just after we got there, and three months later I was shipped off to Korea. I left my wife and our two baby girls with our family in the state of Utah. Just in a few days life was changed. We were happily enjoying family reunions and relatives in Utah and just a few days later I was right up in the action.

Our purpose in going to Korea was to gather data on the causes of morbidity and mortality among the wounded soldiers. I was one of a four-man surgical research team headed by Doctor Feorindo A. Simeoni of Cleveland, a professor of surgery there. He went as a civilian. Assisting him were Major Curtis P. Arts, a career Army medical officer, and two of us who were in for just a two-year stint: Captain George E. Shriner of Georgetown Medical Center in Washington D. C., and I. I was the First Lieutenant, and there was a captain and a major and then a civilian head.

So the four of us went to Korea. We went to the Mobile Army Surgical Hospital, the so-called M.A.S.H. units, visited every one of them. They thought to give us better exposure to the whole gamut by taking us right to the front lines where we saw the 155-millimeter howitzer cannons blazing away, shaking the earth with their impact and recoil. We took trips with the wounded in the helicopters and then after visiting all the mobile army surgical hospitals in Korea we also visited some of the major evacuation hospitals in Japan and in Hawaii. So we tried to get the whole perspective. Basically we found that much of the morbidity and mortality, of course, couldn't be influenced much by medical care. A severe wound is a severe wound. But there were certain things that we could do something about. For example, if blood vessels had been severed we could teach how to restore continuity of blood flow by using blood vessel grafts. Or for those who were dying of kidney failure, one component of our report was that lives could be saved if we would establish an artificial kidney unit in Korea. So not long after we returned and made our report, the artificial kidney unit was established in Korea.

Well, that gives you kind of an overall picture of our assignment there.

****

Yes, as I came to one mobile army surgical hospital one of the doctors who knew that I was a member of The Church of Jesus Christ of Latter-day Saints asked me if I would be willing to see a Mormon boy who'd been hit in the spine with a missile. He was a paraplegic:

wouldn't ever use his legs again and so as I was introduced to this young man he could see that I didn't know what to say. I greeted him and expressed condolences and love as best I could and he said, "Oh don't worry about me, Brother Nelson. I know why I'm here. And I don't use my legs to work out my salvation. I do that with my faith." And I learned a lot from that young man. He was under age. He was only a priest from Idaho Falls. I mean only a priest meaning agewise. He was not even old enough to be an elder, but there he was with great faith facing a future of inability to use his lower extremities. I often wondered what ever happened to that wonderful young man who taught me a lot about faith.

****

I think men in the military, no matter the time, the country or the place are going to be under a lot of surveillance, mostly by their own fellowmen in the military. Their behavior will be watched very carefully so they have missionary opportunities that are really quite unparalleled among their own people. In addition, there's some spill over into the people that you're serving. That was so in Korea and it was so in other conflicts that have come: Vietnam, Cambodia, and now in the Gulf Area. We're always being watched, always by a loving Father in Heaven, and always by our associates. And so what we are becomes very, very important and it shows.

****

I love the Korean people and I think that they have endured much hardship with this political separation of their own families. I've seen those families reunited and I've seen those families divided because of differences among men. I want very much to be part of the message of the Lord which unifies people; rallies them behind His banner. He is the Prince of Peace and we are His disciples. We are His peacemakers so anything that serves the cause of peace is something that causes me to rejoice.

A wounded U.S. Marine awaiting transportation back to a field hospital after receiving first aid at the battle zone. Defense Dept. (USIA)

DANIEL O. NOORLANDER

A veteran of World War II, Daniel was living in southern California when the Korean conflict erupted. He served in Korea during 1951 and 1952. He was commander of an intelligence and reconnaissance platoon in Korea where he obtained the rank of first lieutenant.

Sergeant Hand, John Tomiko, and Daniel Noorlander in Korea 1951–1952.

The major told me he wanted us to find out where the Chinese lines were. The Chinese lines were well-entrenched positions that pocketed the whole mountain to our front.

Deep caves and tunnels penetrated the whole front. I was surprised that the major would think I was so gullible or misinformed that I did not know what was going on.

"Now, Major," I proceeded. "If that is all you want to know, I can tell you exactly where their positions are on a map.

Remember, I flew over this area in a plane before I was grounded?" I had a gut feeling I was being trapped into another one of those National Guard attacks where commanders do all their planning on a map with red and blue arrows, showing the movement of armies without any consideration of human life.

After I asked a couple more questions, I was finally told the real reason for the attack. The major let his hair down a little and confessed that the commander wanted a little publicity for the folks back home. What he was really saying was that jobs back home were at stake and there were some needed recognition and promotions to enhance one's retirement fund. There were few promotions given following a war.

There just was no justifiable military reason for the proposed attack. The Chinese and American lines were stabilized along the 38th Parallel, and the war was winding down. I quickly thought of my men and an alternative out of the dilemma.

"Look," I said. "If you want a little publicity, this can be done, but it has to be done a little differently. Okay?"

He asked me what I had in mind. He was also taken aback a little because I had challenged his position.

"I want a week's preparation, all the artillery support I can get, and I'll take your large 'Los Angeles City Limit' sign." He agreed and I got busy. "If they just want a show, I'll give them one, but on my terms," I thought to myself.

The following week every man in my platoon looked over aerial photographs of the area I had picked to reach our objectives. We memorized every bomb hole and earthen ditch bank that could provide us with shelter in case we needed it. I decided to attack Chinese style with just enough flair to confuse the enemy.

I knew the Chinese understood American tactics, and I wanted them to believe we were going to attack American style. So, I planned a massive fire power against their lines from the division artillery to soften up their positions, but the difference was going to be that I would not attack where the shells were going to land, but between the two areas I had selected.

Each man was camouflaged with white clothing since a full moon was projected for the night of the attack. We were not going up a draw American style, but across the 1000-yard open plain in front of the Chinese lines that were laced with frozen rice paddies and snow.

Each man was provided with a 5-gallon pail of timed explosives, flares, and phosphorous smoke grenades. Several men carried five-gallon pails of napalm, a jellied gasoline. Each pail was fortified with a long stick of black powder with a time fuse attached.

The evening before the attack we drove a half-track, which is a type of armored car, near the division outpost. We camouflaged the vehicle with brush and headed up the hill to the outpost. We planned to depart just at dark with two minutes of twilight left so we could cross the Kumsong River. The river was not deep, but I was glad we wore insulated boots, because the temperature was dropping rapidly.

Just before our departure, I was called to the outpost phone by the major. He told me that some of our tanks had penetrated the area where we were going and that they were fired upon by machine guns. He said that we could back out if we wanted to. He apparently was having second thoughts about this mission. I was glad that at least he appeared to have a conscience.

"No, Major," I replied. "I think we can handle it." I then led the men down the back side of the mountainous outpost to wait for the artillery barrage which was our signal to cross the river.

Inwardly I felt a little uneasy. I said a little prayer as I led the men down the slope. I normally did not petition my Creator for any special help that was involved with the military. It was against my principles to ask for favors that our enemy had just as much right to. I asked myself, "If I were the God of the heavens, and all these combatants were my children, who would I favor and who would I select to win the battle of that day?" I thought of the many men in the division who became immoral in their actions in Japan to the point of total debasement. I thought of the Chinese and the moral principles taught by their great teacher Confucius.

In spite of this thinking I did ask the Lord for some special help that evening. I asked that He would give me the courage to lead my men into combat that night, and that I would not show any fear to them. I also asked for the first time in my military career that I would be able to bring all the men home with me that night. I knew my men were not perfect, nor was I, but I did not believe I could live with myself if just one man was incapacitated or killed for this publicity stunt.

As we crouched down next to the river waiting for the artillery, I looked at my watch. All of a sudden the audible whine of artillery shells went directly over our heads and exploded to our left and right on the Chinese positions as planned.

I motioned the men to follow me as I crossed the rather wide river. In the middle of the river I noticed my men were overly cautious and this was slowing us down.

Then I had a very strange experience. It was as if I was being informed that no one was watching us. I knew that the Chinese could not or were not looking in our direction.

I stood up from my crouched position and waved my men on. They all stood up and walked across the river without any more hesitation. They followed me all the way to the edge of the Kumsong village, long before evacuated because of the war. We traveled rather rapidly in order to not give the Chinese second thoughts about where the attack might take place.

By prearranged hand signals, I directed one squad to the left, and I took one squad to the right. Another squad stayed behind and made a corridor to our rear from which we could escape just in case our flanks were attacked by the Chinese.

Again, my men hesitated. They knew there had been a reported Chinese machine-gun position in that area. As before, I had the same feeling come over me. I knew that no one was watching us or could see us.

At that moment, as before, I stood up from my deeply crouched position. My men looked at me in disbelief. Both squads then went about their business as planned, without hesitation or fear. We planted our explosives throughout the village. We lobbed the smoke grenades closest to us and the flare grenades just in front of the smoke grenades, so the brilliant light would reflect against the smoke and not expose our positions. All the explosives were timed in ten minute intervals so the last ones would go off about an hour after the first ones.

Soon the napalm exploded in what appeared to be small atomic mushrooms rising from the center of the grass-roofed huts. Soon the whole village was on fire. Explosives literally tore up the town and in all my Fourth of July experiences, I have never seen such a beautiful display.

We left the village just as we came in—at a fast trot. I knew the Chinese would counterattack or at least send a patrol to investigate this new type of warfare. As I had promised, we didn't

The Bronze Star

The Bronze Star Medal is awarded to any person who, while serving in any capacity in or with the military of the United States after 6 December 1941, distinguished himself or herself by heroic or meritorious achievement or service, not involving participation in aerial flight, while engaged in an action against an enemy of the United States; while engaged in military operations involving conflict with an opposing foreign force; or while serving with friendly foreign forces engaged in an armed conflict against an opposing armed force in which the United States is not a belligerent party. Awards may be made for acts of heroism, performed under circumstances described above, which are of a lesser degree than required for the award of the Silver Star. Awards may be made to recognize single acts of merit or meritorious service. The required achievement or service while of lesser degree than that required for the award of the Legion of Merit must nevertheless have been meritorious and accomplished with distinction.

Daniel Noorlander receiving the Bronze Star.

LAKESIDE SOLDIER GETS MEDAL

A Lakeside soldier, 1st Lt. Daniel O. Noorlander (right) receives the Bronze Star Medal for heroism from his regimental commander, Lt. Col. Richard F. Lynch, during an informal ceremony near the front in Korea. Noorlander distinguished himself while leading a patrol into Communist territory where his unit destroyed several buildings considered defensible by the enemy, and netted a large number of casualties. He is a member of the 40th Division's 223rd Regiment. (U.S. Army photo)

leave before putting up the "Los Angeles City Limit" sign on a conspicuous post so the whole division could see it with binoculars from our lines.

We returned to our outpost and looked over the inferno we had started. I called for artillery on the Chinese who were by then pouring out of the hills. The artillery officer asked me over the outpost phone when we were going to quit. He assumed he was talking to me over the sound power phone our third squad laid down for us, in case we needed artillery support to get us out of Kumsong. "We left there twenty minutes ago," I responded.

I could not see any artillery shells land on the Chinese, nor did the mortar fire we called for from the outpost hit its prearranged target in the center of Kumsong. I suppose the forward observers thought we were still in Kumsong, but I kind of believe that there just was a chance that the Lord was protecting someone on the other side as well.

When Julian Hartt, the *Los Angeles Examiner*'s war correspondent, came the following day to interview my platoon, I left plenty of credit to my company commander. By doing this, I was able to get every one of my men their long deserved promotions or ratings and the pay that went with it.

I received a Bronze Star for valor, when in reality there really wasn't much risk taken that night. I just put into practice some lessons I learned about military tactics while serving in the Solomon Islands during World War II, and petitioned for the extra help I knew I needed, knowing I had done all I could do myself.

Mt. Fugi. Camp McNair. Japan

Top: Dan in front seat of Jeep, 1951.

Bottom: Daniel Noorlander with Mt. Fuji in the background. Camp McNair, Japan, December 20, 1951.

Right: Photo and caption as it appeared in the LOS ANGELES EXAMINER *shortly after Lt. Daniel Noorlander led a patrol into Communist territory where his unit destroyed several buildings considered defensible by the enemy, and netted a large number of casualties. Noorlander is a member of the 40th Division's 223rd Regiment.*

BAD MEDICINE—Lt. Daniel Noorlander (above), 4807 Angeles Vista Boulevard, Los Angeles, shown armed with a deadly rifle grenade. Noorlander commands an intelligence and reconnaissance platoon. —*Los Angeles Examiner* photo by Julian Hartt

LESTER J. OYLER

Lester served in the U.S. Army from October 1951 to July 1953 during the Korean War. He served with the U.S. Army Reserve, 6th Platoon as a radio operator. Lester achieved the rank of private first class. After returning from the war he purchased a farm and cattle operation. He has also worked for the Utah Department of Transportation, and has been on two missions for the Church.

Lester J. Oyler, U.S. Army, 1951–1953.

I was loaded on a ship with around a thousand other men, my bunk being on the bottom deck, right near a latrine. The bunks were so closely stacked that when I laid on my side, my shoulders touched the bunk above me.

I was sick the total time we were on the water. All I could hear was water slushing back and forth and the smell of oil from the engines. I vomited for four days straight. When I didn't show up for chow call for that long, I heard them calling my name on the loudspeakers. I guess they thought I had jumped overboard. My friend did bring me water and a few crackers during this time.

In Korea, I was assigned to the Communications Division—switchboard and maintenance. Our job was to run phone lines to the command posts stationed on Pork Chop Hill and later, on Jane Russell Hill. We rolled wires, by hand, to the different command posts and installed the switchboard so we could radio messages back and forth, keeping ourselves and the front lines informed of the position of our soldiers, as well as that of the enemy.

Also, we received messages informing us when our lines were out, or had been destroyed. It was critical that our only means of communication were kept open and operable.

When we received messages that the lines were out, we would walk the line, hand over hand, until we found the trouble, then repair, or replace the line. As we had to walk the lines, it would often leave us as an open target for the enemy.

Our communications center was housed in a dugout, made of sandbags. In it was the switchboard, which we operated twenty-four hours a day. We made cots out of old telephone wires to place our sleeping bags on. We did this to keep us off the dirt floor so we weren't quite so handy a target for the rats (which were in abundance). Our food consisted mostly of C-rations, with exception of one hot meal per week.

On one occasion, our dugout was hit by an artillery shell filled with white phosphate. If someone was hit by even a particle of phosphate, it would burn and eat right through him in no time. We were lucky that we all escaped unharmed as a result of this incident. The enemy would go to all lengths to destroy the communication system.

The enemy attacks, most generally, came at night. It was always a sickening feeling when daylight came, and I could see countless wounded and dead soldiers who had not survived the attack. Among the fatalities was a good buddy of mine who took a hit right through his stomach. It left a hole clear through him about the size of a bowling ball. This sickening sight, among that of other bodies, and the stench of it all will be something I shall never forget.

I never see the flag of the United States of America, or hear the national anthem, without it bringing chills up my spine and tears to my eyes when I consider the price that is paid to keep our country free. I am proud to have served my country, and to have had a part in protecting the freedoms that are so precious and important to all of us.

I honor those who paid the supreme sacrifice of their lives. My heart goes out to those who were wounded and whose lives will never be the same because of their disabilities. I hope and pray that my children and grandchildren, and the generations to follow, will become aware of these things and never forget the price that is paid for freedom.

SPENCER J. PALMER

Spencer served in the U.S. Army during the Korean War from September 1952 to April 1956. He served in the 8206th Army Port Detachment at Inchon, 21st Evacuation Hospital for the 8th Army as a chaplain. Spencer achieved the rank of first lieutenant. This account tells of a special experience that Spencer had with Elder Harold B. Lee while serving in this capacity.

In September 1954, Elder Harold B. Lee of the Council of the Twelve was assigned to survey conditions in Korea with respect to the advisability of officially opening that country to missionary work. The land had not been dedicated as a field of labor nor had LDS missionaries been commissioned to work there.

At that early date, there were a considerable number of American Latter-day Saint servicemen living in various camps throughout the peninsula. Koreans, located mainly in Pusan, Taegu, and Seoul, had been taught the gospel and baptized into the Church by these brethren, or through the leadership and example of Dr. Ho Jik Kim, a prominent educator and government official, who had previously joined the Church in the United States.

Elder Lee was accompanied to Korea by President Hilton A. Robertson, president of the Northern Far East Mission, with headquarters in Tokyo. Since American civilians could not live in Korea at that time, Elder Lee and President Robertson were allowed to visit only under the aegis of the U.S. military. Both were required to wear army OD outfits. Elder Lee was given the simulated rank of major general (two stars) and President Robertson was given the simulated rank of brigadier general (one star) during their visit.

There were nearly a dozen U.S. chaplains working in Korea at the time, of which I was one. I was privileged to travel with these two generals. I was a first lieutenant (one silver bar) army chaplain, and I had full opportunity not only to participate in their visits to the various campuses of LDS servicemen, but to see their marvelous spiritual impact on them. I was also aware that this was a very historic experience for Elder Lee, and that not only the Americans and

Koreans were generally greatly affected, but something happened in Pusan that personally and literally changed the rest of my life.

[A special meeting was called in] September. Somehow . . . a sizeable number of servicemen and a significant number of new Korean members of the Church [attended the service]. Elder Lee spoke to the Koreans through interpreter Young Gil Kook. Several of the new Korean converts were called upon to bear their testimonies. I could tell that Elder Lee was deeply touched by these sincere and simple expressions of love and faith. The hymns and prayer and testimonies were delivered with tones of great rejoicing and in tears of gratitude.

Since I had been assigned to personally accompany Elder Lee during his Pusan visit, after the evening meeting the two of us were assigned to sleep in the same Quonset hut in Hialeah Compound. I figured that he was exhausted after such a full day of meeting with army leaders and Church members, but that was not the case. We prepared for bed, then lounged. I could tell he wanted to talk. He told me that this visit to Korea had opened his eyes to many new things. He then said to me, "Spencer, this is the first time for me to visit Asia, to personally meet so many young people from a foreign land, who previously in Church classes I had only thought of in a scriptural or theological way. It was easy to think of them casually if at all. But tonight when I looked into the eyes and souls of these students who shook my hands and expressed their faith and testimony, I realized as never before that the Lord loves them and cares about them very much."

Then Elder Lee expressed to me with a low and resonant voice, and with considerable feeling what he later said publicly in his general conference remarks in October in the Salt Lake Tabernacle, "I feel the signs of divinity in Korea. The work of the Almighty is now beginning to increase with a tremendous surge" (See Harold B. Lee, "Miraculous Power of Divine Intervention Present in Orient," *Church News* [9 October 1954]: 8; also Chaplains Spencer J. Palmer and John R. Connell, Jr., "Elder Lee Visits Korea," *Church News* [October 1954]: 7ff).

Spencer developed a "great sense of compassion" for all the Lord's children while he served as Army Chaplain during the Korean War.

But then, after some hesitation, Elder Lee looked me in the eye and said he had some personal counsel to give me. He said that he saw a great work unfolding in Asia, and in Korea, and that he felt the Church membership was not prepared for it. He said the members of the Church in America are thinking of the war and of their American loved ones who are enduring separation and hardship. But the members are not thinking of the Koreans, their problems, and the future. The Lord is aware of these wonderful people, and we must also become better prepared as a Church to friendship them, to love them, and to bring the fullness of the gospel to them. "Spencer, the Church needs you and people like you to open the work in Asia. I would like you to stay close to these Korean people. Prepare yourself to serve the Lord, as he shall see fit to call you to labor here. We laborers are few, but the work to be done is miraculous and marvelous to contemplate."

Elder Lee really didn't ask me or call me to any kind of position or assignment. He didn't assure me that I would be expected to assume any leadership role. But because of my great love and respect for him as a person, and for his position as an ordained and authorized prophet of God and Apostle of the Lord Jesus Christ, I took his comments very seriously. His words changed the direction of my life.

He returned to Salt Lake [City, Utah], buoyed up by what he had experienced. . . . He recommended that the Church move forward in establishing missions [in Asia] and in sending missionaries to Korea.

The following year, on August 2, 1955, . . . on a hill overlooking Seoul, Korea, Elder Joseph Fielding Smith dedicated the land for the preaching of the gospel, and commanded Satan to free the land and its people from the chains of war and poverty.

In April 1956, through the special assistance of Dr. [Ho Jik] Kim, visas were cleared for the first Mormon missionaries to serve in Korea as part of the Northern Far East Mission, Korea District.

The Korean Mission of the Church was officially organized in 1962. Since that time several missions have been established, sixteen stakes have been organized and a beautiful temple of the Lord has been built in Seoul. Now in 1992, there are about 50,000 Korean members of the Church.

Because of that special moment with a prophet of the Lord in the Quonset hut in Pusan, I made a resolution to stay close to the people of Korea, and to dedicate myself and my life to serve the Lord wherever He may call me to serve.

After my tour of duty as a chaplain, . . . I decided to enroll at the University of California to prepare myself in Korean history, language, and religion, not in the spirit of demanding or expecting that I must be called to serve the Lord in Korea, but in the spirit of joyfully responding to a suggestion of a prophet of the Lord, whose words I could not ignore.

I am deeply grateful that Heavenly Father has seen fit to call me to serve in Korea as a chaplain, as a mission president, and as the president of the Seoul Korea Temple. Shirley [my wife] and I are most grateful that we have had the wonderful privilege and blessing of associating with the Korean members of the Church.

Taken from Spencer John Palmer, "My Turn on Earth: Reflections at Sixty-five" (Provo, Utah, 1992), 96–98.

ROBERT E. PARSONS

Robert served in the Navy during World War II and in the U.S. Army during the Korean War, from June 1950 to March 1954. In Korea he served with the 2nd Infantry Division as a chaplain with the rank of first lieutenant. After the war, Robert taught at Brigham Young University as a religion professor.

In July 1952, while traveling through Salt Lake City, Utah, on my way to Korea, I was set apart as a chaplain and a missionary by Elder Bruce R. McConkie of the First Quorum of the Seventy. In the blessing I was told that this was the second mission to which I was called in the Church and that all former blessings [of my first mission] were resealed upon my head.

I arrived in Korea in August and spent the next fifteen months with the 2nd Infantry Division. While on the way to the front (the United Nations was fighting North Korea) I prayed fervently that the Lord would assign me where I could serve the best. At the last moment my assignment was changed from the 3rd Infantry Division to the 2nd Infantry Division. The reason for this was evident within the week, for when I arrived I found a group of LDS soldiers who had been praying individually for someone to come and begin meetings. Though they were close together they had never met and no one had taken the initiative to organize an LDS group. Our meetings began with only three members, but fifteen months later the group had grown to sixty. I also learned that a Maori battalion was stationed on our left flank, and within a fortnight I had organized an LDS group among them.

Chaplain Robert E. Parsons standing at the 38th parallel in Korea.

My work with the Maoris became so successful that their division chaplain registered a complaint with the corps chaplain and asked that my visits be curtailed. This was entirely unjust as I had received the division chaplain's permission to begin this work and had checked with him regularly concerning my activities. The Maori boys were disheartened, but a turn of events turned their dismay to joy. Almost immediately our division received orders to replace the British Commonwealth in their position. Their entire division went into reserve except for the Maori battalion which was detached from the British and attached to our American division. It was now an easy matter to hold services, and although the 8th Army general would no doubt take credit for the shift, we offered our humble thanks to the Lord.

Right: Many Koreans were taught by the LDS servicemen during the war.

Below: The Brigham Young University branch collected boxes of clothing and shipped them over to Chaplain Parsons. He took it to one of the many poverty-stricken villages who were in need of such donations. Robert is shown in the photo below, second from the left, wearing a flap hat, and the other servicemen shown were assigned to help Robert to deliver the clothing (drive the trucks, etc.). The village is near the 38th parallel.

While occupying this new position we were hit in two places, The Hook and Little Gibraltar. The Chinese got into the trenches and tore up everything. Our men were assigned to clean out the trenches and relay the minefields and barbed wire. They were working about twenty hours a day and there was no time to stop for church even on Sunday. Finally, the men began to request some type of a service so I spoke to the company commander. He was cooperative, but insisted that the work was so urgent that the men could not take time to go to the bottom of the hill for church as was the usual practice. If I desired to meet with them during their 20-minute lunch break I was free to do so. A meeting was consequently arranged.

Normally I wore a flak vest while on line, but that day I could not obtain one because we had lost so many during the Chinese attack. However, I met with the men anyway. I had expected about thirty Protestants, but the Catholics and about fifty Koreans also gathered. This made quite a crowd. The men were nervous and needed spiritual encouragement and a replenishing of their faith in God. What could I give them in ten minutes? I started a hymn—and finished it alone. Then I took off my helmet and offered a prayer. Holding my helmet in my arms, I stood on the hillside and looked at the men in the trenches. Some were battle-hardened. Others had just arrived a few weeks before. "Men," I began, "wherever you are and whatever you're doing, remember that the Lord has the situation well in hand." As these words left my mouth, a Chinese mortar dropped on us. It's the only shell I never beat to the ground. The men all dropped into the trench, and I was left standing by myself. The mortar passed overhead and lit perhaps fifty to seventy-five feet behind me. I braced myself for the explosion but none came. The shell was a dud. As the men slowly looked back up over the trench, I repeated to them, "Remember wherever you are and whatever you're doing that the Lord always has the situation well in hand." I then dismissed the meeting.

* * * * *

While working with the Maoris, an interesting testimony was born by a nonmember. Church services for the Maoris were often a half-day affair. They would come, hold a serious meeting, and then sit around for several hours singing songs, doing action songs and hakas (their native dances) and just enjoy each other. During one testimony meeting, Bill Mulligan, a nonmember, stood and began to speak. He told how during World War II he had first met LDS boys in North Africa. One of the Maori boys had been hit and was expected to die. The doctors gave him up. Then two Maori boys came, laid their hands on his head and prayed. He lived. This so impressed Bill that he inquired what they had done. He found out they were Mormons and claimed to hold the priesthood. Consequently, when he heard of our meetings in Korea, he had started to come. He asked if we remembered the small Book of Mormon (LDS servicemen's edition) that we had given him. We nodded. He said he had treasured it highly, but that week there had been a fire in his tent. It was burned to the ground. He had kept this book in his duffle bag but that was burned too. While poking around among the ruins, he came across his Book of Mormon. The outside cover was scorched, but not a single page was burned. The radio that had been next to it in his duffle bag was completely melted. This so impressed Bill that he had gone to his division chaplain, who was from the Church of England, and bore his testimony that he knew the Mormon Church was true and that as soon as he could overcome some of his bad habits, he was going to join.

* * * * *

It was a great relief when an agreement was reached at Panmunjom to cease fighting. Soldiers on each side warily came out of the trenches and looked across the valley at each other. I cannot remember now why I went into a vacated area (one of the United Nations forces had pulled out) but as I was walking along a path I suddenly felt something touch my leg. I stopped walking in midstep and balancing on one leg looked down to see my lifted leg pressed against a wire. Following it with my eyes I saw that it was booby-trapped to a grenade at the side of the path. I gently lowered my leg and stepped over the wire, grateful to the Lord that my life had again been preserved. Apparently the troops that had vacated the area had not bothered to follow standard procedure and remove all booby traps. They were probably just glad to get off line.

Humble homes and people in Pusan.

Top: Chaplain Parsons conducting Church services near front lines, north of the 38th parallel.

Center: LDS chaplains, 1953. Front L–R: Larry Rast, Leland Campbell, Robert Parsons. Back L–R: Ben Mortensen, Bill Green, unidentified, unidentified.

Bottom left: Baptism of several Koreans and one serviceman. Bottom right: Same event as above. Front L–R: Chaplain Robert Parsons, President Peter Nellson Hansen of Japan Mission, Chaplain Ben Mortensen. Back L–R: Dr. Ho Jik Kim, Sung Ja Lee, Young Sook Kim, unidentified serviceman, unidentified serviceman, Yung Hee Han, LeRoy Uncles (baptized this day), Chaplain Howard Bradshaw, Tai Whan Kim.

Keith Pendleton.

KEITH PENDLETON

Keith served in the Utah National Guard from 1950 to 1952 during the Korean War. He served with Battery B of the 213th Field Artillery Battalion as a radio operator, and achieved the rank of sergeant. Keith served later as a missionary and a temple worker.

We did have a few encounters. I have a hard time remembering some of them because when I came home I blocked them out. We had very few injuries in our unit. We had a couple of boys get wounded, but they weren't serious wounds. We went over with 100 percent of our local boys, and we came home with 100 percent of our local boys. The people started referring to us as the "Second Helaman's Army" because of this.

* * * * *

My buddy Gene Brooks got married just before we went over and he was having a really rough time of it. He came to me one day. I was an elder at the time. (My father had made sure I was an elder before I left.) Gene asked me if I would help him. We would sit at night a lot of times out on the outpost. That is where we were at most of the time and we would sit there and we would talk about our families. I felt I was helping him and of course, I was helping myself. We always ended our talk sessions kneeling in prayer. We became quite close on this.

* * * * *.

There is one thing that I'd like to mention: our battalion commander, Frank Dalley. He was a wonderful man. He had what he called quiet time. He had a white flag that he'd hang out in front of his tent. And when that flag was in front of that tent nobody would disturb him because he was in there talking to his Maker. And to me, his prayers are what brought us home. He felt like he took his kids over there and he wanted to bring them all home. You don't see that too often in a lot of people, but he was a wonderful guy. When he left for the war he looked quite young, but when he came home he looked like he was a hundred—he had white hair. So you can tell what kind of stress he had on him.

Left: Byron "Brooks" Taylor and Keith Pendleton.

Above: Parley J. Lang and Keith Pendleton.

All others: Keith and fellow soldiers of the famed 213th Field Artillery Battalion from southern Utah.

GAIL WESLEY POULTON

Inset: Captain Gail W. Poulton Air Rescue Service SA-16 Grumman "Albatross" Amphibian. "I am giving the ground crew the sign to put the wheel chocks in place."

Captain Gail W. Poulton, Korea 1951. Poulton's helicopter crashed just after delivering a wounded marine to a hospital ship. The crash was caused by a malfunction in the fuel system. There were no injuries.

Gail served in the U.S. Army and the U.S. Air Force. He joined the military in February 1943 and served with the 35th Division, 134th Infantry Regiment, and 12th Tactical Air Command, 64th Fighter Wing, Air Rescue Service, and as a pilot in the Air Force Academy. Gail retired in May 1965, having achieved the rank of lieutenant colonel.

One day on an early mission, I was flying along and thought I should be right over the landing coordinates [of the aid station], but nobody had popped a smoke canister, so I started a right turn to make a large circle, and suddenly I saw a string of tracer fire going up in the air in front of my nose. I thought, "That's funny; they seem to be shooting at me." There was a ridge in front of me, and I started to climb to get to the top of that ridge to look on the other side thinking I was a bit impatient or had a head wind and my ground speed was slower than I thought and I was not quite to the aid station. As I started to climb, another burst of tracer fire came up from

a gun almost below me. It was obvious that they could easily hit me if they were trying, so I concluded they weren't trying to hit me but they were trying to get my attention. I turned back and started to descend toward the weapon that had fired, and I saw a group of men near the weapon waving at me and thought that must be the aid station so I circled them to get into the wind in order to land. As I started down the approach they waved me off and pointed in another direction. I leveled off and turned in that direction and flew a few hundred yards. Suddenly they popped a purple smoke grenade, which was my color, so I went in and landed.

As soon as my wheels touched ground an ambulance jeep came driving up and the stretcher-bearers took the two stretchers and almost ran to the helicopter. My medic had the litter capsule lids off and was ready to take the litters and strap them down with the safety belts. Just as he was doing that, the explosion of mortar rounds went off and the jeep took off in a cloud of dust. One of the litter bearers was assisting my medic with the safety belts, and he yelled at my medic that we had better get out fast because they were under mortar attack and that was why they had not popped the smoke the first time we went over because it gave the enemy mortar gunners a perfect target to shoot at. The medic jumped in and put his headset on and told me what the man had said, and I applied full power and we got out of Dodge as fast as that chopper could whop. As I turned south I looked back at the spot I had just left and a mortar shell exploded right at it.

Left: Captain Gail W. Poulton flying the H-5G Sikorsky Helicopter in Korea 1951–1952. The helicopter is approaching to land on the USS Consolation bringing in wounded from the front line aid station.

Above: Korea 1952 (spring). Captain Gail Poulton standing on the left float of the Sikorsky. It is like the one he flew without floats, during the Jell Green-4 Mission.

When I landed back at the 8055 MASH [mobile army surgical hospital] Captain Heller was standing there waiting for me. When I shut down and climbed out of the cockpit he said, "Captain Poulton, let's go to my tent and I will teach you the rules that we follow up here. Whoever checked you out must have forgotten to tell you." He then advised me that if I didn't get a smoke canister when I arrived at the aid station I was not to search around the area nor land to ask questions. The absence of smoke meant it was not safe to land, and I was to return to the MASH and they [the aid station] would call in the pickup later when it was safe. Then he added that the tracer fire in front of my nose meant to turn around and go back because I was right between them and the enemy.

When he finished telling me I looked at him and said, "I sure wish I could remember the name of the guy who checked me out, I sure would like to discuss it with him!" He looked at me, and we both laughed because he had checked me out. We both learned an important lesson that day.

* * * * *

At Panmunjom the new cease-fire and peace negotiations were being conducted in a large circus-type tent located between the cease-fire lines near the 38th Parallel. That location was picked initially because the negotiating teams were driving from their base camps to the negotiating site in military vehicles and didn't want a long drive to get there. Initially the U.N. team rode in nice new, comfortable four-door sedans and the North Korean team rode in uncomfortable combat-type vehicles. After a few weeks the North Korean side arrived one morning in new, shiny American jeeps they had captured earlier when the Chinese had joined them after General Douglas Macarthur had invaded Inchon and drove the North Korean Army almost to the Manchurian border.

* * * * *

We moved north to Site #4 on the Island of Cho-do. We were located there with a radar unit, which was set up on the top of a small mountain. The unit's call sign was "Denis Charlie" and their equipment could see MiG aircraft taking off from the airfield at Antung, Manchuria, when they were only about three hundred feet off the runway. They could also see our aircraft anywhere over the Korean Peninsula. The island was only about two miles off the North Korean coast, and the North Koreans tried everything they could think of to knock it out. At first they sent their gunboats to shoot it up but the U.S. Navy had a destroyer there within a few hours, and they sunk the North Korean gunboat. Next the North Korean Army moved a long-range artillery unit to a coast site closest to the island and began to shell it. The destroyer immediately sailed in between the island and the artillery unit, and with deadly accurate fire, quickly destroyed every artillery piece in the unit. That destroyer circled that island from then on, and the North Koreans left it alone except for one other time when they flew a Russian AN-2, a small, single engine, biplane over the island at night and dropped some small mortar shells near the mountaintop, but fortunately they didn't hit the radar. The destroyer opened up on it with automatic, radar, slaved, quad, 40-millimeter

Silver Star

The Silver Star is awarded to a person who, while serving in any capacity with the U.S. Army, is cited for gallantry in action against an enemy of the United States while engaged in military operations involving conflict with an opposing foreign force, or while serving with friendly foreign forces engaged in armed conflict against an opposing armed force in which the United States is not a belligerent party. The required gallantry, while of a lesser degree than that required for award of the Distinguished Service Cross, must nevertheless have been performed with marked distinction.

antiaircraft guns and literally filled the sky with shells, but the [men manning the guns] couldn't see him and therefore they couldn't hit him. That was one lucky pilot whom we called "Bed Check Charlie." Occasionally and on a very random schedule he would fly down to South Korea at night and toss a few mortar rounds out, each time at a different location, just to harass the troops. The aircraft was fabric covered, and he flew so low that radar could not track him.

Captain Gail W. Poulton Gary AFB, San Marcos, Texas 1952. The Base Commander Colonel Griffith is presenting the "Silver Star" awarded while serving in Korea.

HARTMAN RECTOR, JR.

This future General Authority joined the Church during the Korean conflict. He served in the military during World War II and met the missionaries as a result of an initial contact made with his wife, Connie, in San Diego. A member of the Air Force, Hartman Rector, Jr. was involved in bombing North Korean railroads and other targets during the war. It was during this period that he joined the Church.

When we arrived in Japan the elders decided I was ready for baptism. So we went to the mission home in Tokyo and announced this to the counselor in the mission presidency; the mission president wasn't there. The counselor said, "Well, how long have you been studying the gospel?"

I said, "Oh, about four or five months, I guess."

He said, "We can't baptize you."

"Why?"

He said, "Well you have to be an investigator for a year in Japan before you can be baptized."

I said, "A year? Look, I read the Book of Mormon; I know it's true. I want to join the Church. I want to be baptized."

He said, "I'm sorry, we can't baptize you. We can't do that."

I said, "Well, what do I have to do?"

He said, "You just have to study longer, that's all."

Well, in LeGrand Richards' *A Marvelous Work and a Wonder*, it says in there you should study the gospel for a year before you're baptized. They were following the procedure, I guess. I said, "Look, you know, every time I leave that carrier deck, when I come back there are holes in that airplane that weren't there when I left. They're trying to kill me out there. And if they do, I'll bear testimony against you at the last day that you kept me out of the Church!"

When I told him that, he thought about that awhile and he said, "Well, maybe we . . . you have to be interviewed."

And I said, "Okay, interview me. I'm willing."

He said, "I can make an exception but I'm not supposed to do this,"

I said, "Well, can I take the responsibility? Let me take the responsibility."

"No," he said, "I will. It's my responsibility. Okay, we'll have an interview." It took an hour and a half. Well, he finally decided that I should be baptized.

And that was February 25, 1952. About forty degree weather, outside baptismal font, and about a half inch of ice on top of the font. This McDonald B. Johnson, who had never baptized anybody, was going to baptize me. And when his foot hit the water . . . I mean, we had to break the ice. . . . he totally forgot the baptismal prayer. He couldn't remember my name, he couldn't remember anything. And so we stood in the water with the ice floating around us while they taught him the baptismal prayer. So, I got baptized. I barely survived.

So we went back inside the mission home where I was to be confirmed. Oh, it was cold! When I quit shaking, the other member of the group who was an elder and the co-group leader of the LDS group aboard the *Philippine Sea* was going to confirm me a member of the Church. He hadn't confirmed anybody either. So they gathered around and laid their hands on me, and he confirmed me a member of the Church but didn't give me the Holy Ghost. And when they had finished, the counselor said, "Now, you have to do that over again

Aboard the USS Philippine Sea (CV-47)

Illustrative of the kind of associations which developed among Latter-day Saints during the Korean War is the group located on the USS *Philippine Sea*. The group began meetings in October of 1951. Among those who joined in the services was Donald Johnson, Fred Gaylord Peterson, Keith Gygi, James D. Martin, Gordon A. Pace, Gordon Wellard, Harry P. Head, Donald Cornwall, Hartman Rector, Jr., Lamont W. Archibald, Kenneth J. Peterson, Richard V. Woods, John W. Todd, Rulon J. Johnson, Darrell G. Mille, Kenneth L. Bodily, Max E. Quick, Ronald T. Madson, Neil Andrews, James F. Laughlin, Adam C. Cartwright, and Jay Gardner. It was rare that the entire group met, owing to the nature of their assignments. After the war, members of the group went on to become accomplished Church leaders serving as future missionaries, youth leaders, bishops, and one of their number—Elder Rector—went on to serve as a General Authority. The following description of the group was first published in the *Deseret News—Church Section* on July 2, 1952:

Aboard the United States Aircraft Carrier *Philippine Sea* on duty in the combat area off the coast of Korea, a few Latter-day Saints, though not at home, are still expressing their desire to serve the Lord. This group, but a handful compared to the large aircraft carrier's complement of over 3,000 men, are advancing their testimonies and knowledge of the divinity of the gospel of Jesus Christ.

Under such adverse circumstances, the need for the principles which the gospel of Jesus Christ gives to all who seek it is more forcibly brought home to these young men who are compelled to spend their time thousands of miles from home, their church, and their loved ones.

LDS Serviceman's Group aboard the USS Philippine Sea *(note that the headline for the* Church News *article mistakenly called it the 'Philadelphia Sea.'). Back L–R: Adam C. Cartwright, Donald Johnson, Donald Cornwall. Front L–R: Keith Gygi, Harry P. Head, Hartman Rector, Jr., James Martin, and Fred Peterson. Both Rector and Cartwright were baptized at the Tokyo, Japan mission home.*

Services Aboard 'Philadelphia Sea' Keep Up Morale Of Mormon Crewmen

By KEITH H. GYGI

SOMEWHERE IN KOREAN WATERS—Aboard the United States aircraft carrier 'Philippine Sea" on duty in the combat area off the coast of Korea, a few Latter-day Saints, though far from home, are still expressing their desire to serve the Lord. This group, but a handful compared to the large aircraft carrier's compliment of over 3000 men, are advancing their testimonies and knowledge of the divinity of the gospel of Jesus Christ.

Under such adverse circumstances the need for the principles which the gospel of Jesus Christ gives to all who seek it is more forcibly brought home to these young men who are compelled to spend their time thousands of miles from home, their Church, and their loved ones.

This group had its beginning while the carrier was still off the coast of San Diego in underway training. It was organized by two young elders who were desirous to learn to obey the commandments of God under all circumstances. After they had been set apart as group leaders by San Diego Stake officer and had obtained permission from the commanding officer of the ship, they began their services in October of 1951. Just those two, Donald Johnson of Magna and Fred Gaylord Peterson of Logan, Utah, as the only members. From that time on, as other Latter-day Saints came aboard, the group slowly grew until at present it has reached a membership of fifteen.

THE NEXT MEMBER to appear in the group was Elder Keith H. Gygi of Salt Lake City, Utah. Following him in rapid succession were Elder James D. Martin of Richmond, Utah; Gordon A. Pace of Woods Cross, Utah; Gordon Wellard, Harry P Head Jr., of Sanford, Colorado; Donald Cornwall of Emmett, Idaho; Hartman Rector Jr. of Moberley, Missouri; Lamont W. Archibald of Grace, Idaho; Kenneth J. Peterson of Murray, Utah; Richard V. Woods, of Visalia, Calif.; John W. Todd, of Ogden, Utah; Rulon J. Johnson, Darrell G. Miller, Kenneth L. Bodily, Max E. Quick of Holladay, Utah; Ronald T. Madson, Neil Andrews of Detroit, Michigan; James F. Laughlin of Coranado, Calif.; Adam C. Cartwright of Los Angeles, Calif.; and Jay Gardner. Elder Martin is now discharged from the U.S. Navy.

Due to the many and varied duties aboard ship, there are very few times when the entire group can get together as a body, however two regularly scheduled meetings are held each week. In addition to these two meetings, there have been very few times when at least a portion of these members have not met together in the evening to offer their prayers and to study the Gospel of Jesus Christ. This nightly study has served to weld the group together.

TO PROVE that missionary work can be carried forward in the service of our country as well as in the organized missions of the Church, three of the members, Hartman Rector Jr., James F. Laughlin, and Adam C. Cartwright Jr., have been baptized and confirmed member of the Church by members of this group in the Japanese Mission at Tokyo.

The group has been kept in constant touch with President Mauss of the Japanese Mission. Members of the presidency and missionaries of the Japanese Mission have their in their turn visited the group aboard the Aircraft Carrier at Yokosuka, Japan, during one of their nightly devotional services.

During its rotation periods from the front lines of Korea, when the ship was tied up at Yokosuka, Japan, members of the group have from time to time attended and taken part in the meetings of the LDS Branch at the Yokosuka, Naval Base.

WE HAVE found it expedient to keep in touch with the LDS Serviceman's Committee of the Church. We have received answers to numerous questions which have risen through their studies of the gospel. We wish to thank Elder Bruce R. McConkie of the Servicemen's Committee for the aid and council which he has given them. Families of the various members have been tireless in their efforts to provide the group with the necessary study materials, for which they are thankful.

To paraphrase General Sherman "War is Hell" which is a most apt description but through the power of the priesthood and through individual reliance on the Lord this has been a rich experience through which we have gained rather than lost.

SUNDAY MORNING ABOARD SHIP—LDS members of the U. S. aircraft carrier "Philippine Sea" hold morning services together with M. B Johnson, extreme right, instructing. The three men on the front row were recently converted to the Church by their crew mates. They are, left to right: James L. Laughlin, Hartman Rector Jr., and Adam C. Cartwright.

Top: Hartman Rector, Jr. in uniform. Center: Hartman Rector Jr. receiving the Air Medal. Citation reads: Lieutenant Hartman Rector Jr., United States Naval Service.—For meritorious achievement while participating in aerial flight as pilot of a night attack bomber in action against enemy supply lines between the cities of Wonsan and Hungnam, North Korea, on 27 May 1952. In the face of intense anti-aircraft fire, he personally destroyed four and damaged eight enemy trucks. Continuing his attacks on a second target he destroyed one railroad bridge, two warehouses, and cut the rail lines in two places.

because you have to confer the Holy Ghost when you confirm a member of the Church. That is what confirmation's all about. You have to give him the gift of the Holy Ghost."

"Oh, yes, okay." So they gathered around and immediately he gave me the gift of the Holy Ghost, but didn't confirm me a member of the Church because he thought he'd already done that. And so they begin to prompt him in the circle. Everybody in the circle got in on my confirmation. Finally he got it all together in order and I became a member of the Church.

Now, I was expecting it to feel something great and tremendous when I received the Holy Ghost. I'd read much early history of the Church by this time. I was reading two to four days or nights a week while we were out on the bomb line. I knew that Heber C. Kimball, for instance, had walked around in a daze for about two weeks, so powerful was the effect of the Spirit when he was confirmed. But I didn't feel anything but relief! I didn't know if I was really going to get in the Church or not!

* * * * *

There was a shack sitting by the railroad track and any time you saw any sign of life, smoke coming up out of the— this little building, see, you figure that was probably one of those repair crews that were there. And I saw the smoke curling up out of there and I rolled over, switched on the master arms switch, and I had a couple of 5-inch rockets I could put right in that shack. But you use your bombsight to fire the rockets. And that whole sight filled up with a mother and a baby in her arms. Now you couldn't see a mother and a baby in her arms from 1500 yards. I was way out, just ready to shoot those two rockets in. And there was a mother, a baby in her arms. For some reason the Lord did not want that done. He showed me what was in that shack. And so I just switched off the master arms switch and pulled away because I know I would have killed a mother and her baby. That's what would happen. It was not a repair crew. So I figured, you know, that you can commit murder out there, but the Lord won't let you do that if you listen to Him. If you listen, if you're tuned, even in war, the Lord still works.

* * * * *

Well, they picked me up and got me aboard ship, after I'd fallen in the water, you know. They took me down to the wardroom and laid me on the wardroom table and took off all my clothes to see if I was injured. I said, "No, I'm not injured. I'm fine."

"Well, we gotta check, we gotta check."

And the CO [commanding officer] of the destroyer came up and had this big bottle of brandy in his hand and a water glass. He said, "You're one of the most fortunate young men in the Navy. You've been picked up by a destroyer that has the largest medicinal spirit supply in the Navy."

He poured out half a glass of brandy, and I said something for the first time I'd ever heard myself say that, "No, I don't drink." Never said that before, because the missionaries had just taught me the Word of Wisdom the week before.

Top: Aboard the USS Philippine Sea*—Rector was Master of Ceremonies for "Coming Home Show."*

Bottom: Hartman Rector, Jr. (left) in Tokyo, Japan.

BOYD J. REDDEN

Boyd served in the U.S. Army from March 1953 to February 1955 during the Korean War. He served in the I Corps headquarters as a Signal Corps instructor, after which he served as a cryptographer and teletype operator for I Corps. Boyd achieved the rank of corporal. He is now a retired educator, and has served in the Church mainly as a ward clerk.

When I got overseas, the war had just ended, but they were still pretty cautious. My first experience with the Signal Corps was when I was sent as a shotgun rider with another soldier to deliver some messages to a battalion on the front lines. I didn't know the area, and he didn't know much more, and we got lost and ended up on the DMZ (demilitarization zone). This was a line between North and South Korea of approximately two miles across. We ended up on their side and three North Koreans came at us with guns; we couldn't understand them; they couldn't understand us. We eventually made them understand we were lost, and they let us turn around and go back. Pretty scary.

The Koreans lived in real small, round huts made of sticks and mud. They were heated by wood underneath the mud or cement floors with a hole going up through the center for the chimney. There were a lot of rice fields where we would see the Koreans in water planting or harvesting the rice. We had to go about two miles from our camp to the communications center where I worked. We watched a very pregnant lady for a while. One day, some of them could see her lying out in the field, and the next day she was in the rice paddy with the baby on her back.

* * * * *

A lot of the messages were delivered by plane. One of the pilots was from Provo, [Utah], and because I was from Utah and LDS, I got to go with him a few times. He would make a trip with about seven to ten stops covering somewhere around three hundred miles. One time, we had a long run back without [a scheduled] landing, and he asked me if I wanted a real ride, but told me I had to keep my hat where I could throw up in it if I got sick. It was a two-seater called an L-19 with just room for the pilot in front, another person in back, and then the bag of messages. The backseat had controls also. I had been up enough that I could tell a little bit about the plane from the gauges. I didn't say a word all the way. When we got back, he was surprised that my hat was still empty. He did a lot of rolls and dives, but because I understood the gauges a little bit, I could anticipate what was going to happen.

ARDEN ALLEN ROWLEY

Arden served in the U.S. Army during the Korean War from September 1948 to October 1953. He served with Company A, 2nd Engineer Combat Battalion, 2nd Infantry Division as a platoon leader driver and radio operator. Following his discharge as a sergeant E5, he enlisted in the Arizona National Guard and earned his bachelor's and master's degrees in teaching. He retired from the National Guard as a major in 1974. Arden spent much of his time in the war as a prisoner of war.

Along with the lack of food to eat was added the complete elimination of the POW's source of tobacco. Added to the lack of proper nutrients for the body, soon causing several horrible diseases of malnutrition and death, was the additional strain on the men's bodies: an insidious craving for tobacco. I am convinced that that problem, in addition to malnutrition, weakened men who smoked. The fact that I did not smoke not only allowed my body to remain in better health, but I was, at times, able to give assistance to my fellow POWs.

The POWs were issued a tobacco ration. Each received a small paper package of what was termed "crimp cut" tobacco. Even though I had no use for it, I took my ration. Observing the Word of Wisdom again proved to be of great value to me. We were barely surviving on a diet of a bowl of boiled millet or cracked corn twice a day. One of my fellow POWs had found a cache of soy beans. He jealously guarded his treasure. However, when I offered him enough of my tobacco for one cigarette in trade for a small handful of soy beans, he took my offer. For many days, I was able to receive a small amount of additional nutrition for my body because I observed the Word of Wisdom. I testify that I am alive today because of the observance of that sacred law.

After the first few nights of marching, we noticed that our toes were becoming sore. In fact, before long, they became sore to the point that we could not bear to have them touch anything or anybody. But, in our crowded conditions each day, it was impossible to keep that from happening, and many a man cried out in pain as his toes came in contact with the men next to him. Thank goodness, after a time this condition ceased to exist.

After several more nights of marching, still half-carrying, half-dragging our wounded, we stopped in a small village for a few days. This was a welcome rest. The Chinese were bringing together more and more prisoners. One morning, they [pulled] us all out of the huts to do some exercises. We figured we would be moving again, that they were getting us out to limber us up for another march. Sure enough, soon we were on our way again. We marched for several more nights, still struggling to keep the wounded and sick up with the main body so that they would not fall out and freeze to death or be shot by a guard as had happened to some. I well remember on

Arden Allen Rowley on August 18, 1953—the day he was released from a Commmunist POW Camp. Photo taken by the Red Cross at Inchon, South Korea, and sent to his family.

Homer Wheeler, Arden Rowley, and A.J. Becker aboard USNS Marine Adder, *August 1953.*

one night's march that another POW and I carried, between us, a short, sandy-haired soldier named Fred J. Propori who had been wounded in one of his legs and could not walk on his own. We were not about to let Fred fall out of the march to suffer the fate of some who did. After that night, I lost track of Fred for the rest of the march, but did see him later at our first permanent POW camp. He had recovered from his wound in the leg. (Fred died in March 1997 of cancer.)

During the night of December 24 we pushed ourselves on with thoughts of home, loved ones, and a cheery, warm fireside. As the Chinese guards crammed us into Korean houses, sometime around midnight, it seemed even colder. It was because it was Christmas, and our thoughts were even more of home, family, and the warm, happy times which we had known at Christmas times past. After settling into our rooms, our thoughts of home were interrupted by the opening of the door and the placing of a large, wooden bowl inside by a shadowy, unknown figure. The dim light of a single candle revealed the bowl's contents: our "Christmas feast" of whole-kerneled field corn submerged in a sea of hot, dirty water. Many a man would just as soon not have partaken; however, this meal, as well as others, just as lacking in palatability, was necessary if we were to survive. Already there were far too many who had died of wounds, dysentery, pneumonia, and of other causes already mentioned; there was no need to add starvation to the list so soon. All possible thoughts were, indeed, of home that night, and after the singing of a few familiar Christmas carols, which were a prayer to God, we drifted off and fell into a period of fitful, yet peaceful sleep, grateful that we had survived another day.

Days passed, and one day, as we were discussing the lecture questions in our room, someone suggested that it was a bunch of nonsense for me to go to the Chinese time after time and give them "Commie pleasing" answers which we did not believe whatsoever. We all knew inside that it was true, and I guess it just took someone to express it verbally to jar us to our senses. So we decided that, this time, I would go to the monitors' meeting and give straight answers to the

American POWs about mid-December 1950. Left to Right: MSgt. William F. Maus, PFC Alfredo Rocque, SFC Wyatt Duncan, PFC James Veneris, Unidentified, PFC Robert Vicaldo, PFC Robert R. Willorial, Sgt. Robert C. Kirk. Arden Rowley (not pictured) was a POW 1950–1953.

Chinese. As the monitors gathered at Chinese headquarters, and our reporting meeting got under way, the other monitors responded with the usual "line of bull." When it was my turn, and a Chinese "instructor" asked me what my men had said about the questions, I told him that we didn't see any sense in lying to them any longer, that we did not believe anything that we were hearing in the lectures and that from now on we would answer the questions straightforward and truthfully, that which we had believed all along. So I went on to report our answers to the questions. To say the least, both the Chinese and the other monitors were surprised. The Chinese kept after me trying to get me to give the "correct" answers to their lecture questions. Time passed, and, when I continued to hold out, the other monitors coaxed me to give in and say what they [the Chinese] wanted to hear so that we could return to our rooms. They said something like, "Come on, Rowley, we're going to be here all day if you don't give in." Eventually, the Chinese let the other monitors leave and kept me there and lectured me on the importance of accepting the truth. I kept telling them that we know what the truth is. They accused me of being a "reactionary" and said

Below: Sergeant Wolmer Bartlett salutes the U.S. flag as he steps out of an ambulance at Freedom Village, August 1953.

Right: An American repatriate steps down from a truck at the prisoner exchange point at Panmunjom, Korea, August 1953.

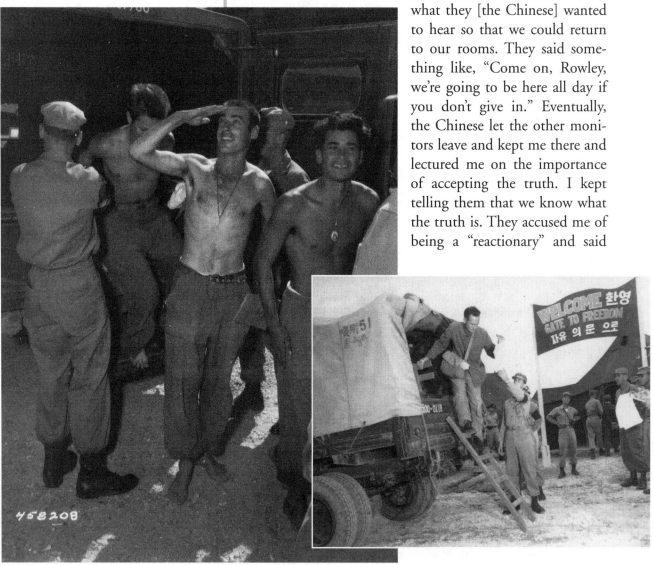

that I was sabotaging the "studies." (We were to hear the names "progressive" and "reactionary" used by the Chinese in referring to certain POWs during the next two and a half years.) The Chinese instructors finally gave up and let me return to my room after unsuccessfully trying to convince me that I wasn't seeing the truth.

* * * * *

My wife, Ruth, calls the following, "The Tuttle–Waterman Story." She has heard it many times through the years since our marriage in November 1953, as I have spoken to youth and civic groups. Allen H. Tuttle, originally a large, robust man from the Seattle area, but now with a thick, black, bushy beard and many pounds lighter, was selected by the Chinese to be among a group of men, one from each room, to be taken to a drafty barn to receive indoctrination lectures each day and to then convey the messages to the men in the rooms. Waterman, from the minute we were assigned to rooms in POW Camp #5, sat down in one corner of the room, pulled a GI blanket over his head, and consumed nothing but water. Tuttle soon contracted pneumonia and became desperately ill. Tuttle's spot in the room, for we did indeed have our "own" little space, was next to mine. During the next few days, I did everything I could think of to help Tuttle eat and hold onto his life. I thinned our millet or cracked corn down to a gruel to feed to him and constantly spoke words of encouragement to him. And Tuttle tried desperately to live. It was obvious to us all that he was suffering so. One day as I was leaning on one elbow next to Tuttle giving him words of encouragement, I decided to petition the Lord to intervene in his behalf. So as Tuttle lay there with his eyes closed, struggling for every breath, I closed my eyes, bowed my head, and offered a silent prayer for him, asking God to bless him that he wouldn't have to suffer any longer. As I finished my prayer, I opened my eyes and looked up. Tuttle's eyes were gazing straight into mine, and he uttered his last words, "Thanks, Rowley." Then he quietly slipped away. Perhaps God had intervened, for who knows what additional suffering Tuttle may have had to endure. In contrast, Waterman remained in the corner with the blanket over his head until he died.

GEORGE R. RUNYAN

George served in the U.S. Navy from August 1951 to May 1952 during the Korean War. He served with Leonard F. Mason DD852 as fire control operator. George achieved the rank of seaman. Throughout his military service and his life, he has been a missionary, both as an official calling in the three missions he has served and as a stake mission president, and informally as well.

While in boot camp, I had many opportunities to teach the gospel. Most of the men were young, and it was their first time away from home. We all lived in a barrack with bunks three high. There was no privacy. I was in the middle bunk so I asked the guy on the bottom if it would be all right after the lights went out if I knelt by his bed to say my prayer. He said okay so each night, I would kneel down; and I could hear the snickers here and there, but an amazing thing happened. I noticed a few others kneeling down. It wasn't long until I was asked questions about religion. It was a great opportunity to teach and help these buddies. I have often thought I had as much opportunity to teach the gospel in the military as I did in the mission field. They were so responsive and open to the gospel.

One of my enjoyable memories was when we would have target practice shooting at airplanes. My job was a fire control operator for one of the 5-inch gun mounts. I was right up on the bridge with an instrument that had radar capabilities. I would follow the target in my scope visually; the instrument would calculate the distance, wind, and roll of the ship so that at any time the captain said fire, I would hit the target. Our targets were mostly a sleeve pulled by an airplane, far enough away so we couldn't hit the plane. If it was a night or in the clouds, the radar scope would be used to locate the target and do all the same things only better. The gun mount which was below me and to one side followed my movements exactly and would fire as I pulled the trigger.

One of my main concerns about being in the service was that I did not want to kill or hurt anyone. With this assignment as my battle station I was the one who would pull the trigger even though it was at the captain's command who was standing right close to me. I prayed a great deal and pleaded with my Father in Heaven that I would not have to hurt anyone. My prayers were answered. One night in Korea there was a small boat (sampan) in our area. This was a problem because these sampans planted mines for us to hit and blow up. I had this sampan in my scope and was ready to fire. When the captain gave the order, it was to the other gun mount, not mine. The next day, we saw the debris floating around and we knew we had hit it. But I did not have to take anyone's life.

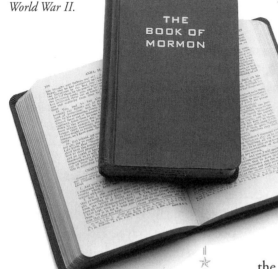

A serviceman's edition of the Book of Mormon was issued by the Church for all servicemen in the Korean War. This compact-size edition was first published and distributed during World War II.

One day, there was a request over the squawk box from some Marines on a nearby island who needed some reading material, and if we had any books, magazines, etc., they would appreciate them. I had several small novels I was through with and three small servicemen's copies of the Book of Mormon, so I decided to send one along in case someone would read it. The books were gathered in one place, and it would two or three days before they were taken to the island. In the meantime some of the fellows went through the books to see if there were any they would like to read. Among these fellows was a man named Fred Hawes, and he saw the Book of Mormon. He had been wishing he had one to read and there it was so he took it. The next day, I saw this guy with my Book of Mormon in his pocket. When I had the chance, I asked him if he was a Mormon. And he said yes and he had been wishing he had a copy of the Book of Mormon and someone to help him with his questions about our church and other churches. He accepted my offer of help, so I had the opportunity to be a missionary again. It was wonderful. I drew him a diagram of the story of the Book of Mormon and tried to help him in reading it. The thing I wanted most to leave with him was the blessing of the Church and my testimony. His reaction was good and what joy it brought to me to share the gospel again. I wish I had known about him sooner. We could have had such a wonderful time during those lonely months. He told me he was from Salt Lake City, [Utah], originally, but his family now lived in California close to Los Angeles. He told me he had been an inactive member, a deacon. His girlfriend was a member, and had told him she wanted to be married in the temple and so did he, but he didn't know how to prepare for it. I'm so happy to have been in the right place at the right time for him. I also gave him a copy of *Principles of the Gospel* for servicemen to help him understand the basic gospel.

KENNETH F. RUSSELL

Kenneth served in the Air Force during the Korean War from June 1951 to September 1954. He served in the 345th Bomb Squadron, 98th Bomb Wing as a B-29 gunner. Kenneth achieved the rank of sergeant. After the war he attended Brigham Young University and then dental school. He has worked as a dentist and served in many areas of the Church.

In January 1951 I had just finished fall quarter at Brigham Young University, and the Korean War was a few months old. The military was gearing up for war after demobilizing after World War II. A group of young men from Springville, [Utah], myself included, enlisted in the Air Force on January 6, 1951, at Fort Douglas, Utah. It looked like most young men would have to go, and we were young and anxious to serve our country, so we chose to enlist in the Air Force.

We traveled by train to Lackland Air Force Base in San Antonio, Texas, where we started basic training. The base was crowded, and we were living in tents. More recruits were coming in every day. Because of the crowded conditions, we were shipped out early by train to have more basic training at our next base. I was sent to B-29 turret mechanic school at Lowry Air Force Base in Denver, Colorado. Because of the urgency of getting men trained, they held classes in three shifts, and I was assigned to a night shift. After graduation they took part of our class and put us in B-29 gunnery school at the same base. This consisted of ground firing and aerial gunnery using gun cameras on a B-29.

After completing gunnery school we were sent to Randolph Air Force Base at San Antonio, [Texas], to be put on a B-29 bomber crew. An LDS pilot, Captain Donald O. Funk, who had been in the Reserves from World War II was recalled to active duty as a B-29 pilot. He requested LDS members for his crew and was able to find eight LDS members out of eleven. Our crew was written up in the December 19, 1951 *Church News*. We trained and learned to function as a crew, and how to operate the systems of the B-29.

After crew training at Randolph we were sent to Forbes Air Force Base in Topeka, Kansas, for combat crew training. This consisted of long-range navigation, simulated combat bombing missions, and more gunnery training.

The last phase of our training was survival training at Camp Carson, Colorado. Here we learned to live off the land and evade the enemy in the mountains in January 1952.

After this we were assigned overseas and took a B-29 to Japan by way of Honolulu, Kwajalein, Guam, and then to Yokota Air Force Base in Japan, arriving in April 1952. At each base where we were stationed we attended church whenever possible. In Japan we attended a branch consisting mostly of military and government employees.

We flew twenty-seven long-range combat bombing missions over North Korea from our base in Japan, each one a story in itself. The missions would last up to twelve hours, and these were flown mostly at night. Our targets consisted of railroad bridges, hydroelectric plants, dams, factories, supply depots, and front line support. Our mission ranged from the 38th parallel to the Yalu River. The enemy had radar-controlled searchlights and flak guns that were very accurate. Searchlights would lock on to our planes and make it possible for their fighters to see us. The flack guns would also lock on and we would depend on the electronic countermeasure officer to jam their frequencies. We crash-landed a plane after one mission with only one injury, and our plane was hit with flak with no injuries. We were the lead crew, and we were decorated for accuracy and determination. We were truly protected and blessed during our time in combat.

When we returned to the States I married, and I served another year in the Air Force. After I was discharged I finished pre-dental training at BYU and went to dental school.

Serving with other LDS servicemen made a favorable atmosphere to help us stay true to our faith and beliefs and to

LDS Bomber Crewmen May Worship in Clouds

RANDOLPH AIR FORCE BASE — Latter-day Saint crewmen aboard a B-29 bomber can hold priesthood meeting above the clouds if occasion requires, according to Chaplain Grant E. Mann, the only Church chaplain in the Air Force.

Eight of the 11-man crew are also Church members, he said. They arrived at the Randolph Air Force Base in Texas individually from various Air Force specialists training schools, and were then grouped together at the request of the crew's 28-year-old aircraft commander, Captain Donald A. Funk of Salt Lake City.

The crewmen can be found attending the San Antonio Branch on Sunday, along with scores of their fellow servicemen.

During the past 41 months nearly 2000 servicemen's kits (containing a servicemen's edition of the Book of Mormon and a little book entitled Principles of the Gospel) have been given out to Latter-day Saint servicemen stationed at Lackland Air Base near San Antonio, according to Chaplain Mann. He has also set apart a good many group leaders among whom have been some 85 returned missionaries.

Kenneth Russell was part of a B-29 bomber crew that was mostly LDS (eight out of eleven). The above article about their crew appeared in the CHURCH NEWS *in 1951.*

resist many temptations associated with military life. I feel we were a good influence on the nonmembers around us. My patriarchal blessing states that I have missionary and genealogical work to do for my ancestors. I didn't serve a mission as a young man, but served a stake mission soon after I moved back to Salt Lake City, Utah, to practice dentistry.

Our crew has stayed close and in 1993 the remaining members of the crew started holding a crew reunion every two years.

GEORGE WOODARD SANDBERG

Woodard served in the U.S. Army from 1953–1955 during the Korean War. He served with the Signal Corps as a radio operator and repairman and achieved the rank of private first class. Woodard is a professional engineer, and has had a career in U.S. Geological Survey and has served a total of four full-time missions for the Church.

It was now the Korean War. Because I had not been in the Army, my draft status remained active. Every six months, I kept being called up and then sent home. I graduated from Utah State University with a degree in engineering, and moved to Shiprock, New Mexico, with my first job and a confident future. I was called up again to report to Salt Lake City, since we still officially lived in Utah. We didn't even take the call seriously; just left all our stuff in Shiprock and drove to Salt Lake City for a nice weekend.

Three hours after arriving at Fort Douglas, Utah, in August 1952, at age twenty-six, I was in the Army. The physical standards had been lowered. I was now deemed worthy to be a private in the U. S. Army. Draftees holding a bachelor's degree were automatically taken into officer candidate school [OCS], but I was not eligible for OCS because of my eyesight. My eyesight was only good enough to enable me to peel potatoes, which I did for the next two years.

My wife was out shopping, enjoying this nice week in Salt Lake City, when I had to call from Fort Douglas to say I would not be coming home that night. I was headed for Fort Ord, California. It was sheer trauma for everyone. Unequivocally unexpected. My wife got up to Fort Douglas in time to see me sworn in and heard the wives being told, "You may expect to see your husbands in eight years; two years in Korea and six more until their army reserve time is served, that is if they come back from Korea." Those were pretty close to the actual words said to all the families present in a mass meeting. In that atmosphere, we parted.

Then, I guess the Lord decided perhaps we had had enough, and a few things started falling into place. After married men finished basic training, they could live off base, so that was a help. [My wife Gwen and I] went on a weekend south to Redondo Beach to watch some unusually high waves. We climbed up on the pilings to watch. A huge 15- to 20-foot wave rocked over the top of the rough cement pilings and washed us back onto the beach. I landed on a rough chunk of cement breakwater, and Gwen landed on me. My ankle was broken, and I next landed in the hospital. The hospital lost my records. I lay forgotten in a cast and watched my company ship out for Korea in the spring of 1953. I think some of them were involved in bloody Pork Chop Hill soon after they arrived; at least the heavy winter fighting was continuing at its worst and POWs were being brainwashed and shipped to China and Russia. We thanked the Lord every day for a broken ankle.

A nice Mormon nurse finally located my records, and I was released from the hospital and finished Radio Signal Corps Training School in the summer. In September 1953 I received orders for France. Gwen went home again to her folks in Circleville [Utah] to have our first baby while I spent the remainder of the Korean War in France.

Again our two sets of parents supported and buoyed us up. The gospel sustained us, and provided us the faith that one day the separation and difficulty would be behind us.

One truly good thing came of the time in France. A group of six or eight Latter-day Saint servicemen regularly got together in the post library and held sacrament services. One morning, another man in the barracks shouted to me, "Where are you going?" (All the others had gone to town for the day.)

I called back, "I am going to church. Do you want to go with me?" He said yes. He went with me; he went again the next Sunday and the next few Sundays. Then I got rotated back to the States and lost track. A short time later, I received a letter from Private Jones saying he had been baptized.

What did my army experience teach me? It taught me I could endure much. It taught me that access to the gospel can be found anywhere, and that my influence for sharing the gospel could be used anywhere. It taught me that the bonds of love and marriage in a temple of the Lord can keep those bonds tight through separation and hardship.

WILLIAM GARTH SEEGMILLER

William served in the U.S. Army from September 1942 to August 1952 during World War II and the Korean War. He served in the IX Corps of the 8th Army as a regimental adjutant in the Transportation Corps. William achieved the rank of first lieutenant, and has since worked as a professional technical writer and novelist.

In February 1952, a young man, Lieutenant Gray from Denver, Colorado, was a patient in the big hospital room with me. There was also a U.S. Army general as a patient just across the hall from us. During my second week there, I was surprised to learn that Gray was a professional artist. The nurse told me that the general had hired Lieutenant Gray for one thousand dollars to do a portrait of the general for his wife who was visiting him. Lieutenant Gray obtained the brushes and color paints for that assignment and spent considerable time in painting that general's portrait.

When Lieutenant Gray came back to our room, he told me what he had done and that the general insisted on paying him the thousand dollars for that large painting. Then Gray stared at me and said, "I would really like to paint your portrait!"

I shook my head and replied, "No way! I'm only a lieutenant, and my salary is sent home to support my wife and three children. I'm not interested in having my portrait done for a thousand bucks because I couldn't even afford to pay the twenty bucks I still have in my wallet!"

Lieutenant Gray grinned at me and said calmly, "Hey, Garth, I wouldn't charge you anything. I really want to do your portrait, for your eyes show the sorrow of war and being away from family."

Therefore, that thoughtful young officer and artist talked me into sitting there on my bed while he did a large painting. A month later I was healed, dressed in my uniform, and in the hall rushing out of there to catch an air force plane returning to Korea. Our Japanese-American nurse from Honolulu, Hawaii, ran up the hall to me and handed me a letter from home. I opened it and was elated to see the three little black and white photos of my children. The nurse said, "Let me see them." I handed them to her and she said, "Hey, these are cute, but they should be in color. Tell me the color of their eyes and hair." Quickly I did, and she scribbled in Japanese on the back of each little photo. Then she exclaimed, "I want to show them to Doctor Smith." She whirled around and ran down the hall to Doctor Smith's office. I glanced at my watch. It was too late to wait any longer. That plane would not wait. Disappointed that she had my kids' photos, I hurried out of the hospital and caught the plane just before it took off.

Soon back into the duties of the Korean War in North Korea, I forgot about those little pictures of my sweet children. Then on Easter morning, a major knocked on my tent door at Hachonjon-ni, Korea, and asked me if I was Garth Seegmiller. I nodded and said, "Yes, I am; what do you need?"

He handed me a long tube package and replied, "I just returned from the Tokyo Army Hospital. The Hawaiian nurse there asked me to bring this package to you that you forgot when you were over there."

I shook his hand, thanked him, and saluted. I could not even imagine what I had forgotten in Tokyo back there in that hospital. Wondering, I opened the tube and with tear-filled eyes and a pounding heart, I was surprised to discover a large painting in color of my three children. A note on an attached paper read, "Dear Garth, Happy Easter from your nurse in Tokyo!"

Now fifty years later in my eighty-fifth year of this wonderful life of earth, I can't forget those thrilling experiences. Even in the hell of war, there is also a little unforgettable heaven, too!

Lieutenant Gray painted this portrait of William Seegmiller. At the time, both were patients in an Army Hospital in Tokyo, Japan.

William Garth Seegmiller taken during his service in WWII

MARC H. SESSIONS

Marc served in the Air Force as one of the first two LDS chaplains in the Air Force who were called up in the Korean conflict. In addition to his primary responsibilities, he arranged Red Cross, Boy Scouts, Church, and other activities.

It was a privilege to serve as a chaplain, and particularly an LDS one, during the Korean War. I developed a deep sense of responsibility as Elder Harold B. Lee, director of the LDS Servicemen's Committee, set Chaplain Grant E. Mann and me apart as the first LDS chaplains called up by the Air Force during the Korean War. I was stationed at Sheppard Field in Texas.

Previously, I had served as the only LDS chaplain in the U.S. Army Air Corps during much of World War II. I had felt very alone at times with my responsibilities to my country and my Church, so it was nice to share that responsibility with other LDS Chaplains during the Korean War.

I didn't fight in any typical battles, but I did fight the war for the servicemen's souls, which I felt was an even greater crusade.

As an LDS chaplain, we had special duties over the LDS servicemen, but also had great responsibilities over servicemen of other faiths as well. It wasn't just giving sermons and conducting meetings on Sunday. I welcomed new servicemen in and encouraged them to attend church.

I loved organizing meetings and teaching gospel insights with the servicemen of all faiths. Regardless of whether anyone ever converted to the Church, I knew that good gospel principles were being shared.

I spent much of my time counseling people regarding morality and other challenges, such as fear of death. I was also a mediator in resolving many grievance cases. I conducted about twenty worship services a month for all faith groups. I visited the sick and the wounded and comforted the bereaved.

As chaplains, we also organized picnics, dramatics, athletics, glee clubs, Red Cross, choirs, Boy Scouts, Mutual, scripture classes, and Primary groups. We arranged community hospitality through local churches, fraternal groups, schools, and USO [United Service Organizations]. We assisted the commanding officers with special events such as Easter service with thousands of servicemen present and other special celebrations.

We helped personnel officers in recommending new duty assignments for others. We helped welcome new recruits each week and helped them make adjustments to new conditions. One of my most interesting assignments was providing spiritual advice to a whole battalion of African-American troops. I felt a special kinship with them, as I had spent my childhood in South Africa while my father was a mission president.

One of my most fulfilling assignments was welcoming servicemen at the conclusion of their assignment and sending them off to civilian life with the challenge of spiritual growth.

Throughout my life, I've had a profound respect for military men who not only commanded and fought, but also spiritually led, such as Captain Moroni. He was a great spiritual military commander and a great example to other LDS servicemen and me.

To share in the spiritual part of a military conflict involving hate, fear, death, and intense suffering was an experience that I will never forget or regret.

ROBERT HENRY SLOVER

Robert served in the U.S. Army from January 1942 to November 1964 during both World War II and the Korean War. In Korea, he served with the United Nations Command as a part of the military government. Robert achieved the rank of colonel. Many years after the war, Robert returned to Korea to serve as the first president of the Seoul Korea Temple in 1985.

Robert Slover, 1944.

On August 19, 1953, I flew from Tokyo, Japan, to Pusan, Korea, as a lieutenant colonel in the U.S. Army, assigned to the Korea Civil Assistance Command (KCAC) of United Nations Forces. Little did I realize that this was the beginning of a long association with the nation and the people of Korea. The truce had just ended the fighting in a long bitter conflict between the communist North Korea and the democratic South Korea. Though the fighting was over, the enmity between the two political divisions did not end. What I saw on that hot August day was a devastated country with millions of refugees gathered in the Pusan Perimeter.

The Korea Civil Assistance Command's (KCAC) mission was to assist with the rehabilitation of South Korea using resources from the military forces. This was the start, at grass roots level, of the rebuilding of what was to become modern-day Korea. My assignment at KCAC began when I was assigned as chief of the Legal and Government Affairs branch, which led to planning and working with the ROK (Republic of Korea) government organizations. At first we were in Pusan; later our offices were moved to Seoul. After May 1954, I was reassigned to Tokyo where I worked for three years as a member of the Far East Command headquarters, with numerous trips back and forth to Korea.

Headquarter's Eighth Army Chapel. "We held our LDS services here on Sunday afternoons." Seoul, Korea, December 1953.

KCAC was headquartered near the then undeveloped and beautiful Pusan Bay. In an effort to describe that part of Korea, as it was in 1953 at the close of the conflict, I quote from my journal, "Most of the houses are of the adobe type, and almost all have straw roofs. The people are miserable. As a rule the smaller children wear no clothes at all this time of the year. Pusan has become the refugee center, for not only the people, but also the government. It is the only major city that was not touched by the combat phase of the war. It has grown from a population of one-half million to three and one-half million. In many areas, as far as the eye can see, the hills are covered with refugee shacks."

I compare the situation then with my visit to Pusan in December 2001. Pusan is a thriving, modern, and highly developed city, including modern hotels, businesses, apartments and homes.

My first Sunday in April, I made my first Korean Church contact when I attended the Sunday School meeting of the LDS serviceman's group at the Pusan Port chapel. There were

Mr. Lee Ho, ROK Vice Minister of National Defense, presents Lt. Colonel Robert H. Slover with the Order of Military Merit, Ulchi, with the Silver Star at a ceremony at the ROK Ministry of Defense in Seoul, Korea. 30 April 1954.

about seventy-five people present, including some twenty-five Koreans. The group leader was an army dentist, Lieutenant Gibbons. Grant Heaton, who later would become the first mission president sent to Hong Kong, was his counselor. There was a separate class for the Koreans, and I again quote from my journal, "One elder, a professor who was educated at Cornell, [was their teacher]." That was my first contact with Dr. Ho Jik Kim and the beginning of an association that would continue through the early period of Church development in Korea, which included both of us being present at the dedication of Korea by Elder Joseph Fielding Smith in August 1955.

Until KCAC headquarters moved to Seoul, I participated in group meetings in Pusan. In Seoul, I was called to a group leadership position.

In Tokyo, President Hilton Robertson asked me to serve as servicemen's coordinator for the Far East Mission, which included branches and districts in Japan, Korea, and Okinawa.

The president of the Republic of Korea, Syngman Rhee, gave KCAC a citation for service to his country, which reads in part: "The Korean Civil Assistance Command, by its tireless efforts and resourcefulness, distinguished itself by its humanitarian services and achievements in the prevention of disease, starvation, and unrest among the civilian population." The citation further describes the work performed in improving the economic situation of the war-torn nation.

KCAC helped plan and put into effect projects for both ROK and U.S. military units. They arranged for shiploads of

Robert Slover took these photos of Elder Joseph Fielding Smith's visit to Korea, during which he dedicated the land for the preaching of the gospel.

Below: President H. Grant Heaton, Elder Joseph Fielding Smith, and Rodney Fye. 24th Infantry Division, Korea, August 4, 1955.

Bottom left: APPE/8A Chaplain (Colonel) John Woods, Elder Joseph Fielding Smith, and Pres. Hilton Robertson standing in front of the headquarters for the U.S. Army forces, Far East and 8th Army. Seoul, Korea. August 2, 1955.

Bottom right: L–R: Dr. Ho Jik Kim, Elder Joseph Fielding Smith, Socker Lee, Rodney Fye, Sergeant Case, and Pres. H. Grant Heaton in front of the Korean War Shrine. August 2, 1955.

grain and other foodstuffs to be sent to Korea; roads and schools were built by ROK and U.S. Corps of Engineers; Signal Corps units rehabilitated communication facilities; while medical units assisted with the building of hospitals, and the deployment of medical supplies.

Several members of KCAC, including myself, were awarded the Korean Order of Military Merit, Ulchi, with the Silver Star by the ROK minister of defense.

* * * * *

In 1955, I was assigned as a lieutenant colonel in the U.S. Army to the United Nations Far East Command (UNFEC) headquarters at Pershing Heights, Tokyo, Japan. With my family (Rosemarie, Robert II and Cindy) we had an apartment in the Pershing Heights Complex. Hilton Robertson was the mission president for the Far East Mission. Under his direction I still served as LDS servicemen's coordinator. In July of that year, Apostle Joseph Fielding Smith, accompanied by his wife, Jessie Evans Smith, visited the Far East Mission.

Elder Smith divided the Far East Mission into two missions, which were called the Northern Far East Mission with headquarters in Tokyo, retaining President Robertson as mission president; and the Southern Far East Mission with Grant Heaton, who was with Elder Smith, as mission president with headquarters in Hong Kong.

Elder Smith wished to then go to Korea to visit the servicemen's groups and to dedicate that land for the preaching of the gospel. At this time, Korea had not yet been opened for civilian travel. Through the UNFEC headquarters, Elder Smith was given an honorary rank of U.S. Army brigadier general. Accompanied by President Robertson, Grant Heaton, and myself, Elder Smith was given permission to visit Korea. Sister Smith also wished to go, but this could not be arranged. Instead she sent with us a recording of her singing. The four of us took a military flight to Seoul.

With rank of brigadier general, Elder Smith was assigned a house on the outskirts of Seoul for billet, and given a jeep and a driver. He was also provided with a light plane as he wished to meet with all the LDS Groups from the DMZ [demilitarized zone] in the north to Pusan in the south. July and August in Korea are very hot and humid. The roads were not paved so there was a lot of dust while traveling. We persuaded Elder Smith to change his usual coat and tie for a white sports shirt that I gave him. He visited the Church groups at each military base and gave inspiring talks, for the most part based on the scripture from Alma in the Book of Mormon, "Wickedness never was happiness." At each base we put Sister Smith's "record singing platter" on the military base loud speaker system, so she sang to everyone on the base.

I took pictures along the way showing Elder Smith at the DMZ looking into North Korea, visiting 8th Army headquarter, etc., along with Brother and Sister Ho Jik Kim.

On August 2, 1955, we were with Elder Smith at his quarters when he indicated we should use that day to dedicate the land of Korea for the preaching of the gospel. Nearby the house where he was staying was a hill that overlooked the city of Seoul. (In 1955, this location was on the outskirts of the city. Now, in 2003, the site is completely surrounded by the city.)

We proceeded to the site on top of the hill where Elder Smith gave the dedicatory prayer. Unfortunately the prayer was not recorded, but I did take a slide or photo of the event.

After completing his mission in Korea, Elder Smith, with President Robertson, President Heaton, and myself returned to Tokyo. It was not too long after this that Paul Andrus, the successor to President Robertson, became president of the Northern Far East Mission and sent the first missionaries to Korea. This part of my association with Korea and the developing Latter-day Saint's Church ended in the spring of 1957 with my military assignment to the States.

DEAN MORRIS SMITH

Dean Morris Smith was a Corporal in First Calvary Company D. A product of Morgan, Utah, Dean was involved in Korea serving both at Inchon and later in Pusan. Most of Dean's time was spent on duty in Japan.

Dean Smith using his snowshoes at Camp Carford, Japan, in winter 1952.

Dean Smith and another soldier friend sitting with a group of (Japanese) youth.

MERLIN J. STEPHENSON

Merlin served in the U.S. Army from August 1950 to July 1952 during the Korean War. He served in the B Battery, 145th Field Artillery Battalion as an ammunition corporal, working in direct support of infantry in Korea. Merlin achieved the rank of corporal and retired from the Reserves after thirty years with the rank of command sergeant major.

We landed at Pusan, Korea, in early October 1951 and shortly after were transported by ship up the western coast of Korea where we landed at Inchon, Korea. From there we went inland and then went north to a place called Sugong-ni, Korea. There had been a city there at one time, but all that was left of the city were the foundations of the buildings and homes. We gave direct support to the infantry and also supported the ROK (Republic of Korea) troops.

Merlin Stephenson in front of what could have been the first LDS chapel built in Korea. It took his artillery battery approximately 6 months to build the chapel. Stephenson's LDS group had on average 25 people attending each week.

The unit was about 90 percent LDS members so we decided to build a small chapel. We asked for and received permission from our stake president to build it. It was built from materials that were left from the destroyed city. We even had a dedicatory service, and I was honored to give the dedicatory prayer. This was one of the highlights of my life. The chapel may have been the first LDS chapel built in Korea. It served its purpose as a meeting place and a sanctuary for us from the daily drudgeries and fears of war and combat. It was also a place to receive the sacrament. The dimensions of the chapel were about ten feet wide and twelve feet deep. The interior contained six benches and a pulpit.

DEAN ALAN SUDWEEKS

Dean served in the U.S. Army from June 1952 to May 1954 during the Korean War. He served with the 10th Special Services Company, 10th Corps in the 8th Army as a bandsman and achieved the rank of staff sergeant. Dean is a civil and structural engineer, and has served in many positions in the Church.

I was drafted into the Army on June 17, 1952, after being married to Carolyn Fowers on June 4, 1952, in the Logan Temple. I received my draft notice upon our return from a short honeymoon in southern Utah. I was inducted only thirteen days after our marriage. I was sent with several others from Utah to Fort Ord, California, for infantry basic training. I was assigned to L Company, 20th Infantry Regiment of the 6th Infantry Division. During the first week of basic training I auditioned to get into band training as I played the trumpet. A few days later, two of us (out of twenty-six) were notified that we had been accepted and would leave our company after eight weeks of infantry basic training and go into band training. We spent the next ten weeks in band training taking lessons and also playing in the Fort Ord Army Band every Saturday for review.

Dean Alan Sudweeks at the Kwandi Ree Valley, Korea in spring 1954.

I received orders in November 1952 to report to Camp Drake in Japan to be assigned somewhere in the Far East. I had a bandsman MOS number. I arrived at Camp Drake on December 17, and while there auditioned for a position in an army special services company located in Korea that was ready to begin rehearsing in Pusan. This was the 10th Special Services Company, 10th Corps in the 8th Army. This special services company was made up of all army personnel and our platoon consisted of a 12-piece band, singers, dancers, comedian, and composer. Our company had four platoons and each put on different shows for the army troops in Korea. Our platoon's show was called "Face the Music." We rehearsed in Pusan, Korea, in January and February 1953 and then traveled by rail north through Seoul to where the 1st Marine Division was stationed near Munsan, Korea. The 1st Marine Division was on the front line and we camped at their headquarters. We performed two shows a day for them—mostly for the troops on the front lines. One morning show was for a reconnaissance group who had had 40 percent casualties the night before. It was a very solemn occasion.

We moved to the Army's 2nd Infantry Division on March 24, 1953. We continued to entertain the army troops and played shows there within 1500 yards of the front lines. We were there about four weeks and then we were assigned and moved to be with the British Commonwealth Division that was on the front lines also. We performed shows for British, Australian, Canadian and Dutch troops. We stayed there for six weeks and moved to the 7th Infantry Division near the end of May 1953. They were also on the front lines.

We continued to perform shows for them until we were assigned to operate the 10th Corps Recreation Center. That was in late June 1953 and was located at Kwandi Ree Valley. The facilities included a ball diamond, a skeet range, and a Quonset hut with pool tables, an ice cream machine and donut making equipment, a photo hobby lab, a hobby shop and a

Dean Sudweeks played the trumpet in the 10th Special Services Company, 10th Corps in the 8th Army. His platoon put on a show for the troops in Korea called "Face the Music." His group performed for troops as close as 1500 yards from the front lines. This photo shows the group performing for Headquarter Troops.

Inset: "Face the Music Show" for the Front Line Troops.

lounge area. The troops on the front lines were brought here one day per week for rest and relaxation. I was in charge of both the hobby shop and the photo hobby lab.

While in Korea we lived in tents most of the time, away from any cities or towns. The weather was similar to the weather in northern Utah. Bathing was often a luxury and sometimes took place in rivers, or we took sponge baths from our helmets.

In August 1953, LDS chaplain Mark Money set me apart as first counselor to the group leader, Douglas Orchard, in the 10th Corps LDS Servicemen's Group. We met in the 4th Signal Battalion chapel at Kwandi Ree Valley, Korea. We usually had about ten to fifteen in attendance at our sacrament meeting each Sunday.

On October 27, 1953, an LDS conference was held at the 10th Corps headquarters. Five LDS chaplains were there and held two sessions. I left Kwandi Ree Valley the first part of

April 1954, was processed at Inchon, and left to come home by ship on April 17, 1954.

The thing I most appreciated about my army experience was the opportunity I had to meet with LDS servicemen, partake of the sacrament, and be spiritually uplifted. I was able to attend sacrament meetings most of the time I was in the Army. I had wonderful support from home. My wife wrote to me every single day and my mother wrote every week. I felt the influence of their and other's prayers for my guidance and protection. Praying and reading the scriptures were a regular practice, and my testimony and desire to serve the Lord dramatically increased. I was truly blessed and protected as my patriarchal blessing had promised me. I really did appreciate the servicemen's LDS scriptures that the Church gave me at the time I entered the service.

Servicemen from Sanpete County, Utah, in attendance at LDS Conference at 10th Corps Headquarters on October 27, 1953. Front row: Paul Peel, Dean Sudweeks, and David Mumford. Back row: Doyle Larsen, Roger Mellor, and Dean Anderson.

Left: 10th Corps LDS Servicemen's Group Sacrament Meeting, October 25, 1953. Front Row: Doyle Larsen, Charles Masterson, Douglas Orchard, Dean Sudweeks, and Stewart Pierce. Back Row: Sergeant McCoy, Keith Hoffman, Erick Sandstrom, Lee Hansen, and Barney Black.

VICTOR LEMAR TERRY

LeMar served in the U.S. Army from 1951 to 1953 during the Korean War. He worked on telephone lines and as a telephone operator. LeMar was blessed with extraordinary protection in various dangerous situations at this time in his life. One such experience is described here.

Victor LeMar Terry was twenty-one when this picture was taken in his Army uniform.

Twice our division went into action. The first time, there were five in our group who came back—myself and four others. The next time, three of us returned; the rest were slain. One time our water supply became contaminated, and our medical men told us not to drink the water for it would mean certain death. My buddies, of course, decided not to drink of the polluted water, knowing that if they were to enjoy the momentary pleasure of quenching their thirst, they would not live long enough to enjoy the many pleasures that awaited those who would return home from the battlefields. But I trusted in the Lord and in the blessing [the stake patriarch] gave me, which I knew was given through the spirit of revelation. I drank the water and have never tasted better water in my life; it was deliciously sweet and, more importantly, quenched my burning thirst. My companions were completely dismayed and distressed by my actions and feared that they would certainly witness my agonizing death within a very short time.

Contrary to the statement of the medical authorities and to the wonderment of those about me, my health was not injured in any way, and I was permitted to continue the work that I was asked to do in the service of my country and fellowmen. I then had a chance to explain the gospel to many of those boys who had watched me drink that contaminated water without harmful effects and had wondered and marveled at how that could be. I gratefully took advantage of the opportunity to explain the Word of Wisdom and the power of the priesthood to give blessings of protection to those obedient to the gospel of Jesus Christ; they began investigating the Church. I don't know how many of them finally accepted the gospel. I soon finished my tour of duty and was sent home. But I do know that many of them studied the scriptures and read the literature I had given them that explained the Church of Jesus Christ and its principles.

THAYNE LLEWELLY THOMAS

Thayne served in the Army Air Corps and the U.S. Air Force. He joined the military in 1942 and retired from it as a lieutenant colonel in April 1965. He served as a pilot in World War II and the Korean War. Afterward, he worked for the Civil Service at Hill Air Force Base in the contracting and procurement section for sixteen years.

I flew my fifty missions in Korea from November 1952 to April 1953. We were assigned to the "flare" squadron. True, we dropped flares along the front line between North and South Korea during battles, but we also dropped espionage agents and sundry other types of South Korean teams at various places in North Korea. These drops were made at an altitude between three and five hundred feet, and they were made at night on some rugged mountain ridge or plateau. The Koreans that jumped were laden down with so much gear, such as radios, explosives, and electronics, they could hardly get out the door of the airplane. I often wonder what shape they were in when they slammed into the ground with such a heavy load. They must have been successful landings and missions because we kept it up despite the hazardous flying since it was at night in deep, dark canyons or up on craggy peaks all the way north to the Chinese border.

I made a couple of missions so far to the northeast that we could see the lights of Vladivostok, Russia. It was not the lights of the city direct, but reflection of the lights from the Korean coast when we would see the searchlights start coming on. We never knew if we caused them to come on or whatever. Our flights were always at such a low-level altitude we didn't think the Russian radar sites could pick us up. It could be we were spotted because the searchlights would eventually turn and beam right in our direction and hold. It was a happy day when I finished my tour there.

Thayne L. Thomas.

LT. MELVIN E. TIETJEN
... new Air Force chaplain

New Chaplain Set Apart For U. S. Air Force

MONROE—First Lt. Melvin
Tietjen, 24, of Monroe, Sou
Sevier Stake was set apart l
Elder Clifford E. Young Ass
tant to the Council of Twelv
as a chaplain to serve with t
armed forces.

Lt Tietjen will report Au
7 to Sampson Field New Yo
where he will under-go f
weeks of indoctrination trai
ing. From there he will recei
assignment to a regular esta
lished Air Force Base.

The newest LDS chapla
was born Nov. 15, 1927 a s
of H. Roland and Genevie
Willardson Tietjen. He marri
Dolores Christensen of Ric
field, Feb. 6, 1948 in the Ma
Temple. He graduated from
South Sevier High School
1946 after which he attend
the BYU and the University
Utah prior to going on a m
sion to the Northwestern Sta
in 1948. While in the missi
field, Elder Tietjen served
a counselor in the mission pr
idency for six months.

Upon returning home fr
his mission in 1950, he return
to the University of Utah
graduated this spring in
School of Business.

The new Air Force chapl
has been active in the Mut
Sunday School and Priesth
organizations, and is at pres
teaching the Elders Quorum
the Monroe North Ward.

MELVIN E. TIETJEN

Melvin served in the U.S. Air Force during the Korean War from July 1952 to July 1954. He had earned a college degree from the University of Utah and had served a full-time mission for the Church. These things, along with an endorsement from the First Presidency, allowed him to become a chaplain. Melvin served on the Sampson Air Force Base, and achieved the rank of captain.

Over a period of a few months I noticed that there was a great deal of profanity among the permanent base personnel. This was quite disturbing to a boy raised in Monroe, Utah, so I decided to put together an antiprofanity campaign to see if we couldn't reduce the amount of swearing that was going on. In those days, as opposed to now, the issue seemed like something that could possibly be accomplished. This campaign turned out to be quite successful and got a lot of press over a period of time.

* * * * *

A second lieutenant on our base had just experienced the death of his one-month-old child. He needed to ship the body back to Salt Lake [City, Utah], but that was financially prohibitive. He heard that I was flying out to Salt Lake for April conference and came to inquire whether I would be willing to take the baby along. I said I would try. After the baby was embalmed, it was placed in a little military casket with brass handles; however, the casket very much resembled a footlocker. A plane couldn't take off from our base as it didn't have a runway. Syracuse, just north of us, was the nearest base that did have a runway, but its only flight out was heading to San Antonio, [Texas]. I got a base taxi to take me and my precious locker to Syracuse, and we boarded a B-25. The pilot of the plane looked suspiciously at the locker, but waved me on board. In San Antonio I had to hitch a ride to Tinker Air Force Base in Oklahoma City. From Tinker I caught a plane up to Great Falls, Montana. I had to go up and down the continent just to get to Salt Lake City.

When I got to Great Falls, I found out that there were no planes going to Hill Field [Utah], in the foreseeable future. I began to worry that I would be stuck there. Girding up my loins, I called the base operations officer to see if he could authorize a training flight to Salt Lake or Hill Field. I'm sure he thought that was quite presumptuous on my part and asked the purpose of my trip. I said I was accompanying the

body of a baby who had died at Sampson Air Force Base whose father was an officer there. He replied, "You're taking what?" I repeated that it was a little baby, and he said what I had done was against all regulations. He also said that he was surprised that I had gotten that far, and that he was sorry, but I wouldn't be going any further on military aircraft.

My only recourse at that point was to find a Trailways bus that was leaving soon. Fortunately there was one that was going to leave in fifteen or twenty minutes, so I asked the driver if he could please wait as I didn't think I could be there in

Servicemen at Sampson Air Force Base were given the opportunity to submit slogans reminding all to avoid profanity. Signs such as this were a result of the submissions. Chaplain Tietjen's campaign against profanity received nation-wide attention.

While serving as a chaplain in the Air Force, Melvin Tietjen was disturbed by the tendency among airmen towards heavy swearing. As an expression of his distaste for the habit, Tietjen commenced an anti-profanity campaign to combat the practice. As the project gathered momentum, various media outlets took notice of Chaplain Tietjen's efforts including the New York Daily News *which made mention of the project which offered incentives for those willing to abandon the habits.*

time. He said he would do his best. I got there just as they were locking up the bus, and in the confusion, I got the casket on board without notice. This was fortunate, as I later found out that Trailways also had regulations against transporting a body. At any rate, we traveled all night and got there the next morning. I think it was around ten or eleven o'clock in the morning when I called ahead to the father of the lieutenant. This was, of course, the baby's grandfather, and he hurried to meet me at the bus station. As we were going up to recover the little casket traveling as a footlocker, one of the workers remarked that the little footlocker looked very much like a casket. I thought, "Oh my goodness, not now!"

Thankfully, the man walked away and another fellow walked up to help me. I hurriedly remarked that I had to get my luggage quickly as I had people ready to take me. So he got if for me right away and put it in the trunk of the grandfather's car. We were both grateful for the obvious divine intervention that brought the infant to a final resting place.

Left: Melvin stands by one of his posters which makes reference to an order given by General George Washington in July 1776. General Washington was concerned about the conduct of the men and their use of profanity.

Below: "Be sure the word you have in mind is not one of profane kind." Another one of Melvin's campaign signs.

Terrel R. Tovey

Following the surrender of Japan in 1945, U.S. troops occupied not only Japan but also other Asian countries. Terrel was one of those stationed in Korea from 1945–1947. The LDS servicemen groups organized at the time were the forerunners of the Church groups that followed during the Korean War a few years later. While in Korea, Terrel served as a young private assigned to the Korea Base Command. Terrel has since served as a bishop, a stake president, and a missionary to Samoa with his wife Catherine. The following are excerpts from his journal:

October 30, 1946, Ascom City, Korea.

Monday morning I went on a truck to pick up garbage. When we unloaded it, I saw the most pitiful sight I've ever seen. A truck from the mess hall had unloaded in front of us and there were as many Koreans as could gather around picking stuff out of the garbage. A couple of women had a small sack and it looked like chicken entrails they were putting in it. When we unloaded we had paper and a few little boards, and they waded right into the garbage that had been dumped from the kitchen to get the paper and small boards. It about made me sick to see the little kids trying to get some. As little as they are they realize that they're helping. The other day I saw a little girl about the age of Leslie (one of my younger sisters) with a big log trying her best to get it home. I hope things are different for them soon.

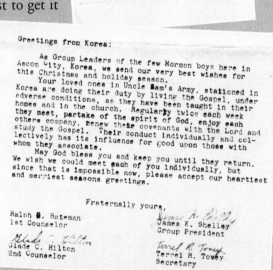

December 1, 1946, Ascom City, Korea.

Today is fast Sunday and we had testimony meeting in church. I'll never forget it I don't think. About four of the guys have their orders to go home and this was their last Sunday. By the time we had sang the last song, which was "God Be with You Till We Meet Again," we all were so choked up we didn't sing very well. Three of the guys had tears in their eyes and I wasn't far from it. It was really a swell meeting though. After church we went to Johnny Mckay's (President McKay's nephew from Kellogg, Idaho) mess hall for dinner.

December 21, 1946, Ascom City, Korea.

Church is at 9:30 tomorrow in Seoul so we'll have to leave here about 8:00. I guess they have a program arranged and I think they're going to baptize a captain after church. (He was baptized in a bathtub in a hotel.) Probably not quite cricket but the best they could do. His wife was a member in the States and he was surprising her as a Christmas present. Even though we're not supposed to baptize in a body of water that both can't get into, it was a tear jerker.

Troops stationed in Korea prior to the war organized LDS groups. These groups provided Church services and activities for the servicemen. Terrel R. Tovey served as the secretary to the group presidency in Ascom City, Korea. For Christmas 1946, the group presidency sent to the families of the servicemen in their group a Christmas letter recognizing the faith of the LDS servicemen in Korea.

NED MARTELL VOWLES

Ned Martell Vowles served in World War II and the Korean war in both the U.S. Army and U.S. Air Force. Stationed in Korea for the majority of his time overseas his assignments were as an Adjutant and Personnel Officer and received a "spot" promotion to the office of major while there. After his service he worked 31 years for the Utah Department of Employment Security.

Ned at his desk as Group Director of Personnel in Seoul, Korea 1953. Ned was apart of the LDS Group Leadership until his return to the States.

Picture of Ballard T. White in OG uniform at Pusan, Korea, December 12, 1954.

BALLARD T. WHITE

Ballard served in the U.S. Army from June 1953 to May 1955 during the last months of the Korean War. He served with the Judge Advocate General Section KCOMZ in Pusan, Korea, as a stenographer and confinement clerk. Ballard achieved the rank of sergeant. While in Korea, he remained very active with the Pusan LDS Group and valued his association with other members.

This is being written in 2002, forty-eight years after it occurred. Therefore, what I write at this time is, in some cases, somewhat different from what I would have written shortly after it happened.

While in Korea my contact with The Church of Jesus Christ of Latter-day Saints was very important to me. I was the only member in my barracks, and there was one other member on the compound. He was less active and had Word of Wisdom problems. Fortunately there was a strong LDS servicemen's branch and a good LDS chaplain to keep an eye on us. There was a Criminal Investigation Division (CID) unit close by with quite a number of returned missionaries so we had a fairly active branch. I served as Mutual secretary, editor of a monthly branch newspaper, and helped organize the first LDS-sponsored Korean Boy Scout troop.

As I think back on my experiences in Korea, there are three things relating to the Church that stand out. These are (1) the opportunity I had to help teach and to baptize a Korean named Kim Bong Tae, (2) the visit of Elder Harold B. Lee, and (3) the opportunity to attend a religious retreat in Japan.

Kim Bong Tae was an orphan who lived on our compound and served as a driver of the jeep assigned to transport us, usually the warrant officer. Kim had not finished high school and was sleeping on a wooden bench in a room that was used to contain a working water heater. The water heater no longer worked, the door had been removed, and the windows were broken out. So Kim was sleeping in a rather drafty room with no bedding. This was not too bad a sleeping arrangement during the summer. However, as winter approached, he would be pretty cold at night. Our chaplain, Spencer J. Palmer, arranged for a sleeping bag for Kim to help keep him warm. With the help of some of the returned missionaries in the CID unit and Chaplain Palmer, I initiated teaching the gospel to Kim. We met on a weekly basis. In March 1955 a baptism service was held in which nine Korean Saints were baptized. I had the honor of baptizing Kim. (A photograph identifying those who baptized and those who were baptized appeared in the April 16, 1955, issue of the *Church News*. This same photograph later appeared on page 566 in the book, *The Story of the Latter-day Saints* by James B. Allen and Glen M. Leonard.)

When I approached our supply sergeant about using some cook's whites for the baptism, he was surprised we would be doing it at this time of the year; the water was still quite cold. He remarked that doing so would require a lot of faith. To which I replied, "It would." The supply sergeant showed up at the baptism; he was a less-active member of the Church whom no one knew about. We were not successful in reactivating him. Because the baptisms were performed in the ocean, we needed to time the actual baptism with the waves, or the baptizer was baptized with the convert. I almost made it.

After I left Korea I continued to correspond with Kim for several years. He finished high school, married, and raised a family who was active in the Church. At one time, he was a branch president. I have not had contact with him for many years so I do not know more about him.

At this time, forty-eight years later, what I remember most about Elder Harold B. Lee's visit to Korea in September 1954 was the wonderful spirit he brought with him. The Spirit of the Lord, which accompanied him, lifted the spirits of the servicemen and Korean Saints and gave them greater determination to live the gospel of Jesus Christ. We were able to forget for a short while that we were in a war-torn country with lots of poverty and shortages. While Elder Lee was in Korea we had sort of a mini-conference with great talks and a program of songs and dances by the Korean Saints and their children. It was spiritually uplifting, delightful, and very colorful with the native costumes of the Koreans.

What I now remember of the religious retreat in Oiso, Japan, in March 1955 is how great it was to get away from the "business at hand" in Korea, feel the strong Spirit of the Lord, and associate again with so many members of the Church. We had great accommodations and food and were extremely grateful for the wonderful opportunity and appreciative of the effort put forth for us. An account of this retreat was prepared by me shortly after it occurred and appeared in the *Church News*, April 16, 1955.

Below: Ballard T. White helped organize the first LDS-sponsored Korean Boy Scout Troop.

Below: Group shot of part of the attendance at the Latter-day Saint services conducted at the chapel in the 8069th AU compound, Korean communications zone. Some of those present are Elder Harold B. Lee, President of the Quorum of the Twelve Apostles of The Church of Jesus Christ of Latter-Day Saints, President Robertson of the Japanese Mission, Brigadier General Richard B. Whitcomb, and Commanding General Pusan Military Post.

QUENTIN H. WHITE

Quentin served with the U.S. Army from January 1952 to December 1953 during the Korean War. He served with the 308th Command Information Center Detachment, 8th Army headquarters in Seoul, Korea. Quentin worked in intelligence and achieved the rank of corporal. Following the war, he served a mission to Finland and has since taught at the university level and been a manager for the Church in international physical facilities.

It was at Camp Drake, Japan, where I first bore my testimony. The Sunday after my arrival I inquired about the likelihood of an LDS meeting on the base and was informed that there was a regular one held in the classroom of one of the barracks in another company area. There were dozens of barracks, and I left to find the one according to the directions I had been given. As I was approaching the area, I could hear the singing of a hymn and immediately knew where to go. As I approached closer, another soldier walked up and inquired as to whether I was going to church. I replied in the affirmative and told him that it was an LDS service. He then asked if I thought he could attend as well so I took him with me. The classroom had two doors and about thirty to forty chairs.

We entered by the back door and sat on the last row. All the others (about twelve to fifteen) were sitting together on the first two rows. They had just finished with the opening prayer. Several turned around and looked at us when we came in, and it was immediately evident that most were officers. The group leader, who was a colonel, was just announcing the "two-and-a-half-minute talk" which was followed by the "sacrament gem," and the sacrament. As the sacrament was prepared, my new friend quietly asked what it was and whether he had to participate. I quickly and quietly explained what they were going to do and that he was not obligated to participate but could if he desired. All the brethren who blessed and passed the sacrament were officers. My friend took the sacrament just as I did. As soon as it was over the time was turned over to testimony bearing.

It was a little strange even for me. The presiding brother, the colonel, bore his testimony followed by everyone else in order of their seating on each row. During the fourth or fifth testimony my friend asked if it was required that we all testify. I assured him that it was completely voluntary and that it would not even be expected of him inasmuch as he was not a member. However, the longer it went, the more nervous he became and he inquired again. And I again assured him that it was not necessary and to prove my point I told him that I had been a member of the Church all my life and had never borne my testimony. He seemed reassured. But when all the men on the front rows were through, and everyone had born his testimony, they just sat there, obviously giving us time to stand if we so desired. Some turned and looked. My friend was fidgeting and obviously uneasy and asked me again and at the same time noted that most were officers and that we were both privates. I shook my head and patted his knee.

The next minute or so seemed to take an eternity and again some turned and looked at us as if to tell us to get on with it. It made me nervous, but I was determined to hold my ground. Suddenly my new friend could stand it no longer. He stood and thanked the Lord for blessings as he had heard others do and even testified that he believed in Christ. When he sat down the silence continued and some again turned to look at me as if to say get up as we are tired of being here. I knew from long experience that they had to close the meeting, officers or no officers, and I was determined to sit it out. But I was very nervous now, and my friend had joined the others in looking at me with encouraging expressions. I finally broke by standing and bearing my first public testimony. It was not that bad an experience, and I made it a point from then on while in the service to bear it each fast day.

* * * * *

The Church was a big part of my life in Korea. Rulon Teerlink was our local group president. I was the clerk. We held Sunday meetings at the 5th Air Force headquarters located on the Seoul University campus. There were some buildings with only minor damage there. We held regular Sunday services and usually had forty to fifty people in attendance, many of whom were front-line soldiers on pass for a day or two. We generally had Sundays off and even when on duty we were permitted to attend church.

Rulon left Korea for his home in Salt Lake City, Utah, on my birthday in 1952. I drove him the twenty or so miles to Inchon where he boarded a troopship to return to the United States. That was a sad day for me, but I was happy for Rulon. He was married and anxious to get home. Life for me went on just the same. I got a new LDS roommate, but he turned out to be LDS in name only. I began to associate with Calvin Beck who became our new group leader. Calvin was from Tooele, Utah. He was an officer assigned to the Photo Interpretation Unit which we relied heavily on for up-to-date information about several locations in North Korea.

With Calvin as our Church group leader, we began to hold MIA on Tuesday evenings, and we had a pretty good turnout. At the same time we began to hold an English class prior to MIA for several Korean young people we knew. Among them was I Ho Nam, a young man who worked in Calvin's unit and several others who worked in Calvin's unit and in my unit. It started out small but within two or three weeks the class had grown to more than a hundred, and it continued to grow until we were almost overwhelmed. We held several simultaneous classes in the old university of Seoul University campus where we held our Church meetings. The classes included grammar, vocabulary building, and two or three levels of conversation. I am sorry to say that I do not remember the names of the several servicemen who acted as teachers. The students came from all over the city of Seoul. And because there was no public transportation, Calvin and I both sought and received permission from our commanding officers to use one of our trucks to bus some of the students between two or three points in the city and the university. Consequently, Tuesday evenings started early and ended late as we each took two trips to and from the university. But it was a meaningful and interesting time. Several of those students became interested in the Church and a number of them eventually joined.

* * * * *

Seoul was devastated, having been the focal point of four hard battles as first the North Koreans took it over, and secondly as the U.N. forces took it back, followed by the Chinese, and finally again by the U.N. forces. There were still about a million people there, but they were a mix of former residents and evacuees who had stopped there on their flight south. Most lived in bad conditions of the kind that might be imagined in a war zone. Among them were several thousand orphans who lived on the streets and were the worst off of all. The winters there are bitterly cold. The majority of the orphans had little clothing and that often consisted of only a sack with a neck and arm holes cut into it. They huddled together at night in rather large groups consisting of fifty to a hundred individuals. If they were lucky they were able to build a small fire for warmth, but most often they had nothing to shield them from the cold. Many died and each morning the Korean government sent a truck to the main locations of these groups to pick up the dead. One group of orphans was not far from our unit, and I often watched from the top of our building in the early morning as the dead were picked up. At times the truck was loaded with bodies as if it were wood. The condition of the orphan children was the single most depressing element of my Korean experience.

Calvin Beck and I were affected the same way and we were determined to help with the orphan population if at all possible. There were several orphanages in the city, one not too far from where we were located. We went to visit. It too was a depressing sight. The children were poorly fed and had little

Korean refugees forage for food and other items in a garbage dump.

of what we could expect as civil amenities. The people who were running it were about as bad off. We began to give them a little money to help them out.

Sometime in the fall of 1952 I became acquainted with Captain Bill Durdan who was with one of the forward divisions working as an artillery spotter using a small plane. At his invitation I flew with him on a couple of his assignments. More importantly, however, I learned while at the front that the division had many expendable surplus supplies of which they would be happily relieved. They were required to keep certain amounts on hand for emergencies but the shipments to them were automatic and regular, resulting in huge amounts over their needs, which were stored in the open. I went to my commanding officer and requested permission to obtain some of those supplies rather than liquor to pay our informants. He agreed and gave me permission to take our small truck to retrieve what I thought appropriate. Calvin went with me and we had no trouble getting a full truckload of canned meats, canned cheese, sugar, salt, flour, canned vegetables, dried milk, socks, sleeping bags, and other clothing. We were also invited to return for more. When we returned to Seoul I separated those supplies needed for our informants, and we delivered the balance to a couple of orphanages. It was illegal to give military supplies to anyone but it was an exhilarating experience that resulted in repeated trips.

The following trip we took a large truck and filled it full. I again took a small portion for our official needs and we divided the balance among the orphanages and the families of some of the Koreans who were beginning to attend our Church services. Word had also gone to an adjacent division that resulted in an invitation to come relieve them of some of their surpluses. Calvin and I were delighted to oblige. The next trip was on Thanksgiving 1953. This trip was completely illegal because our unit needed no further supplies for informants. This time we planned ahead with some of our Korean friends to establish drop-off points, and we each drove a large truck, and we had a couple of Korean helpers along as well. We arrived at Bill Durdan's unit just as they were starting to serve a hot Thanksgiving dinner. We were invited to join them, but our Korean helpers were obliged to remain in the trucks. Bill arranged to take them some food. While he was out, the cook came around with eggnog for those who wanted it. I like eggnog so I took a full glass. It was good and while the cook was returning to the kitchen he served me another. I drank them both. When Bill returned he warned us that the eggnog was spiked with gin. I should have known better. Fortunately, Calvin didn't like eggnog and had not imbibed. We had a good meal with all the trimmings and left for the supplies. We obtained a full truckload of the usual supplies and a full load of waste timber ends from bunker construction that could be used for fuel in Seoul. On the way back down the winding dirt mountain roads I was in the lead when Calvin began to honk and honk. I stopped. Calvin came running forward and as he did I stepped out of the truck and fell flat on my face. I was drunk, and Calvin had been honking because I was all over the road. It was a dilemma because we were loaded with illegal cargo, and we had no relief driver. I had to drive but it was late that evening before we arrived in Seoul. As before we unloaded the trucks without incident in an illegal, off-limits area of Seoul to the delight of many Koreans. But we also became aware on that occasion that we could no longer control who received the supplies and decided not to press our luck further and ceased our furtive operations.

At some point later on we became aware of an old Japanese estate for sale. It was a walled-in parcel of about five acres located in the center of the city near the capital building. It had a two-story house on it that had been hit on one corner by an artillery shell. Otherwise it was in fairly good shape. The selling price was $2,500. We decided it would make an excellent orphanage and thought we could get the LDS Church interested in buying it. We approached the mission in Japan but were turned down. The Church was not yet established in Korea. We then decided to raise the money and buy it ourselves, but we soon found out that foreigners were not permitted to buy real estate. Then Calvin found a Korean gentleman who was already trying to help some of the orphans and was willing to help us buy the property in his name. We knew that we would have no legal claim, but we went ahead and raised the money. The purchase was made and we placed five children off the streets to start with.

If my memory serves me, the oldest of the children was a twelve-year-old girl whom we placed in charge. She had the duties of mothering, cooking, washing and ironing. The other children had daily duties to find food and more importantly twigs, weeds, and any other burnable material for cooking and warmth. We were furnishing the food and clothing for the time being. We knew that our sources were not permanent so our Korean partner was trying to work things out with the government to get a regular ration of rice. I was ordered home at about that time. I don't know what became of the orphanage or the property.

FRANK J. WILLES

Frank served in the U.S. Army from 1951 to 1953 during the Korean War. He served with the 108th Signal Repair Company as a repairman. Frank achieved the rank of corporal. After the war, Frank worked for the Navy as a civil service employee, as a draftsman, and as an electrician's helper. He later became a school teacher, and has always remained active in the Church. (See also account of Richard Henstrom who administered to Frank Willes in his moment of greatest need.)

In Korea, I went to the 108th Signal Repair Company near Chunchon and remained with them until my return and discharge. One day in October 1954, I was working on the roof of a shower we were building out of corrugated steel. I began to feel dizzy and developed a severe headache. Because it was so terribly hot (even in October), my first thought was that I might have sunstroke or heat exhaustion. I felt that the best thing to do was to go to my tent and lie down. This took place about midmorning.

I remained in my tent through the noon meal and tried to sleep. The headache kept getting worse and worse until, by early evening, I became delirious. When the others in the tent returned after the evening meal and found me the way I was, they reported the situation and had me taken to a MASH [mobile army surgical hospital] unit just north of Chunchon. They later told me of sitting on me in the jeep to keep me from jumping out.

When we arrived at the hospital unit, my temperature was very high and most of my right side was paralyzed. The medics decided that I had either malaria, polio, or both. The only way they could tell if polio was the culprit was to take a spinal tap and try to grow a certain type of culture in it. Even though I remember only parts of what happened, I'll never forget the spinal tap. The process called for my doubling up while they put a long needle into my spine. Of course it hurt. I recall nurses holding me; medics sitting on me; and doctors cursing me. They put the needle into my back nineteen or twenty times before they were finally able to draw out the fluid they needed.

By morning, they decided that no matter what I had, they wouldn't be able to help me; so they strapped me to a helicopter and took me to Seoul. The first thing they did there

"Bravest of the Brave"

A perspective shared from a soldier not of the Latter-day Saint faith:

I was an infantry platoon leader in the 2nd Platoon, L Company, 180th Regiment in Korea from July 1952 to June 1953. I am sorry, but I don't remember the names of my medics during that period, but they were, for the most part, Mormons, and they were the bravest of the brave. Many times, they and I would go into the trenches under withering artillery and mortar fire looking for our wounded. During an artillery barrage, our phone lines to the individual would be cut, so we had to go in person to find casualties.

One time on Bloody Ridge, I called on the phone to the medic who was in a bunker near me, and told him that we had to start looking for the wounded. He said he would be right up. After a few minutes when he didn't show, I went to his bunker. He sat there stunned and almost unable to speak. There was a hole in the roof of his bunker, and a 120-mm mortar round lay near him, unexploded. He told me later that the round came through the roof, hit him on the head a moment after he had put on his helmet, and almost knocked him out. In a few minutes, he picked up his medical supplies, and we went into the trenches.

Without exception, they were all very brave.

Jim Morgan
Santa Fe, New Mexico

In bitter fighting on Hook Ridge, Marines threw back 800 screaming, bugle-blowing Chinese. Shown above, a wounded Marine is given a drink of water by buddies as he awaits evacuation to a rear area aid station. November 1952. T. Sgt. Robert Kiser. (Marine Corps)

was—you guessed it—take a spinal tap! They were much more proficient and managed to acquire a sample of my priceless fluid in only three or four attempts. (My back was black and blue up to my shoulder blades for about a month after.)

I was placed in the critical ward while I was still unconscious. Their hospital was an old, bombed-out hotel in downtown Seoul. When I finally came to my senses, I asked the young medic on duty where I was, what I had, etc. He answered that I had encephalitis. Because of the high rate of venereal disease in Korea at the time, I thought he had said something else and began to protest that it was impossible. He repeated the word more slowly and clearly, adding that it was a type of brain fever which was transmitted from the water buffalo by the mosquitoes. When I asked him just what that meant to me, he replied in a very diplomatic way, "Oh, you'll probably die."

As soon as what he had said really registered, I called for the chaplain of the hospital. Soon a colonel and a minister of the Baptist or Methodist faith arrived. I asked if he could locate two Mormon elders for me. In about an hour, two men arrived. One was a chaplain in the Army and one was from the Air Force. Both were from Utah and both LDS elders. What a happy sight! They laid their hands on me and anointed my head with oil. They blessed me with blessings I'll never forget! They said that I would live to return home and see my newly born son, that I would again see my lovely wife and other loved ones. They even said that I would completely recover and that I would have no lasting effects from the illness. Such a blessed relief! I asked them to return the next day and almost immediately went to sleep without delirium.

I awoke feeling much better, though terribly weak. I couldn't help but notice that the man next to me who was ill with the same malady was noticeably worse. They took the needle out of my arm, and I ate a pretty good meal. I asked the doctor about the two men I had asked to return and he indicated that he had asked them not to return—that I wouldn't be there. He said that if it appeared that I would live, they would fly me to Japan for treatment. There was so much improvement, though, that they felt I should stay. We discussed at length my illness and the two chaplains. He told me that he was amazed by the almost immediate improvement. He indicated that I shouldn't be too optimistic because of the high fever that I had had. He said that it was likely I would never regain complete use of my still-paralyzed right arm or that some other effect would make itself known. The fever, he said, had been too high for too long not to have caused some permanent damage. He predicted permanent paralysis.

Within the next two or three days, my whole right side was back to normal, and I was able to eat my meals in the hospital mess hall. The doctor, a Seventh Day Adventist, was amazed! When he reported to the head doctor that I was nearly ready for discharge, the commanding medical officer replied that I must not have had what the original diagnosis indicated. My doctor told me, however, that there was no question about what I had had and about my past temperatures, and began asking more questions about the Church.

Within two weeks from the first trip to the MASH unit, I was waiting for the men from my outfit to come get me. The doctor kept repeating his amazement. He told me that it was a miracle that I had survived with only one scar—I had developed a severe stutter. The day I left Seoul, the doctor indicated that he was planning to talk further with the "Mormon chaplains."

I returned to my camp; the captain was very happy to see me. He had already lost his executive officer and one of his senior noncommissioned officers to encephalitis and didn't relish the thought of writing a letter to another new widow. (An epidemic did develop and at least fifty Americans and hundreds of Koreans died.)

It was no more than a week or two until I had completely stopped stuttering and as the Lord, through His servants in uniform had promised, I had completely recovered. There are undoubtedly those who would say "coincidence" or "chance," but there is no power on this earth that could make me believe any other than that which I know to be true—that God, through the bearers of His priesthood, and for purposes not known to me, gave me another chance at life. God is as close to us as the sound of a voice and all He needs to answer us is to be asked.

RICHARD D. WILSON

Dick became a U.S. Marine at the age of seventeen, arriving in Korea in November 1951. He served with Fox Company, 2nd Battalion, 5th Marines, 1st Marine Division, and he achieved the rank of sergeant. His company commander reported that he was the youngest buck sergeant in the Division and possibly the entire U.S. Marine Corps.

Fighting a war without having your scriptures is like being baptized without going in the water. During the twelve months I served in Korea, I never experienced the abiding comfort and the feeling of the Spirit you receive when attending a sacrament, Sunday School, or priesthood meeting. My scriptures had been lost someplace between getting aboard the troop transport ship in San Diego and when I arrived in the port of Pusan, South Korea. But I did pick up a small copy of the New Testament provided by a Protestant chaplain. I think I had taken having the scriptures for granted until I got into a war.

I found that in those months in Korea between 1951 and 1952 that my experiences would forever change my life's perspective. Without personal prayer and scripture reading I don't think I would have been able to keep my sanity or my beliefs intact. Why? Because an 18-year-old seems to view himself and his life as immortal. I quickly found it not to be the case. It happened shortly after I arrived at the front. I met a Marine much older than I that everyone called "Preacher." Most of us seemed to pick up a nickname. He got his because he always carried his Bible wherever he went. He liked to read us various verses that seemed to fit the moment. He was married, had some kids, and was a nice guy. I really liked him a lot. Then one day about noon he was walking to his bunker carrying his Bible as usual and an incoming mortar exploded a few feet from him, and he was killed instantly. It happened that quickly. One minute he was there and alive and the next he was gone and dead. He was the first person in my life that I knew as a friend and that had either died or was killed. Later when they were gathering his personal belongings someone murmured the question, "How could someone so good, so spiritual, and so religious lose his life while others who are not so good and some who have never even attended a church or read the Bible live?" I remember thinking about that for a long time that night.

That was the first time I realized how quickly you can meet your Maker, lose your life and a friend. I think that day we all asked ourselves if we were ready to face the ultimate sacrifice. It took me a long time to deal with that event—if I ever have!

* * * * *

In early spring of 1952 some of our company was assigned to occupy a hill; I think it was called "Warsaw." It was about four to five hundred yards in front of the MLR (main line of resistance). We had daily and nightly contact with the North Koreans and Chinese which amounted to mostly mortar fire and enemy probes to test our resolve to hold the hill. Next to that hill was a slightly less elevated hill where there were several reinforced rifle and machine-gun squads. Forward of the main bunker and trench line was a sniper's hole. It was dug on the forward slope about forty to fifty yards. It was camouflaged with scrub brush, and it was almost impossible to see. The routine was that an hour or so before sunrise one of our snipers would belly out to that sniper's foxhole and wait for sunrise.

With his sniper's rifle, silencer, and high-powered scope, he could observe throughout the day and especially in the early morning the movement of enemy troops in the trench line and bunkers across the shallow valley. They were his target.

For several weeks he did his job. Then one day just after dark, which was the usual time for the

Dick Wilson with gun.

sniper to crawl back to the safety of the trench line and his buddies—that night he was late. He never showed up. They tried to make contact but with no luck. Finally, under the cover of darkness a fire team of three from his unit crept down to his sniper's foxhole and found him slumped over his rifle with a single bullet in his head. An enemy sniper had somehow caught him during a split second of exposure and with just enough time to get off a single shot. It was a very sad day for all of us. Everyone placed a special value on these courageous Marine buddies. Unfortunately it did not end there.

A couple of days later his replacement showed up and took his position in that same sniper's foxhole each morning before sunup. Three days or so went by and one night after dark he was late and did not return. The word quickly spread and all of us could not believe that we might lose another one. It would be too much. We still felt the deep pain from losing our other friend. That night the fire team crawled down to his foxhole and found him with a single bullet to his head. The word spread. No one would believe it. But this tragedy and deep loss was even more staggering when we found out that they were brothers!

Even as I write this story that occurred a half century ago. the personal heart-wrenching emotion of that day brings a lump in my throat and tears to my eyes, and I can hardly contain myself. That was the last time they used that sniper location.

Dick Wilson with fellow soldiers of the Fox Company, 2nd Battalion.

L. KENT WIMMER

Kent served with the U.S. Army from November 1950 to July 1951 during the Korean War. He served with the 25th Division, 65th Combat Engineers, operating a D-8 Caterpillar and making airstrips. It was in this work that Kent lost the use of his eyes. Since his very painful release from the Army, he has run a private law practice.

Near an ordinary work-day's end, I began grading back toward our motor pool. En route, one of my lieutenants came alongside the Cat-12 to interrupt my routine schedule of returning. He ordered me to go back a short distance to where personnel of the Canadian Princess Pat Brigade were roughing out another of many emergency landing strips, presumably in an area under their jurisdiction. They needed to have someone more accurately level their newly developing runway areas.

On reaching the far end of the runway, I quickly turned the Cat-12 around, to begin doing my artistry of feathering new materials out over the runway. Actively tuft-tossing workers were doing their best to rid the runway surface of all remaining insidious tufts of rice roots. The entire team was really working harmoniously that evening.

In every move around that large emergency landing strip, I as usual systematically kept the Cat-12 strictly within a clearly designated safe lane. For me to do otherwise would be really foolhardy and asking for genuine trouble. Each day or night, the peaceful silence was harshly shattered by man or animal wandering onto some form of live armament. Then someone had to go out and pick up their widely scattered pieces, if any could be found.

And then totally unexpected, it happened!

I had graded perhaps one-sixth of the distance back along the runway, and was beginning to believe we could finish the bulk of smoothing that large runway surface that evening, when I saw my last earthly image!

Though I don't remember a sound, I clearly saw the fiery red flash! And for years later, whenever any loud noise occurred near me, some type of unknown cross-over link in my nervous system immediately re-created that fiercely blinding red flash all over again!

After that intense second of fiery blast, my memory continues to recall only isolated islands of fuzzy and disjointed occurrences. Such is most understandable, especially after carefully discussing the aftereffects of devastating damage to my old Cat-12 with Harold Vowles. Just like me, after returning from Korea, Vowles began attending classes at the University of Utah. As soon as he learned my home address, he came to visit with me. In his initial visit, he told me about assisting in evacuation of my old grader from the emergency airstrip. His too candid description was harsh and raised hair on my neck all over again. According to Vowles, one front wheel was gone! Apparently, it was blown off by the tremendous force of an explosion. Then Vowles added another hard fact. The powerful blast had kinked the main frame of my old Cat-12! Such harsh factual disclosure was difficult for me to imagine. Many, many times in using the old machine to grade roads or airstrips, the weight of the grader was fully supported by the blade, when harshly hanging up on a rock. But according to Vowles it appeared to him as if the blade had been directly over the massive explosive charge when it detonated and the blast thrust the blade assembly upward with such force that it produced cracks in the paint along its main frame! In so many, many ways, I firmly believe I am very, very fortunate to be alive today.

One item must be noted. Because of the heavy weight of my steel helmet, when no real danger lurked nearby I often removed the steel and simply wore a lighter helmet liner in working pieces of heavy equipment. That practice minimized the terribly disquieting soreness of my scalp from the weight of the steel helmet. But that evening however, my lieutenant was there, so I wore my steel to avoid even a minor violation of regulation. More than likely, a steel helmet saved the top of my head from the severe damage of vicious, tearing pieces of jagged metal and flying earthly debris! OH! Thank the dear Lord for even small favors!

WESLEY HAROLD WORKMAN

Wesley served in the U.S. Navy Armed Guard during World War II, and in the U.S. Army from 1948 to 1964, participating in the Korean War. He served with the 24th Infantry division, 21st Infantry Regiment as an infantry and athletic instructor, and achieved the rank of sergeant first class. In his twenty years of service, Wesley visited over thirty-five countries and forty states in America.

On June 28, 1950, I was packed and ready, with my orders in my hand. I was taken to the train depot by our company clerk. Many of the men in the company had given me a set of Noritaki china to take home. How elated I was, knowing I was to be with my loved ones soon! I was standing at the depot waiting for the train to leave when a jeep came down the road to the depot and stopped near me. It was the First Sergeant Haley, ordering me to return to the company. A Red Alert warning had ordered us to proceed to Korea where a war was erupting—a war that should never have been our country's problem. I was truly heartsick. Had I not been of sound mind and body I would have lost my mind.

My company was rushed to Sasebo, Japan, where we embarked on a slow freighter to Korea. The rains started July 1, and we were drenched before we boarded the train's flatcars in our trucks. I rode in the cab of the truck as we traveled up to Chochiwon, Korea. We were nearly choked into unconsciousness from the long tunnels the train went through. The smoke from the locomotive was taking away all the oxygen in the tunnel. We finally got smart and donned our gas masks before we came to another tunnel.

We arrived at Chochiwon, not too far from where the South Koreans were battling with the communist troops. The rains continued to drench us. We each slept in our pup tents on the hillside and during the night we were literally washed to the bottom of the hill. I thought that naval battles were rough. Naval battles were heaven compared to this muddy hell. I was to live this way for months. The filth in Korea was worse than India due to the wars these poor people had to endure for generations past. Deprivation prevailed in Korea.

My company was sent up to the front lines directly behind the South Korean Army to represent support forces in retaliation of the enemy's infiltration south of the original demilitarized zone (DMZ). This was either July 3 or July 4, 1950. Our leaders were confident that a show of American forces would discourage the North Koreans and a compromise would be forthcoming. What a terrible misconception in the minds of our commanders. The enemy wasn't impressed when they saw us. Most of their troops carried opiates, and when they were preparing for an attack they would take this opium and death was their objective.

Our duties for many weeks to come were to delay action forces until other regiments could arrive to bolster our remaining troops. Many times we heard through the grapevine that we would be relieved by other regiments and return to Japan, but to no avail. We traveled up and down the countryside of Korea so many times I knew the terrain better than the state of Utah.

One sergeant I knew was a heavy gambler. During one of our rest periods he won several hundred dollars in a card game. That night he was assigned an outpost nearly two hundred yards forward of our position to listen for the enemy. The next morning he didn't show for his report so the men went out looking for him. He had received a direct hit from a mortar. The money belt he carried all his winnings in had blown up with him and money was all over the hill.

We were assigned by the commander of the 21st Regiment to furnish the necessary transportation for the Marines from Chonju to Wonju, a distance of thirty-five miles. Our convoy of two dozen army trucks went immediately to Chonju to start our shuttle of men and their equipment through dangerous mountain passes. One mountain pass was very narrow in the turns and had been blown up by enemy cannon fire. Our engineers had worked night and day to repair the pass by building a wooden structure to support our trucks. We drove several nights and days without any rest. We knew it would save lives, so we did our utmost to complete the mission. We were then instructed to return to our regiment as soon as was feasible. We moved separately down the road as a tactical maneuver. I was the last to leave so I sacked out in my sleeping bag and slept for hours. I awakened and drove madly down the road toward my regiment. This move was my untimely encounter with General Mathew Ridgway, the commander of all forces in Korea.

I was following the road signs "Danger Forward" which was the code sign for the 24th Division. I was in a hurry to get back to a normal life of showers and shaves. I was a pitiful sight. I took off my steel helmet and set the speed as fast as possible. A convoy was parked on the side of the road, elements of the 1st Cavalry Division. I saw no reason to slow down, so I kept my speed. What a mistake! As I rounded a curve passing trucks like picket fences, I spied a tall individual standing in the middle of the road, legs apart, hands on hips, glaring at me. I started pumping the brakes and fishtailed to a dusty stop a few feet from this human road block. He slowly raised his right hand and moved his index finger. I slid out from under the wheel and walked cautiously forward. Holy smokes, General Ridgeway! His first remark, I remember well was, "How long have you been in Korea, Soldier?"

"Since June 28, 1950, General Ridgway," was my reply.

He countered, "Have you ever been apprised of my orders to all commanders here of existing speed regulations, especially passing roadside convoys?"

"Not to exceed 20 mph, General," I replied.

He finalized our brief meeting by a minute smile I hardly noticed and said, "Now get your butt back in that vehicle, put that steel helmet back on your head, and drive like the Army taught you!" I almost felt my rank melt off my arms! The chaplain couldn't have driven more carefully.

THE VIETNAM WAR

The first Europeans to arrive in Vietnam were Portuguese explorers who established a trading post there in 1516. Missionaries intent on converting the Vietnamese people to Christianity soon followed the traders. After a period of general peace throughout much of the seventeenth century, a series of civil wars created the political instability that later characterized Vietnam. During these years the French Society of Foreign Missions and the French East India Company worked together to become a dominant European influence in the country. At the beginning of the nineteenth century a rising spirit of Vietnamese nationalism led to the expulsion of the representatives of the French government and Catholic Church from the country. The French responded with a display of military might that subdued the Vietnamese and secured their colonial domination of Vietnam as part of French Indochina.

VIETNAM SERVICE MEDAL

Criteria: a. Awarded to all members of the Armed Forces of the United States serving in Vietnam and contiguous waters or airspace thereover, after 3 July 1965 through 28 March 1973. Members of the Armed Forces of the United States in Thailand, Laos, or Cambodia, or the airspace thereover, during the same period and serving in direct support of operations in Vietnam are also eligible for this award. To be eligible for award of the medal, individual must:

(1) Be attached to or regularly serve for one or more days with an organization participating in or directly supporting military operations; or

(2) Be attached to or regularly serve for one or more days aboard a naval vessel directly supporting military operations; or

(3) Actually participate as a crewmember in one or more aerial flights into airspace above Vietnam and contiguous waters directly supporting military operations; or

(4) Serve on temporary duty for 30 consecutive days or 60 nonconsecutive days in Vietnam or contiguous areas, except that the time limit may be waived for personnel participating in actual combat operations.

The medal was designed by sculptor Thomas Hudson Jones, a former employee of the Army's Institute of Heraldry. The medal is bronze with an oriental dragon behind a grove of bamboo trees above the inscription "REPUBLIC OF VIETNAM SERVICE." On the reverse, a crossbow surmounted a by a torch above the arched inscription "UNITED STATES OF AMERICA." The ribbon is yellow, with three red stripes in the center, and a green stripe on the outside edge.

The awfulness of war is poignant when you must transport one of your comrades from the battlefield..

THE VIETNAM WAR

THE THREE SERVICEMEN *statue stands in a small grove of trees facing the west side of the Vietnam Veterans Memorial (see map on pg. 4), and was sculpted by Frederick Hart. The statue was dedicated on Nov. 11, 1984. It is shown here decorated fo*

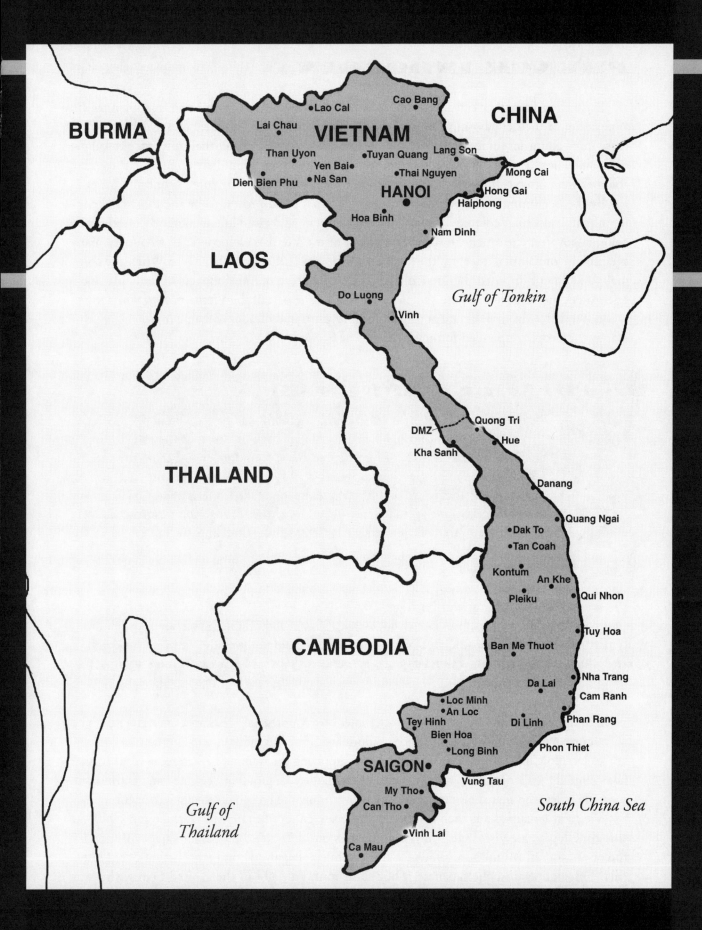

FRENCH INDOCHINA

Expanding French colonial ambitions during the nineteenth century eventually led to the annexation of the neighboring countries of Laos and Cambodia into French Indochina. With these three countries under their control, the French hoped to expand their influence throughout Asia. Their desires did not come to fruition because they soon discovered that their new colonies were often difficult to manage and did not provide the anticipated economic benefit.

By the beginning of the twentieth century, Vietnam had proven to be the most challenging of the Indochina colonies. Relying on sometimes cruel and violent methods, the French colonial government sought to suppress the will of the Vietnamese people. In a country managed solely for colonial interests, the local people became little more than serfs. When the colonial government imposed the French language and culture on most aspects of daily life, local resentment increased and fostered a determination on the part of the Vietnamese to win national independence. In this climate of unrest, local revolutionary leaders became increasingly popular as the people responded to their promises of freedom for Vietnam.

Ho Chi Minh (1890-1969)

At the time of Ho Chi Minh's birth, Vietnam was part of French Indochina. Expelled from French schools for rebellious activities, Ho traveled abroad, finally settling in Paris in 1917. Here he became a founding member of the French Communist Party. He then traveled to Moscow. After receiving training in Moscow, he moved to China where he organized Vietnamese exiles in an attempt to liberate Vietnam from the French. In Hong Kong he founded the Communist Party of Indochina and remained there until his arrest in 1932. After a short stay in Russia he returned to China to help with communist efforts there. In 1941 he returned to Vietnam to found a communist independence movement. At the end of World War II, Ho's group, known as the Vietminh seized power in the northern provinces of the country. Frustrated by the United States' and Europe's refusal to recognize his government, he fought the French to a standstill in 1954. He then increased his efforts to unify Vietnam. Serving as the leader of North Vietnam, he guided the war effort until his death in 1969. In his honor Saigon, the capital city of Vietnam, was renamed Ho Chi Minh City in 1976.

During World War I the French attempted to suppress all resistance movements. The Vietnamese responded with public demonstrations and acts of terrorism. In 1925 a new revolutionary leader, Ho Chi Minh, appeared on the scene. Applying the training he had received in Russia, he organized the Communist Party in Vietnam and gathered a group of dedicated and enthusiastic revolutionaries who shared his determination to overthrow the French colonial government.

Vietnam remained a French colony until the surrender of France to Germany in 1940. At that time Japan, an ally of Germany, took possession of French Indochina. The revolutionary forces of Ho Chi Minh, now known as the Vietminh, began to conduct a China-based guerrilla campaign against the Japanese. They soon found an ally in the United States who was willing to trade weapons and other military aid in exchange for intelligence information about the Japanese Army. Throughout the war, Ho Chi Minh made a concerted effort to convince the United States that the Vietminh was the legitimate government of Vietnam.

1945
POST-WORLD WAR II VIETNAM

With the surrender of Japan in 1945, the Vietminh attempted to fill the political vacuum by declaring itself the legitimate government of Vietnam. After establishing their headquarters in the northern city of Hanoi, the Vietminh worked to encourage a general uprising in support of national independence. Ho Chi Minh was frustrated when the war-weary French refused to recognize his government. France's decision to disregard Ho's declaration was based on its interpretation of the agreements made between the Allies at the end of World War II.

The Truman Doctrine

Following the end of World War II it became evident that communist Russia and China intended to expand their influence throughout the world. In response to communist aggression, President Harry S. Truman issued a presidential pronouncement in 1947 that declared the United States' intent to provide financial and military aid to any country facing communist insurrection. The balance of power between the communist nations and the United States became known as the Cold War that dominated the latter half of the twentieth century.

President Harry S. Truman enters Cecilienhof Palace to attend one of the meetings of the Potsdam Conference, 1945.

The United States complicated the matter by also refusing to recognize Vietnam's independence and chose instead to support the French claim. While the Vietminh had proven themselves a valuable ally in the fight against the Japanese during World War II, their communist affiliation was considered unacceptable in the postwar era. Guided by the Truman Doctrine, the United States declared its preference for French colonialism over a communist government. This treatment led Ho Chi Minh to take an ultranationalistic position that prevented any long-lasting cooperation with the Americans. Recognizing this as an important opportunity, the Soviet Union did not hesitate to embrace the Vietnamese cause and offer training and military support in their drive for national independence.

The year 1946 marked the beginning of what some have referred to as the First Indochina War, a nine-year struggle between Vietnamese communists and the French colonial government. This war had the general support of the Vietnamese people and was characterized by the Vietminh's guerrilla tactics rather than direct confrontation with a superior foe. In 1949 the new communist government of China escalated the war by providing the Vietminh with much-needed military aid. This action shifted the balance of power and allowed the Vietnamese to take the offensive for the first time.

President Truman responded to the unfolding events in Vietnam by supplying the French with financial aid and military advisors. But because he had more than enough to keep him busy—the occupation of Japan, the reconstruction of Europe, and the Korean War—Truman preferred to leave Vietnam to the French. By the time Dwight D. Eisenhower became president in 1952, France had grown desperate over the situation.

As early as 1953, John Dulles, the U.S. secretary of state, encouraged President Eisenhower to directly intervene in Vietnam. Fresh from the experience of the Korean War, the president did not want another war in Asia. However, the United States did continue to provide financial and military aid to the French to support their struggle against the communist rebels. The number of U.S. military advisors in Vietnam continued to grow until there were almost one thousand by the end of Eisenhower's term of office. Throughout his presidency, Eisenhower used the "Domino Theory" to justify U.S. involvement in Vietnam. This theory proposed that communism must be stopped or it would spread throughout Asia like dominos falling one after the other.

After nearly a decade of fighting, the Vietminh overwhelmed the French forces at Dien Bien Phu in May 1954. When America refused to send troops to their aid, the French determined that the war was too costly and surrendered to the revolutionary army. Both sides then agreed to seek international help in settling the conflict.

The Geneva Conference of 1954 convened to first consider the situation created by the Korean War and then settle matters between the Vietnamese and the French. Modeled after the decision to divide Korea at the 38th parallel, Vietnam was temporarily divided into two countries at the 17th parallel: in the north, the communist Democratic Republic of Vietnam; and in the south, the state of Vietnam (later the Republic of Vietnam)—a country led by Vietnam's traditional emperor who sympathized with the French. The agreement further called for free elections in 1956 to unify the country under one government.

THE SOUTHEAST ASIA TREATY ORGANIZATION

The United States was dismayed over the recognition of Ho Chi Minh's communist government and refused to sign the Geneva Accords. Instead, it chose to establish the Southeast Asia Treaty Organization (SEATO). Following the example of the North Atlantic Treaty Organization (NATO), an effort to oppose communism in Europe, the member nations of SEATO reached a similar agreement to oppose the spread of communism in Asia.

With the support of SEATO, the United States provided massive amounts of aid to the newly created Republic of Vietnam (South Vietnam). This enabled the new government to

SEATO (Southeast Asia Treaty Organization)

In 1954, representatives of Australia, France, New Zealand, Pakistan, the Philippines, Thailand, Great Britain, and the United States signed a collective defense treaty. This treaty was a response to the growing communist influence in Southeast Asia. While Vietnam was not a member, it was under the protection of SEATO because of its status under the 1954 Geneva Accords. Like NATO, its European counterpart, this organization depended largely on the military strength of the United States to enforce its directives.

Manila Conference: SEATO nations leaders group portrait in Manilla, Philippines, 1966. L–R: Prime Minister Nguyen Cao Ky (South Vietnam), Prime Minister Harold Holt (Australia), President Park Chung Hee (Korea), President Ferdinand Marcos (Philippines), Prime Minister Keith Holyoake (New Zealand), Lieutenant General Nguyen Van Thieu (South Vietnam), Prime Minister Thanom Kittikachorn (Thailand), President Lyndon B. Johnson (United States).

hold its first election in 1955 and elect Ngo Dinh Diem as its first president. Recognizing that the promise for a national referendum would not be honored, the communist government of North Vietnam rejected the legitimacy of the government of South Vietnam. The resulting conflict between North and South Vietnam then became the Second Indochina War that consumed much of the next two decades.

North Vietnam sympathizers, now better known as the Viet Cong, (the Vietnamese equivalent of "communists") joined with regular troops from North Vietnam to mount a determined military offensive against the government of South Vietnam. Fearing that increasing numbers of South Vietnamese citizens might sympathize with the North's efforts to reunite the country, Diem's government launched a cruel and oppressive attack on its own citizens. President Diem made it illegal to be a communist or even a communist sympathizer in South Vietnam. This resulted in the arrest of thousands of citizens and the placement of strict restrictions on basic individual freedoms. The outcries of the offended citizens were met with even more oppression as the government viewed all opposition as communist inspired. Throughout all this, the United States continued to support Diem's regime, believing that it was the best hope for stopping the spread of communism.

In 1960 the government of North Vietnam officially declared its intent to openly assist the Viet Cong in their attempt to overthrow the government of South Vietnam. This resulted in the creation of the National Liberation Front, an organization of North and South Vietnamese people dedicated to overthrowing the Diem government and unifying Vietnam. This only encouraged Diem to increase his dictatorial oppression over his people, which in turn resulted in even more resistance.

1960
THE KENNEDY RESPONSE

During the 1960 presidential campaign, John F. Kennedy expressed his strong anti-communist stand. Kennedy proposed an increased national military presence in the world, which he felt would bring a quick end to the Cold War. Following his election, reports from Vietnam dismayed the new president. His concern increased, as it appeared that Diem's government would fall to the communists. In an attempt to strengthen South Vietnam's army, Kennedy approved the use of combat air support and sent an increased number of military advisors to aid the army of South Vietnam. The primary purpose of these U.S. forces was to help the South Vietnamese Army increase its combat effectiveness.

By 1963 Washington realized that the corruption in Diem's government was contributing to his lack of success in meeting the communist offensive. Increasing numbers of South Vietnamese citizens publicly protested Diem's oppressive tactics. Notable among these demonstrations were the Buddhist monks who responded to Diem's unfair treatment of their order by setting themselves on fire. These developments led the Kennedy administration to accept a proposed military coup by Diem's own generals and provide the support they requested. In November 1963, the rebellious South Vietnamese officers carried out their plan and, much to Kennedy's dismay, assassinated Diem and his brother. While successful, the military coup did little to halt the advance of the communist forces. This was due in part to an extended period of government instability created by a series of different military governments. This enabled the Viet Cong to further penetrate South Vietnam and expand its influence with much of the population. In response, the number of U.S. troops serving in Vietnam as advisors, known as the American Military Assistance Command, increased to over 16,000.

A Buddhist monk commits ritual suicide in protest of government anti-Buddhist policies. October 5, 1963, Saigon, South Vietnam.

Increasing numbers of South Vietnamese citizens publicly protested Diem's oppressive tactics.

1964
GULF OF TONKIN RESOLUTION

After the assassination of President Kennedy, Lyndon B. Johnson became president of the United States. After review-

The Technology of War

Because the Viet Cong relied on outdated weapons, surface-to-air missiles supplied by China, and handmade booby traps, the United States used its technological superiority to great advantage. In previous wars, helicopters were used to increase troop mobility, but the Vietnam War was the first war in which technologically advanced helicopters were extensively employed as gunships. Besides helicopters, the United States also employed armored personnel carriers, electronic sensors, and satellite technology.

THE MCDONNELL F-4 FIGHTER BOMBER

The F-4 proved itself as the leading fighter plane of the Vietnam War. Used first in 1965 the plane soon proved suited for a variety of attack and bombing purposes.

Left: Two F-4B phantoms of the 1st Marine Aircraft Wing on their way to support ground troops in 1969.

THE GENERAL DYNAMICS F-111 FIGHTER-BOMBER

The Air Force introduced this plane in 1968. The advanced TFR (terrain-following radar) system enabled the fighter-bomber to fly under enemy missile radar to accomplish its mission.

Right: Commonly known as the "Aardvark," this fighter-bomber is a long-range, all-weather aircraft. One of its unique features is the "swing wings," which move from a straight to a swept-back position. This allows for slow speed flight as well as Mach 2 capability. The F-111 was first employed in the Vietnam War in 1968.

BELL UH-1A (HUEY) HELICOPTER

Introduced as a utility helicopter in 1959, this aircraft soon became a real workhorse throughout the war. It was used extensively for combat attack, transporting combat troops, and medical evacuations. Later modifications made the aircraft useful in supporting night and patrol and reconnaissance missions.

Left: UH-1D helicopters airlift members of the 2nd Battalion to a new staging area during Operation "Wahiawa" in 1966.

AH-1G COBRA ATTACK HELICOPTER

Much faster than the Huey and equipped with extensive weaponry, the Cobra proved to be a formidable attack aircraft. Because of its attack capabilities, the Cobra provided strong support for the Huey, which carried troops and evacuated the wounded.

One of the Cobra helicopters of the 9th Infantry Division in for repairs.

M-16 ASSAULT RIFLE

The M-16 was first used by U.S. troops in Vietnam in 1963. It was a gas-operated weapon, capable of fully automatic firing from a 30-round clip. The rifle weighed just over six pounds and was characterized by is unique carrying handle on top of the rifle. The rifle could also be fixed with a grenade launcher or a bayonet.

M-48 PATTON TANK

High-tech warfare was also seen in the tanks and other military vehicles used in Vietnam. The M-48 Patton tank was used most effectively throughout the war. Powered by engines reaching 750 horsepower, the tank was both quick and mobile. To counter the Viet Cong rocket grenades, the tanks were covered with special armor.

Marines riding atop an M-48 tank cover their ears as the 90mm gun fires during a road sweep southwest of Phu Bai in 1968.

OTHER VEHICLES

Wheeled vehicles such as the M-37 cargo 3/4 ton 4x4 truck built by Dodge proved valuable. A variety of boats were also used to patrol rivers and carry supplies. One boat, termed "Zippo," was outfitted with a flame thrower to burn vegetation along the shore.

American gunships transporting troops downriver to a new location.

President Lyndon B. Johnson shows his support for the American troops in Vietnam.

ing the situation in Vietnam, Johnson was convinced that increased U.S. intervention was needed to support the government of South Vietnam. Johnson selected General William C. Westmoreland to direct an increased war effort. As the army of South Vietnam continued to struggle, Westmoreland called for an invasion force of 200,000 U.S. troops, which he believed would bring a quick end to the war. The president hesitated to escalate the war and did not grant the request.

In August 1964, the situation intensified when North Vietnamese patrol boats attacked the USS *Maddox,* a naval destroyer stationed off the coast of North Vietnam. The *Maddox* quickly repelled the attack, but this incident in international waters gave President Johnson the impetus to ask Congress for greater military involvement. Soon after the attack on the *Maddox,* Congress passed the Gulf of Tonkin Resolution, allowing the president broad control over the use of armed forces in fighting an undeclared war in Vietnam.

While it is unclear what really happened in the Gulf of Tonkin, the incident became the major turning point in U.S. involvement. The number of military personnel in Vietnam increased dramatically until it reached a high of over 540,000 in 1969. The countries of South Korea, Australia, the Philippines, and New Zealand also sent forces, bringing the total number of servicemen to over 600,000. When added to the estimated number of forces fighting for the Viet Cong, the total number of combatants on both sides reached almost one million.

1965

OPERATION ROLLING THUNDER

General William C. Westmoreland was selected by President Lyndon B. Johnson to direct an increased war effort.

Several raids on U.S. installations resulted in numerous casualties that brought the war into sharp focus for the American people. With characteristic directness, Johnson responded swiftly, using the broad powers granted by Congress to launch the sustained bombing of North Vietnam. These bombing missions were known by the code name "Rolling Thunder." Massive air raids continued for the next three years in an attempt to quell the enemy's ability to wage war. In March 1965, the first detachment of 3,500 combat Marines arrived in Vietnam. Thousands more followed as Johnson committed an increasing number of combat troops to the

General Westmoreland called for . . . 200,000 U.S. troops, which he believed would bring a quick end to the war. [President Johnson] hesitated to escalate the war and did not grant the request.

war, bringing the total to nearly 200,000 by the year's end. To complement the increased military effort, the United States also quietly suggested various "peace initiatives" to provide an incentive for the North Vietnamese to end to the conflict.

During this time a debate ensued over the best way to wage the war in Vietnam. General Westmoreland felt that it would take an all-out offensive to defeat the communist forces. Johnson disagreed and defined the war as a defensive effort. This resulted in a limited war that was characterized by conflicting and unclear objectives. The Viet Cong understood this and modified their

Protests Against the War

Military police guard the pentagon as anti-Vietnam demonstrators protest the Vietnam war.

The antiwar protest movements took many forms. Some groups favored peaceful demonstrations (e.g. the Catholic Defense League), while others believed that only violence would force an end to the war (e.g. the Weathermen). One prominent group was the Students for a Democratic Society. Composed mostly of university students, this loosely organized group sponsored demonstrations across the nation. The effect of antiwar demonstrations was magnified by the extensive press coverage given such events.

tactics to prolong the war, hoping that the Americans would tire of fighting, as had the French. Attacks, such as the bombing of the American Embassy in Saigon in 1965, which resulted in the death of over fifty people, demonstrated the enemy's resolve to continue the war by any means. By the end of the year, the United States had over 350,000 troops stationed in Vietnam.

The growing number of combat troops reflected in some ways the failure of American government leaders to allow their military commanders to conduct the war in the most effective manner. Complicated procedures required field commanders to coordinate their efforts with their South Vietnamese counterparts as well as political leaders in Washington. This often resulted in decisions that compromised military effectiveness in the field.

The situation grew even more complicated as the domestic response to the war turned increasingly negative. These feelings only intensified when the government expanded the draft to meet the growing number of soldiers needed to fight the war. The resulting voices of opposition to the war included not only college students, but also prominent government leaders. Magnified by the disturbing images televised from Vietnam and the sometimes-biased media reports, public tension increased as the war divided the nation. As a result, public protests held to denounce the war became common throughout America.

During much of 1967, the American forces fought a series of seesaw campaigns that did not result in a clear victory. This led Westmoreland to recognize the need to secure an area located south of Saigon known as the Iron Triangle. During this campaign it became apparent that when faced with a superior force, the Viet Cong would simply withdraw or retreat across the border into Cambodia. Later, they would return to occupy their original positions, showing little adverse effect. U.S. leaders were frustrated that direct military action had so little impact on the Viet Cong. They requested that the president further escalate the war by raising the number of troops

Guerrilla Warfare

Despite their technological disadvantages and smaller available forces, the Viet Cong proved remarkably resilient to attack. They made up for their disadvantages through tenacity and mobility. Their lighter equipment and knowledge of terrain often gave them an advantage over the foreign forces. Their preference for guerrilla warfare tactics in which they determined who, how, and when to fight amplified these strengths. Bolstered by the clear objective to liberate South Vietnam and unify it with North Vietnam, the Viet Cong also had a mental advantage over the allies whose purposes were often less apparent.

The Viet Cong used these advantages to frustrate the forces of the United States and South Vietnam. Scattered among the general population, the Viet Cong were virtually indistinguishable. Because they did not have a highly organized structure, they could avoid planned U.S. military attacks by splitting up and blending into the population. They could also escape by fleeing over the border to Laos and Cambodia, which were demilitarized zones. The Viet Cong could escape to the north as well. U.S. policy prohibited penetration farther than twenty-one miles into North Vietnam. When military pressure eased, they regrouped and attacked again. Guerilla warfare tactics frustrated allied leaders who were accustomed to traditional front lines.

serving to almost 700,000. But 1967 ended quietly in Vietnam, leading U.S. commanders to hope that the Viet Cong's will to fight was decreasing and that a cease-fire was imminent.

1968

THE TET OFFENSIVE

In 1968 things went from bad to worse for Washington, both in Vietnam and on the domestic front. The influence of the antiwar movement put increased political pressure on the government leaders at home, while in Vietnam the Viet Cong escalated the war by launching a broad offensive campaign against key military and civilian positions in South Vietnam. On January 30, the beginning of Tet, the Vietnamese New Year, large numbers of Viet Cong attacked more than fifty cities and hamlets throughout South Vietnam, including Saigon, the nation's capital. After defending forces recovered from the unexpected intensity of the attack, some cities were quickly secured by the allies while others, including Saigon, continued to suffer devastating

President Johnson anguishes over tape recordings sent from his son-in-law, Marine Corps Captain Charles Robb, in Vietnam.

destruction. This offensive resulted in the deaths of thousands of civilians and extensive damage to the communities involved. The Viet Cong hoped that this offensive would incite South Viet-

The Tet Offensive was a demoralizing experience for those who had thought that the war was winding down.

Viet Cong member captured during the attacks on the capital city during the Tet holiday.

namese to rise against their government and by so doing weaken America's determination to continue the war. While, for the most part, their intentions failed, the Tet Offensive was a demoralizing experience for those who had thought that the war was winding down. Furthermore, it convinced many in America that the war must come to a speedy end. Ironically, the Tet Offensive proved most costly to the Communists who lost 32,000 solders and much of the equipment and supplies they needed to continue the fight. Had the United States known how vulnerable this offensive had left the North Vietnamese, they might have forced a quicker end to the war.

Following the Tet Offensive, representatives of the United States and North Vietnam began meeting in Paris to discuss a peaceful solution to the war. On another front, President Johnson expressed his lack of confidence in General Westmoreland's management of the war, and replaced the field commander in Vietnam with General Creighton Abrams. A string of smaller offensives followed during the next six months. The Viet Cong hoped that their continuing attacks would eventually gain sufficient momentum to overwhelm the resistance of

The Ho Chi Minh Trail

Besides the bombing missions over North Vietnam in which the United States dropped hundreds of thousands of bombs, the United States also went to great efforts to block the Viet Cong's supply route from the north known as the Ho Chi Minh Trail, which wound its way from North Vietnam through the mountainous areas of Laos and Cambodia to South Vietnam, supplying the Viet Cong fighting in the south. Arms and munitions passed over that trail, as well as communications between northern and southern divisions of the Viet Cong. The U.S. and South Vietnamese forces mined and bombed sections of the trail, only to find that within a few days the route had shifted by a couple of miles and that the supply process continued.

Left: The Ho Chi Minh Trail consisted of a network of jungle footpaths, trails, and roads that functioned as a supply route from North Vietnam through Laos and Cambodia into areas controlled by South Vietnam.

Right: An Air force F-105 Thunderchief swoops over a bridge in communist North Vietnam as billows of smoke from hits by other aircraft hide the target. On this flight, four Thundercheif pilots destroyed this bridge, damaged another, and damaged about 15 barges with 750-pound bombs, 2.75-inch rockets, and 20-mm cannons.

the South Vietnamese and American forces. However, because of the heavy losses that the communists continued to suffer, their political infrastructure began to weaken. The Americans took advantage of this and stepped up their efforts to seek a peaceful end to the war. It was apparent to U.S. commanders that the years of bombing and direct military action had done little to weaken the communist resolve to unite Vietnam under one government.

Later that year, President Johnson decided not to run for reelection. After a vigorous campaign, Richard M. Nixon was elected president of the United States with the promise that he would bring "peace with honor" in Vietnam. U.S. commanders petitioned the new president

Booby Traps

Lacking the advanced technology of the U.S. forces, the Viet Cong devised a variety of ingenious booby trap devices that, when concealed, could wound and kill unsuspecting soldiers. Booby traps hindered troop movements, made jungle patrol dangerous, and demoralized the soldiers. Although primitive, booby traps accounted for almost 20 percent of the injuries and deaths suffered by combat troops in the field.

Booby traps came in two types. One relied on explosives to kill or maim, while the other used stakes and traps to inflict injury. The explosive traps were powder-filled coconuts, grenades covered with mud, trip wires, etc. that exploded when triggered by an unsuspecting soldier. Booby traps using stakes were made with sharpened poles of bamboo that were placed in holes and camouflaged to hide them from view. Stakes were also mounted on bent saplings, which, when triggered, would sweep across a trail impaling anything in its path.

Above: Sharp spikes were attached to a piece of green bamboo. This was bent around another post and held in place with a trigger line. When the bamboo post was released by a trip wire the pole snapped forward, propelling its spikes into the victim. Below: The cartridge trap was made from an unexploded cartridge placed in a piece of bamboo. This was buried in a camouflaged

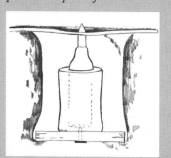

hole in the ground. A nail was driven through the bottom of the bamboo, which rested on a solid board. When the cartridge was stepped on, the nail at the bottom of the cartridge caused it to explode upward, usually hitting the victim in the foot.

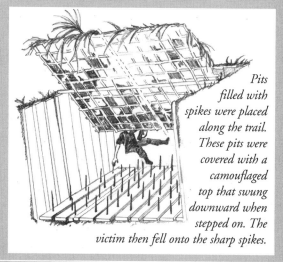

Pits filled with spikes were placed along the trail. These pits were covered with a camouflaged top that swung downward when stepped on. The victim then fell onto the sharp spikes.

for 200,000 additional troops, feeling that the added strength would be sufficient to bring an end to the war. Nixon refused their requests and instead explored other alternatives.

1969

NIXON'S PLAN FOR VIETNAMIZATION

In 1969 Nixon introduced a new policy, which he called "Vietnamization." This policy required that the South Vietnamese gradually assume full responsibility for fighting the war. This would allow increasing numbers U.S. troops to be sent home. As part of the process the United States planned to provide additional training for the South Vietnamese Army. Under Nixon's plan, the number of U.S. troops serving in Vietnam decreased from a high of over 540,000 in 1969 to a low of 150,000 by the end of 1971.

However, for the soldiers still fighting in Vietnam, the president's plan did not seem to be working. Battles such as that at Ap Bia Mountain (Hamburger Hill) where over fifty Americans lost their lives vividly demonstrated to the American pubic that Vietnamization had not brought the immediate success the President had promised. Understanding this and desiring to end the war more quickly, Nixon approved the increased bombing of North Vietnam and provided additional funding to the South Vietnamese Army. However, he did continue to fulfill his commitment to bring increasing numbers of U.S. troops home.

As part of Vietnamization, the South Vietnamese Army, supported by U.S. forces,

Many young men from the South Vietnamese Army were trained by U.S. forces in order to better protect their villages.

Vietnamization had not brought the immediate success the President had promised.

launched a campaign into the surrounding countries of Cambodia (1970) and Laos (1971). These countries had become harbors for the Viet Cong due to border-crossing regulations respected by the United States. Targets in Laos and Cambodia included several important communist bases, which lay just over the border. During these raids, the United States lost more helicopters to antiaircraft artillery than at any other point during the war, and the Viet Cong fought more savagely than ever. Though they suffered heavy losses, the South Vietnamese Army was able to neutralize several key enemy bases and destroy thousands of tons of supplies. But the Viet Cong demonstrated their resilience by moving deeper into these countries where they could wait for an opportunity to renew the conflict.

As Nixon accelerated his plan, U.S. advisory teams in Vietnam recognized that Vietnamization would leave the

South Vietnamese unable to defend themselves. While the advisors were told to turn over to their Vietnamese counterparts all responsibility for the war, their orders prohibited them from leaving in Vietnam equipment and supplies desperately needed by the South Vietnamese to succeed. Many expressed frustration with orders to "burn, bury, or blow up" what they could not take with them rather than give it to the South Vietnamese Army. Vietnamization continued and by the end of 1971 there were approximately 60,000 U.S. troops remaining in Vietnam.

Recognizing the continuous decline in the number of U.S. forces, the North Vietnamese launched a sweeping attack

Opposite: In war, time drags as soldiers await going home to family and friends. A sky trooper keeps track of the time he has left on his "short-time" helmet.

Media Coverage of the War

Walter Cronkite and a CBS camera crew use a jeep for a dolly during an interview with the commanding officer of the 1st Battalion, 1st Marines, during the Battle of Hue City, 1968.

The media coverage of the Vietnam War was extensive. Never before had war become so personal for the American public. The images daily broadcast over the nation's television networks did much to shape public attitude toward the war. Journalists provided both general coverage of the war as well as human interest stories related to the experiences of the individual troops.

known as the Easter Offensive. It began with North Vietnamese troops overrunning South Vietnamese forces at key positions throughout the country. To stem the attack, the United States provided a massive amount of air support. The communist attacks then lessened but nevertheless continued until stiff resistance by the South Vietnamese, aided by U.S. fighter aircraft, brought an end to the offensive. Angered by the attack, Nixon ordered an extensive bombing campaign and the mining of Haiphong Harbor in North Vietnam. He believed that by taking the war to the North Vietnamese citizens he could

This issue of LIFE MAGAZINE, Nov. 26, 1965, featured a Viet Cong POW.

Recognizing the continuous decline in the number of U.S. forces, the North Vietnamese launched a sweeping attack known as the Easter Offensive.

War: Where boys have no choice but to become men. Courageous soldiers, especially young ones, attempted to protect the freedom of other nations.

encourage their leaders to seriously consider a cease-fire. The effect of the new laser-guided bombs and other advanced weaponry had a devastating effect on the cities of North Vietnam. The result was a renewal of the peace negotiations between Henry Kissinger, the U.S. secretary of state, and North Vietnamese representative, Le Duc Tho. This was good news for Nixon who was preparing for the presidential campaign of 1972.

1973

PARIS PEACE AGREEMENT

The war was a major issue in the presidential election of 1972. Many did not consider Vietnamization a success and as a result opposed Nixon's continued leadership. This was compounded by the revelation that representatives of the president had illegally entered a committee office of the Democratic Party in the Watergate Hotel. Using wartime executive privilege, Nixon was able to forestall for a time the investigative process, but the Watergate scandal continued to hamper the president.

In October 1972, Kissinger announced that the end of the war was near at hand. The timing of this announcement was most beneficial for the Nixon presidential campaign despite the fact that an actual peace treaty had yet to be signed. Following the presidential election, Kissinger encouraged the reelected president to further increase the bombing of North Vietnam to ensure that the promised peace agreement would be achieved. The North Vietnamese responded with a sincere effort to reach a cease-fire agreement. In January 1973 representatives of the United States, North Vietnam, South Vietnam, and the Viet Cong signed the Paris Peace Accords.

The peace agreement, among other provisions, called for the immediate removal of all U.S. military personnel from Vietnam. By March, three months after the cease-fire, all U.S. troops had left Vietnam. However, this did not bring an end to the fighting as the North Vietnamese continued to take the offensive against an increasingly helpless South. The "burn, bury, or blow up" plan of the departing Americans further weakened the South Vietnamese Army. By taking or destroying equipment and supplies, the Unites States left South Vietnamese troops woefully unprepared to meet any military threat.

> **By taking or destroying equipment and supplies, the United States left South Vietnamese troops woefully unprepared to meet any military threat.**

During this time the government of South Vietnam refused to acknowledge the impending doom by assuring the international community that life had finally returned to normal. Some U.S. officials declared that the war was over and even encouraged American businesses to invest in South Vietnam. The government of South Vietnam optimistically opened a tourist bureau and encouraged travelers to vacation there. For the next two years the government of South Vietnam continued this façade while it waged a losing battle with the Viet Cong.

1975

THE FALL OF SAIGON

Close-up of a Vietnamese woman who is leaving her village to escape the conflict. Many South Vietnamese people fled their country as refugees rather than submit to the repressive communist regime of Ho Chi Minh.

The Watergate scandal finally forced President Nixon to resign in disgrace in August 1974. Gerard R. Ford succeeded him as the next president of the United States. While this brought some stability to the American domestic scene, chaos was increasing throughout Southeast Asia. The Khmer Rouge threatened to overthrow the government of Cambodia, and antigovernment riots filled the streets of neighboring Laos. In Saigon, the government of South Vietnam faced certain destruction as the communist forces advanced on the capital.

In 1975, sensing that victory was near, the Viet Cong swept southward forcing the South Vietnamese Army to retreat in disorder. The few units that stood firm were quickly overwhelmed. Believing that the United States would again come to their aid, South Vietnamese leaders appealed to President Ford. Their cries for help were ignored and on April 30, 1975, North Vietnamese troops captured Saigon bringing an end to several decades of war in that country.

The agricultural countryside had been devastated . . . and most of the country's urban industry had been destroyed . . . It would take years for the country to recover from decades of war.

Thirty years after Ho Chi Minh's initial declaration of independence, North and South Vietnam were again united as one country. The new communist government exercised their dictatorial power by promptly imprisoning all those who had supported the South Vietnam government. They then forced upon the people a repressive communist dictatorship. Rather than submit to this regime, many fled the country as refugees. Those who remained faced economic hardships. The agricultural countryside had been devastated by bombings and repeated applications of deforestation chemicals. In addition, most of the country's urban industry had also been destroyed during the war. It would take years for the country to recover from decades of war.

Vietnamese people evacuating a village to get away from the conflict.

CONCLUSION

Over 2,600,000 American men and women fought in the Vietnam War, and about 58,000 of those died, over 300,000 were wounded, and more than 2,500 were listed as prisoners or war or missing in action. Less important, but still significant, the United States spent about $200 billion on the war, which had a detrimental effect on the U.S. economy. The United States had failed to achieve its objectives in Vietnam, and communism prevailed. Those who participated in the war did not receive the recognition they deserved, as had those who had fought in previous wars.

The role of the United States in the Vietnam War remains a controversial subject, with hundreds of books scrutinizing every aspect of the war. Regardless of the controversy, it remains a significant part of United States and world history. Regardless of the arguments, there can be no debate over the value of the many lives offered in defense of democratic ideals and the cause of freedom. It is fitting and proper that the veterans of the Vietnam War receive the gratitude they deserve for the service they rendered the American people during a most difficult period of history.

BIBLIOGRAPHY

Addington, Larry. *America's War in Vietnam: A Short Narrative.* Bloomington, IN: University Press, 2000.

Anderson, David L. *The Columbia Guide to the Vietnam War.* New York: Columbia University Press, 2002.

Edmonds, Anthony O. *The War in Vietnam.* Westport, CN: Greenwood Press, 1998.

Gilbert, Marc J. *Why the North Won the Vietnam War.* New York: Palgrave, 2002.

Hall, Mitchell. *The Vietnam War.* New York: Longman, 2000.

Langguth, A. J. *Our Vietnam: The War, 1954–1975.* New York: Simon and Schuster, 2000.

Lind, Michael. *Vietnam, the Necessary War: A Reinterpretation of America's Most Disastrous Military Conflict.* New York: Free Press, 1999.

Logevall, Fredrik. *The Origins of the Vietnam War.* New York: Longman, 2001.

Moise, Edwin. *Historical Dictionary of the Vietnam War.* Lanham, MD: Scarecrow Press, 2001.

Tucker, Spencer C., ed. *Encyclopedia of the Vietnam War: A Political, Social, and Military History.* Santa Barbara, CA: ABC-CLIO, 1998.

Vietnam Veterans Memorial

The Vietnam Veterans Memorial in Washington, D.C. is mobbed by veterans and their families on the day of its dedication. November 13, 1982.

In 1979, Vietnam veteran Jan C. Scruggs first conceived the idea for the national Vietnam Veterans Memorial. He headed a public fund-raising effort that generated enough money to privately fund the building of the monument. It is located on the Mall in Washington, D.C., between the Washington Monument and the Lincoln Memorial. Dedicated in 1982, the memorial consists of two freestanding black granite walls each 250 feet long set in a "V" shape. Maya Lin designed the memorial using the Western or Wailing Wall of the old temple in Jerusalem as her inspiration.

Known simply as "the Wall," the memorial is one of the most visited sites in Washington. Visitors come to view almost 60,000 names of soldiers killed in the war engraved on the two walls.

Using a directory provided on site, visitors can locate the name of their friend or family members killed in the war. Many visitors place pieces of paper over the name and rub the name onto the paper as a keepsake.

Adjacent to the Wall are two other monuments related to the Vietnam War. The first is a sculpture of three Vietnam soldiers dressed in battle gear. The second is a Vietnam Veterans Women's Memorial showing servicewomen helping a wounded soldier.

THE INFLUENCE OF THE CHURCH DURING THE VIETNAM WAR

1962-1973

Although dark and devastating, war has often served to introduce the gospel message into countries where it did not exist before. Vietnam was one of those countries. The LDS servicemen[1] who served in the Vietnam War were pioneers in a new country, and they experienced some of the same trials and blessings that are common in such work. They often longed for Church associations, made special efforts to gather with other Latter-day Saints, and had to make do with limited resources in creating a Church environment. Such experiences made it possible for many of the servicemen to grow spiritually in ways not possible had they been at home. Because combat realities often limited Church organization to small isolated groups, many LDS servicemen had the opportunity to serve in missionary and leadership positions. Through such service they grew in their understanding of the gospel and the missions of the Church. They felt particular joy in sharing the gospel with other servicemen and local Vietnamese citizens. Through such efforts these "soldier-saints" participated in the beginnings of the Church in this part of Southeast Asia.

Captain George A. Willmore works in humanitarian efforts to help the people of Vietnam, especially the children. His philosophy was that the humanitarian efforts in conjunction with military support would in time enable the Vietnamese to solve their own problems.

CHURCH SUPPORT FOR MEMBERS IN THE MILITARY

In 1965 when the United States increased the number of combat troops in Vietnam, the Church published an editorial in the *Church News.* Among other things, the article declared, "Our Church is committed in upholding, honoring, and sustaining the law, and for this reason, we honor our young

men who enter the military service in defense of our liberty and rights."[2] While other groups often protested the war, the Church preferred not to criticize government actions. When requested by Selective Service officials to limit the number of full-time missionaries called, the First Presidency imposed a quota that limited each ward in the Church to one missionary each six months.[3] While the Presidency recognized that this directive would result in some young men not being able to serve missions, they felt that it was important to support Selective Service efforts to increase the number of young men drafted into military service.

Representatives from the Quorum of the Twelve Apostles . . . traveled to Vietnam . . . to provide encouragement.

Fall of 1968. Elder Bruce R. McConkie with son Joseph McConkie outside of Saigon.

Recognizing that the young members who entered military service would need support and spiritual sustenance, Church leaders endeavored to support LDS servicemen as much as they were able. Upon entering the service, each LDS serviceman received a packet of materials that included pocket-sized scriptures and basic instruction booklets. Church leaders also promoted regular correspondence between servicemen and families, wards, and local priesthood leaders. In addition, they requested that each military man also receive some form of Church literature, such as the *Improvement Era* or the *Church News*.[4] Representatives from the Quorum of the Twelve Apostles and other general Church leaders traveled to Vietnam to meet with LDS servicemen to provide encouragement and support. Later in the war, the Church organized servicemen's seminars at key military training bases in the United States to help prepare new inductees for the challenges they would confront and the missionary opportunities that would be theirs in military service.

The LDS chaplains who served during the war were also a great strength to the LDS servicemen. They helped organize

servicemen's conferences, assisted with weekday worship arrangements, and provided spiritual leadership as needed. During the Vietnam War, military leaders raised the qualifications for chaplains. The Church was most affected by the requirement that all chaplains complete ninety hours of college course work related to their ministry. Due to this restriction, the Church was not able to fill its quota with qualified applicants. Petitions by Church leaders resulted in the military allowing LDS applicants to substitute a two-year mission for sixty of the required credits, thus allowing for a greater number of qualified individuals. At the high point of U.S. participation in the war, the servicemen were fortunate to have up to twenty-seven LDS chaplains on active duty during the war.[5]

LDS servicemen in Cam Ranh Bay ready to board plane to attend conference in Pleiku, Vietnam, on Christmas morning 1966.

The growth of the Church in Vietnam paralleled the escalation of the general war effort. It is estimated that the percentage of Church members serving in the military stood at a rather constant one percent of all servicemen throughout the war.[6] At the high point of U.S. involvement in 1968, Church leaders in Vietnam estimated that out of the more than 500,000 soldiers serving, "between four and six thousand" were LDS.[7] Knowing all the while that peace could be found through the gospel, Church leaders were dedicated in obeying the laws of the United States.

LDS SERVICEMEN'S GROUPS

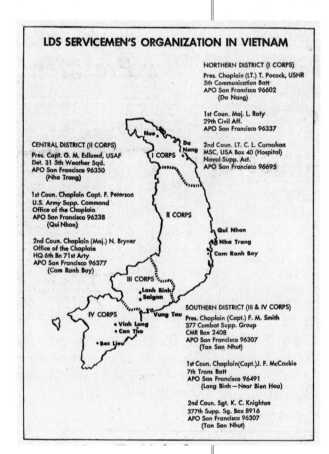

LDS SERVICEMEN'S ORGANIZATION IN VIETNAM

NORTHERN DISTRICT (I CORPS)
Pres. Chaplain (LT.) T. Pocock, USNR
5th Communication Batt
APO San Francisco 96602
(Da Nang)

1st Coun. Maj. L. Rafy
29th Civil Aff.
APO San Francisco 96337

2nd Coun. LT. C. L. Carnahan
MSC, USA Box 40 (Hospital)
Naval Supp. Act.
APO San Francisco 96695

CENTRAL DISTRICT (II CORPS)
Pres. Capt. G. M. Edlumd, USAF
Det. 31 5th Weather Sqd.
APO San Francisco 96350
(Nha Trang)

1st Coun. Chaplain Capt. F. Peterson
U.S. Army Supp. Command
Office of the Chaplain
APO San Francisco 96238
(Qui Nhon)

2nd Coun. Chaplain (Maj.) N. Bryner
Office of the Chaplain
HQ 6th Bn 71st Arty
APO San Francisco 96377
(Cam Ranh Bay)

SOUTHERN DISTRICT (III & IV CORPS)
Pres. Chaplain (Capt.) F. M. Smith
377 Combat Supp. Group
CMR Box 2408
APO San Francisco 96307
(Tan Son Nhut)

1st Coun. Chaplain(Capt.)J. F. McConkie
7th Trans Batt
APO San Francisco 96491
(Long Binh — Near Bien Hoa)

2nd Coun. Sgt. K. C. Knighton
377th Supp. Sg. Box 8916
APO San Francisco 96307
(Tan Son Nhut)

In early 1962, a handful of Latter-day Saints served in Vietnam as military advisors. During that time, Bud Cavender and five other LDS servicemen began holding Church services at the Tan Son Nhut Air Base near Saigon. This was the first time that LDS Church meetings had been held in the country. In response to this interest, Robert D. Taylor, president of the Southern Far East Mission, organized the first LDS servicemen's group in Saigon on June 30, 1962. By fall, the Saigon group roster reported fifty-five members, all Americans, including three families and eight children.[8]

As the number of Church members in Vietnam increased, more LDS groups were formed. Groups typically consisted of several Church members who were stationed near one another. While a few groups had an information organization, most groups had a group leader who had been called and set apart. He functioned as the presiding elder. District and zone leaders appointed by the mission president supervised the groups under their jurisdictions. This type of organization provided many servicemen with a variety of leadership experiences that strengthened their faith and testimonies. For the LDS servicemen, the group was a source of strength and fellowship that sustained them throughout the war. LDS groups also provided support and fellowship for new converts.

THE FIRST
CONVERT BAPTISM

★
★
★

Captain John T. Mullenex of the U.S. Air Force was likely the first convert during the Vietnam War when he was baptized on November 3, 1962.[9] Because the small group had no baptismal font and the nearby waters were polluted, Brother Mullenex was baptized in a 500-gallon water purification tank that had been "dressed up" with white sheets and palm leaves. One of the brethren had welded together some steel steps leading up and then down into the rubber "font."

The next year, two Vietnamese women were baptized in that same tank. They had been taught the gospel by Patricia Bean, who was working with the Vietnam American

A baptism at Long Binh, Vietnam.

Association teaching English.[10] It is thought that these two sisters were the first Vietnamese baptisms during the war.[11] This small group of Saints consisting of servicemen and their families along with the new converts, both Vietnamese and American, increased to a group of over two hundred members despite the escalation of the war.[12]

"NO SUNDAY IN VIETNAM"

Since members of LDS groups had to travel to church services over dangerous roads sometimes watched by Viet Cong guerillas, the American and Vietnamese Saints often went to church fully armed. Throughout the course of the war, weapons were a common sight at religious services because, as one chaplain explained, "There's no Sunday in Vietnam." [13] Unfortunately this was because of a constant need for readiness in case of attack. Elder Gordon B. Hinckley, upon returning from visiting LDS servicemen in Vietnam, described the common sight of weapons in Church meetings in a conference address: "Their automatic rifles were stacked along the rear pews, and they sat in their battle fatigues, many of them with a pistol on the right hip and knife on the left."[14] Even the garments worn by the endowed servicemen reflected the realities of war. This was the result of a July 1966 directive from the First Presidency that authorized the use of green garments that complied with existing military regulations.[15] Those who regularly attended Church meetings in Vietnam grew accustomed to these sights, but for newcomers, the reminders of combat in the chapel served as a poetic contrast to the soldiers' dedication to their faith.

Because the Saints were spread so far apart, it was not uncommon for a small group to gather together on Sunday. One soldier gave this report: "I've just attended services held in a tent. . . This group may be small in numbers but it is large in faith."[16] Another veteran tells of the time in combat when he heard someone whistling a familiar tune. Recognizing it as "We Thank Thee, O God, for a Prophet," he crawled below the crossfire and learned that the fellow was a faithful member of the Church. The two men immediately decided to hold an impromptu sacrament meeting in the foxhole.[17] If only to sing a hymn and administer a makeshift sacrament with crackers and canteens, Church brothers found spiritual refuge in such meetings. In extreme situations, some servicemen who were isolated completely from other members worshipped alone, often singing hymns by themselves and reciting memorized scriptures.[18]

THE FIRST LDS MEETINGHOUSE

Some LDS servicemen were fortunate enough to serve on military bases where LDS groups didn't have to worship in foxholes. They met in rented rooms or huts. But members of one LDS group, however, wanted a building of their own. In September 1965, LDS servicemen at the Bien Hoa Air Base near Saigon assisted in the construction of the first and only Church meetinghouse built during the war. Thirty-five servicemen, having heard that a local contractor needed help moving some supplies, volunteered for the job. In exchange for their services, the contractor helped build a chapel for their group.[19] The building, twenty-three by forty-six feet, was made of surplus aircraft hanger material and contained a handful of backless benches.[20] In spite of the humble accommoda-

The Bien Hoa chapel was the only Church-owned building in Vietnam during the war.

tions it was a "spiritual retreat" for many servicemen" and served the Saigon district throughout the war.[21] The Bien Hoa chapel was the only Church-owned building in Vietnam during the war.

It was common for LDS soldiers to donate part of their pay to secure suitable meeting places. At one point, Church leaders asked each member to donate one month's combat pay, which was termed "peace pay." Funds raised through these donations were placed in reserve for meeting local member welfare needs and for securing needed meetinghouses.[22]

Depending on the number of members, the Saints would meet in a variety of rented or borrowed locations for Sunday meetings. In Saigon, the members were able to rent a twelve-room home to use as a meetinghouse. The home had originally been the residence of a Buddhist leader who had moved from the city. One advantage of the residence was the large rain reservoir in the backyard of the home that served the branch as a baptismal font. A well-known Vietnamese lawyer who was not LDS assisted the Church in its efforts to secure this building for Church purposes and gain official government recognition for the Church in South Vietnam.[23]

Above: Front L–R: (Bro. Thach's children) Vu, Nga, and Huong. Second row L–R: Howie Whittington, Jim English, Steve Bland, unidentified, Peter Bell, unidentified, unidentified. Third row L–R: Unidentified, Unidentified, Thayne Green, Warren Soong, unidentified, Brother Thach. Back row L–R: Virgil Kovalenko, unidentified, unidentified, unidentified, unidentified, unidentified, unidentified, unidentified. Inset: A hand-drawn sign above the doorway at the entrance of the Bien Hoa LDS group chapel.

Above: LDS ward in Dong Tam. They met in an inflatable hospital Quonset hut. Sometimes before they could start the service, they had to patch the holes from the shrapnel that were made the night before. Then the Quonset hut could be re-inflated. While serving in the 9th infantry, Terry M. Jorgensen was one of five members to be set apart as a missionary by Major Allen C. Rozsa. While there, the man on the young lady's left side was baptized. Later the two were married.

Right: The "New" Mormon chapel replaced the original tent chapel in Cam Ranh Bay..

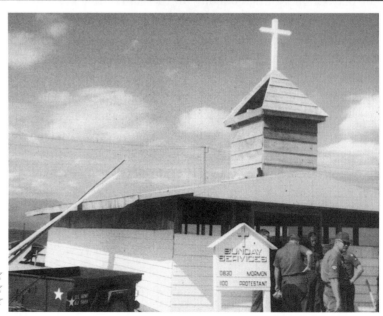

DEDICATION OF VIETNAM

By December 1965 there were 1,500 LDS servicemen in Vietnam, and the Vietnam zone of the Southern Far East Mission had been subdivided into three districts to better serve the increasing number of LDS servicemen. Further evidence of Church growth came on October 2, 1966, when Nguyen Cao Minh became the first Vietnamese member to receive the Melchizedek Priesthood. Minh had joined the Church in 1963 while attending school in the United States. His conversion proved providential because over the next ten years he played a vital role as a missionary and local leader of the Church. Brother Minh served faithfully as a local priesthood leader, continually encouraging missionary work and the translation of Church literature.[24]

In October 1966, when the number of LDS soldiers had grown to over 2,200, Elder Gordon B. Hinckley of the Quorum of the Twelve, with Elder Marion D. Hanks of the Quorum of the Seventy and President Keith E. Garner of the Southern Far East Mission visited the troops in South Vietnam and held a district conference at the Caravelle Hotel in Saigon. Over two hundred members of the Church participated in this historic event.

At that conference, under the direction of the Spirit and with the approval of President David O. McKay, Elder Hinckley dedicated the land for the preaching of the gospel. In the dedicatory prayer Elder Hinckley expressed gratitude for the Constitution of the United States, as well as for the missionary work that had already been done among the Vietnamese people. He prayed that there would "come upon this land an added measure of [the Lord's] holy spirit to touch the hearts of the people and the rulers thereof."[25] Following the conference, Elder Hinckley visited several other LDS groups outside of Saigon in a DC-3 ("Gooneybird") made available for his use by the Air Force.[26]

Top: Program for the conference where Elder Hinckley presided and dedicated the land of South Vietnam for the opening up of the preaching of the gospel.

Bottom: Farrell Smith (District President of southern district), Joseph McConkie (1st counselor of southern district), and President Keith Garner (President of the Southern Far East Mission).

Top: Major James M. Harris, pilot at Bien Hoa and district missionary who taught the gospel to Nguyen Ngoc Thach, his wife Tran Thi Xuan, and their children. Brother Harris is pictured with six of the Thach children.

Bottom: A neighborhood swimhole and shallow ford discovered by Lt. Harold C. Lynch as a possible site for his batism to be held. His group leader agreed, and the baptism took place in this very spot. Lt. Lynch used nearby bushes as a dressing area.

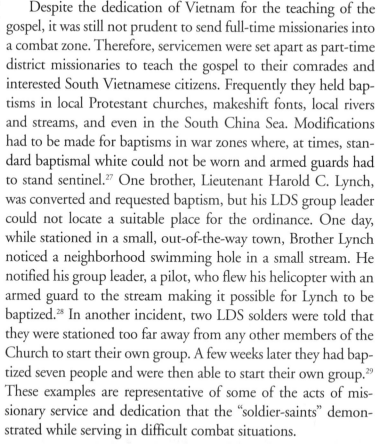

Despite the dedication of Vietnam for the teaching of the gospel, it was still not prudent to send full-time missionaries into a combat zone. Therefore, servicemen were set apart as part-time district missionaries to teach the gospel to their comrades and interested South Vietnamese citizens. Frequently they held baptisms in local Protestant churches, makeshift fonts, local rivers and streams, and even in the South China Sea. Modifications had to be made for baptisms in war zones where, at times, standard baptismal white could not be worn and armed guards had to stand sentinel.[27] One brother, Lieutenant Harold C. Lynch, was converted and requested baptism, but his LDS group leader could not locate a suitable place for the ordinance. One day, while stationed in a small, out-of-the-way town, Brother Lynch noticed a neighborhood swimming hole in a small stream. He notified his group leader, a pilot, who flew his helicopter with an armed guard to the stream making it possible for Lynch to be baptized.[28] In another incident, two LDS solders were told that they were stationed too far away from any other members of the Church to start their own group. A few weeks later they had baptized seven people and were then able to start their own group.[29] These examples are representative of some of the acts of missionary service and dedication that the "soldier-saints" demonstrated while serving in difficult combat situations.

"NO MORE DEVOTED OR CAPABLE MEMBERS WILL BE FOUND ANYWHERE"

In an October 1966 general conference address, Elder Hinckley praised the LDS servicemen in Vietnam, claiming that "no more devoted or capable members of the Church will be found anywhere in the world."[30] He had observed during his visits that the LDS troops lived gospel principles in the midst of the rigors of combat, the absence of friends and family, and the great challenges of disparate military lifestyles. In fact, many servicemen reported being able to find some good in their experiences during the Vietnam War because of their upbringing as Latter-day Saints. They frequently described how the principles of the plan of salvation "provided a greater sense of purpose and moral anchor."[31] These faithful members studied the gospel from the standard works, their serviceman's copy of *Principles of the Gospel,* and periodicals such as the *Church News* and the *Improvement Era* sent from their home wards and stakes. Because there was not an official servicemen's edition of the *Church News* as there had been during World War II, home bishops and quorum presidencies assumed greater responsibility for sending Church periodicals to those serving from their wards. Later in the war, arrangements were made so that the servicemen themselves could directly subscribe to the Church periodicals.[32] The Saigon LDS servicemen's group published their own Church periodical, a 16-page magazine called *The Soldier Saint.* This magazine was useful in efforts to contact the many members who were scattered around the country away from LDS groups. One of the editors reported, "Our concern was that of the 250 members in the division . . . only 80 were in our base camp. Yet we were responsible for all 250. *The Solder Saint* was one way to reach out to all of our members for whom we're responsible."[33] The publication included not only directories, but also messages from wives at home, letters from servicemen to other servicemen, a Book of Mormon study guide, and even scripture-based crossword puzzles.[34]

Church literature provided comfort to the LDS soldiers. One brother stationed in a helicopter ambulance

THE SOLDIER SAINT *magazine: begun by the Cu Chi group of the South Vietnam District in September 1970 (Volume 1). It was continued by the Long Binh Group (Volume 2).*

unit wrote a thank-you note to the editors of the *Improvement Era*. In that message he described taking his copy of the magazine on wounded-recovery missions to read whenever he had a break. He wrote, "I can never forget the warm and helpful inspiration I've consistently found in reading. . . . It has without a doubt been one of the biggest single guides in keeping me close to the church."[35] Another brother, visiting Vietnam as a correspondent, suggested that servicemen should receive "one good LDS book a month" and rationalized that even if the books never returned to the United States, at least "they will become tools of learning for someone else."[36]

Although helpful, Church literature did not replace a direct association with other members of the Church. As a result, Church leaders in the military sought to contact every LDS serviceman in their jurisdictions to let them know that gospel fellowship was available. Such contact was comforting, especially for those in situations that would not allow them to attend Church meetings. Typical of the efforts to maintain contact with Church members were those of Louis T. Bowring, a helicopter pilot who served as a Church leader in the southern district. He flew over 250 flight hours throughout his district to meet with members of the Church. Those who looked forward to his visits named his helicopter Hereafter 472.[37]

From the pulpit at General Conference in October 1966, Elder Hinckley invited all young men serving in Vietnam to contact the Church, and advised all young men who go to the war to make their presence known to the priesthood authorities in the military.[38] He also advised parents to send information about the location of their children in the military so they could be fellowshipped. But in spite of this effort, it was sometimes difficult for chaplains and leaders to account for all the LDS servicemen in Vietnam. One chaplain reported that in spite of their best efforts, he was "afraid that only about 10–15 percent of the Church members know where the groups are" and urged families to send information about their relatives to Church leaders.[39]

CONTINUED CHURCH GROWTH

By 1968, when there were 5500 members in Vietnam, the *Church News* printed a map of the three districts with the names and addresses of each district presidency.[40] Church leaders hoped that it would aid servicemen in contacting the nearest priesthood leader. At this time, W. Brent Hardy became president of the Southern Far East Mission. His monthly visits to Vietnam strengthened the districts and gave encouragement to the LDS members living there.

After the surprising Tet Offensive by the North Vietnamese in early 1968, the district president and the high council of the southern district decided to revise the home teaching program to focus on two specific challenges faced by LDS soldiers: physical injury or death, and immorality. Home teachers were counseled to contact their charges once a week, primarily to ensure that all was well with them.[41] The goal was that no Latter-day Saint soldier, no matter how isolated, should feel alone and deprived of gospel fellowship.

Consistently throughout the Vietnam conflict, faithful LDS soldiers served as a source of virtue in the military. Besides sharing the gospel with military buddies and South Vietnamese locals, one of the most important things they did was to strengthen each other. They gathered

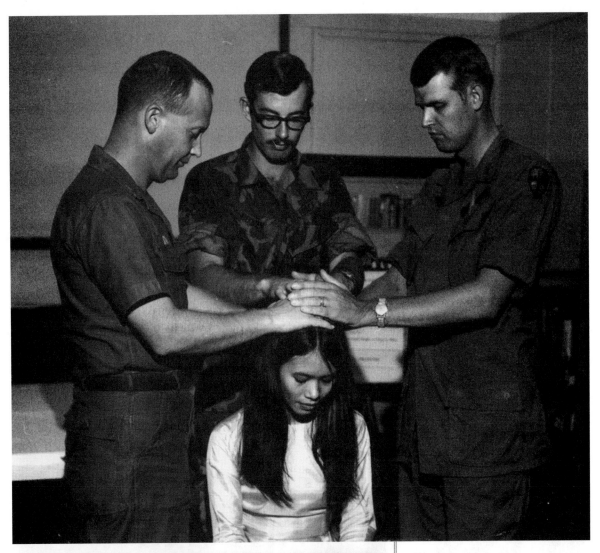

Above: A South Vietnamese young woman being confirmed shortly after her baptism. This photo is indicative of the kind of missionary work that went on throughout the country of the Republic of Vietnam, also known as South Vietnam, during the war.

Left: Paul Simkins gives a talk in the Bien Hoa chapel in 1972. Facing him directly in white civilian clothes is Nguyen Cao Minh, who was the first Vietnamese man to receive the Melchizedek priesthood.

Certificate issued to Steven Marshall in the fall of 1966 giving him authorization to conduct meetings, perform ordinances, and carry out all other Church functions as the Phu Bai LDS Group Leader.

Hartmann Rector addressing soldiers in the Vietnam conflict at the Mt. Fugi Conference in 1970.

in "families" and participated in family home evenings; they administered to sick or wounded comrades; and they served as volunteers to deliver food and supplies to impoverished South Vietnamese civilians. Time and again, these "soldier-saints" demonstrated selfless acts of heroism in assisting others within their platoons and companies. In spite of the ravages of war, they often expressed publicly in meetings their gratitude to their Heavenly Father for the opportunity to serve their country. These members of the Church constituted a great force for good during the war.

By February 1969, there were eighteen servicemen's groups and 7,500 members in South Vietnam. Any LDS soldier near a major base camp had an opportunity to enjoy the blessings of the Church. The programs of the Church were organized and functioned well enough that faithful servicemen could continue to progress in the gospel by being ordained to the Melchizedek Priesthood, receiving temple recommends, attending meetings, and doing missionary work.[42]

CHURCH-SPONSORED MILITARY TRAINING CONFERENCES

As the demands of the national draft increased, the Church Military Relations Committee developed a training program similar to that which a missionary would receive before his mission. The first of these training sessions was held in December 1968. One of the leaders present at the meeting, Elder Boyd K. Packer, compared this meeting to a meal: "We hope that this will be a great survival meal for you, to sustain you in the field. . . . That's the purpose of this."[43] Another of the Twelve, Elder Mark E. Peterson, said, "It's a different kind of mission, but yet you can accomplish many of the things that the proselyting missionaries accomplish."[44]

In a later servicemen's training conference, held in the Salt Lake City Missionary Home, Elder Harold B. Lee told the prospective soldiers, "You young men will be on a type of mission. Some of you returned missionaries, after your service, will be able to say you did as much missionary work in the service as you did in the mission field."[45] The response from the young men to talks given by the Brethren was positive. One young LDS serviceman said, "After today's meetings, I think I'm ready to go in the service, knowing that the Church supports me."[46] Another brother, upon returning from military service in Vietnam, recognized the value of his training and suggested that his combat experience was "the greatest missionary experience of his life."[47]

DEPARTMENT OF THE ARMY
HEADQUARTERS, XXIV CORPS
APO SAN FRANCISCO 96349
OFFICE OF THE STAFF CHAPLAIN

AVII-CH   11 February 1972
SUBJECT: The Church of Jesus Christ of Latter-Day Saints (Mormon)
Conference for MR-1

To Whom It May Concern:

1. Purpose: To announce a conference for all personnel of the Church of Jesus Christ of Latter-Day Saints (Mormon) in MR-1; to encourage all chaplains to disseminate information and to help provide maximum opportunity for Latter-Day Saint personnel to participate.

2. Information: The LDS Conference will be held at XXIV Corps Chapel, Camp Horn, on 6 March 1972. Participants are responsible for providing their own meals and billeting. Dining facilities are available on the compound.

3. Transportation: Individuals requiring local transportation within the Da Nang area should contact one of the individuals listed in Para 5 below.

4. Schedule: Meetings will be held Monday, 6 March 1972 as follows:

a. Leadership Meeting for Group Leaders, Counselors and District Councilmen at 1100 hours.
b. General Session from 1330 hours to 1600 hours.
c. Fireside Meeting from 1900 hours to 2000 hours.

5. Coordination: Need for transportation and questions concerning the Conference may be referred to one of the following:

Walter Clifford, CPT, USA, (District President), 277th S&S Bn, Da Nang
951-2224
Omar Green, DAC, (1st Counselor) US Army Mortuary, Da Nang, 957-4441
Louis Eldridge, DAC, (2nd Counselor) CORDS, Da Nang, 957-3341
Douglas Whitney, CPT, USA, (District Councilman) XXIV Corps, Da Nang
951-2141

Joseph C. Rowan

JOSEPH C. ROWAN
Chaplain (LTC), USA
Staff Chaplain

Above: John Robert Mallernee's copy of the official military announcement for the LDS District Conference in Da Nang.

Left: Mt. Fugi Conference 1970.

EZRA TAFT BENSON VISITS

Elder Ezra Taft Benson and other Church leaders at the April 1969 Servicemen's Conference at Mount Fuji, Japan, April 1969. The Servicemen's Conference was an annual event and conference attendees included military personnel and their families from throughout the Far East, including those who had come from Vietnam after requesting that week in Japan for their "R & R."

Elder Ezra Taft Benson addressing servicemen at the 1969 LDS Servicemen's Conference in Mt. Fugi Japan.

In April 1969, Elder Ezra Taft Benson of the Council of the Twelve visited the war-weary servicemen and held conferences in Da Nang, Bien Hoa, Nha Trang, and Saigon—covering all three Church districts in Vietnam. The scream of jets and the whirr of machine-gun fire often interrupted Elder Benson's sermons at the air bases, but he recognized "a high degree of spirituality" among the servicemen. In these conferences, Elder Benson told the men and women, "I bring you the love of President McKay and all those who serve with him. In fact, I bring the love of all the folks back home. I would remind you of the message of President McKay, 'Remember who you are, and act accordingly.'"[48] Included as a part of several of these meetings the congregation sang the hymn, "I Need Thee Every Hour." This hymn seemed to express the silent thoughts and prayers of those in attendance.[49] Encouraged and uplifted by Elder Benson's remarks, LDS servicemen and Vietnamese Saints continued sharing the gospel. Their success gave rise to a new mission.

The new Southeast Asia Mission was organized in November 1969 with G. Carlos Smith as president. Vietnam then became a zone in this new mission the next year. Later, the Vietnam zone was transferred to the Hong Kong-Taiwan Mission where it remained for the duration of the war.

THE VIETNAMESE SAINTS

By 1971 the conflict was winding down, and in answer to many prayers, LDS servicemen were being sent home. However, for the Vietnamese members the work was just beginning. In May 1971, Nguyen Cao Minh accepted a call to serve as the president of the Saigon branch. He was the first Vietnamese member to serve as a branch leader. At this point, there were enough Vietnamese members to translate during missionary discussions and even do missionary work themselves. One serviceman wrote home to report his experience in laboring with Vietnamese members. "We have been teaching the gospel to our associates. . . . Right now we are using five Vietnamese who have already joined the Church, as interpreters. . . . It takes a

It soon became evident that a Vietnamese translation of the Book of Mormon and other scripture was necessary.

lot more explaining to get the point across, but you can always see and feel the Holy Ghost working with you."[50]

Another account tells of Nguyen Van The who was initially introduced to the gospel by Roy Moore, an LDS serviceman. "Tay," as the servicemen knew him, became a leader in the Church and later served as the last president of the Saigon branch. During the fall of Saigon in 1975 he provided courageous leadership for the branch members left behind to face the invading North Vietnamese Army.[51]

It soon became evident that a Vietnamese translation of the Book of Mormon and other scripture was necessary. Sister Cong Ton Nu Tuong Vy, who was converted after having helped to translate Joseph Smith's First Vision, was asked to

Top: Nguyen Cao Minh was called to serve as the first Vietnamese member to serve as a branch leader. Photo taken Sept. 30, 1986 in the United States.

Bottom: LDS members with President Brent Hardy of the Hong Kong Mission at Conference in Saigon. Others in background: Chaplain Joseph McConkie, Brother Payne (Navy Officer) and Chaplain Smith. Sisters are some of our Vietnamese and Chinese members.

Saigon Branch, 1971.

complete a translation of the Book of Mormon. In order to find the peace to do so, she bought a small bit of land in the mountains and moved there in 1972. She prayed and read the English Book of Mormon several times, as well as other books on the life of Christ. She spent two years studying and working to complete the first Vietnamese translation of the Book of Mormon.[52]

In June 1971, William S. Bradshaw became president of the Hong Kong mission; he became responsible for the Vietnam zone. In the closing years of the war he demonstrated his commitment to this part of his mission by maintaining a rigorous schedule of visits to the servicemen's groups throughout Vietnam.

In 1973, the Paris Peace Accords ended U.S. involvement in the war and all the armed forces were removed from

Vietnam. Several thousand LDS servicemen returned home, including some who had been prisoners of war. While the accounts of the POW illustrate the awful conditions under which they lived, they also demonstrate the great faith and even some cheer in these impossible situations. One brother tells of how he was nominated chaplain by his fellow prisoners. In his room each of the denominations took one Sunday to talk about their religion. This brother took twelve Sundays because he had so much to say.[53] Another brother remembers trying to remember the verses of "Did You Think to Pray." After coming up with the first three verses, he struggled trying to remember the fourth. He found upon his release "that there are only three verses. I have the only fourth verse."[54]

From Elder Hinckley's dedication of Vietnam until the beginning of 1973, the Church had not assigned full-time missionaries to Vietnam. But in February of that year President Bradshaw of the Hong Kong mission visited Vietnam to determine if it was time to send full-time missionaries. Finding conditions appropriate, he requested permission to assign several missionaries to the country. He was overjoyed to read the reply from the Brethren: "After consideration of the matter, it was determined that you might be permitted to send four missionaries to Saigon."[55]

When the first missionaries arrived, they found a branch of Vietnamese members who had been converted through the work of the recently departed servicemen and their families. In as little as one year, the missionaries helped to balance the number of Vietnamese adult members with the number of the youth, and the number of brethren with the number of sisters.[56] The number of full-time elders increased until there were fifteen missionaries serving in Vietnam.

The network of Latter-day Saints during the Vietnam War was a bulwark of righteousness, and, as Elder Hinckley said during one of his conference addresses, a "silver thread in the dark tapestry of war."[57] He described the thread as being an enlargement of the Lord's program in a troubled land. In spite of the war, the LDS servicemen had been able to remain full of virtue and faith. They were able to share the gospel with friends they might not have met without the call to battle. Many Vietnamese people learned of the gospel, and the scriptures were prepared for later generations of Vietnamese members. Out of the bitterness, despair, controversy, and destruction of the Vietnam War came conversion, testimony, hope, and brotherhood.

EPILOGUE[58]

By March 1973, with the release of American POWs by the Hanoi regime, all combat forces departed, with the exception of a marine guard stationed at the U.S. Embassy complex in Saigon. During the two-year period that followed, the members of the Saigon branch enjoyed the service of full-time missionaries from the Hong Kong mission. Membership grew quickly despite the fact that the North Vietnamese Army continued to push south. The period of peace was short-lived as the North Vietnamese Army approached Saigon. During this time a fierce battle at Bien Hoa resulted in the destruction of the LDS chapel, which had been a place of refuge for so many over the years.

As the enemy troops drew near Saigon, panic drove thousands of South Vietnamese to escape by whatever means they could. Many were evacuated by emergency airlifts of American aircraft of all kinds. Finally, it was necessary to withdraw the missionaries and by April 4, 1975, all remaining missionary elders were safely in Hong Kong.[59] On April 14 President Jerry Wheat of the Hong Kong mission sent Elder Richard Bowman back to Saigon for the purpose of bringing a copy of all branch membership records to the mission office.[60] This proved useful in the later attempts by the Church to assist members leaving Vietnam. On April 30, 1975, the Republic of Vietnam fell. The Church then ceased to function when many Saigon branch priesthood holders were subsequently imprisoned by the North Vietnamese communists.

Membership grew quickly despite the fact that the North Vietnamese Army continued to push south.

In this picture a soldier is clearing the land for a pig farm, as a helicopter brings in supplies needed to build structures. During the war, humanitarian projects like this one were established to help the Vietnamese people. Pigs and other animals would be brought in and the Vietnamese people would be shown how to run these farms.

For the next fourteen years, floods of Vietnamese fled their homeland by whatever means they could, usually by unsafe boats launched at night in the South China Sea. Many died, while others became stateless refugees washed up on the shores of numerous countries in Southeast Asia. Among the refugees were members of the Saigon branch. The Church quickly organized a program to find, interview, and help arrange for sponsors for these Vietnamese Saints. Among the Church members who were relocated to the United States by the Church's refugee effort were Nguyen Van The and Nguyen Cao Minh. After a few years, the effort concluded when the Church believed that all Vietnamese members were either dead or out of the country.

Recognizing that more needed to be done, LDS veterans voluntarily searched through refugee camps and made inquiries of international rescue agencies regarding Church members. Interest in this effort increased when in March

1982, a letter from Xuan, the wife of Nguyen Ngoc Thach arrived at LDS Church headquarters from Vietnam. Her humble plea for contact with the Church led to the formation of an independent LDS veterans organization known as Veterans' Association for Service Activities Abroad (VASAA). One of its objectives was to find as many LDS families from Vietnam as possible and to reunite them with family members and help restore their contact with the Church.

Between 1982 and 1998, VASAA processed more than one hundred refugee and immigration cases involving six hundred people in family reunification programs. In addition, VASSA provided help in obtaining needed financial, medical, and educational aid for many of these families. VASAA representatives repeatedly traveled to Vietnam between 1985 and 1992 in an attempt to search out Church members. They found twenty-three LDS families there and were able to help sixteen of those families immmigrate to Canada, Australia, and the United States.

As a direct result of the VASAA's projects, LDS Church General Authorities returned to Vietnam beginning in late 1992. Since then, the Church has sponsored medical and educational teams to assist the Vietnamese. Branches of the Church were organized in Hanoi and Saigon in May 1996, which resulted in President Gordon B. Hinckley returning to rededicate Vietnam in a special sacrament meeting in Saigon.

A fitting culmination to the LDS veterans' efforts came on October 29, 1996, when several of them gathered at the Jordan River Temple to witness the sealing of Brother Nguyen Ngoc Thach to his wife Xuan and some of their children, including two who died in Vietnam. LDS servicemen had promised that family on July 24, 1971, that they would never forget them and would help them receive the blessings of the temple. Elder Marion D. Hanks performed the sealing ceremony that fulfilled this promise.

Veterans' Association for Service Activities Abroad (VASAA) was a not-for-profit tax-exempt war veterans' charitable organization. The Association was founded in 1982 as a result of a specific plea for help from former allies in Vietnam. The logo shows the chapel at Bien Hoa Air Base built in 1965 by American servicemen who were members of The Church of Jesus Christ of Latter-day Saints (LDS). The open doors and windows represented that the Association was open to all who believe in helping those in need.

L-R Wayne Allen, Sister and Brother Thach, Mel Palmer in front of the Jordan River Temple the day the Thachs were sealed.

ENDNOTES

1. In using the word "servicemen" the authors acknowledge the women of the Church who also served in the military in Vietnam. While fewer in number than the men, their contributions and sacrifices were no less significant.

2. Editorial, *Church News* (4 December 1965): 16 (hereafter cited as *CN*).

3. "Statement from the First Presidency," *Improvement Era* (November 1965): 952 (hereafter cited as IE).

4. Victor L Brown, "With the Servicemen in Vietnam," *IE* (December 1968): 99.

5. Joseph F. Boone, *The Roles of the Church of Jesus Christ of Latter-day Saints in Relation to the United States Military, 1900–1975* (Ph.D. diss., Brigham Young University, 1975), 558–566.

6. R. Lanier Britsch, *From the East: The History of the Latter-day Saints in Asia, 1851–1996,* (Salt Lake City, UT: Deseret Book, 1998), 426.

7. Keith E. Garner speaking at the Oakland Servicemen's Conference (7 December 1968) as cited in Joseph F. Boone, *The Roles of the Church of Jesus Christ of Latter-day Saints in Relation to the United States Military, 1900–1975* (Ph.D. diss., Brigham Young University, 1975), 473.

8. Britsch, *From the East,* 418.

9. NA, "First Convert Joins Church in South Vietnam," *CN* (24 November 1962): 7.

10. Richard C. Holloman, "The Snap of a Silver Thread: The LDS Church in Vietnam," unpublished paper, 1977, Saints at War Archive, L. Tom Perry Special Collections Library, Harold B. Lee Library, Brigham Young University, Provo, Utah, 3.

11. Britsch, *From the East,* 418.

12. NA, "First Convert Joins Church in South Vietnam," *CN* (24 November 1962): 7.; Britsch, *From the East,* 419, 420.

13. NA, "Chaplain Is Man of Courage, Almost a Legend in Own Time," *CN* (23 August 1969): 5.

14. Gordon B. Hinckley, "A Challenge from Vietnam," *IE* (June 1967): 52.

15. Vietnam Zone Historical Report (VZHR), entry: 12 July 1966.

16. Gordon B. Hinckley, "Appreciation for our Men in Military Service," *IE* (December 1966): 1122.

17. Robert Hillam, "Peace amidst War," *Ensign* (April 1989): 10–11.

18. Mary Jane Woodger, "A Latter-day Saint's Response to their Church Leaders' Counsel during the Vietnam War," Vietnam War Generation Journal 1, no. 2 (August 2001): 40.

19. NA, "A Chapel in a War Torn Land," *CN* (11 September 1965): 11.

20. Sgt John B. Mahony, "Not Fancy but the Spirit Is There," *CN* (10 December 1966): 13.

21. Britsch, *From the East,* 420.

22. NA, "Vietnam: Church Is Moving Ahead," *CN* (16 September 1967): 4; Maj. Scott Lyman, "A High degree of Spirituality," *CN* (10 May 1969): 4; Holloman, "Snap of a Silver Thread," 11.

23. Holloman, "Snap of a Silver Thread," 12.

24. Lanier Britsch and Richard C. Holloman, "The Church's Years In Vietnam," *Ensign* (August 1980): 25–30.

25. Spencer J. Palmer, *The Church Encounters Asia* (Salt Lake City, UT: Deseret Book, 1970), 143.

26. George L. Scott, "South Vietnam, Thailand Dedicated for Missionaries," *CN* (19 November 1966): 5.

27. Hinckley, "Appreciation for our Men," 1122; NA "Baptismal Service in Vietnam," *CN* (19 July 1969): 13.

28. NA "A Baptism in Vietnam Waters," *CN* (25 February 1967): 8, 15.

29. NA "Church Strong in Vietnam" *CN* (1 February 1969): 4.

30. Hinckley, "Appreciation for our Men," 1122.

31. Woodger, "A Latter-day Saint's Response," 33.

32. Boone, *Roles of the Church,* 679–681.

33. Peter Cookson, personal correspondence to Roan McClure in possession of the authors.

34. NA, "Home Evenings: Soldiers in Vietnam Assigned as Families," *CN* (28 November 1970): 6.

35. Brent LeBaron, "A Letter from Vietnam," *IE* (November 1966): 963.

36. Hack Miller, "Send Vietnam GI's Good Reading Material," *CN* (26 March 1966): 15.

37. Louis T. Bowring file, Saints at War Archive, L. Tom Perry Special Collections Library, Harold B. Lee Library, Brigham Young University, Provo, Utah.

38. Hinckley, "Appreciation for our Men," 1122.

39. NA, "Survey Indicates Servicemen Not Receiving Mail," *CN* (1 February 1969): 4.

40. NA, "LDS Servicemen Well Organized in Vietnam," *CN* (2 March 1968): 13; NA, "How to Help Servicemen," *CN* (15 June 1968): 8.

41. Desmond L. Anderson, "Meeting the Challenges of the Latter-day Saints in Vietnam," *BYU Studies 10* (Winter 1970): 189–191.

42. NA, "Church Strong in Vietnam," 4.

43. Boone, *Roles of the Church,* 748.

44. Ibid., 749.

45. Stephen W. Gibson, "A Seminar for Servicemen," *CN* (14 June 1969): 8*10

46. Woodger, "A Latter-day Saint's Response," 32.

47. Maj. Scott Lyman, "A High Degree of Spirituality," *CN* (10 May 1969): 4.

48. Hinckley, "Appreciation for our Men," 1122.

49. Nguyen Van The, "The Saigon Shepherd and the Scattered Flock," unpublished manuscript, Saints at War Archive, L. Tom Perry Special Collections Library, Harold B. Lee Library, Brigham Young University, Provo, Utah.

50. Cong Ton Nu Tuong Vy, "Out of the Tiger's Den," *Ensign* (June 1989): 44–45.

51. J. M. Heslop and Dell R. Van Orden, *From the Shadow of Death: Stories of POWs* (Salt Lake City, UT: Deseret Book, 1973), 83.

52. Ibid., 111.

53. Britsch, *From the East,* 433.

54. Britsch and Holloman, "Church's Years in Vietnam," 29.

55. Gordon B. Hinckley, "A Silver Thread in the Dark Tapestry of War," *IE* (June 1968): 48.

56. Much of the prologue is courtesy of Virgil Kovalenko, the past president and a founding member of VASAA (Veteran's Association for Service Activities Abroad).

57. Holloman, "Snap of a Silver Thread," 39–40.

58. Jerry Wheat (talk given at the tenth anniversary of VASAA, Temple Square, Salt Lake City, UT, 1992). Copy in possession of the authors.

BYU group performing at the 1969 LDS Servicemen's Conference in Mt. Fugi Japan.

DAVID D. ADAMS

As a young 24-year-old army medic, David served a year's tour of duty as a clinical specialist with the 1st Medical Battalion in the 1st Infantry Division. After Vietnam he graduated from the Physician's Assistant Program at the University of Utah. He has been a practicing PA since 1972. He currently lives in Idaho.

It was my mother who was the greatest help during this time of great concern in my life. As the days went quickly by, I became more and more anxious about going off to war. I knew my anxiousness and concern were upsetting Mom also, but I just didn't know how to handle it. On the day before I was to travel back to Salt Lake City and catch the plane to Oakland, California, to be shipped overseas, Mom told me she wanted to talk to me. As we sat down together, she picked up a copy of the Book of Mormon. Mom turned to a chapter in the book of Alma, and began to read about a group of 2,000 young men who were going off to fight in a war at that time. These young men never had fought in a war before, and yet in their own words they said to their leader Helaman, "Father, behold our God is with us, and he will not suffer that we should fall; then let us go forth. . . . Now they never had fought, yet they did not fear death; and they did think more on the liberty of their fathers than they did upon their lives; yea, they had been taught by their mothers, that if they did not doubt, God would deliver them" (Alma 56:46–47).

Above: David Adams in his hooch (living quarters) in DiAn, Vietnam.

Below: Specialist 6th Class Jim Spencer and Dave Adams standing in front of the Clearing Station (much like a hospital) in DiAn, Vietnam.

Right: Dave with the guys who shared a hooch in Daug Tieng, Vietnam—an area near the Michelin rubber plantation that was known as the "fish-hook" of Vietnam. L–R: Ron Webb (Dave baptized Ron in the Saigon River), Tom Rodgers (who also joined the LDS church while in Vietnam), Ray Santher, and Dave Adams.

I have often wondered if my mother knew this was my favorite scripture. I had often pictured in my mind as a child those valiant, young warriors going off to battle with no fear because of their faith and the teachings of their parents. I had always hoped that somehow I could exhibit those same kinds of courageous qualities if I was ever in a similar situation. As Mom and I talked and sat together, on that solemn day in our lives, we discussed both her and my hopes and aspirations. She said that she didn't think she measured up to being a good mother as well as those mentioned in the Book of Mormon. I assured her that she had always done her very best to teach me to have courage, never to doubt, and to put my utmost trust in God. We made a pact on that special day that whenever either of us was afraid, lonely, discouraged or concerned while I was away at war that we would pick up the Book of Mormon. We would turn to those sacred passages and whatever concerns we may have had would be swept away with the faith exhibited by those 2,000 plus valiant young men. Many

Left: Dave with the guys he trained with to become a clinical specialist at Letterman General Hospital in San Francisco, California. This picture was taken just before they shipped out to Vietnam. L–R: Jerry Halsey, Cliff Beuregard, Dennis Allison, Dave Adams, and Troy Britton (Troy joined the LDS church while serving in Vietnam).

Below top: A group of medics taking wounded soldiers from a helicopter on litters and getting them into the Clearing Station for treatment. Dau Tieng, Vietnam.

Below bottom: Dave treating a Vietnamese patient in the Clearing Station in Dau Tieng, Vietnam.

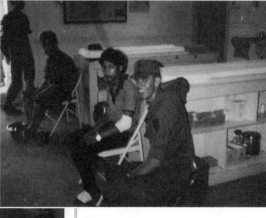

times during my tour of duty in Vietnam, both Mom and I put this pact we had made with each other, to the test. It always consoled and comforted us. The prayers my darling mother offered up to God to protect her son were the same prayers offered by those loving mothers long ago for their sons, as they followed that great leader Helaman into battle.

* * * * *

There were six of us that lived in the hooch together in Dau Tieng: Tom, Ron, Dennis, Al, Cliff and myself. I was the only member of the Church when we first moved in together. Ron W. was a young soldier and medic who had extended his tour of duty twice, six months each time for a total of one year. As Ron and I easily became close friends it was evident to me that he was a troubled young man who could not get a realistic grip on life and what its meanings were in regard to him. We had many close and personal talks with one another. One time when I asked him why he had extended his tour twice, he reflected on the question and then answered, "I really don't know why." He couldn't put his finger on just one reason; there apparently were many reasons.

However, a few months later, I had the privilege of blessing and baptizing Ron in the Saigon River. As he came up out of the water he looked into my eyes directly and said, "Now I know the real reason I extended my tour." I chokingly fought back the tears, realizing just how much the gospel had changed this young man's life and perspective.

D. LARRY ANDERSON

Larry served in the Army in Vietnam from August 1968 to June 1970 as an infantry sergeant in the Infantry Delta Company of the 198th Infantry Brigade. He is currently the director of the Utah Division of Water Resources. He has served in numerous Church callings, including bishop and high councilor.

The men I served with had a belief in and a love of God. Being in a situation where you could see death and injury at any moment causes you to look for strength and answers to questions of why, how come, from a Superior Being. Many carried Bibles with them and some of the guys would meet together from time to time for Bible study. It was my experience that everyone had a belief in God. I believe the old statement that

When given the choice of whether he wanted to carry the radio or machine gun, Larry Anderson said that it was an easy choice. He had walked point (the first man in a column of soldiers that was most likely to trip a mine or walk into an ambush) enough to know that he did not want to do it any longer. He enjoyed carrying the radio, because he knew exactly what was going on at all times.

there are no atheists in foxholes is true. I also believe that most of us offered a silent prayer often for protection.

Those who were called to serve their country in Vietnam were good men who left families and loved ones to put their lives on the line. Many did not return home and others returned with terrible battle scars and wounds. I pray we will never forget them and someday they may be recognized for their sacrifice and patriotism.

I still remember the day at the Salt Lake [Utah] airport just like it was yesterday when I had to kiss Cozette and Eric for the last time and tell them that I loved them as I boarded the plane. It may have been the most difficult time of my life as I loved them both very much and knew Cozette would worry while I was gone. It was emotional to say good-bye, especially finding out the day before that Cozette was now two months pregnant. She had a miscarriage about five months later.

I do believe God watched over me and my family while we were apart. I never felt I was going to be hurt in Vietnam. In fact, I had a strong conviction I would be okay and would return home safely, which is exactly what happened. Questions have haunted me for years, such as why God would allow such a terrible war to

Jim Maness sleeping in a NVA hammock in the jungle, ready to answer his radio at any time.

occur? Why were so many great young men killed or seriously injured in a war we were not allowed to win? Why was I protected and able to come home uninjured? I guess I have felt some guilt for returning home unhurt while many of my friends were injured or died. Over the years I have concluded I am not going to find the answer to my questions here on earth, but I suspect I will understand it some day when I have a chance to meet Christ.

* * * * *

One of my company commanders was Captain James A. Fivian, a great CO [commanding officer] who I have the greatest respect for. It was his third tour of duty in Vietnam and he was about twenty-nine years old. He remained our commander for six months. He found out that three of us were LDS, and every Sunday when the Tabernacle Choir broadcast was on the Armed Forces Radio Network (many carried transistor radios with them in the field), he stopped the company for a rest break. He never told the rest of the company why he always stopped at the same time each week, but he told us it was so the Mormon boys could go to church. It certainly wasn't a traditional religious service, but it was an opportunity to be with Doug and Doc and listen to the choir and the *Spoken Word*.

The U.S. military adopted a program in Vietnam that allowed enemy soldiers who had surrendered (Chieu Hoi [Open Arms] Program) to be retrained and serve with an American unit as a Kit Carson Scout. They usually served directly under the company commander and traveled with the command post. There could be one or two Kit Carson Scouts assigned to a unit. You were always a little concerned when they first joined the unit, not knowing for certain if they had given up their loyalty to North Vietnam. During my time in Vietnam we had two scouts: one was an ex-NVA officer about twenty-eight years old named Cong, the other was an 18-year-old ex-Viet Cong soldier who had been wounded named

Top: Much of the terrain in Vietnam was dense jungle. These squad members on a jungle trail had to be very quiet so that the enemy would not hear them.

Bottom: Douglas Murphy of Vernal, Utah.

Opposite: Marines cross the Cam Lo River on a search and clear mission near the demilitarized zone.

Chieu Hoied. Cong was a Buddhist and was married with a child. His family lived in a city in South Vietnam. They were all brutally killed by the NVA while he was serving with our company. Vang was a Catholic who had been rounded up in his village in South Vietnam at the age of sixteen and told he was now fighting for the Viet Cong. I wasn't certain I ever trusted Cong, but I became very good friends with Vang during the three months we traveled together. We ate together and shared the same tent each night. During the rainy season Vang would get up and

Kit Carson Scouts

During the spring of 1966, the United States Marines began recruiting disaffected Viet Cong to serve as scouts and advisors for patrols into enemy territory. From the tradition of the Indian scouts who assisted the United States Cavalry in the nineteenth century, these Vietnamese scouts became known as Kit Carson Scouts.

The scouts soon demonstrated their value to their American allies. They proved to be capable soldiers with useful understanding of local conditions and enemy strategies. Vietnamese locals trusted the scouts and provided them with information that they would not share with Vietnamese army regulars or the United States Marines. In addition to providing a military advantage, the scouts also served as a useful propaganda tool.

Nearly 7,000 Vietnamese served as Kit Carson Scouts. At the end of the war in 1975 over 4,000 were in active service. After the fall of Saigon, the North Vietnamese systematically identified the scouts who had worked for the United States. These individuals were killed or imprisoned in special camps. The ultimate fate of the Kit Carson Scouts remains unknown.

go out and find something to cover up the end of the tent so I would not get wet. He always said, "Andy number one, VC number ten." Between Vang's Pidgin English and the thirty Vietnamese words I knew we got along great. I've often wondered what happened to the Kit Carson Scouts especially after the U.S. left and the North Vietnamese took over the country.

* * * * *

We had been firing and throwing hand grenades into an area where we thought the NVA [North Vietnamese Army] was hiding for about an hour. Captain Smith, who was just around the bend in the river, (three hundred feet away) said the only way to find out where a sniper is, is to draw fire. He took his .38 pistol in one hand and a hand grenade in the other and started running across the river channel instructing everyone to open fire to give him cover. He got about halfway across the river channel and was shot. He fell in the channel a few feet from Gump and Joey. No one could get to him and he gradually died. Captain Smith was only twenty-two years old, and had a goal to be the youngest major in the Army. He had been in Vietnam continuously for almost two years and had gone through a divorce while in Vietnam.

Our biggest fear as infantry soldiers was tripping a land mine or booby trap. In the nine months I was in the field, we had over 20 soldiers killed and 40–50 injured in my company.

Of that amount about two thirds were killed or injured by mines and booby traps. To have a buddy killed by a mine or booby trap was a devastating and emotional blow. One moment they were walking just in front of you, the next moment there was an explosion and they were dead or seriously injured. The worst part was there was no one to shoot at or relieve the anger and frustration you felt. The booby trap may have been placed several days or weeks earlier, so the guy who had set it was long gone.

One morning about three-and-one-half months after arriving in Vietnam, one of our platoons hit a booby trap that

Top: ARVNs cooking a water buffalo lunch that they had earlier shot for both their company and the American company with them.

Left: The life of a soldier includes amenities such as this shower.

Right: Platoon members: Terry Lowery, Doug Murphy, Glen Shaler (Gramps), Ray Whitman. (Ray was killed a few weeks later.)

killed five and wounded six. They had set up around a tree and there was either a booby trap in the tree or someone had tripped a Bouncing Betty mine. The platoon leader, platoon sergeant, platoon RTO [radio telephone officer], medic and one other person were killed and six other guys seriously wounded. The entire platoon was wiped out in a split second.

I saw men who had tripped a land mine get a leg blown off. I have talked with them while we waited for a dust-off to take them to a hospital. They did not feel anything. They generally were not bleeding. They were in shock. The reason we kept so much distance between us when we moved through the rice paddies was the concern we had with mines and booby traps. The theory was if you stayed at least thirty feet apart and someone set off a mine; in most cases they were the only one that would be injured. Your buddy in front or behind you in most cases would be unhurt. This worked most of the time and only on rare occasions did more than one person get hurt.

STEPHEN ANDERSON

Stephen was born in Washington. While in Vietnam he served in the Army's 8th and 4th Artillery from 1967–1971. Currently he is the owner of a painting company in Arizona and is first assistant in the high priest group leadership of his ward.

In Vietnam I was stationed on the DMZ [demilitarized zone]. This was a strip of land between North and South Vietnam or better known as no-man's-land, which both the North and the South tried to claim. On the DMZ there was a hill called J. J. Carroll. We were dug in deep and lived underground like moles and we had large bunkers with the tops covered with several layers of sandbag. Even though we were hit almost every day by rockets or mortars after a time of getting used to that we felt somewhat safe there. The times we did not feel safe were when we left that hill and went out on what we called missions. This was when we would go to locations to help with the infantry and try to hold off some of the many big attacks that happened out on the bush.

We never knew what was going to happen and the fear we went through was extremely intense. I had been on a few missions and I knew what to expect. After one or two missions it wasn't quite so bad. One evening we got a call that gun two and three were to pack up and be ready to go out first thing in the morning. They never told us where we would be going, only that we would be told when we were on the road or just before we left. In some cases we would have an idea of how long and could try to load up on supplies. My gun was Gun Two. As I said before, I had some idea what to expect but for whatever reason I felt really bad about going out on this specific mission. I tried to convince myself that this was just fear setting in and that all would be okay, but as the night went on I felt worse. I knew if I were to go out on that mission I would not be coming back alive. I had heard that some men knew just before they died that they were going to, and I just knew that my time had come. I was not a member of any church at the time, but I felt I knew God and I believed He listened to prayers. That night I went off to some place alone, and I said a prayer to my Heavenly Father. In the prayer I said something that I didn't understand at the time and never gave it much thought until later.

I told my Father in Heaven that if He could somehow stop us from going out on that mission that day I promised I would baptize my son. The next morning a jeep had arrived from the rear carrying some mail and the one who was driving that jeep was an ex-point man from

VC TERRORIST CAPTURED PLANTING PRESSURE MINE IN ROAD NEAR TUY HOA

Viet Cong terrorist Phan Hoa, 22, who confessed that he and a companion had laid 16 land mines, five of which caused 72 civilian deaths in the past five weeks, is shown at Tuy Hoa District head-quarters after his capture, March 22.

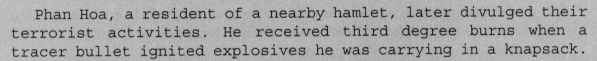

The terrorists were caught in a government ambush just outside of Tuy Hoa, the capital of Phu Yen Province, about 380 kilometers or 240 miles northeast of Saigon.

When surprised on the road by a hidden unit of the 47th Vietnamese Division the terrorists were preparing to plant yet more pressure sensitive mines. One terrorist was killed in the shooting that followed.

Phan Hoa, a resident of a nearby hamlet, later divulged their terrorist activities. He received third degree burns when a tracer bullet ignited explosives he was carrying in a knapsack.

The government ambush was just a few kilometers from the site of minings which began with separate detonations on February 14, in which 54 Vietnamese civilians were killed and 18 wounded in an explosion under a large bus, and later under a three-wheel Lambretta.

On March 18, another 15 Vietnamese civilians were killed when another Lambretta three-wheel bus touched off a Viet Cong mine.

Other mines killed three additional civilians.

Authorities believe the mines were used to terrorize villagers returning to their homes from refugee camps in the area. The Viet Cong also have been seeking revenge against the area's villagers because they cooperated with a large-scale Allied operation earlier this year which succeeded in denying thousands of tons of rice to the guerrillas.

the infantry. The man said, "They know you are coming." At the bottom of the hill on the road out there he had spotted a land mine. This was not your ordinary land mine. This land mine was buried underground with only a tip the size of a dime poking up. It would take something very heavy to set it off like a 175 tank, the same one I would have been taking down the hill. It was my gun that would have been first. The captain cancelled the mission for a different day. I knew God had saved me that day and from that day forward I felt I was going to make it home alive. This gave me some comfort for the rest of my tour.

DONALD G. ANDREWS

As a Florida resident, Don served in Vietnam as a commander of the 17th Assault Helicopter Company in the Army. Currently he lives in Utah and is a commercial aviation pilot. He has served as a bishop in his ward.

During this second tour I was involved in combat on a daily basis, flying assault helicopters in the areas where people are shooting at you and so forth. I think the fact that I was a member of the Church, that I had been to the temple, and that I had received a blessing prior to coming to Vietnam that I would be protected gave me a feeling of assurance. I was flying and involved in some pretty intense things and I don't know if it was a conscious or just an unconscious feeling that I felt I would be okay.

The Sundays where I had an opportunity to gather with other members of the Church was a very strengthening thing to me. In my first assignment we could find only three members of the Church on our base. The three of us would meet at the end of our long days, no matter what time of day it was, and on Sundays, we would get together and have a sacrament service. We would often come in muddy and dirty and stack our rifles in the corner of the tent and meet. I remember joking that if one of us couldn't be there, we would really be disappointed because one guy had to bless the sacrament, one had to pass it, and the other one had to give a talk.

* * * * *

I have always had a love of country. A deep love for this wonderful country that we live in, and I think that one of the first impressions that I have of combat is the camaraderie that there is amongst Americans. I recall one of my very first missions in which there was an aircraft shot down and it wasn't in our unit. It was in a completely different unit miles away from where we were operating, but we stopped everything that we were doing to go over to rescue that American crew; to surround them, and to pull them out safely. I was impressed that one single American life is so important and that you know you don't leave anybody behind. You do everything you can to get everybody back. There was no hesitation to do that. It was almost instantaneous that you know, when you have to go rescue somebody you go do it. There are no questions, no ifs, ands, or buts. I think there is a sense of loyalty amongst Americans that are serving under those kinds of trying circumstances that is wonderful to observe and be a part of.

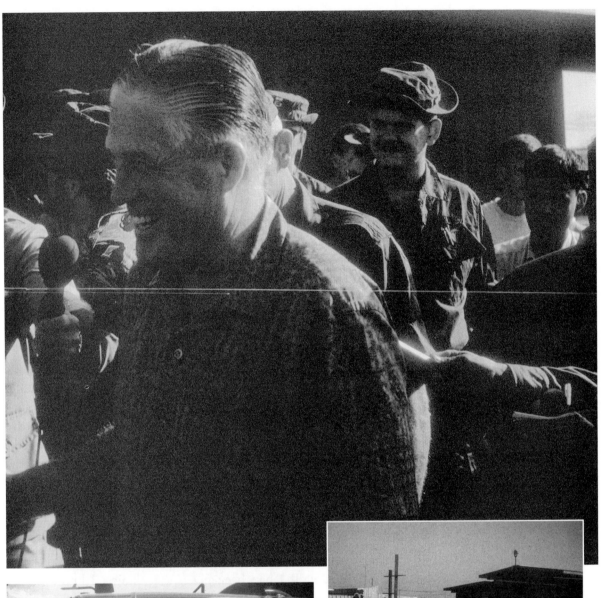

Above: Presidential candidate George Romney (December 1967) visits LDS servicemen at Chu Chi, Vietnam.

Above Inset: Governor Romney's visit at Chu Chi.

Left: Colonel (then Major) Donald G. Andrews.

ROBERT K. BANZ

Robert served with the U.S. Army during the Vietnam War from 1965–1968. He was part of the 135th H.E.M. Company, 69th Maintenance Battalion. He is currently working in education, and has taught at the LDS Church College of Western Samoa. He has earned his B.S., M.S., and is working on his doctorate degree in education.

Top: Sp/4 Robert Banz playing his guitar at Cam Ranh Bay.

Bottom: Sp/4 Robert Banz was at Cam Ranh Bay from 1966–1967.

In the fall of 1966 word went out that Apostle Gordon B. Hinckley and Elder Marion D. Hanks would be visiting Vietnam. By the first of December we knew that Apostle Hinckley would be visiting the central region of Vietnam and that a conference would be held on the military base at Pleiku on Christmas day. The prospect of attending a conference with an Apostle seemed unreal. The thought that someone who had a wife and a family waiting for them back in Salt Lake [City, Utah] would voluntarily be in Vietnam on Christmas day made no sense. I knew that he had willingly accepted an assignment to be with us. We had to be in Vietnam on Christmas; he didn't. The decision he made to be with us, foregoing the pleasures of spending Christmas day at home with his family, has always been a witness of President Hinckley's willingness to sacrifice his own for the welfare of others. I have always appreciated that. If I had been given that choice, I know exactly where I would have been.

Elder Hinckley greeted us the best he could. It was the largest gathering of Saints I had seen since attending a stake conference in Nashville, Tennessee, while I was stationed at Fort Campbell, Kentucky. We were taught by him. We were encouraged by him. We learned that it was okay to be doing what we were doing. The spirit was great. When I left that meeting I was walking on air. The spirit lingered the whole day. That day was my best day ever in Vietnam. The conference came to a close. The brethren basked in the spirit as we mingled and shared our experiences. We didn't want the day to end.

I don't recall much about the trip back to Cam Ranh. I was so filled with the spirit of the day. I do remember climbing the hill to my compound and feeling that my day was the best ever. As soon as I entered camp I could feel a different spirit around me. My buddies had, of course, had Christmas day off too. They had slept in late but had started their Christmas party early. For the most part, they were all drunk. I learned that there had been a number of fights; one guy even had to be taken to the hospital. I found several friends passed out, inebriated. As usual I helped clean them up and get them into their bunks. The tent and compound were in shambles from the partying, but that could be cleaned up in the morning. I crawled onto my bunk, reminiscing about my activities of the day and the glorious experiences the Lord had provided for me.

One Sunday I learned that a Church conference was going to be held. The conference was going to be held at the airfield

Sp/4 Robert Banz outside his hooch. He has just returned from the field in Cam Ranh Bay.

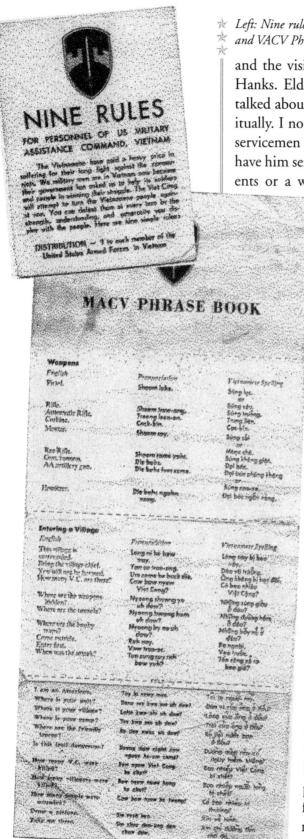

and the visiting authority was going to be Elder Marion D. Hanks. Elder Hanks took time to visit with each of us. We talked about our concerns and about how we were doing spiritually. I noticed that he took the time to compile a list of the servicemen he visited with. He asked us if we would like to have him send a note to anyone special back home such as parents or a wife. He took down the addresses. The personal priesthood interview he conducted that day was one of the most uplifting events in my life. It came at a time when it was needed most. He brought the Savior's peace to us in a place that had very little peace. I will forever be grateful to him for his willingness to serve us. His service to us went far beyond that which was expected.

RICHARD W. BEASON

Dick advanced to rank of Lt. Colonel during his service in the Marines. He joined the Church in 1962 and held many callings while in the service. His military responsibility in the Marines was directing bombing strikes on enemy positions.

While stationed as a marine major in Da Nang, South Vietnam, I came across a message about an upcoming Latter-day Saint military conference at Mount Fuji, Japan. I hurried to the senior chaplain and asked him if our 180 Latter-day Saint servicemen could attend. The chaplain, who recognized that Vietnam was an arid spiritual environment, was enthusiastic about letting us participate. He soon obtained the commanding general's permission.

Our sole obstacle was transportation: the men could go to the Fuji conference only if they could find spare seats on military flights to Japan. A member of the Church who worked at the Cam Ranh Bay flight operations building had recently promised to help any member find transportation from Vietnam, but when we reached the building, no one could find him. Our large group anxiously watched jets arrive and depart. Each plane to Japan was full to capacity.

After ten hours of disappointment, a Latter-day Saint colonel, realizing that we had been relying on the arm of flesh, suggested that everyone find a private place to pray. We quickly dispersed.

Soon, a miraculous chain of events occurred in Japan. As a certain jet prepared to depart for a round trip to Vietnam via Saigon, Cam Ranh Bay, and Da Nang, a sudden snowstorm covered the runway and caused a delay. Then a tire blew out

Major General Ormand Simpson USMC (L) presents the Bronze Star with Combat "V" to Major Richard W. Beason USMC (R) 1969, at the Marine Corps Supply Center in Albany, Georgia.

and the plane had to be towed to a hangar. To make up for lost time, the repaired airliner was routed directly to Cam Ranh Day, where we waited.

When our group was paged for boarding, we wondered how many of us they meant. To our amazement, the plane had 180 vacant seats. Combat-hardened veterans wept and hugged each other, shouting for joy. All of us boarded the flight and buckled our belts gratefully.

Only those who have experienced war know the physical sensation of leaving a combat zone: it feels like you are shedding a great weight. Tension flows out of your body as the plane gains altitude, and pretty soon you realize that you've made it out alive. After we were airborne, a flight attendant came down the aisle with a cart.

"Would you care for a beer?"

"No thank you, ma'am."

"How about coffee or tea?"

"No thanks."

After ten rows of such replies, she paused and asked, "What's the matter with you guys?" Several men shouted in unison, "We're Mormons!"

The conference rejuvenated us spiritually, emotionally, and physically. Even after twenty-five years, I often recall my gratitude for being part of that divinely orchestrated exodus.

Taken from "Our Prayers Took Flight" August 1994, *Ensign* p. 56.

STEPHEN G. BIDDULPH

With only three hours' notice, Stephen was on his way to South Vietnam, leaving behind his two children and an expecting wife, Elaine. He became a spotter for the 1st Vietnamese Marine Battalion and participated in two major attacks behind enemy lines. He was wounded on the second attack, and after rehabilitation, returned to full duty and completed twenty years of active duty service, retiring in February 1990.

The last night in Saigon I was very nervous. The next day we were to be assigned and fly to our areas, which brought it even nearer. I couldn't sleep, and about 1:00 A.M. I got up and fumbled in the dark for my patriarchal blessing and padded downstairs. It was deserted, so I went in one of the toilet stalls and sat down. It was very hot, and as I sat there the sweat dripped from all over my body. I needed to think, so I took out the blessing, read it, and then reread certain parts.

I've always had a deep reverence for and belief in the origin of that blessing. Certain parts seemed particularly to stand out at that time and give me strength. I remember in particular that I was told to be bold in defense of truth, to be a representative of the Church. So I took courage because the Lord told me to be bold. I was also promised that the Comforter should tell me the Lord's will and forewarn me of danger. I was promised that the sea, land, and air would be safe to my travel. I should be numbered among the most faithful of my ancestors and have faith likened even unto Paul of old and exercise faith particularly in the Lord's promise to seek ye first the kingdom of God and all else will be added. I pondered those things in my heart and then prayed and asked our Heavenly Father to help me gain this strength and do His will.

After my prayer I was consumed by a spirit so real and yet so natural and compatible with my nature that it seemed to embrace me and immediately, with no word of communication, all fear was dispelled. I imagine that the experience could be compared to the soothing phenomenon of a father picking up his crying son and comforting away all his fears. I felt literally freed from all cares and woes that had plagued my soul less than a minute ago. I felt as if I was in the very embrace of the Holy Ghost and all worry fled suddenly from my soul. In a matter of less than thirty seconds the fears that had literally caused me to tremble were removed and I felt "calm as a summer's morn." There in that toilet stall with the filth written on the walls, the Holy Spirit reached out and touched my troubled heart. I got up, picked up my blessing, went to bed, and slept peacefully until morning.

Somewhat later, after this experience, I received a letter from Howard. He related to me that on an earlier date he had worried and contemplated about my state of affairs. He had prayed about this concern, and he felt as though he could almost perceive me. It was dark where I was, and he could see that I was troubled. He prayed that I would be comforted and saw by the Spirit that I was. Since that time he had no real worry about my safety, for a statement from a revelation was impressed on his mind as it was on mine: "Thy days are known and shall not be numbered less." Our mutual experience is a testimony to the beautiful truth of the power of the spirit of the Comforter.

* * * * *

At eventide, our unit moved into a small village recently destroyed by battle. The stench of death was everywhere. As I walked along a small paddy dike, a dead enemy soldier lay in the adjacent field. By that time I had become accustomed to the ugly face of death. But I was interested when I heard that our soldiers had found papers on the dead enemy, a diary of sorts. This piqued my interest, and I became obsessed with finding out what the final thoughts of this hated enemy were.

I was able to obtain a rough English translation of the diary entry, which I read that night by the light of my flashlight. The enemy soldier wrote about being sent south to fight the American invaders, how they fought bravely, but how he hated war. He missed his family in the north. He missed nature, the birds, animals, and forests. He just wanted to go home. I sat stunned by what I had read. We were not enemies. We were brothers. We were alike despite our cultural and political differences. That diary had a profound influence on changing my attitude about war and the enemy, and I realized at that point that I was not a man of war, but one of peace. The power of the gospel and the universality of man descended upon me powerfully.

* * * * *

There were two bunkers in the house. The house itself was thatched and made out of flimsy wood with all sides relatively open. One evening as we lay talking, a recoilless rifle started shooting at us. The shell roared in and exploded just short of our house, sending everyone scurrying for cover. It caught us by surprise, but in a matter of two seconds everyone but me was stuffed in a bunker underground. The little bunkers were built for Vietnamese, not burly Americans, and anyway my legs were too stiff and I could hardly move. I got to my feet and in sheer desperation walked behind a three-foot sandbagged wall and lay down. I had on a flak jacket and I pulled my helmet down over my face, but all I had over my head was the thatched roof. My feet and head were unprotected, and I felt like a duck on an open slough.

There was deadly silence while everyone waited for the enemy gunners to make their corrections and fire again. Only the occasional crackle of the radio could be heard in those few seconds. Yet it was in those hallowed seconds of deadly silence when it seemed that certain physical destruction was the only future that I had on earth, that I had one of the most beautiful and moving experiences of my life. It was a time when the veil was pulled, and I became acutely aware of those things that are real in this life,

Marines search a North Vietnamese Army trooper who surrendered to them during a firefight on Operation "Prairie II."

not the material things that swell the heart with false pride, but the simple things of the spirit and of family and of eternity. And I found, for the first time, that beautiful and simple means of communication—real communication—with our Heavenly Father. I was up there before Him, pleading with Him, trying to tell Him I could accept whatever He had in store for me, but praying I'd be spared for my family—my wife expecting a baby within a few months, and my two little sons, scarcely more than babies themselves. I also prayed a lot for the others. Stripped away were the formalities that all too often bog us down, and there flowed forth a sincere supplication with a willingness to abide by the will of the Lord and I felt Him there listening and loving me. In the silence of that moment there was a transmission of power that bore the spirit up and made it equal to the task.

Then came a huge roar followed by the hiss of the round. It sounded like a huge freight train bearing down on one tied to the tracks. It screamed just over the roof of our house and exploded just beyond, sending pieces of metal crashing into the roof above my head. Now they had their data. The next one we knew would be right on top of us and so we waited.

I don't know what thoughts the others had, but I talked with God. I never was petrified at the thought of dying. I was scared but calm enough to lie there and meditate on the whole thing. Ever since coming to Vietnam I had not worried about being killed. I had received a message from the Comforter that first night in Saigon when I worried so much. So here I was now, shot through both legs, lying behind a wall with bullets and bombs crashing in, and I just had to ask again if everything was really going to work out for my protection. I don't believe I ever really felt I was going to die. I guess no man does. Yet my reason told me that we could not survive that next shot which was sure to be corrected to an accurate hit.

As I look back on those worrisome moments in the field waiting for the helicopters to come, I remember a row of Vietnamese marines and myself lying on our backs behind a small dike in the hot sun. Gently there was a touch on my sleeve; no word. I looked over, and a Vietnamese looked at me with a thirst I could see in his eyes. He lay immobilized by his burns. His lips were parched and his face showed pain. I leaned over and put the canteen to his lips.

Then I saw an entire row of men in the same condition—all worried, all tired, all burned terribly. They lay with swollen, still arms and scorched faces under the blistering sun. Down the row I crawled, across the hard ground and poured the precious water into their upturned lips, and I found joy in their relief. Then I spotted one lying on a stretcher who was nearing advanced stages of shock. I crawled over there and gave him some water. It trickled out the sides of his mouth and as I lay by him I saw his eyes go glassy and bright. I could see that they were now blind. His jaw rhythmically jutted out for a period of about one minute and then he was perfectly still. His unseeing eyes stared toward heaven; his unspeaking mouth was slightly open; his dead body lay upon the ground to which it would return. There were about thirty-six bodies on the LZ [landing zone]. There was no water left.

Only later did I find out just how much I was blessed. About two hours after we left the field, the NVA [North Vietnamese Army] put about ten direct hits with their recoilless rifle on the very house I was in, reducing it to rubble and burned timbers. Some say I was extremely lucky, and others think it a marvelous coincidence, yet I know where this luck came from. All the doctors I saw marveled at the simplicity of my wounds. The left leg was a clean shot clear through with little muscle damage. A little higher and it would have severed the artery and I would have died. The right leg had infection in it from the three-day exposure, but an operation took care of that. I could have lost my leg, but as it was, only the muscle was destroyed. No major nerves or arteries were hit, no broken bones. The bone was visible from the kneecap down, and the artery was pulsing in view. That is how close I came to death. I would be grossly blind and ungrateful not to give my Father in Heaven my undying thanks and dedication for His miracle to me.

RONALD BILLINGS

Ronald was born in Arizona. As a Marine, he served in the 2nd Platoon, Mike Company of the 1st Marine Division. His assignments included that of pilot, intelligence, forward observer, radio operator, and navigator. He was involved in the "Truoi River Bridge Security" Operation, and Operation "Houston Phase II." He is currently living in Washington where he is a wildlife photographer.

During this day we continued with Operation Houston Phase II and followed a dry riverbed to the base of a mountain. We proceeded to follow the rest of the company up the mountain trail. As we approached the top, there were two routes leading down: a side that had been shelled where not too many trees were left standing; and a side that had not been shelled, still with a lot of jungle. We were supposed to take the shelled side down, but because it was more difficult our company commander decided that we should take the jungle side down instead, where we would be picked up somewhere on the beach. As we started down, most of the company was in good spirits; there were even some sounds of humming in the air. It was more like a walk in the park. We looked like a bunch of Seven Dwarves marching along that trail. We had traveled down the mountain trail, maybe three hundred or four hundred yards, when crack, crack, boom, boom!!! A grenade had landed near my feet, injuring my right eardrum. The force of the explosion picked up a boulder and dropped it right on the tip of my nose, not really hurting me, except for my ear, and my head was really confused and foggy. For a moment I did not even know where I was: A feeling that did not last very long. Our radioman that was right behind me was killed! Our staff sergeant, who was behind him, was wounded in the upper arm. He wrapped our comrade in his poncho and dragged his lifeless body down the trail towards me. Just a few days before, I had pulled a large thorn out of his hands. He was just like a big, gentle kid. I will never forget taking hold of that poncho and continuing to drag and carry my friend's lifeless body down the trail.

It was then my job to make out the KIA [killed in action] tag and attach it to his boot. It was a sorrowful thing I had to do. We could hear many more sounds of crack, crack, and explosions further down the trail. We knew that 1st and 3rd Platoons were getting hit hard. My 2nd Platoon stayed the night in a clearing further up the trail. During the night, helicopters from Da Nang flew over 1st and 3rd Platoons positions. We would watch machine-gun tracer rounds shooting up from the ground, hitting the choppers as they flew in to help. The gunfire from the ground was too intense for the choppers to stay around. The next morning word came back that the corpsman from our platoon was needed up. That meant me! So, along with several Marines, I headed down the trail to meet with the 1st and 3rd Platoons. As we approached the command post, there were several wounded Marines, as well as our severely wounded senior corpsman. At least one of our corpsman had been killed. I could hear small arms fire and numerous explosions going off. I was so frightened. The next thing I heard was something that to this day causes me great grief; there was an explosion and out of that explosion came the cry and screams of a young Marine, screaming the words, "Mommy, Mommy!" I will never forget hearing him and the terrible sounds of war. The next thing I heard was, "Corpsman up" and someone else said, "Doc, it's your turn." So like a scared rabbit, I headed up the hill to see what was needed, all the time not wanting to look up, fearing that the minute I did, I would be shot. I made it to the top of the hill where another Marine was crouched behind the tree. First thing he saw was my hand bleeding and said, "Doc, you've

got your first Heart." He then proceeded to tell me that there
was a wounded Marine farther down below his position in a
gully. I could not believe that I was heading down the hill to find
the Marine that was wounded. The whole time I was praying to
my Father in Heaven for his protection and never looked up. I
finally made it to the wounded Marine. How, I don't know, but I
did. He had been hit with shrapnel from a grenade. His face and
body were covered with wounds. I treated him the best I could
and then helped him get back to the CP [command post].

There were numerous times that my Father in Heaven
protected me. He kept me from taking someone else's life by

*American soldiers making their way
through the thick brush of Vietnam.*

accident. He kept that first grenade from hitting me directly.
He kept that sniper from killing me. He kept me from being
in that first platoon that walked into an ambush. He preserved
my life while I was lying in a foxhole. He kept me from getting on that first helicopter that crashed. He kept the chopper
blades from hitting me. He protected me as a cable lifted me
up by a rescue helicopter. He delivered me home safe and to
this day, yet I did not fully understand at the time. If it had
not been for my Father in Heaven, I would not be here today.

C. ELDON BITTER

Eldon Bitter received his bachelor's and master's degrees from BYU. He served in World War II and Vietnam. He was awarded the Legion of Merit in Vietnam.

CRAIG S. BRADFORD

Following his graduation from the University of Utah, Craig served 24 years as a fighter pilot, Pentagon strategist, and U.S. diplomat. He completed three combat tours in Southeast Asia. He is now retired from the Air Force and living in California. His account relates his experience with O. Leslie Stone, who presided over the Salt Lake Temple at the time he received his endowment prior to leaving for his first tour in Vietnam.

On July 21st, I received a letter from the Salt Lake Temple President, O. Leslie Stone. He had been moved by our acquaintance, but not because of any wisdom from my lips. Having walked together through several Temple corridors, we stood silently in the same doorway where a Heavenly messenger nearly three quarters of a century ago informed President

Lorenzo Snow, amongst other things, that my grandmother would be born to this 82-year-old prophet of God and his 42-year-old wife. I tingled all over as we became immersed in the Spirit, yet little did I realize my reverent escort had been functioning on a different page. The Holy Ghost was busy impressing him that the young men and women entering military service during those trying times needed special guidance from their spiritual leaders.

Later that day he discussed his experience with a member of the Quorum of the Twelve Apostles, which soon resulted in special assignments being given to the Quorum of the Seventy, one Seventy in particular. President Stone then looked up my grandmother, who was known to the General Authorities, to find my address.

This humble temple president explained in his letter that he had prayed on my behalf and received the following inspiration:

a. I should wear my temple garments day and night.

b. Especially important, I must do everything possible to keep the Lord's commandments while fighting in Southeast Asia.

c. I should bear in mind that our mission in Southeast Asia was to help those who could not help themselves—to protect people from Communist oppression. This moral obligation actually towered above every American's inherent duty to serve his or her country in times of war.

d. If I behaved righteously and fought in the interest of preserving free agency, my life would be spared. Moreover, upon my return from Southeast Asia, I would marry my queen for eternity, whom the Lord would select, and enjoy the blessings of raising righteous children. My patriarchal blessing stated the same blessing—the Lord would find a wife for me.

e. Compelled by the Spirit, President Stone quoted from the Book of Mormon:

> Now Moroni, leaving a part of his army in the land of Jershon, lest by any means a part of the Lamanites should come into that land and take possession of the city, took the remaining part of his army and marched over into the land of Manti. And he caused that all the people in that quarter of the land should gather themselves together to battle against the Lamanites, to defend their country, their rights and their liberties; therefore, they were prepared against the time of the coming of the Lamanites. (Alma 43:25, 26).

These verses indicated the wisdom of projecting national power into other lands to fight against common enemies of liberty. In partnership with the People's Republic of China, North Vietnam and its insurgent factions (such as the Pathet Lao and the Viet Cong) intended to conquer all of the non-Communist nations in SEA, one after the other. President Dwight D. Eisenhower accurately exposed this long-term Communist strategy, naming it his "Domino Theory." President Stone, the Scriptures, and ministering of the Holy Ghost thus gave me the invaluable knowledge that U.S. involvement in the Vietnam Conflict was the right course of action for my country. I believed I would not die while fighting this war as long as I honored the covenants I undertook in the temple.

DOUGLAS CHARLES BRAITHWAITE

During the Vietnam War Douglas served as a captain in the Marine Corps, 1st and 3rd Battalions from 1962–1965. His assignments included that of combat advisor to the South Vietnamese Army. Currently he lives in Utah, and is a consultant and a businessman. He has served in many Church positions such as an ordinance worker for the Boston Massachusetts Temple and elders quorum president.

I was set apart as a group leader while in Vietnam, but I did not once find an opportunity to have services with other LDS troops. When in the bush I privately prepared sacrament for myself—always with tea and usually with rice. I think that I had the sacrament brought to me once in the hospital, but I was in a drug-and-fever-induced stupor. I went to the mission home in Hong Kong while on R&R [rest and recuperation] and brought back a lot of Church material. They were lost along the way. I also misplaced my triple combination for a long time. This was serious because much of the Book of Mormon is written, and all is edited by great military men; and their accounts resonated with me on both tactical and scriptural levels.

By the end of my tour I was just praying that I could do my best and take what was dealt to me like a faithful child of God. At a fundamental level, one cannot control one's role but one can control how it affects one. Alma 62:41 says, "But behold, because of the exceedingly great length of the war between the Nephites and the Lamanites many had become hardened, because of the exceedingly great length of the war; and many were softened because of their afflictions, insomuch that they did humble themselves before God, even in the depth of humility." This verse became my touchstone in Vietnam and forever since.

DONALD Q. CANNON

Donald served in the office of the chief of staff for Army Intelligence. Serving as an intelligence analyst he achieved the rank of captain. One of his assignments was to gather intelligence related to the situation in Vietnam. In addition he also gathered intelligence about the 1967 Six-day War between Israel and neighboring Arabic states. He is now a professor of Church history and doctrine at Brigham Young University.

When I graduated from the University of Utah in 1961 I was also commissioned as a second lieutenant in the U.S. Army. The Army assigned me to the Intelligence branch.

Fortunately, the Army allowed me to delay my active duty while I worked on an M.A. and Ph.D., which I received from the University of Utah and Clark University, respectively. Since four years had passed, I had achieved seniority and was now a first lieutenant.

In October 1965 I began my basic infantry training at Fort Benning in Georgia. Even though we were all intelligence officers, we were required to take infantry training before attending intelligence school. Near the end of our training cycle the four hundred men in our class were informed that we would all be going to Vietnam.

In the meantime, two of the four hundred were given orders to serve at the Pentagon in the Office of the Assistant Chief of Staff for Intelligence. The two were a lawyer from New York City and myself. We both had longer time in grade than the others in the class at Fort Benning.

Our work at the Pentagon was fascinating. First, in order to go right to work while our security clearance was being processed, we were given a lie detector test. This gave us a temporary clearance. The men in our unit prepared daily intelligence briefings for the chief of staff, the secretary of the army and other army generals stationed at the Pentagon. We arrived at work at 5:00 A.M. and prepared our sections of the briefings. Then, at 7:30 A.M. we each presented a set number of intelligence briefings in the offices of the recipients. My responsibility was western Europe, and I did daily articles as a well as background articles for our briefings. As we presented the briefings, however, we were expected and required to be informed on all aspects of intelligence, especially on Vietnam.

One day as we engaged in casual conversation, I mentioned how unusual it was for two of the ten in our unit to be Latter-day Saints. The others assured me that such a case was not unusual and the Mormons tended to play a very large role in intelligence matters. I was pleased to become part of that tradition!

While at the Pentagon, Donald was promoted to the rank of Captain. Here, the commanding officer of his intelligence unit is pinning the captains' bars on his uniform.

LARRY (LUCKY) CHESLEY

Larry, also known as Lucky to many, joined the Air Force in 1956. He was shot down in 1966 while flying over Vietnam and spent the next 2,495 days, just short of seven years, as a prisoner of war in Vietnam.

In the fall of 1965 I was stationed in Florida and volunteered to go to Vietnam. We went to Georgia on our way to Vietnam. While we were there, we would go into the officers' club to enjoy ourselves, and I would stand off by myself and watch people. One particular night I was looking at the crowd and my eyes stopped on this young man and the Spirit told me that this man would not be coming home. I thought "What a horrible thought!" and dismissed it. My eyes were moving around the room and they stopped on another young man and the Spirit said he's not coming home and then the Spirit

Chesley flew an F-4 Phantom for the USAF. Built by McDonnell Douglas, the F4 Phantom was large for a jet fighter with a length of 62' 10" and a wingspan of 38' 5". It had two General Electric J79 engines producing a combined total thrust of 34,000 lbs. It could reach speeds in excess of 1400 mph and cruise at almost 600 mph. The jet had a range of over 1300 miles.

said, "And neither are you." On our very first mission over Vietnam that first man was shot down, in March the second man was shot down, and in April I was shot down.

We were on a low level mission over Vietnam going 760 miles per hour. I grabbed the handle to eject myself, but it didn't work, so I reached for the rings above my shoulders to pull a face curtain over my face to block the wind, but I couldn't find the rings, so I reached up with one hand to pull a ring down, and I finally ejected myself. It knocked me unconscious and broke my back in three places. I floated to the ground very quickly and I could see the Vietnamese coming to capture me and they did almost immediately. They stripped me of all my clothes down to my garments and my socks. They didn't know how to use buttons, zippers, or snaps. They just cut my clothes from my body with a machete. There I was, surrounded by the enemy . . . with a broken back, in my underwear, scared to death, and something inside of me said "Larry, pray." Prayer wasn't a new thing to me. I had prayed every morning and every night for years as a young boy before I had ever got into this predicament, but I didn't know what to pray for. So I kind of dismissed it but the feeling came really strong, "Larry, Pray." So I looked toward heaven and said a very simple prayer. I said "Father in Heaven, I may have to walk a long way and I can't do it without my boots." Within one minute they brought back my boots—the only things they ever returned to me. I didn't know what a great blessing it was to have those boots until some days later when we reached Hanoi and saw men who had walked to prison barefoot and had worn the meat off of their feet all the way to the bone. And then I knew what a great blessing it was to have those boots.

We marched for about five miles until we got to a truck. They threw me in the back of the truck, tied my arms behind my back, tied my wrists together, and tied them to the top of the bed of the truck leaving me hanging with my arms behind my back, and we started down the road. And again I said, "Dear Father in Heaven, this is killing me. Can't you bless me?" Within about five miles that knot came undone on top of the truck, I fell into the truck and I was able to loosen the cords and get circulation back in my hands. Another simple little prayer and a simple little answer.

The next day we stopped, and I was guarded by a Vietnamese soldier. He was very sadistic; he had an AK-47 automatic weapon, but he also had a stick about eighteen inches long and an inch or an inch and a half wide and he loved to beat me with that stick. He beat me across my head and shoulders, and even my broken back, but he mostly beat my arms. He beat my arms until they swelled up to be three to four times their normal size, and I still carry a scar on my left arm from his beatings. That night as I knelt to pray I said, "Dear Father in Heaven, isn't there somewhere you could send this sucker, like the front lines or something?" The next morning the guard was gone.

Within twenty-four hours I had asked for three little things and I had gotten all of them.

In 1969 they moved a group of us out of Hanoi to a camp called Son Tay. Son Tay was the worst camp, of the nine camps, I ever lived in. Every night and every morning I prayed individually, we prayed as a room and we prayed as a whole camp that the Lord would move us to a better camp. Finally the Lord said okay. On July 14 they came in with trucks, we rolled up our gear, we got in the trucks and we went to the new camp. It was a better camp but compared to anything you can think of it was still hell. But it was so much better than the hell we had been in, we liked the new hell. That night we got on our knees and we thanked our Father in Heaven for the blessing of being in a new camp. On November 22 of that same year, the Green Berets, America's finest fighting men, crashed in the Son Tay camp and liberated an empty camp. I would have come home two and a half years sooner if God hadn't answered my prayers. I learned a great lesson. I had been taught it all my life. Thy will be done at the end of my prayers. I say that with more fervency than I ever have in the past when I pray now.

I received no medical treatment for my broken back. I rode twenty-one days on bombed out roads, and went through my initial torture sessions with a broken back. I know that God lives and that He is my Father and that He knows me by my first name. When I got home and they took X-rays of my back, they said that yes my back had been broken in three places and that there was nothing they could do for me. It had healed perfectly. A muscle had grown down the right side of my back, about the size of my forearm to hold it as a brace.

I only cried twice in prison other than when I was being tortured. The first time was when my mom wrote me and told me my wife had divorced me, and the second time was in March 1966. The pain had overcome me. I started to cry. My roommate's name was Jim Ray. Jim saw that I was crying so he crawled up into the window of our room and started screaming for a doctor. We heard a guard coming so Jim got back down off of the window and onto his own bunk. The guard came in and started beating him and so Jim jumped off of his bunk, picked up the guard and threw him out of the door and up against the wall. The guard took off his rubber sandal and started shaking it at Jim. The guard was probably 5'4" and Jim was 6'2". The guard didn't speak English and Jim didn't speak Vietnamese. Jim said, "If you hit me with that I'll take it away from you and beat the hell out of you with it." The guard slammed the door and left.

When the guard left, Jim and I knelt down by our bunks and took turns praying. Jim is a Baptist and I am LDS. We prayed that the Lord would soften the hearts of our enemies. The first rule of prison was eat everything you get and the second rule was never hit a guard. We heard the commotion coming, and we knew what was about to happen. An English-speaking officer came in and told Jim that he would be severely punished because he couldn't hit a guard and go unpunished. He ranted and raved and after a few minutes shut the door, locked it, and left. Jim and I got on our knees again and prayed that our Father in Heaven would have mercy on our souls. The guards didn't come back that night which was a good sign. The next morning was Tet. Tet is their New Year's. At their holidays they would usually take us out and give us a hot cup of tea and a sugar cookie. This day was no different. They came and took Jim and me out of our room into a room that was decorated. They gave us our cup of tea and cookie and we ate it and were about ready to go back to our room and the English-speaking officer said to Jim, "You can't hit our guards and go unpunished. Go stand in the corner for one minute." That was his punishment. Jim and I believe that God, who can touch the hearts of our enemies, soften them, and that is what He did for us. The importance of that story is Jim loved me; Jim loved me more than he loved himself. And there aren't very many people like that today.

Transcription taken from a video sent by J.A. Moss, P.O. Box 17, McLean, VA 22101 of Larry Chesley giving a fireside in Virginia.

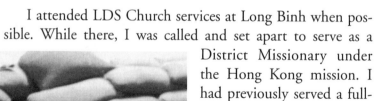

TERRY E. CHILDS

During Vietnam Terry served as a military patrol supervisor, achieving the rank of sergeant. He was awarded the Bronze Star for his services. Before the war he served a full-time mission to Australia. Currently, he is an agent with the U.S. Defense Investigative Service.

Sgt. Terry E. Childs: C Company 720ᵗʰ MP BN 18ᵗʰ MP BDE; Long Binh, Republic of Vietnam 1972.

I attended LDS Church services at Long Binh when possible. While there, I was called and set apart to serve as a District Missionary under the Hong Kong mission. I had previously served a full-time mission to Australia and this was a very different mission experience. While on duty, I carried weapons of war (M16 rifle, M72 grenade launcher, M60 machine gun, etc) and then carried a Bible and a Book of Mormon while trying to teach the gospel in the evenings. You would hear the Cobra helicopters flying overhead and hear the mini-guns firing into the jungle on the outskirts of our base, and we would be trying to teach the gospel and join in prayer with those we were teaching. I think, in a very small way, I could relate to Mormon, (in the Book of Mormon), who was engaged in war with the Lamanites, and yet would also try to teach the gospel in a warlike condition. I always kept my pocket-sized Book of Mormon and servicemen's guide with me, and they gave me a great deal of comfort.

Illegal drug use and prostitution were rampant on our base. Even though most of my time was serving with the military police, the MPs were as much involved in illegal drug use and living with prostitutes as anyone else. We made a post raid one day and picked up 198 prostitutes on our base that were living with GIs, and those were just the ones we found. In our company of about two hundred men, I can only recall three of us who did not have a prostitute living with them at one time or another: myself, my roommate Jerry Carter (who was also a returned missionary), and a kid named Tom Bird. Tom was

CERTIFICATE OF APPRECIATION

FOR SERVICE IN THE ARMED FORCES OF THE UNITED STATES

TERRY ELIOTTE CHILDS SERGEANT 566 74 6634   17 FEBRUARY 71-18 NOVEMBER   72

I extend to you my personal thanks and the sincere appreciation of a grateful nation for your contribution of honorable service to our country. You have helped maintain the security of the nation during a critical time in its history with a devotion to duty and a spirit of sacrifice in keeping with the proud tradition of the military service.

I trust that in the coming years you will maintain an active interest in the Armed Forces and the purpose for which you served.

My best wishes to you for happiness and success in the future.

Richard Nixon

COMMANDER IN CHIEF

DD FORM 1725
JAN 70

from Tennessee and a devout Baptist. As you walked through our company area you could smell the marijuana coming from the hooches where the men lived. I continually thanked the Lord for the gospel to guide me in this time of my life. I was not involved or interested in the illegal drugs or being involved in out-of-marriage sex. The gospel was a real anchor in my life.

Certificate of appreciation given to every soldier when they came home from Vietnam.

SID CLARK

Sid was born in Texas. During the Vietnam War he served in the Army's 1st Infantry division from 1970–1971. He is currently a Produce Manager. He has served in several Church assignments and is currently the High Priest Group Leader.

Did any of your church leaders talk to you prior to your leaving for Vietnam about your going; give you any advice, counsel?

Yes, my bishop did. I had a real hard time with going. With the fact that I knew I was going to be in artillery and I knew I was going to be on the front line, but there is no such thing as a front line in Vietnam, and that I would be killing people. I had a hard time with that because I didn't want to kill somebody and find out that because you killed somebody you are not going to make it to the Celestial kingdom. He talked me through that and basically told me that I am doing what my country wants and it's not going to be a sin that's going to be upon my head for things that I do over there as long as it's morally right. The killing that I do, did, is not the same as premeditated, or murder type thing over there.

Did you have any chance to share the gospel with anybody over there? Did you talk to them about it?

Not per se, I just lived it. Anytime we would go into the Combat base itself, they always made sure that Sid had his 7-Up to drink or his Coke to drink and that he was the designated walker-backer, because you walked wherever you went, and we couldn't get a jeep.

Did you find any other Church members down in that area?

Yes, I was the second Mormon in that battery. It was an Alpha battery also; A-battery. There was a Mormon brother and he was in Fire Direction Center and lived underground and so we never got to have actual contact with each other. Just when I came into battery, the Lieutenant said, "Oh, another Mormon. We've got one in the FDC."

So during your entire time in Vietnam you weren't able to go to Church?

No, I did get to go to church and it would be really neat because we'd sit there and we'd have sacrament and you'd have a captain passing sacrament to Spec-4's and you're just going, wow, this is cool. There is this church; it's not army right now. I even got to go to conference once. I arranged it with my battery commander and they had conference and those other two returned missionaries and I got to hop a chopper and we got to fly up to Denang, and we got to go to conference, Vietnam conference, not General Conference.

We were out away from Kasan, shooting for an insertion into Laos, which at that time we weren't going into Laos but we were shooting current insertion into Laos and we were getting a re-supply. We had three guns in, three guns out and I was on one of the three guns that was out on this maneuver, because we leave three guns back so that the three guns can cover the three guns that are out so we can leap frog our rounds basically. We weren't out of range of them but we were shooting for an insertion into Laos and we were in the process of getting a re-supply and when we were so far out we were getting resupplied by shanook. We had three shanooks coming in and each shanook had a Cobra escort. We were in the middle of a fire mission; we had gun two shooting at a fire mission. It was a contact fire mission and we were trying to get re-supplied at

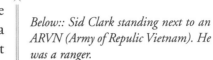

Below:: Sid Clark standing next to an ARVN (Army of Repulic Vietnam). He was a ranger.

Left: Ranger Ridge out of Khe Sahn – 102 Artillery.

Below: Sid Clark spent more than a year working on Battery Gun 1, 155 self-propelled artillery at Fire Base Miloc.

the same time we were to get this fire mission going and the battery commander thought it would be better if the shanooks dropped the powder and the Joes closer to the guns so we wouldn't have to hump them so far. We got gun two in the middle of a fire mission, you've got excess powder behind the gun that we're not using because, I couldn't even tell you what charge it was, but you had excess powder that you weren't using behind the gun. The battery commander pops a smoke. First shanook comes in, drops the powder, well what happens to the smoke canister? It gets blown into the powder that's open, the excess powder. It catches on fire, so your other two shanooks hang back because we're flagging them off, we've got gun two's pit on fire, we've got all this other powder that's open, ready to go into the gun it catches on fire. They're scrambling to get gun two, somebody into the gun and pull it out because everybody jumps out of the gun and runs, and we finally got a guy into the gun so that he could drive it out of the pit. We had to call the grunts that we were shooting for, and tell them that we had a disaster going and we had to quit shooting for them so we could pull gun two out. So we've got this powder that burns majorly hot. It burn so hot that it will melt the sand together and it will make glass when you burn the excess powder. The only thing that we can think of is that there was a LAW (light anti-tank weapon).

So we think that a LAW somehow got fired off because of the excess head, it blew up basically. One round actually fragmentized and the other round split open and did not fragmentize. Okay the killing radius of a 155 is 50 meters. There were three of us, because everybody ran to gun two to try and get everybody out of there and help them get out of there. There were three of us left within that fifty meters, two of them got sent out, not by medivac, but by the next chopper out, and one was bleeding through the ears, the other one had minor fragmentations, and I stayed there. Nothing happened, As a matter of fact, I was able to pick myself back up and flag the choppers, the shanooks to a safer place to drop the powder and Joes, because we needed the powder and Joes and they weren't going to leave. They couldn't go back with a full armament payload. They're basically sitting ducks out there.

So I picked myself up, ran quite some distance away from where my gun was to a safe position to where I felt was safe, and flagged into the other two shanooks so that they could drop their load and get out of there. Yeah, Heavenly Father was looking out for me.

JERRY CLAYTON

During the Vietnam War, Jerry was assigned to the 75th Infantry Company as part of a long-range reconnaissance patrol. His assignment included that of a gunner/observer on a hunter-killer team. Currently he lives in Provo as an electronic technician and teaches the Valiant 9 class in Primary.

I had just been assigned to the 1st Brigade Scouts, a hunter-killer team. The team was made up of a Cobra gunship and two light observation helicopters, this type of configures was called a white team. As an infantryman on the ground I had had the occasion to look up and see these hunter killers checking our area for signs of the enemy. Flying out in the open in full view and sights of the enemy was something I thought only the bravest or craziest men would do. I was new to the unit and trying to fit in as one of the guys. I was now part of this elite unit and felt proud to be a part of it. In fact, I felt very lucky that things had happened in such a way that allowed me to move into the unit.

I was told that I was to go to a party at the officers' club for the door gunner who flew with Pops. This man, Pops, was considered the ace in the unit and everyone looked up to him. At the party things were okay. They were drinking and toasting the door gunner and having a good time telling stories of past missions. All of a sudden Pops came up to me and asked what I was drinking. I told him I was drinking a soda. He became very stern and called attention to all in the room that I was not drinking. All eyes were on me as Pops grilled me on the fact that I was not toasting his door gunner with a proper

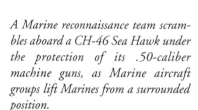

A Marine reconnaissance team scrambles aboard a CH-46 Sea Hawk under the protection of its .50-caliber machine guns, as Marine aircraft groups lift Marines from a surrounded position.

drink. He lectured me on being a part of the unit, saying I had to drink a real drink to be part of it. He tried to give me his drink and I just stood there. I felt as I if I had shrunk to only two feet tall and was aware that all eyes were on me, watching to see what I was going to do. I felt sick as I realized that if I didn't take the drink, I would not be a part of the unit; I would be an outcast.

It is hard to describe what it meant to me to be in the unit and now I was seeing it slip away because I didn't drink. Again the drink was pushed my way and I was told to drink. I finally told him I could not and would not drink because it was against my religion and I was a Mormon. As the word left my mouth I felt as if I had just signed my own death warrant. To my surprise, Pops put his arm around me and told me he was testing me to see what type of a man I was. He told me he wished he were as strong as I was and I could fly with him any time. He told me that he had found out that I was a Mormon and saw a chance to see how true Mormons were to their faith when confronted without other Mormons around. I was glad that I had chosen the right even though I thought no one knew of my religion. I often wonder what impact I would have had if I had taken that drink. I would have failed the test and after that how would Pops look at the Mormons?

American soldier in a bunker watching for Viet Cong.

* * * * *

The soldiers from the South Vietnam army unit who were working with us shot down a big bird that flew over our campsite one night. We were with an armored cavalry unit. The tanks and armored personal vehicles were all gathered into a circle like covered wagons of pioneer times. Some of the ARVNs [Army of the Republic of Vietnam] told us it was bad luck for them to have shot down that type of bird. The next day we found out how bad our luck was to be. We were sweeping through the jungle looking for the NVA [North Vietnamese Army]. They found us.

That morning was uneventful. We were dropped off on one side of the jungle by the armored unit. We were to walk through the jungle until we came to the other side where they would pick us up and take us to another area to repeat the process. There had been intelligence that an NVA unit had moved into the area and we were looking for them.

Part of my unit was dropped off at one area and we were taken to another one. We had just started our push through the jungle when the first element reported they were taking fire. We got back on the armored vehicles and headed back to the contact area. Along the way we started taking fire from the wood line. We stopped and returned fire. It was decided to assault the wood line and go through the jungle to link up with the unit that was dropped off first. The entire unit fired into the jungle, then the tanks leading the way in three columns started toward the wood line. The tanks were crashing the trees down. To our left we could hear mortars crashing. We thought it was friendly fire but found out later it was the enemy. We kept moving forward trying to keep up with the tracks when all of a sudden they stopped. Then I heard some explosions and gunfire. We had made contact with the enemy and were under intense fire. I kept moving forward, passing the forward most tanks and APC [armored personnel carrier]. One APC looked like a can would look if you put a cherry bomb in it, blown inside out. I passed some wounded men who the medics were treating and passed the lead tank into an area that had some mounds in it. Termites pushed up the mounds of dirt. I got behind the mound and looked over to see the lead element. The point man, the Lt. [lieutenant], and others lying there were wounded or dead. I went over the mound and helped push the wounded back behind the hill. I took over the M60 machine gun that was there. The gunner was wounded and left with the others, leaving only me alive in that area.

I kept firing the gun in a 180-degree arc. Left to right, then right to left, only taking time to reload new belts. I found that as long as I was firing it seemed that the enemy would fire back. Someone who took it from the tracks was tossing me ammo, the belts were many times longer than the ones we normally used and allowed me to fire longer between reloading. I noticed a grenade lying next to me. I didn't see it thrown at me. I waited for it to go off but it didn't. During the wait I wondered if time stood still before you died, as it seemed an eternity waiting for it to explode. Waiting and waiting, I finally started counting until I got to ten and decided it was a dud. As I continued to fire I was hit with an explosion and wounded in my arm. Another grenade had been tossed at me and went off, blowing everything up and over me. I was dazed by the concussion but kept firing. The gun was getting so hot that I was being burned as I handled it. Left to right, right to left, I kept swinging the gun in that 180-degree arc. Looking at the bodies of those dead around me I started to think of them and cry for them. Some people got back over the mound and started to push the bodies back to the other side. A medic was with them. He was lying by me looking at my arm. The next moments I can only say what I felt and saw.

While the medic was treating my arm the belt of ammo ran out. I grabbed another and jammed it into the M60. It only took seconds to do this, but time had switched to slow motion. I saw the enemies' rounds coming at us; green tracers in slow motion hitting the last man going over the mound and knocking him over it. Then I watched the rounds come at me. Then they went around me, and I watched them hit the medic in the head, exploding it and throwing his brains all over me. The round lifted him up and he came down on me. I rolled him off and continued to fire. I was scared to death, witnessing such a thing happen to someone who was trying to help me. I was terrified as I fired the gun. I felt like my life was in the gun and as long as I kept it firing, I was okay. How long I was in that state, I don't know. I just kept the gun going and thought about the medic. I was alone with the dead medic and the loneness hit me strong. I wasn't afraid of dying, I was afraid of dying alone; that no one was there to comfort me as I accepted death. I started to pray and plead with my Father in Heaven that I was frightened and that I did not want to die alone and that I wanted someone to be there with me to comfort me and to let me know he was there. As I prayed, suddenly, I felt as if I were radiating and filled with light and a calm peaceful feeling came over me. Inside my head a voice was telling me I was not alone. He was there, and I would be okay.

During all this I kept the gun going, loading and reloading. They had tossed ammo all over me and I had only to reach for a new belt. The gun was so hot, it was firing itself and finally it blew up. I had projected my safety into the firing of the gun and when it blew up, I got up and started running over the mound past the tanks and down the path they knocked down. I ran until I was in the open area. Someone tripped me and I remember the water being poured over me. Some of the guys told me that I had rounds going all around me as I ran. I was medevaced to one hospital where they pulled pieces of wood from the wounds in my arm and treated my burns. I was sent to another hospital in Phu Vinh the division headquarters. I recall them giving me a shot, and I slept for days before I was rested enough to talk to the doctors. One of the doctors I talked to was Major Hefner. He asked me if I wanted to go home and about how I felt. I told him I wasn't hurt enough to go home but I wanted to know why all those people died and why the medic was killed and not me? I was torn up inside that I had survived and those around me were killed, especially the medic who was trying to help me. I told the doctor I had just told the medic to go and I was okay and then he was shot. I felt bad and guilty of his death.

Major Hefner sent me to see a chaplain at division headquarters—Chaplain Newby. Chaplain Newby was an LDS chaplain. He talked to me for a while and I told him what had happened and my feelings. Then he asked an odd question of me. "Do you have your patriarchal blessing with you?" I told him I did. I had gotten it the year before and put it away. I had been told by one of my priesthood leaders that it was a beautiful one, but I had found it not to be what I expected. I thought it would tell me what to become and what to do with myself. Just before I went to Vietnam I was given a servicemen's copy of the Book of Mormon and *Principles of the Gospel.* I had folded up my patriarchal blessing and placed it in the book and had forgotten it until I was asked for it. I pulled it out and gave it to the chaplain. He unfolded it and read it. I had had no idea that I would be in Vietnam or in a war when I got it, but Chaplain Newby told me he had the answer to all my questions.

There were the answer promises given by the priesthood and from Heavenly Father. I was told there that I would be experiencing these things but I would be shielded from them and that guardian angels would be around about to protect me. We talked about the blessing and what it meant and how it was fulfilled with the events that happened to me.

My testimony of the blessing was sure and the rest of my tour I felt invincible and volunteered for everything because I knew I would not be seriously hurt. After I had received it and felt it did not answer my questions I had put it away. After the firefight and talking to the chaplain, I realized what Brother Sunderland had meant by my having a beautiful blessing, one that was fulfilled and proven many times in Vietnam.

GERALD S. COLEMAN

During the Vietnam War Gerald served in the Army's 1st Air Cavalry Division from October 1967–May 1969. His assignment included that of a combat medic during the Tet Offensive and other various battles. Currently he lives in Washington and is a physical therapist. Gerald has served in numerous Church callings and is currently a temple worker.

This A-6A Intruder, of Marine All-Weather Attack Squadron-242, with jet engine starter attached, is in the final stages of preparation for a night mission over North Vietnam. With its self-sufficient radar system, the Intruder can find and bomb a predetermined target.

During the evening, I was visiting some of my friends in their poncho tent when I had the impression come over me around 10:00 P.M. that we better break up our conversation and return to our own tents. I went back to my tent that I was sharing with our Vietnamese scout. Suddenly the night air was filled with several bursts of AK-47 rifle fire, and two B-40 rockets slammed into our company position. I heard someone call for a medic to come quickly to the side of one of the platoon sergeants who had been hit by a bullet from the VC [Viet Cong] raid. One of the rockets had blown apart the tent that I had just vacated a few minutes earlier. I crawled to the side of the injured sergeant, checked his vitals, and shined my infrared flashlight into his eyes to check his pupils for dilation. He wasn't responding at all, and then I felt blood on the back of his head. His breathing was shallow and his pulse was weak. He was barely alive. We needed to call for a medevac chopper right away to airlift him to a MASH [mobile army surgical hospital] unit. Luckily, no one else was injured during the VC raid on our camp.

* * * * *

I was kneeling on a high spot between two large bomb craters where the rest of the troops were digging in and facing out for a possible enemy attack. I was praying with all of my heart to my Heavenly Father for protection. I asked Him through the power of the priesthood and in the name of Jesus Christ to please protect us from harm through the night until daylight when we could see clearly to mount an attack on the enemy around us. I felt a burning go from my head through my entire body to my toes, and a peaceful calm came over me, and I knew we would be protected from harm during the night. I went to the side of several of my buddies in the bomb craters and told them not to worry; we would be protected all night. For hours we watched the plane circle overhead pouring gunfire into the enemy position and listened to the artillery rounds whistle over our heads and explode just beyond us.

GARY E. COX

Gary was born in Pocatello, Idaho. He graduated from Brigham Young University's Air Force ROTC in 1959. Late in the Vietnam War, Gary served as a lieutenant colonel in the U.S. Air Force. His assignment was that of a pilot in a reconnaissance squadron. He served as a tactical fighter/reconnaissance pilot until 1975. After the war, he became a military plans officer. He retired from the Air Force in 1981.

My time to serve in the Vietnam War came late in the history of that conflict, May 1971–1972. Consequently, I had foreknowledge of what to expect, both in combat and the living conditions. I was assigned to the 12th Tactical Reconnaissance Squadron. Because the war was winding down, the wing's manpower levels were being reduced. I flew only a few missions before being transferred to the Airborne Command, Control and Communications Squadron where I completed my tour of duty.

My primary concern was how to cope with the living conditions in Southeast Asia. I wasn't concerned with the physical environment like the climate, a place to sleep, the food etc. I was concerned about the moral degradation and the temptations I had heard of from friends who had already completed their tours and returned. I had been separated from my family for shorter periods of time, but never for a full year, and I was worried about how to survive spiritually.

Before leaving my family, my wife and I determined we would do several things: write daily letters, conduct family home evenings via audiotapes shuttled through the mail, and call via the military MARS radio system as often as possible. Additionally, I decided I would read the complete standard works during the year, pray twice daily, and complete a military education correspondence course. My father gave me a blessing assuring me of my family's well being and the promise that I would land safely from every mission.

Despite these goals, commitments, and promises, I was still anxious about how I would perform under the conditions I knew awaited. Once departed, I began my personal reading and upon arrival I found the LDS servicemen's group and attended meetings. The fellowship with the group of member servicemen of all ranks was warm and helped relieve the loneliness. I would associate with my squadron friends at socials, at the pool, the mess hall, etc. Whenever possible I carried and studied a textbook or two from the Industrial College of the Armed Forces correspondence course. From this my aircrew buddies knew I had embarked upon a major obligation and did not question my absence from the squadron hooch. The hooch was the daily watering hole where the aircrews went to drink, exchange stories, view movies or other materials that were not always compatible with my commitments.

It was November 1971, six months into my tour, that I had not had one tempting thought, nor lingering image in my mind from an occasional and unintentional exposure to certain material. I was pleased, but amazed. Such had not been my experience on previous, but shorter, absences from home. I was in the Doctrine and Covenants in my scriptures study program. Having recognized the protection I was experiencing, wondering how it was so and asking in prayer, I came to Doctrine and Covenants 6:16, which reads: "Yea, I tell thee, that thou mayest know that there is none else save God that knowest thy thoughts and the intents of thy heart."

My wondering at the protective care I had received ceased. I knew the means that God had prepared by which we could participate in protecting ourselves from the evils of the world. Daily prayer, scripture study, and letters from my wonderful wife, along with the recorded voices of my family during our weekly family home evening times put my thoughts and intents above the level where temptations from sources, seen and unseen, were effective.

This experience sustained me through the remainder of my tour and has been a source of inspiration and strength since. I have shared it with friends, family, and other Church members as a testimony of the love of our Heavenly Father who has provided the way by which we can return to Him.

RICHARD D. COX

Richard served as an Air Force pilot for twelve years. During his Vietnam tour he served with the 20th Special Operations Squadron at Nha Trang Air Base. His assignment was to transport long-range reconnaissance patrols from forward operating locations near the Cambodian border into preselected landing zones.

My first combat mission in Vietnam was very nearly my last. Certainly there's little unusual about that with men who have confronted war. But this wake-up call occurred after I'd been in the Air Force for nearly twelve years. I was a seasoned pilot with thousands of hours of flying time, and to find myself so quickly and impolitely exposed to hostile fire came as a considerable shock. For years I had flown multi-engine aircraft, most lately KC-135 tankers performing routine midair refueling in the U.S. Only recently I had come off from being grounded because of the treatment for cancer I had received. I considered that in the best interest of being promoted, I had better get my papers in for duty in Vietnam.

This was in 1968 and the war was heating up. To my surprise I was assigned to fly helicopters, which involved conversion from fixed wing to rotary wing training. Frankly, I was quite delighted because I was wearied of flying the flagpole—in other words taking off, flying straight, refueling a bomber and then returning to base and practicing approaches and landings. The missions usually went on for several hours total and I was sick of it. Chopper duties with frequent flights and shorter missions seemed very attractive.

I was off to Texas for three months of learning to fly the UH-IF Air Force Huey and then to Florida for special operations training. I'd been assigned to the 20th Special Operations Squadron at Nha Trang Air Base in Vietnam and could find very little about the specific mission of our unit.

Cpl. John D. Linton uses a rocket circuit tester to check for stray electrical voltage, which could cause accidental misfire of the two rocket pods attached to Huey helicopter gunships. Richard D. Cox was retrained from flying fixed wing to the rotary-wing Huey helicopters.

People in the U.S. who did know weren't talking and others seemed uncomfortable when I even mentioned it. Stateside orientation involved only general discussion with very few specifics. Without being too coy or theatrical, I soon discovered there was a good reason for the confidentiality factor—I was going to be doing something that we weren't supposed to be doing. I was going to be flying clandestine missions into Cambodia. This was 1968, and we weren't supposed to be there. Not yet, anyway.

The 20th SOS [special operations squadron] was assigned a mission code named "Daniel Boone." Our job was to transport six-men and seven-men long-range reconnaissance patrols from forward operating locations near the Cambodian border into preselected landing zones. We were to quickly drop them off and let them roam about in bad guy country to gather intelligence such as tapping into communication lines, identifying hostile forces, counting sampan traffic in streams, and even taking prisoners for interrogation when possible. When the LRRP [long-range reconnaissance patrol] guys had completed the mission, or when they encountered enemy forces, our job was to get them out as quickly and as quietly as possible. This was seldom possible. Our visits annoyed the North Vietnamese forces, and they could be spiteful rascals. They were also very dedicated, committed, and expert at demonstrating their resentment. This was their house and we were not welcome.

On my first mission I was assigned to fly copilot for a brave, young captain who was flying his last mission. This was SOP [standard operating procedure]—brand new guys with experienced types. They knew the ropes and we had to learn from scratch. I should add here that the LRRP team leader, a veteran Green Beret sergeant, was a rather extraordinary individual (see Looney Tunes) who enjoyed an incredible reputation for bravery or courage or whatever such insanity can be called. His reputation was legendary throughout Southeast Asia. The NVA [North Vietnamese Army] actually had a price on his head. Here I was, the essence of innocence, being led into the valley of the shadow of death by an ex-Ohio State halfback, smart, skilled, and a much decorated Green Beret without the slightest appreciation of either discretion or cowardice.

Accompanied by two Huey gunships, the forward air controller directed us into the LZ [landing zone]. We dropped down into the hole, actually a spot in the jungle barely large enough to accommodate the arc of our rotor blades and before we touched down, the team leader, radio operator, and four Montagnard tribesmen jumped out and headed for the tree line. Oh, yes, did I forget? These particular LRRPs usually included indigenous personnel, in the case four of the hill people who inhabited the central highlands of Southeast Asia. For this effort, they had eschewed their traditional loincloths, and all were dressed in NVA combat fatigues (even the tall, blond, insane team leader), and all carried various types of communist-made weapons.

Following the insertion (military jargon for putting troops in) the pilot lifted off and pulled out of the LZ. He flew the chopper at treetop level to build up speed and was just getting ready to pop up or climb for altitude as quickly as possible when we heard the radio operator wheezing, obviously out of breath from running. "We're in contact!" he said. The enemy had been waiting for them in considerable force.

The pilot immediately performed a 180-degree turn and headed back for the LZ. I thought, "Okay this is the way it's done; the way it's supposed to be." I was polite, unquestioning, obedient and abysmally stupid. Again the FAC [forward air control], from high above, guided us back into the original LZ. We dropped down, skids settling into the high grass, and looked out for the team members. Nothing.

Suddenly from all sides, a Vietnam version of the Second Battle of the Marne erupted. Actually, nothing like it at all, but to my tender ears it sounded and felt like every enemy gun in Southeast Asia was blazing away at us. Our two gunners on board, each with an M60 machine gun, were standing on the helicopter skids and hollering on the intercom, "We are taking ground fire." Gee, what a surprise, bullets were whizzing by us, ripping holes into the chopper, shattering the instrument panel and windows, and spraying glass into the pilot's face. Debris flew from the cockpit, and now the gunners were yelling, "Firing out!" The sound of the M60s became a staccato roar and the unmistakable stench of cordite filled the cockpit. The rotor blades were whipping up grass and leaves and contributing to the total noise and confusion. Not a team member was in sight. Just four of us, sitting there on the ground without a clue, while scores of little men were trying desperately to kill us.

Our gunships, also Hueys, flew pass after pass over us, spraying minigun fire around us into the trees and heavy foliage where the offending ground fire originated. We heard their chatter on the radio. We had little time to be comforted by their protecting cover. It all happened in seconds, and it seemed as if everything was playing in slow motion. The sights, sounds, smells were as vivid as if they were being played over and over again. What was amazing was that I felt absolutely no fear. The realization of what happened would come only later when we were safely back at our FOL [forward operating location]. And it would come, big time! I had been unwittingly introduced to what I can only refer to as a resolution. I knew I was going to die there in that place and there was nothing I could do about it. There was no time to go through the standard steps of denial, anger, bargaining, acceptance, etc. No, I was going to die and that was that. No time to think of family, home, the gospel, or reflect upon my life. No time for regret or guilt or sorrow. Only time to die and not necessarily willingly, but rather to simply take the bullet and die.

I was not in any way contemplating issues of duty or bravery or even Mom, the flag, and apple pie. By some irrational sense, everything was resolved for me in those very brief moments. It was an emotion I would experience many more times afterwards. And while I never suffered a single scratch from combat, I believe that I was at least in someway profoundly affected from this and subsequent events.

Yes, I had survived cancer. But that was different. It had occurred and I had dealt with it. I had had time to reconcile with the tumor and its threat. Fear, resentment, accommodation, and acceptance had all enjoyed their seasons. But not this. Not other men willingly, eagerly, trying to kill me. No, in those moments I never thought about others on the helicopter or the team out there somewhere. That time I was encapsulated in a surreal, albeit vivid cacophony of sights, sounds, and numbed sensation.

This was not the place to be at all. The same instant that all those hellish events occurred, we realized we had to get out of there. I followed the pilot on the controls as he lifted the collective and we felt the chopper respond. Still bullets were whipping by us and our gunners were returning fire. As we moved up and forward, more debris flew through the cockpit; the controls grew sloppy and a bit unresponsive. Finally, we cleared the trees and started picking up forward speed. Only a hundred feet or so off the ground, our left gunner yelled on the intercom, "I've been shot in the head!" We had started recovering our wits and his exclamation struck me once as both startling and contradictory. If he had been shot in the head, how could he possibly be able to say that? I looked over my shoulder, and there he was, sprawled back inside the compartment, his eyes wide, and face pale and very shaken. He was clawing at his helmet strap, frantically trying to get it unfastened. The other gunner had thrown himself inside too and was helping him get the headgear off. Fumbling at the connection, it finally came free and he jerked it away. Two small,

Lance Cpl. William F. Clover refuels his helicopter while the Sea Knight's gunner, Sgt. Roosevelt Thomas checks for battle damage. The helicopter had been hit twice that morning by VC sniper fire during troop insert.

boat shaped bullets tumbled out of the helmet and clattered to the metal helicopter deck. Again, this all happened in seconds. The pilot was still picking up airspeed and the gunner was happily not seriously injured. Two AK-47 rounds had pierced the front of the helmet, spun around inside the foam-like liner, and stopped harmlessly, offering only a gentle scuff to the gunner's scalp, and resulting in a very stiff neck.

What about the LRRP team still there on the ground? Reality hit brutally. We had failed. They were hopelessly outnumbered and trying to run. Surely by now they were dead men. My first mission. The pilot's last. What a way to begin and to end. The chopper was not responding normally, but it was flyable, so the mission leader told us to return ASAP to the forward operating location back in Vietnam. Senses now returned, we felt no exhilaration for our escape. We could only think of those six men still there unaccounted for. We heard nothing on the radio to encourage us. The pilot told us to take time and check ourselves for wounds. It was a classic combat veteran's response. I had heard that sometimes with the intensity of combat people are hit and fail to recognize it until later. But I checked myself—no problems. I took the chopper while he counted his arms and legs. Except for facial cuts from flying glass, he was fine too. Neither of the gunners had been hit either, except for the two rounds into the helmet.

We landed safely and went about checking the helicopter. We lost count of the hits we'd taken. As I inspected my side, I found a hole in the door over me, behind and under. Our chin window was gone, bullet fragments littered the floor, and engine and flight instruments were shattered. How many rounds had passed between the pilot and me? Miraculously the engine itself hadn't been hit and likewise the main and tail rotor blades and the flight controls had been only minimally impacted. A miracle? Not yet, but one was about to happen. We had waited back at the FOL for less than half an hour when the other choppers in our flight came into view. All were there whopping back toward us with that distinctive Huey sound. Four gunships—two primary, two spares. And the fifth, our backup transport chopper trailed behind. They landed in a usual swirl of red, central highlands dust. Engines shut down; men exited right and left from the clumsy-looking birds. Now the miracle! Out of the backup tumbled six, tired, dirty men. The team was safe, uninjured, and intact. How do miracles happen? Maybe it wasn't really a miracle, but it shouldn't have been either. No way should we or the team have gotten out. But there we were all safe and sound and the odds had been absolutely against us. Why? Well, it happened this way. The enemy didn't do a very good job at all—to our good fortune. It seems that when we went back to extract the team, the NVA troops turned from the team to us. They wanted our chopper, so they concentrated their fire on us. The team, meanwhile, saw their chance to get out of there. While the enemy poured fire into us, our spare slick pulled in one hundred meters behind us and picked up the entire team without taking a single hit. Quite unwittingly, by our ill-considered tactics, we'd saved the LRRP. Of course, the mission was a bust. Nobody had time to gather any intelligence in those frantic moments.

There was more that we would find out some weeks later. It would be both a grim and saddening postscript. Another team was inserted into the area after it had time to cool down. They scoured the area and located the shallow grave of no fewer than 116 NV soldiers who had been slaughtered by our gunship that day. How many more were wounded and would later die? How many were maimed and crippled? We had no way of knowing. For our side it was a smashing victory. Certainly there would be 116 fewer NVA troops facing our young soldiers and Marines farther south in Vietnam. Surely it stretched the enemy's capabilities a bit more, but what a price they paid. I paid a price, too. Later on. It took me a while to recognize it, but in those exhilarating moments following the mission I found myself delighting in the blood of my enemies. How easy it was to lapse into those same grisly sentiments that afflicted the Book of Mormon peoples.

ALMA L. DAY

Alma grew up in Utah and served a mission in Scotland. Following his mission, he served in Vietnam for two years as a member of the U.S. Marine Corps. He was awarded the Purple Heart for being wounded in action. He was a special education instructor at Victorville High School in California. He is the father of ten children.

Top: While serving in Vietnam, Alma's home ward (Highland Ward, American Fork Stake) sent boxes of food, clothes, and goodies for him to pass out to the children. Here he is passing out candy to 70 Vietnamese children.

Bottom: Marine, Alma Day, stands with children at the well that was found in the middle of the peasant village.

We [my father and I] went to the temple in Logan five days before I left for Vietnam. Its quieting peace and harmony absorbed us. We both knew that even death could never mar nor destroy our relationship. No panic of threatening separation mocked us. It was while in those walls of the temple peace that my dad told me that if I were to die while fighting for my country, he would not feel it as a tragedy. Honor and service and willingness overarched the sliver of death, in his thinking. It was then that a pearl of quiet surety told me that I had nothing to fear. All would be well. I would be wounded, no doubt, but not killed. This assurance lifted my mind from foreboding and erased the thought that I would be alone in Vietnam. My own mother, who had died eight years before, seemed close once again.

* * * * *

Then the glad news came that President Hugh B. Brown and

Elder Gordon B. Hinckley were going to visit the island in a week. This was such a rare event. I was told that a General Authority hadn't visited them in fifteen years. As I listened to their wise and wonderful words, the squalor of Vietnam faded from my mind. I felt that God still ruled in the affairs of men, in spite of all the seeming savagery. The old principles they reviewed lifted me above the sordidness of man's groveling. I felt a comfort and closeness with ideals and views they taught so freely. Somehow all would turn out for the best.

President Hugh B. Brown added testimony to these thoughts, "You have your difficulties, no doubt, but like the great eagle, you can rise above the adversity and soar to the heights in majesty and command. Spread your wings to the lifting winds of adversity. Let it carry you to where you can see all the great horizons in all the mastery of the victor."

I returned to war-torn Vietnam a little more prepared. Such gladness and sense of purpose still lingered with me as our plane dipped down into my former world of sadness and perplexity, for I had been touched by men who understood the real forces which impinge upon human development.

Top: Alma Day served in the marines and was the computing mortar man that searched for booby traps.

Bottom; Alma Day helping during a typical morning madcap. He treated a girl who had boils up and down her lower legs. After lacerating and bandaging the boils, he gave her soap, which was the only thing that they could do to stop the spreading. However, the natives would work in knee-deep rice paddies all day after they had received this help, which totally defeated the purpose.

* * * * *

After a month of working together, Sergeant Reece and I grew to be personal buddies.

Our chats at night turned from superficial talk to open treatment of topics that stirred in our hearts. One night when we were alone he told me that he was a Mormon. He didn't want to tell me earlier, he said, because he felt it would be a catastrophe. He told me all the reasons that made him believe that a religion couldn't be lived on the battlefield. He listened to my counterviews. I was surprised to learn that my every word and act had been studied through the previous month.

He especially liked the way people respected me, and wanted to learn to work with people in the way I had. He recalled the drunks that would come in at night half unconscious, and pour out the loneliness of their lives to me.

Sergeant Reece knew the terrible pang of a man who had turned from his Creator and his own parents. He said, "I'd never want my family to ever know what happened over here. They'd disown me forever. From now on I want to be proud of my life." We talked late into the night. He threw away his cigarettes, and forsook the ration of beer. Every man, I reflected, has to find his own pathway. Each one leads through gardens of Gethsemane. He has to make these awesome journeys of life pretty much alone. Great crises demand all our resources and these reservoirs of strength must be earned through our own individual assignments. Friends can encourage and help, but life is often a lone, lone battle, I have learned, in the short travels I have had with her.

* * * * *

Then came August 16. Two PFs, or popular forces, from the nearby village came running in with excitement. They wanted two grenades as they had trapped a VC [Viet Cong] in a hole and wanted to flush him out. When we arrived there were a dozen people gathered around. I noticed they wouldn't even go near the hole, so I volunteered to take a look. I got so restless, I told Red I was going down and started to descend. The sarge told me to get my hide out of that hole. He saved my life from that gruff order. Some PFs now brought the little brother of the woman being questioned. He was thirteen years old. "If there is no one in there, you won't mind if we send your brother, will you?" they mocked her. They gave him a small oil lamp and down the tunnel he went. I reasoned that if there was anybody down there, he would not a hurt a small boy without a weapon.

Then all was silent. I stood waiting. I wondered what had happened. Where was the boy with the excitement in his eyes? He didn't come up. I thought the boy was coming through the smoke and darkness. "Red, come quick!" I yelled. "He's coming out, and he needs help." Red stretched to see what I saw, gasped in horror, and simultaneously dived for cover. I tried to follow Red, but was a split second too late. The grenade exploded as I turned from the hole. Our own grenades took six to eight seconds to explode, the Cong's blew up in three. I had just enough time to turn my face away. I was lying in a pool of blood eight feet outside the hooch. I felt numb. I gazed at the hard-packed ground. "It can't be a dream," I thought. A cold chill shivered through me. A sinister feeling told me that the Cong was looking down his rifle sighs at my back.

Someone yelled, "Look out!" I knew they were hollering at me. I picked myself up knowing that I'd find out how bad, and where the pieces of hot shrapnel hit me.

"There he is!" they shouted. I scrambled to safety, surprised that I could move. Maybe by some miracle I would be all right. I lay back and tried to assess reality. Confusion was everywhere, especially in my own mind. I waited for the din to cease and bring the dull pain that comes after shock.

Minutes before the activities began a squad of Marines from Charlie Company had happened to be on patrol in that area. They saw the people clustered around and came to investigate. Luckily they had a corpsman with them. He patched up another Marine who had been grazed on the neck. In the excitement of the firing at the VC, he didn't see me. I was too near unconsciousness to call to him. For several seconds I just watched blood spurt from my arm. I thought how fascinating and pretty blood looked. I wondered why I was not in a wild panic. All my clothing was getting soaked. The grenade must have gone off just a few feet from me and sprayed me with steel. I had twelve holes in me, but I only felt the one in my right leg. Somebody noticed me and hollered to the doctor. "You'd better get Day before he bleeds to death!" The nineteen-year-old green corpsman looked scared as he ripped off my clothing. I joked about him taking it so seriously. He mumbled something about trying to find the worst wound. The task now was to carry me to an opening where the chopper could land. It was exciting; especially when the merciful chopper dipped down to lift me out of death's bleeding hands. Safety and all the luxury of modern medical attention were only five minutes away. I breathed a prayer of relief and gratitude . . .

After all the to-do of settling me into the infirm's bed, I heard the full account of what had happened back at the village. I had come terribly close to death. My buddies said I surely must have had a guardian angel near, as on at least four accounts I should have been gone. First, if the Cong had thrown any other type of grenade, Red would not have seen it. The type he had thrown was an old Chinese make that shot out tiny sparks when its pin was released, letting Red see it in the darkness, and giving me the time to get those precious feet away. Not a ghost of a chance would have been mine if our own type had been tossed. Second, the odds of having one of those dozen scorching pieces of metal hit me in a vital spot must have been ten to one. Third, when I was lying at the tunnel's entrance, the Cong came from his hiding and could have plastered me easily. Instead he decided to make a quick run for it. He had an AK-47 rifle, and saw me move, but likely thought if he could sneak up into the rafter unnoticed, he could make out better. He tried to escape, instead of finishing me off. Fourth, if that squad from C Company hadn't happened along, the wild bleeding would not have stopped, nor would we have had a radio to call for the helicopter in time. I felt lucky!!!

JOHN DECKER

As a California native, John served in Vietnam as a staff sergeant in the Army's 1st Infantry Division from 1968–1969. His assignments included defending portions of the Ho Chi Minh Trail. Currently he is a safety specialist for the federal government. He has served in many Church positions and is currently a counselor in his high priest group.

In 1969, I was nineteen years old, and not real sure as to what direction I was going. My mother had passed away when I was seven, my father wasn't a member of the Church, and so I really had no one in my family to nudge me towards going on a mission. What direction I was going in was soon answered, however, by my receiving a draft notice. It was right after I received my patriarchal blessing. Receiving this blessing, I would soon discover, would play a significant part in my life. In my blessing it stated that as long as I would live a righteous life, the Lord would protect me, as a shield, from harm. Why I received this blessing, I really don't know, other than I do have a great family today. But here I was, going to Vietnam as an infantryman, carrying this blessing in my backpack, and every two weeks or so I would pull it out and read it again. While I knew that this blessing might be significant, it isn't really what drove me to live with conviction of my beliefs. I was fortunate in my youth to have had great spiritual leaders and to have great friends with high morals. This is what carried me.

I was assigned with the 1st Infantry Division, Mechanized Infantry (armored personnel carrier). It was in Vietnam that I discovered that being LDS and having high morals does carry respect from others. Because very often, especially infantrymen

John Decker on patrol south of Chu Lai, Quaing Nai Province.

live for today, thinking that today might be their last day. Many partied when they had the opportunity. A few on the other hand, looked to the Lord, as I did. Let me give you four examples why I believe I was blessed to live. I was fifteen feet away from a mine when it went off, killing my driver and my captain. It also severely wounded my platoon leader. Yes, I was hit too, a small piece of shrapnel hit my chest, but I was so stunned by the explosion, I didn't even know I was hit. I was the second closest to the mine, yet it was as if I wasn't hit. I was medevaced to a MASH [mobile army surgical hospital] unit and spent two weeks in a rear arca, then reassigned to the Americal Division, in the same area where the My Lai massacre had taken place a few months earlier.

It was shortly after I reached my new assignment that my company was assigned to sweep an area, along with two other companies of infantry. The battalion commander made the terrible decision to bivouac in an area that already had foxholes dug. The Viet Cong were intelligent enough to booby trap the area. A planted artillery shell in a tree was set off, killing eighteen GIs all around me. I wasn't touched.

Because I was in the jungle for the most part, I was only able to attend an LDS Church service once in Vietnam. I was finally given one week of R&R and chose to go to Hong Kong where I did attend church. I will never forget seeing, for the first time, LDS people who were not Americans. It was a neat experience for me. But, while I was in Hong Kong my platoon got hit really hard. In fact, when I got back to my unit, half of my squad was gone.

A few weeks later my company was transported by helicopter to a new mission. My squad was the first one to land, and we started down a trail. I was walking third in line. We came to a fork in the trail. The squad leader radioed back to the platoon leader and asked if we should take the trail to the left or the right. We were told to take the trail to the right. The squad behind us took the trail to the left. Ten minutes later the squad that took the trail to the left was ambushed. The person who was walking third in line was hit through his heart, killing him instantly. When we found out, everyone in my squad turned and looked at me, and the only thing I could say was, "I know."

John Decker, Many missions were started and ended by helicopter. Photo taken somewhere in the Quaing Nai Province.

THALES A. DERRICK

Thales was assigned to the 481st Tactical Squadron, which was deployed to Vietnam in June 1965. This was one of the first full squadron deployments of the war even though individual pilots had been involved as advisors to the South Vietnamese Air Force for years. His assignment was as assistant operations officer and mission scheduling officer. Thales's responsibility was to match pilots with planes and combat missions, as well as fly an equal share of combat missions in an F-100D Super Sabre jet.

I scheduled myself to lead a flight of four F-100Ds against an emplacement of Viet Cong troops that were shelling and

attacking the U.S. Army and South Vietnamese Army forces. I conducted the regular preflight briefing, which outlined our target-attack tactics for dive-bombing using 750s—general-purpose bombs. We learned from the intelligence officer, that we could expect fairly heavy automatic weapons fire from the Viet Cong. Because this was Captain Parker's first combat mission, I stressed that we would vary our attack headings.

Soon, we were on our way to the target. The weather was clear and this was both good and bad. It meant that we would have a clear view of the target area, but the ground gunners would also have a clear view of our F-100Ds. I contacted our forward air controller [FAC], who was our linked with the friendly forces on the ground. Our FAC was airborne in a small L-19 Bird Dog aircraft, and he had been assessing the best location for our bombs and also getting current locations of the friendly forces. He relayed all the information to our

Captain Thales A. "Tad" Derrick in the F-100D MORMON METEOR.

Inset: The "Super Sabre" was used extensively during the Vietnam War. Although production of this aircraft ended in 1959, it remained useful when equipped for "wild weasel" missions. This particular aircraft is housed in the Hill Airforce Museum in Roy, Utah.

Above: Captain Thales A. Derrick's plane at 500 knots.

Right: The group is discussing the nose fuse of a 750-pound bomb. Left to Right: Major Pat Berry, 481st Ops Officer; Hack Miller, DESERET NEWS; Captain Thales A. "Tad" Derrick; Airman, Major Berry's Crew Chief.

four fighters as we approached the target. He then shot a smoke rocket for a reference point and told us that the bad guys were along a small canal that was connected to a jungle forest on the north. He suggested we bomb the north bank of the canal and the adjacent forest where the main concentration of enemy forces were located. I led the attack and dropped two 750s. They impacted the desired area. The number two aircraft attacked from a slightly different heading and number three adjusted his attack to again confuse enemy gunners. Then I saw pieces and fluid coming from Captain Parker's aircraft. He had been hit by ground fire. He pulled out of his dive and began climbing for altitude. I went into afterburner and quickly caught up with Captain Parker's aircraft. He had a large hole in the right wing and was losing fuel rapidly from that wing tank. He was also losing hydraulic fluid. His radio was shot out and we had to communicate by hand signals. John indicated that I would lead him home and that we would go out past the South Vietnam shorelines in case he had to eject. The water was a friendlier place than the VC [Viet Cong] infested jungle.

I made radio contact with our tactical air control center and told them I was bringing home a badly damaged Number four. The center picked us up on radar. As I looked to my right to check on John, I noticed that he was pointing frantically to his right wing. I pulled my aircraft up slightly to look over the top of his plane and saw that his right wing was totally engulfed in flames. He gave me the signal that he was going to eject. I moved left to give him lots of room. Fooom!! Off came the canopy followed immediately by the ejection seat and John strapped to it. John separated from the seat cleanly and his parachute opened automatically. A nice, fully blossomed chute! As I circled John, he signaled to me that he was okay and he deployed his life preservers and life raft since he was definitely going "in the drink."

The water that exits the Mekong River at most times of the year is kind of a muddy yellow. It was this color as John hit the water with his yellow life raft and became immediately invisible. Before his parachute sank, I marked the spot with reference to some landmarks on the coast and began to circle. It was at this time that I noticed the boats!

There were four good-sized, sail-powered fishing boats, each about ninety degrees apart, around the circle I was making. John was in the center of the circle. Suddenly, I noticed that all boats had altered their courses and were heading for the center of the circle and John. Who were these people? Innocent fishermen or Viet Cong running guns up or down the river? I didn't want them messing with John either way! I called the center and asked if they had any ideas about how to handle the boat issue. They came back with a non-helpful, "Use your own discretion." At that time I assessed my options. I had two 750 bombs left. One bomb would more than destroy one boat, so two boats could be sunk with bombs. I still had a full load of 800 rounds of 20-millimeter, high explosive shells that could be split out of four cannons at a rate of 1,500 rounds per minute per gun. The guns could make kindling wood out of the other two boats. But what if they were innocent fishermen? I prayed, "Father, I want to protect John, but I don't want to kill innocent fishermen. What shall I do?"

The answer came immediately. "You don't need to destroy them. You can scare them into stopping." I can remember smiling to myself. A fighter plane itself can be pretty intimidating, without firing a shot. I pushed the throttle up full bore and the aircraft accelerated quickly to five hundred knots. I dropped down using the height of the nearest boat for gauging my distance above the water. I ran at the boat lower than mast high and just as I got to the boat

I pulled up abruptly and lit the afterburner. Ka-Boom! I don't know if I blew the sail down with jet-wash or if the fishermen dropped the sail; they were afloat, but stopped still in the water. The same tactic was used on the other three boats. All sat motionless. A prayer of thanks, "Thank thee, Father, that was great."

Now, where was the rescue helicopter? I was starting to get low on fuel. The center indicated that a helicopter had me in sight and would come up on our frequency. I got the chopper pilot on the radio and said that the downed pilot was in the center of my circle. He acknowledged and said he would begin a low level sweep of the circle center. Soon, he spotted John.

When John got back to the base and was cleared by the flight surgeon, I gave him a hug. I never forgot the generous blessing of a loving Father sending the message of the Spirit to me at five hundred knots.

JOHN DINKELMAN

John was born in Holland and later immigrated to the United States. During the Vietnam War he served as a chief warrant officer in the Army. He served in the Army for thirty-five years. Early in his 35-year army career he participated in the World War II Battle of the Bulge as a member of a tank crew. Currently he is a U.S. State Department Foreign Service officer stationed in Turkey.

I served two tours in Vietnam. I was the master of LCU (landing craft, utility)—the same as an LCT, a landing craft of World War II vintage. Several times I felt the Spirit as I was moving my boat with 120 tons of artillery shells in a river too narrow to turn around as Charlie, the name of the enemy there, was dropping mortar shells in front and back of me. All I could do was to keep steaming. Twice rockets hit my boat and neither exploded as they penetrated the hull; and you can well imagine what would have happened with 120 tons of ammunition on board.

When I was able I would attend LDS services with a small group at a nearby navy base in Da Nang. Often the song selected to sing was, "We are all enlisted till the conflict is o'er," and the sailors would sing, "Sailors in the navy, Happy are we" etc., always getting a chuckle. There was a navy LDS chaplain, Pocock, who was admired and loved by us LDS fellows and he had called a conference at China Beach near Da Nang. At the services were being held, the speaker would have to pause often because the helicopter noise would drown him out. He [Chaplain Pocock] had a classic statement he often used, "Don't keep the gospel. Share it!!"

BILL ESSEX, JR.

Bill was born in Arkansas. During the Vietnam War he served as a captain in the Army's A-411, 5th Special Forces Group from 1966–1972. His assignments included patrols and ambushes. He is currently a Utah police officer and has served as a Sunday School instructor.

In January 1968 I was a first lieutenant en route to Vietnam. Shortly before leaving, my father gave me a blessing. In the blessing he promised me that my life would be spared if I obeyed the Lord's commandments and lived the gospel. A few days later, I was attending a general priesthood meeting. As I entered the meeting our stake president, Cecil Burningham, asked me how I was doing. I told him that I had had a headache for several days that I couldn't seem to shake. He told me that I didn't need to put up with that and offered to give me a blessing before the meeting. After the blessing of health and the almost immediate departure of the headache, President Burningham went on to promise me that my life would be spared if I obeyed the Lord. It seemed that he had used the exact words my father had used in his blessing.

I was assigned to the 5th Special Forces (Airborne) in the Republic of Vietnam in the middle of February 1968. During

1st Lt. Bill Essex, MSG Peter Astolos, SSG Jim Turley, SGT Taylor, SGT William (Flip) Howell (back row) receiving Bronze Star Medals for Valor.

the middle of March I was assigned to lead an operation that involved setting up a blocking force, or anvil, for the 9th U.S. Infantry Division to drive communist forces into. I had been troubled for several days because the captain had asked me to accept responsibility for the camp funds from the lieutenant I had replaced. He had asked me not to report a shortage and to make up the shortage in the paperwork. I had done what the captain had asked and felt very guilty for doing it. The night before the operation, I couldn't sleep; I felt that I had not lived up to my part of the blessing I was promised and therefore had no protection. I was sure that I was going to be killed because I had been dishonest. Needless to say, I fell asleep on my knees.

As we flew away from the camp the next morning I looked around believing that I would never see it again. I wasn't afraid; I just knew that I was going to die. When we reached the landing zone, the first lift (my lift) was inserted without incident. Just as the second and final lift reached the landing zone we began taking heavy fire. We were receiving fire from machine guns, rockets, and mortars from a force much larger than ours that were dug in the tree line. To make matters worse I was not given direct control over the artillery and air support for my part of the mission. I had no way of contacting them except through the commander of the American unit. He was busy doing other things and could not be bothered with my problems. To add insult to injury, helicopter gunship pilots saw my Vietnamese troops and started strafing us. The VC [Viet Cong] had us pinned down tight; they didn't really need the air support that our side was giving them.

Once the engagement began, I forgot that I was supposed to die, and got busy consolidating my troops and trying to coordinate effective fire. Eventually I was able to contact a forward air controller that got me some support. While I was making our position with a panel, a bullet struck the inside edge of the ammo pouch just to the left of my belt buckle. Upon reaching the back of the pouch, it turned left and cut the back off the pouch. It continued cutting three inches out of my shirt, one inch out of my garments, went into the top of my canteen and out the bottom. I was spun around and knocked down, and I felt a burning pain exactly like the feeling guys that had been shot described. Jim Turley, the medic, ran to me and started checking me for wounds. We were both surprised to find none. The bullet had traveled in a complete semi-circle around my waist and exited my web gear behind my back in a direct line from where it first hit me. During the several hours that we were engaged, five of my NCOs [noncommissioned officer] and about sixty-five of my strikers were wounded. No one was seriously hurt and I didn't lose a single man. Under the circumstances, I had to believe that I wasn't the only one the Lord was protecting that day. Later, as the 9th Infantry started to join us, another sergeant and I were lying on either side of a young private from the 9th. At that point we were strafed for the last time. The machine-gun fire shot to within inches of the sergeant, hit the private, killing him, missed me and started hitting within inches beyond me. That evening I gave thanks to God for sparing me and giving me another chance. I also thanked Him for protecting my men and freeing us from a terrible situation.

Military Medals and Awards

Medals are listed from highest ranking down, and list is not all-inclusive of every medal that could be earned.

BRONZE STAR: Awarded for heroic or meritorious achievement of service, not involving aerial flight in connection with operations against and opposing armed force. Bronze "V" device worn to denote valor.

THE LEGION OF MERIT: Awarded for exceptionally meritorious conduct in the performance of outstanding service.

Medal of Honor [Army, Air Force, Navy (which includes the Marines & Coast Guard)]
Distinguished Service Cross
Navy Cross
Air Force Cross
Defense Distinguished Service Medal
Distinguished Service Medal (Army, Navy–Marine Corps, Air Force, Coast Guard)
Silver Star
Defense Superior Service Medal
Legion of Merit
Distinguished Flying Cross

THE AIR MEDAL: Awarded for meritorious achievement while participating in aerial flight. Bronze "V" device worn to denote valor.

REPUBLIC OF VIETNAM GALLANTRY CROSS WITH PALM UNIT CITATION: Awarded by the Republic of Vietnam to units for valorous combat achievement.

Soldier's Medal
Navy and Marine Corps Medal
Airman's Medal
Coast Guard Medal
Bronze Star Medal
Purple Heart

Defense Meritorious Service Medal
Meritorious Service Medal
Air Medal
Aerial Achievement Medal
Joint Service Commendation Medal
Army Commendation Medal
Navy Commendation Medal
Air Force Commendation Medal
Coast Guard Commendation Medal
Joint Servce Achievement Medal
Army Achievement Medal
Navy Achievement Medal
Air Force Achieverement Medal
Coast Guard Achievement Medal
POW Medal
Combat Readiness Medal (Air Force)
Good Conduct Medal (Army, Navy, Marine Corps, Air Force, Coast Guard)

(Left) THE DISTINGUISHED FLYING CROSS: Awarded for heroism or extraordinary achievement while participating in aerial flight. Bronze "V" device worn to denote valor.

STEPHEN E. FEATHERSTONE

During the Vietnam War Stephen served in the Army's 101st Airborne Division from 1965–1966 and 1971–1972. His assignments included division aviation officer and command helicopter. He currently lives in Utah, after serving a 21-year U.S. Army career. He is also a personal business management consultant. He now serves as second counselor in the presidency of the Mount Timpanogos Utah Temple.

In a ceremony during which I assumed command of the 158th Combat Assault Helicopter Battalion, General Hill offered me a glass of champagne to toast the battalion and my assumption of command. I spoke softly to him. "Sir, I don't drink, I am a Latter-day Saint."

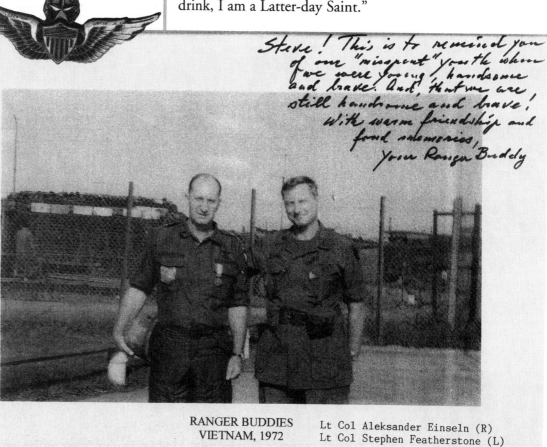

Steve! This is to remind you of our "misspent" youth when we were young, handsome and brave! And, that we are, still handsome and brave!
With warm friendship and fond memories,
Your Ranger Buddy

RANGER BUDDIES
VIETNAM, 1972

Lt Col Aleksander Einseln (R)
Lt Col Stephen Featherstone (L)

He just looked at me and said, "Drink, it's a tradition." I just shook my head slightly indicating that I would not drink the champagne. I had planned for this eventuality, knowing this was likely to happen. My battalion clerk had placed a clear glass of 7-Up with the can still on the tray. I took the glass and as General Hill began his toast he politely reached out, and we touched glasses. Several of my men were LDS returned missionaries and were watching me with trepidation that tradition might pressure me to break the Word of Wisdom. It did not.

Stephen E. Featherstone's Dog Tag.

Below: UH-1 D Helicopter, RVN June 1966 Operation Near Cu Chi.

BERNIE FISHER

The Medal of Honor was awarded to Major Bernard F. Fisher, U.S. Air Force, for his courageous rescue of Major Jump Meyers. When Major Jump Meyers's plane crashed in flames on a Viet Cong-held airstrip, there appeared to be no chance of rescue, yet Bernie decided to try. He performed this rescue in the face of some two thousand hostile troops. His determination and his incredible display of courage in the face of a resolute and heavily armed hostile force reflected service above and beyond the call of duty.

As a young man, prayer was always an important factor in my life. While in the Air Force, I had many opportunities to call on God for His help. The sheer terror of flying in weather that at best many times was below minimums, gave me the privilege of calling for help. The day of the rescue, March 10, 1966, probably changed my life forever. I remember watching Jump Meyers' plane, flaming like a torch at the back past his tail after he was hit, and my telling him to dump his bombs and pull his gear up so he could belly it in. As I watched in horror, he skidded down the runway and off to the right. The plane burst into a huge ball of fire. I thought he was probably killed in the crash. Then a gust of wind seemed to blow the flame from the right side and Jump came smoking out across the wing. It looked like he was burning as smoke and flames seemed to trail him. He jumped into a ditch at the side of the runway to hide from the enemy troops that were dangerously close. I called for a helicopter rescue, but they said it would be about twenty minutes. I went back to the battle with many thoughts racing through my mind. Going in to pick him up was not a good idea. However, I had such a strong feeling, so I decided to take a few minutes and seek counsel with my Heavenly Father. I said, "If this is what you want me to do, I need your help. You have never let me down." A calm peaceful feeling came over me, and I knew what I must do. My wingmen, John Lucas and Denny Hague, bless their hearts, said they would cover me. They were strafing right along the side of the runway, keeping the Vietnamese heads down. Denny said, "If one of them had raised his head, we would've gotten him." I will always be grateful for the Men In Blue that I flew with and for those dedicated troops on the ground that kept the planes in tip-top condition and kept us flying. I will be eternally grateful for the help and protection I received that day from my Heavenly Father.

Taken from Colonel Jimmie Dean Coy, *A Gathering of Eagles* (Mobile, Alabama: Evergreen Press, 1991), 17.

DAN FOOTE

Dan served in Vietnam as a Marine. Following his service he completed his education under the GI Bill program.

I turned twenty-two on one of the combat operations. We were sitting in a rice paddy, and the guys decided that we were going to celebrate my birthday. It was a big thing. At twenty-two, I was the oldest man in the squad. We pooled our money and bought this big GI can full of Ba Mui Ba, which is thirty-three beers, and sodas. About half the guys were looped by midnight. I was LDS, so I drank sodas while the rest drank beer. About one o'clock in the morning, we were still sitting there. I looked over at Al Echols and asked, "What's crawling across your leg?"

"I don't know." By this time nobody cared about light security. We turned on the flashlight and the next thing we saw was a king cobra backing up and spreading its hood. If you

Air Force Medal of Honor

FISHER, BERNARD FRANCIS. Rank and organization: Major, U.S. Air Force, 1st Air Commandos. Place and date: Bien Hoa and Pleiku, Vietnam, 10 March 1966. Entered service at: Kuna, Idaho. Born: 11 January 1927, San Bernardino, Calif.

U.S. Air Force Major Bernard F. Fisher was awarded the Air Force Medal of Honor, by President Lyndon B. Johnson at a White House ceremony. Major Fisher received the Medal of Honor for his rescue of another Air Force pilot, Lt. Col. Dafford W. Myers.

CITATION: For conspicuous gallantry and intrepidity at the risk of his life above and beyond the call of duty. On that date, the special forces camp at A Shau was under attack by 2,000 North Vietnamese Army regulars. Hostile troops had positioned themselves between the airstrip and the camp. Other hostile troops had surrounded the camp and were continuously raking it with automatic weapons fire from the surrounding hills. The tops of the 1,500-foot hills were obscured by an 800 foot ceiling, limiting aircraft maneuverability and forcing pilots to operate within range of hostile gun positions, which often were able to fire down on the attacking aircraft. During the battle, Maj. Fisher observed a fellow airman crash land on the battle-torn airstrip. In the belief that the downed pilot was seriously injured and in imminent danger of capture, Maj. Fisher announced his intention to land on the airstrip to effect a rescue. Although aware of the extreme danger and likely failure of such an attempt, he elected to continue. Directing his own air cover, he landed his aircraft and taxied almost the full length of the runway, which was littered with battle debris and parts of an exploded aircraft. While effecting a successful rescue of the downed pilot, heavy ground fire was observed, with 19 bullets striking his aircraft. In the face of the withering ground fire, he applied power and gained enough speed to lift-off at the overrun of the airstrip. Maj. Fisher's profound concern for his fellow airman, and at the risk of his life above and beyond the call of duty are in the highest traditions of the U.S. Air Force and reflect great credit upon himself and the Armed Forces of his country.

Men of the L Co., 3rd Bn., 4th Marine Regt. slog through the rice paddies in a sweep-and-destroy patrol.

ever wanted to see something hilarious, this was it. There must have been twenty drunken Marines chasing a king cobra across the rice paddies at two o'clock in the morning.

* * * * *

It was sort of fun being the "Mad Mormon." I had every rank from private to colonel sitting on the edge of my foxhole talking about the Church, and many of them ended up joining the Church. I had a Book of Mormon with me and had to send some people out on OP [operations] so I could read it myself. A lot of men were looking for something over there and there were many opportunities to talk about the Church.

I learned that the Lord will take care of you if you live right and communicate with Him. There is a lot of guidance and counsel available if you are in a leadership position and will only listen. Before missions I would go off by myself and have a word of prayer. My men would always check to see if I had made "commo" with the Lord. After a while, a couple men asked if they could join me while I prayed and then finally it became our custom to kneel in prayer before and after each mission.

I've been all over in the jungle, in the desert, and in the Arctic. If you look for it you can find something beautiful anywhere. I survived partially because I looked for the beautiful; by finding the good in people and by trying to be the best Marine I possibly could be. There were negative things like pain and death, but in the long run I profited from Vietnam.

DAVID GARDNER

As a resident of Idaho, David enlisted in the Air Force. After his tour of duty in Vietnam, he was assigned to serve in the Pentagon. During his service experience, he served as a branch president.

It was difficult. I do not care who you were, if you were in Vietnam, the possibility was always there. We would walk down into Saigon three times a week. You would hear shooting going on and the reality, and the possibility of death hung over everyone's shoulders who was in Vietnam as soon as you entered the country. I think I can honestly say that I faced the whole possibility prayerfully. I wanted to go down on record that the greatest thing I felt that I had going for me was my faith in God, my relationship with my Heavenly Father, and the prayerful moments that I spent on my knees.

Before I left for Vietnam, I went out and spent a day alone in the woods of Idaho and poured out my soul to my Heavenly Father and asked him to bless me, to keep me so that I could come home to my wife and my newly born little baby daughter, our first child, who was at that time four months old. I pleaded with Him to preserve my life and asked Him and promised Him that I would sacrifice and serve Him the rest of my life. That was a promise that I made.

Before I got on the plane to leave for Vietnam, my father gave me a father's blessing and promised me that my life would be preserved and that I would perform a great mission while I was in Vietnam. He actually promised me in the blessing that I would perform a second mission for my church. I did not realize how that was going to be fulfilled until a few months after I got there. I was called as the branch president of the Tan Son Nhut Air Force Base group of servicemen. I began to realize that all of that was being fulfilled right before my very eyes.

GARTH LOWE GEDDES

Garth was born in Idaho. During the Vietnam War he served as lieutenant colonel in the Army's 1st Air Cavalry Division from 1965–1966 and 1968–1969. His assignments included that of aviation battalion commander. Currently he works as a business analyst in Utah.

I wanted to be alone so I walked away from the airfield to the white coral beach that encircled the island. One who has not been there and done that can hardly imagine the emotions that one feels who is on his way into combat for the first time. As well, I felt keenly the loneliness and heartache that I would experience . . . again, so soon after a year away from my family in Korea. Had I been in one of the landing craft chugging toward Omaha beach on D-Day, June 6, 1944, I doubt that I could have been more frightened and distraught than I was. I was physically sick. I was emotionally drained. I was worried about my wife and family, which I had literally dumped at her parent's home. I recall thinking to myself, "Buck up, you sissy. You are not an eighteen-year-old kid. You're thirty-five years old and you've been through some pretty tough times before . . . and you did just fine. You know how to deal with stress. Stiffen your back and your resolve and deal with this!" But my lectures to myself were ineffectual. I just needed to get away from everyone for an hour or so and perhaps, in prayer, I could draw some solace, some comfort, some reassurance that I would make it through a year in combat alive and that my family would be all right.

I walked down the beach, not knowing where I was going . . . I just wanted to be alone. I looked back along the beach and could see a single set of footprints in the sand trailing back almost as far as I could see. I was very alone, but I pushed on, slowly walking and fervently praying for strength to endure faithfully and cheerfully what now would be required of me. I walked past several old broken and overgrown concrete bunkers, which gave stark evidence to the terrible battle that had raged there during World War II between the Americans and the Japanese.

After a while, I came to what remained of an old heavy timber bridge which at one time stretched across a narrow inlet into a small, deep-blue lagoon. It was sort of eerie. The jagged skeleton of the bridge now stuck up in the air like the hulk of an old abandoned ship. Most of the bridge had long since been destroyed by the sea or by bombs and shells which rained down on the island during the battle which had raged twenty years before. With some effort, I climbed up onto the old bridge and stood leaning on what remained of a weathered, wooden railing. I was very, very alone. With the soft rush of the surf gently pounding over the reef about two hundred yards to my front, I prayed. I had never prayed like this before. My need had never been this great.

Somewhere in that prayer, I lifted my head and gazed out onto a thousand miles of clear, blue ocean; praying, pondering, pleading, waiting. After a time, I became aware of a swimmer, so far away that he appeared only as a little dot in the foaming surf. He worked his way over the reef into the small blue lagoon over which I stood. At a point directly beneath where I stood, he pulled from his belt a small cloth bag containing crusts of bread which he released; a handful at a time, into the crystal clear water. When he did so, hundreds of beautifully colored tropical fish streaked from the bottom of the pool to take the bread. The water literally churned as the fish fought over the small scraps of bread.

When the sack was empty, the swimmer raised his mask and for the first time, became aware that I was there. We exchange greetings, and I casually asked, "Where are you from?"

He responded, "I'm from Salt Lake."

Without thinking, there tumbled from my mouth the words, "Are you a Mormon?"

"Yes." He quickly made his way to the edge of the lagoon and I raced down the incline of the bridge where, though having never before met, we embraced as brothers. We spent several wonderful hours together talking about and comparing notes about our families, praying together and strengthening one another as brothers in the gospel of Jesus Christ.

As we talked, I became aware that he too had been lonely, that he too had been praying for strength and reassurance; that he too felt, as did I, alone and forgotten. We had each come to a point in our feelings where we felt that perhaps God did not know where we were and that He did not care.

But there on that tiny speck of an island in the middle of the Pacific, I had found my Sinai; I had come to my sacred grove. Like Paul on the road to Damascus, I too had met my God face to face. In my own way, I too had talked with God. Later that evening when I boarded the aircraft whose next stop would be Vietnam, I left without any assurance that my life would be spared during the hostilities that lay directly ahead, but I did take from that experience the sure knowledge that God was real, that He did know my pain, that He did share my loneliness and that He knew and cared deeply that I was afraid.

As I have reflected on that experience, I have come to know that our meeting on that small island so far away from anywhere was not chance. A loving and caring God had caused our paths to cross, and that meeting indelibly blessed both our lives. Through that incredible happenstance, God reassured both of us that He knows who we are . . . and he cares. My experience there was not at all unlike the experience of the Prophet Joseph Smith. In my own way, I heard God speaking to me as He did to the Prophet Joseph Smith in the dark cell of Liberty Jail, "Know thou, my son, that all these things shall give thee experience and shall be for thy good. The Son of Man hath descended below them all. Art thou greater than he? Therefore hold on thy way . . . fear not . . . for God shall be with you forever and ever" [D&C 122:7–9].

EARL LEROY GUNNELL

Earl graduated from the Air Force Academy in Colorado Springs before entering the Vietnam War. For his service both he and his crew received the Distinguished Flying Cross.

We got up to go on a regular mission that morning and the crew that was scheduled into this particular airfield was sick that morning so they reassigned us to take this flight. It was during April 1970, when the U.S. Forces were starting the Cambodian Offensive. The field we were to go into was on the border of Cambodia. We loaded up that day with two 105-howitzers and quite a bit of ammunition to supply those guns, about twenty-five ground troops, and several other miscellaneous things. We had a heavy load going in.

They asked us to go into an airfield that was only 2,500 feet long, a dirt strip, which is the minimum that you could land a C-130 aircraft. As we approached that day, we got clearance for landing, but we could see it was like a beehive of activity down there. There were helicopters all around and in fact, there was a helicopter sitting right on the far end of the runway creating a dust storm. We could hardly see and you could see fighters delivering ordnance about two miles to our left just over Cambodia and we went down and landed.

As we touched down on that short field we aimed for a spot two hundred feet from the end of the runway. We had between a 200- and 500-foot spot that we had to land in, or we couldn't be assured that we could get the airplane stopped in time. We put it down in the first 200 feet and then as soon as I touched down, I threw it into full reverse and literally stood on the brakes and pushed as hard as I could with full reverse and hoped I could get it stopped in time. This day we got about midway down the field and the dust from the helicopters was so thick that we couldn't see a thing, and we didn't even know where the end of the runway was. Fortunately, we got it stopped by the time we got to the end and pulled off and started to unload.

C-130 Hercules

Only a few aircraft have earned the description "legendary." However, the C-130, named "Hercules" from the mythical Greek hero renowned for his great strength, has become a true, real-world legend. More than 2,200 C-130s have been built, and they are flown by more than 60 nations worldwide, in more than 70 variations. [The aircraft was engineered by Lockheed Martin Aeronautics Company, and there have been numerous modifications throughout the years.]

In truth, there is no airlift mission the C-130 has not flown. It carries troops, vehicles, and armaments into battle; drops paratroopers and supplies from the sky; serves as airborne and ground refuelers; provides emergency evacuation and humanitarian relief; and conducts airborne early warning and maritime surveillance. It has recovered space capsules, and worn skis in Antarctica. Surviving the toughest flights, the roughest landings and the constant pounding of heavy cargo, many of the earliest C-130s are still active today. In the history of aviation design, the preeminent symbol for strength, durability and multimission success unquestionably belongs to the C-130 Hercules. (Lockheed Martin Aeronautics, www.lmaeronautics.com/products/airmobility/c-130/index.html)

The usual unloading procedure at a field like this was to leave an outboard engine running to provide power so that if we could get the other engines started we would be able to leave in a hurry. The ground forces didn't maintain a lot of ground power units to help start up aircraft, so we needed to leave our engine running. That day we heard the noise of our engine running and several helicopters hovering around doing their thing. We could see them while we were in the aircraft that was being unloaded. I remember at this time there was a helicopter about fifty feet away from us starting to set down into a tall grassy area just to the side of the runway. As they approached the ground we heard this scream over the radio, "Don't touch down, helicopter, I repeat, don't touch down! There are mines over there!" They just hovered there for a while and then went back up. It was hard to follow all the action there. There were all kinds of people that were doing all kinds of things all at once and nobody seemed to be controlling anything. It is a wonder they didn't kill more of their own people than the enemy did.

We left everything there and then we had to fly to another field near central South Vietnam. It was another hotbed at that time. We went over that day and picked up some more troops and things, and then we were to return to the original field a second time. By the time we had done this, we had used up most of the day. When we got back that evening, just at dusk, we came in and landed again with much the same kind of activity still going on. As we were unloading, darkness settled over the area, and about that time another C-130 came into land. Boy, if you have ever seen an airplane have a hard landing, this guy came down and he landed so hard that he bounced about fifteen feet back into the air. And knowing that he'd never get it stopped, he just shoved the power to it and went on around and went on back to Tan Son Nhut and called them when he got there and told them he'd see them the next day.

In an airfield that was that much of a hotbed of activity the ground control team wanted to leave each night and return to a more secure airfield. The usual procedure was to use the last plane in for the day as their transportation out. As the ground crew watched the last plane bounce and take off again, they were very eager to make sure we didn't leave before they got aboard. By the time we got everything unloaded and ready to go, it was pitch black and then suddenly from all the activity and noises that had been going on, it was just like someone had given a signal and a dead silence had come over the whole jungle. Everything was just black, quiet, and calm. You didn't know where the enemy was or what was going on. We loaded up that air force ground control team and then took the runway. Usually, in such a short runway, you back the airplane up all the way to the end of the runway and then hold the brakes and put full power on the engines. One gets it revved up and then lets her go and hopes to not lose an engine. As soon as we broke ground we turned off the lights so that we weren't the target for somebody. That was kind of an exciting experience and they gave my crew the DFC [Distinguished Flying Cross] for that one-day activity.

DOUG T. HALL

Before Doug served in Vietnam he was a member of the Army's 1st Special Forces Group, stationed in Okinawa. He trained in Thailand, Korea, and Taiwan before going to Vietnam in 1966. Doug volunteered for the Army in order to serve in Vietnam as a member of a special forces radio operator.

Right after we had ambushed the Viet Cong we knew that all the noise we'd made was going to alert everybody else in the area. We had moved down the trail after the ambush and found the Viet Cong's hooch, (sleeping tent) and set it on fire and then called for an extraction. The patrol leader moved us into a clearing on the trail. There was a lot of overhead cover, but very little ground cover and he said, "Okay, stop right here." I thought, "Why is he having us stop in the middle of the clearing? Why don't we at least go into the woods for cover?" I'm sitting there thinking and it runs through my mind that there could be Viet Cong or NVA [North Vietnamese Army] at that very moment sticking their guns out of the jungle right at us and I panicked; I wanted to jump up and run for the woods. I didn't, I controlled it, but for that one moment it hit me that I had never had that experience before. It made me appreciate the book, *The Red Badge of Courage.* Stephan Crane talks about how those kids go into battle and all of a sudden these guys are dropping their guns and running. I know, I understand the feeling, I can understand why they would do that, and I could not accuse them of cowardice. I don't think that's cowardice at all. Sometimes something runs through your mind and you just panic. You just react to that and I don't think anyone can blame anybody in those kinds of situations for that. At least I couldn't anymore.

As a kid I had seen a lot of war shows and they always talked about how these guys would come and they'd say, "Here, Sergeant, take my stuff, take my letter to my girl, I just know I am going to get it in this next battle." And then they'd get killed; it always happened that way. If I ever have a feeling like that about a mission, I am not going to go. We got a mission, and I had a funny feeling and I thought, "I shouldn't go on this mission." I told our leader I had this funny feeling and I said, "I promised myself that if I had a funny feeling that I wouldn't go." He was not going to force me to go with him. I sat and stewed upon it for about an hour and then changed my mind and said, "Okay, I'll go."

And he said, "Fine." So we packed up all our stuff and headed off to Budop, which was his old special force's camp and from there we'd run our operation. On that operation several things happened.

The first thing is that we moved out to the river that separated Vietnam and Cambodia and at that river we sat up for the night with the idea of crossing at a fording area the next morning. The next morning when we got up, I tried to raise our air cover on the radio and I couldn't get anything. I checked that whole radio out, and I could not make it work or make communication. And we couldn't operate without the radio and so we decided we'd go back into Budop so we turned around and walked back to Budop.

When we got back to Budop and checked the radio, we discovered the only thing that was wrong with it was that the antenna post was loose which would have normally been the first thing that I would have checked, but I didn't this time. So we tightened up the post and everything was fine. While we were sitting there getting ready to go back in, one of the camp spies came in to report that he had crossed that ford earlier that morning and had walked right into an NVA patrol that was lying there in ambush which would have been there when we would have crossed. Had the radio not caused a problem we would have walked right into them that morning.

KENT HANSEN

As a native of Ohio, Kent served as a chief petty officer assigned to naval support activities. His assignment in that capacity included that of a combat journalist. He joined the Church during his service in Vietnam. Currently he is the communication director of the Utah Travel Council. He has served in many Church callings and is currently his ward's high priests group leader.

The camp library offered little information about the LDS Church. I walked over to the Camp Tien Sha chapel to see what I could find. In the foyer was a massive rack of pamphlets segmented into Catholic, Protestant, Jewish and Other. In the "Other" section, I found one LDS tract on tithing. Finally, I asked one of the chaplains where I might find a Mormon. "Oh, you mean the L-S-Ds. You might ask over at the post office," he said. "Their lay leader is a postal clerk named Orvin Shepard."

A few minutes later, I arrived at the post office and asked for Shepard. A man stopped what he was doing and came over to me. "I am Shepard," he explained. "What can I do for you?" With all the arrogance of youth, I explained that I wanted to disprove Mormonism and needed to borrow a Book of Mormon. He told me to wait and slipped into his hooch. He returned carrying a stack of tracts such as only a Mormon could collect, which consisted of a Book of Mormon and a doctrinal compendium titled "Principles of the Gospel."

Below: Kent Hansen was a cartoonist for the U.S. Naval Support Activity (NSA), Da Nang Public Affairs Office.

Right top: Some of Kent Hansen's cartoons depict experiences that happened to him. Others are just too absurd to ever happen, but they are humorous.

Right bottom: Soldier drawn by Kent Hansen.

Roy serviceman enjoys work in public affairs office

by JO2 Dwight D. Rowin

Da Nang — Comic books are usually considered entertainment for youngsters. However, for Journalist 3rd Class Kent Hansen of Roy, they've been an instrument of learning.

Hansen, cartoonist for the U.S. Naval Support Activity (NSA), Da Nang Public Affairs Office the past 18 months and assistant editor of the command newspaper, "Elephant News," learned basics in drawing from the "super hero" comic books.

"I've had very little formal training," said Hansen, son of Mr. and Mrs. Robert K. Hansen, 2587 W. 5750 S., Roy. "Most of what I learned has been from comic books such as Batman, Superman, Spiderman and similar comics.

"For a couple of years I spent most of my time tracing and then copying the comic strips and books. It wasn't until a couple of years ago that I developed my own style."

Hansen's first artwork to appear in the command newspaper "Elephant News" (then the "White Elephant News") was Sept. 20, 1968.

"It was a simple drawing emphasizing that everyone from the Admiral to a Seaman reads the newspaper," Hansen remarked.

Since that time, Hansen's artwork has been in every publication of the command newspaper. In August 1969, Hansen began a cartoon character named "Halfhitch Harrigan."

"The ideas for my cartoons come from various places," the 22-year-old 1966 graduate of Roy High commented. "In a lot of instances the cartoons depict experiences that happened to me. In other cases, the incidents are so absurd that they

couldn't happen — but are funny.

"Mainly, I try to put Halfhitch in a sympathetic position. This is so the lower-rated people can associate with him. He will occasionally strike the "powers-to-be" sometimes accidentally, and other times on purpose.

"At the same time, the senior NCO's and officers can associate with the cartoon since they can see what is going to happen to Halfhitch for his errant ways."

However, Halfhitch Harrigan made his last appearance in the March 13 edition of the "Elephant News."

Hank Ketcham, noted cartoonist and creator of the "Dennis the Menace" comic strip has started a syndicated strip entitled simple "Half Hitch." Incidentally, the strip will be about the Navy.

Hansen is changing his format from the one-frame cartoons to the four-frame cartoons. His new series will be entitled "Sea Bats." The characters in the new strip will be Captain Lee Helm, Ensign Buster Butterbar, Boatswain Mate Chiefs Marlon Spike and Tiger Sharkey, Seaman Gangway Gordon and Poopdeck Parker.

"I actually hate to see 'Halfhitch Harrigan' go overboard," Hansen stated. "If anyone was going to use that for a name of a cartoon strip, I'm glad it was Hank Ketcham. He's always been one of my favorite cartoonists."

Hansen and Ketcham have been corresponding the last few months, and in a recent letter to Hansen, Ketcham noted he was sorry to see the young artist's Halfhitch "mothballed." However, Ketcham is actually reviving a character he first used in the early 1940's.

About his tour at NSA Da Nang, Hansen feels he's

profited from the 18 months in the Republic of Vietnam.

"There is no doubt that the experience I've picked up will be an asset later," Hansen, who attended Utah State University at Logan for a year, remarked. "I've been fortunate in that I've worked with people who have a vast working knowledge in their respective fields. This includes writing, photography, layout, drawing and other aspects of journalism.

Since reporting to NSA in August 1968, Hansen has done just about anything a journalist could possibly do. He's drawn cartoons for internal publications, including the cruise book, written stories and poems, taken photographs, edited and rewritten copy, planned layout for the command newspaper, conducted radio interviews and escorted civilian media representatives.

Hansen hasn't remained tied to his desk for the past 18 months, however.

"I've traveled all over I Corps, from Sa Huynh to fire support bases near the DMZ," Hansen commented.

"I've enjoyed traveling to places in the field, especially to the detachments. I've visited every NSA detachment and I can honestly say that the morale there has been as high as you'll find anywhere."

Hansen's vast area of activity doesn't end with his working hours at the public affairs office.

While at NSA, Hansen became a member of the Da Nang Area Choral Group and the Vietnamese-American Association, formed and directed a choral group of Vietnamese girls and was group clerk for the Tien Sha Latter-day Saints group of the Southeast Asia Mission.

What does the future hold for Hansen?

"My next duty station is Commander, Service Force Pacific Fleet in Hawaii and I hope to do much the same type of work there that I did here," he remarked. "Afterwards I would like to have a syndicated cartoon strip. I will definitely continue to draw cartoons. This isn't work for me — I enjoy it too much."

He seemed a little too cooperative and suspiciously I told him that I wanted to be left alone and that I didn't want to see any missionaries. My promise to return the books as soon as I was finished was countered by a quiet smile. He said I could keep them. I was puzzled by his kind helpfulness.

I retired to the barracks to begin my attack. I knew it would be unfair to attack beliefs, but in order for the Church to be all it claimed to be, it had to be completely logical. Therefore, I would attack the logic. I decided that *Principles of the Gospel* would help me get right down to the doctrines, so I started there. My fine-tooth comb cut into page one and a day and a half later emerged—empty. For the first time in my life, I couldn't logically discount a book.

The Book of Mormon was another story. Joseph Smith certainly couldn't have known as much about the Bible as I did. He had only a third-grade education and I had studied for the ministry! The Book of Mormon would provide my loophole. I found it on page 520. "And when ye shall receive these things, I would exhort you that ye would ask God, the Eternal Father, in the name of Christ, if these things are not true; and if ye shall ask with a sincere heart, with real intent, having faith in Christ, he will manifest the truth of it unto you, by the power of the Holy Ghost" (Moroni 10:4).

There it was. I knew the heavens were shut. If I accepted Moroni's challenge and received no answer, I could look any Mormon in the eye and declare him a liar. I had read in the Joseph Smith's testimony pamphlet that Joseph had knelt down and prayed out loud. Because I was sincere and wanted to do things right, I resolved to duplicate Joseph's effort.

The next problem was finding a suitable place to pray. Unlike young Joseph, I had no grove of trees in which to retire. Any tress outside the compound would have been filled with those who would be only too happy to kill me. Camp Tien Sha, where I lived, was an old French fort. Behind my barracks was one place that could work. It was bordered on two sides by a high, thick concrete wall.

A few feet inside the wall was a large tree. At night, a person kneeling behind the tree would be invisible in the shadows but could see anyone who might approach. In mid-August 1969, I knelt in that secure spot behind my barracks and prayed aloud.

I told God that I had read the book that the Mormons say is from Him. I admitted that there were good things in it but that it said near the end that if I wanted to know if it were true, God was compelled to tell me. Well, I wanted to know if it was true. No sooner had I closed my prayer than I heard a voice so very clearly and it said this to me: "What you have received is true and now that you know that it is true, you know what you must do, for not to do it is to sin." This wasn't supposed to happen. How could this be? It was not the answer I was seeking and certainly not what I had expected. But I had asked and now I had my answer and all the responsibility that went with it. The Church of Jesus Christ of Latter-day Saints was the only true church on the earth! I knew it. I dared not deny it. What would I do? What could I do? I smoked, drank, and was not a righteous man by any means. I knew my family would disapprove. Could I hurt them that way? Membership in the LDS church would mean a complete commitment to change my lifestyle. But that didn't really matter, did it? I knew the Church was true and there was only one thing for me to do.

That Sunday, I ventured into the chapel for LDS services. I arrived early because I was unsure of what to do. As I approached them to ask questions, they swarmed me, inquiring who I was. "I'm Kent Hansen," I said.

"Well, Brother Hansen," one of them said, "Would you speak in Sacrament meeting today?"

I said, "Wait a minute! I am not even a member of your Church."

"That's okay, they said. "We'd still like to hear from you." I looked toward the front and there, just finishing a personal prayer, was Orvin Shepard. He turned and smiled. I spoke in the meeting that Sunday, telling them about my experience behind the barracks. I asked if there was someone there who

Thu and Lieu had invited us over to celebrate Tet. They were the laundry ladies at the navy Headquarters. Left to right: SN Kent Hansen, Mama-sau Thu, Mama-sau Lieu, JO3 Rich Lizotte.

might assist me in preparing for baptism. Almost half a dozen elders nearly injured themselves vaulting the pews to get to me first.

When I got back to my barracks I wrote to my friend and mentor, Dr. Rowley, and told him that I was going to get baptized. He wrote back immediately and told me he was very happy for me but warned me not to be baptized unless I was absolutely sure. "The Church," he said, "isn't something you can put on and take off like a coat. It is real and it is true and it is forever." I smiled as I read it. Of course, as usual, he was right. But I was sure, and I knew it was true and I was in it forever.

Within the next few days, all of my questions were answered. But the answers to my questions were secondary compared with the testimony that now burned within me. I was baptized in the South China Sea off China Beach near Da Nang, Vietnam, on September 21, 1969. I was confirmed at the water's edge and ordained to the office of a deacon.

SCOTT HANSEN

Scott's assignment in the U.S. Army was as a truck driver and door gunner. During his combat experience he received the rank of SPC/E-4. Before arriving in Vietnam, he had completed a full-time Church mission in the Great Lakes area.

I was assigned to the 1st Air Calvary Division (airmobile) unit as a door gunner on a Huey helicopter. One of our missions was to fly in support of an infantry company. Our job was to call in artillery and mortar fire in support of the troops on the ground. Late in the afternoon they came in contact with the enemy. At that time they had some wounded and called for us to medevac them out. It was dark when we went down in and picked up the wounded and took them to their firebase.

The firebase had triple constantina wire around the compound. Then there were forty feet of cleared area and then another triple constantina wire. In the forty feet of cleared area was where the helo pad was. Normally we would land on this helo pad, but this one night we decided to land next to the medical bunker inside the firebase. We came in blackout (lights out until about a hundred feet above the ground). Upon landing, as we were taking the wounded off the chopper, mortars started to hit where the helo pad was. After unloading we took off but realized that we still had someone in the chopper. I asked him what he was doing and he said that he had radios on the chopper that he was accountable for, so he had jumped back on before we had taken off. We had to return him to the firebase compound. We landed next to the medical bunker and not on the helo pad as we were supposed to because we knew that we could be blown up. Mortars hit the helo pad as he jumped off with his radios. Upon taking off we heard a loud boom and felt like something hit the chopper. We headed back to our base camp at Tay Ninh where we inspected the chopper and found the main rotor blade had hit

Scott A. Hansen next to a Scout Bird with an AK-47 rifle.

Scott A. Hansen was a door gunner on the Huey pictured in Tay Ninh Vietnam.

the tail boom. As we came out of the firebase compound our main rotor blade hit a radio whip antennae. That is what caused the main rotor blade to hit the tail boom. This caused the rotor blade to be dented and unbalanced which caused the chopper to vibrate. When the main rotor blade had hit the tail boom it cracked the shaft that drives the tail rotor. The mechanics that checked it out said that the chopper should not have been able to be flown, but should have crashed on the flight back in. On our flight back in, because of the vibration, we thought that we were going to crash land, so I checked my .45-caliber pistol and my M16 rifle, as they were extra weapons that we carried besides the M60 machine gun. At that time I was worried about my family and how they would react if I was missing in action. During the flight I found myself saying several silent prayers knowing that my Heavenly Father was watching over me and would let me return home safely. My patriarchal blessing states that my life will be spared in difficult conditions.

DAVE HERBERT

During the Vietnam War Dave served in the 173rd Airborne Brigade, A Company. He single-handedly eliminated an enemy gun bunker during a battle before being seriously wounded. His head injury required that he learn to read, speak, and walk again. His testimony sustained him through the ordeal of combat and recovery. The following were provided by Dave as news clippings from the BOX ELDER NEWS, *Brigham City, Utah.*

"PARENTS FIND 'LOST' GI IN DENVER HOSPITAL"

BRIGHAM CITY- For more than a month Mr. and Mrs. Jay Herbert knew their son had been seriously wounded in Vietnam—but didn't know where he was. The Brigham City couple was reunited Wednesday with their son, Pfc. Dave Herbert, 19, at an Army hospital in Denver, CO. It took phone calls around the country and the aid of the Red Cross to help find him, but their anguish isn't over. The war injuries left their son paralyzed and seriously impaired his speech. He was wounded Nov. 12 in South Vietnam, but his parents didn't learn until just before Christmas that he had been taken to Fitzsimmons General Hospital at Denver on Dec. 16. Mr. and Mrs. Herbert, former Ogden residents, were notified late in November that their son had been wounded on Nov. 12 and taken to a Tokyo hospital. Word of their son's injuries came in a telegram from the Army adjutant general's office about a week after he had been wounded. After receiving the telegram notifying them of his battle wounds, Mr. and Mrs. Herbert heard nothing more concerning the extent of his injuries or his whereabouts. All they knew was that he first had been taken to a hospital in Tokyo. Mrs. Herbert had heard that wounded service men normally were taken to military hospitals closest to their hometowns. The father, a police sergeant with the Brigham City Police Department, sought help from the Red Cross. Phone calls also were made to legislators in Washington, D.C., in an effort to learn the young man's whereabouts. It was finally discovered that he had been transferred to the Denver hospital on Dec. 16 and his parents were notified a week later. The young soldier, who had been in South Vietnam for about 4 months, suffered "severe injuries to the brain" during a seek-and-destroy mission in the Dak To area. He is a grandson of Mr. and Mrs. Algie Herbert of 1329 5th Ogden. His grandmother said today he is paralyzed and his brain severely damaged by a bullet, which entered the side of his head. For some time he was left completely without the ability to speak, but he is slowly being taught how to recite simple words from memory. Pfc. Herbert's parents left for Denver on Christmas Day and are expected to return home this weekend.

* * * * *

"BRIGHAM CITY GI WINS BRONZE STAR"

BRIGHAM CITY. A Utah soldier was awarded the Bronze Star Medal for Heroism in ceremonies at the Salt Lake Veterans' Hospital Wednesday. Pfc. Dave W. Herbert, son of Mr. and Mrs. Jay Herbert, of Brigham City, won the award for valor in the face of the enemy in the Vietnam conflict. Pfc. Herbert is being treated in the Veteran's Hospital for head wounds received at the time of the action for which he was cited. In that action, he knocked out one North Vietnamese machine gun nest single-handedly and attacked another before being wounded. The order granting Pfc. Herbert the Bronze Star lauds him for his "outstanding display of aggressiveness and devotion to duty."

Bronze Star Medal
Awarded for Heroism

Taken from the presidential announcement of February 8, 1968.

Dave Herbert single handedly eliminated an enemy gun bunker during a battle before being seriously wounded in the head. The above photo was taken in 1967.

Reason: For heroism in connection with military operations against a hostile force. Private First Class Herbert distinguished himself by exceptionally valorous actions in the Republic of Vietnam on 12 November 1967 near Dak To, Republic of Vietnam. On this day, Private First Class Herbert was point man for Company A, 1st Battalion (Airborne), 503d Infantry, as they moved toward the crest of a hill. After finding fresh signs of the enemy in the area, Private First Class Herbert found a North Vietnamese Army rucksack, fresh bandages, and footprints. After informing his superiors, Private First Class Herbert spotted what he thought was a fresh grave, but then took cover when he spotted movement and came under fire. After returning the fire, Private First Class Herbert moved toward the enemy position and eliminated it with fire from his rifle, After moving still father forward, Private First Class Herbert located a machine gun bunker and attacked it. He killed the gunner with his rifle and then neutralized the position with a hand grenade after crawling very close to it. Private First Class Herbert then spotted another machine gun bunker and as he maneuvered forward to attack it he was seriously wounded in the head. With the initial enemy threat eliminated by Private First Class Herbert, his company managed to withdraw from the hill and allow air strikes to be effectively placed on the enemy positions. After evacuating Private First Class Herbert, the company managed to rout the enemy force and capture the hill. Private First Class Herbert's outstanding display of aggressiveness, devotion to duty, and personal bravery were in keeping with the highest traditions of the military service and reflect great credit upon himself, his unit, and the United States Army.

The citation read: "Pfc Herbert found a North Vietnamese ruck sack, fresh bandages and footprints and deliberately began searching the area for the enemy.

"Pfc Herbert spotted what he thought was a fresh grave but then took cover after he spotted movement and came under fire. After returning the fire, Pfc Herbert moved toward the enemy and eliminated it with fire from his rifle. After returning the fire, Pfc Herbert moved toward the enemy and eliminated it with fire from his rifle. After moving farther forward, Pfc Herbert located a machinegun bunker and attacked it. He killed the gunner with his rifle and then neutralized the position by hand grenade after crawling close to it.

Pfc Herbert then spotted another machinegun bunker and as he moved forward to attack it, he was seriously wounded in the head. With the initial enemy threat eliminated by Pfc. Herbert, his company managed to withdraw from the hill and allow air strikes to be effectively placed on the enemy positions."

BOB HOUGHTON

Bob served in the Air Force's 433rd Tactical Fighter Squadron. He was involved in a uniquely heroic air force incident, called Pardo's Push. Bob is currently a retired air force major.

Never before nor since has history recorded an aviation rescue attempt in the combat zone of war like Pardo's Push and saving the lives of another aircraft crew. In that incredible rescue in the sky over North Vietnam and Laos, four brave Americans of the United States Air Force were facing sure death or capture after both planes were hit.

The aircraft commanders of two F-4 Phantom Jet Fighter Planes were Captains Bob Pardo and Earl Aman. The special military mission assignment for the two U.S. Air Force F-4 Phantom Fighter Planes was twofold. First, with their missiles they were to protect the strike force of the other F-4 and F-105 aircraft against any threatening North Vietnamese MiGs, and second, to bomb that important target. Before the Aman-Houghton plane even approached the target, heavy fire from the enemy's antiaircraft guns erupted and filled the sky with deadly shrapnel. As the U. S. strike force continued flying toward Thai Nguyen, the sky was soon blackened with the enemy's exploding antiaircraft cannon fire.

Suddenly, while the Phantom Fighter was 75 miles from the target, an exploding shell burst from a North Vietnamese antiaircraft gun. Flak smashed into their F-4, shaking it violently. They knew their plane was hit, so they called to see if either of them had been wounded. Neither one had been hurt, so they hurriedly checked their gauges and discussed whether or not to return to the Thailand air base or continue with their mission to bomb that strategic target.

They decided to complete their mission and bomb the target. Aman and Houghton dived their F-4 fighter down in the midst of heavy firing by the enemy and dropped their bombs on that target, as did their other comrades in the armada of U. S. Air Force F-4 and F-105 fighter planes. Several American aircraft were shot down over the target. Aman and Houghton felt their quivering plane take two more hits and witnessed Pardo's and Wayne's F-4 fighter also being hit hard by an enemy cannon shell over the Thai Nguyen steel plant target.

The initial exploding enemy shell badly damaged the F-4 fighter aircraft of Aman and Houghton, and it quickly started losing its 5,000 pounds of fuel. Deadly gunfire was saturating the sky with heavy smoke clouds and shrapnel exploding all around their plane. The danger of death was now rapidly confronting them. Due to the sudden loss of fuel, it was evident they could not make it back to the refueling tanker. There only choice was to radio their flight leader that they had been hit by the fusillade of the North Vietnamese antiaircraft gunfire.

Captain Pardo and Lieutenant Wayne steadfastly refused to leave their comrades there to bail out of their plane into sure death or capture by the swarming and shooting enemy troops on the ground below. At the risk of their own lives, Bob Pardo and Steve Wayne were determined to help Earl Aman and Bob Houghton escape from that deadly debacle. Both planes were still in the danger zone southwest of Hanoi between the Red and Black rivers. After asking Aman to jettison his drag chute, Pardo tried to put the nose of his aircraft in the empty drag chute compartment of Aman's F-4. That effort failed quickly because there was too much jet wash coming off Aman's engines.

Pardo attempted to put the top of his fuselage against the belly of the crippled F-4 as Aman and Houghton did their best to steady their falling aircraft, but that also quickly failed.

There was too much jet wash turning the Pardo-Wayne plane away, making any rescue attempt in that manner absolutely impossible. In defiant desperation, Pardo shouted to Aman over the radio to drop their plane's tail hook and said he was going to push them on the tail hook of their crippled plane. This was a seemingly impossible venture!

Aman and Houghton were both shocked to hear this previously unheard of rescue attempt. They were well aware that the steel tail hook that was engaged by Air Force crews was only for emergency landings to snag barrier cables to stop a plane's forward movement.

What Captain Bob Pardo was planning to do had never before even been attempted. Neither plane was safely equipped for such a uniquely dangerous and incredible aerial maneuver. Nevertheless, they had to let Pardo try it for the alternative was certain death or capture for both Aman and Houghton. Captain Earl Aman dropped the tail hook, and it automatically locked in place, but the slipstream of the lead F-4 was swaying the tail of the plane and made it extremely difficult for Pardo's glass windscreen to maintain contact with the steel tailhook. Aman's and Houghton's plane was now down to only 400 pounds of fuel, and it was rapidly draining out. Their aircraft was descending at 3,000 feet per minute. The plane was flying at a speed of 250 knots, approximately 300 miles per hour. Pardo carefully brought his plane's nose up under the rear end of the other plane to nudge the tailhook against the glass windscreen of his F-4 fighter. Any pushing attempted had to be extremely careful because the glass is only one inch thick. If the windscreen would break, the tailhook would be in Pardo's face. Then Pardo began carefully "kissing" his windscreen onto the tailhook for only 2-20 seconds at a time before the turbulence would thrust his plane aside. The other plane's rate of descent was now being slowed down. Suddenly, dangerous cracks zigzagged in the glass windscreen, so Pardo backed off a little and managed very carefully to position his metal square at the junction of the glass windscreen and the radome against the tailhook. Then he delicately continued to push the other plane a few seconds at a time before the turbulence would move Pardo's plane aside. This effort reduced the descent of Aman's and Houghton's F-4 Fighter Aircraft from 3,000 feet to 1,500 feet a minute.

With the crippled plane's engines running, the jet blast complicated the task of maintaining contact with the tailhook. Aman and Houghton quickly discussed that problem and shut down the engines of their fighter. With the engines off, the jet wash was significantly less. Then Pardo again gradually made contact with the tailhook and steadily pushing the lead plane. The two F-4 Phantom Jet Fighters were now flying on only one pair of engines.

The F-4 of Pardo and Wayne had pushed the F-4 of Aman and Houghton about 58 miles southwest from the North Vietnamese target to the border of Laos across the Black River and was now also running out of fuel. These four U. S. Air

Navy Aircraft, A1H "Skyraider."

Force men quickly decided they all had to bail out as a last possible resort to preserve their own lives. They radioed their location to the Air Force search and rescue crews. As they were losing altitude rapidly, Captain Aman and Lieutenant Houghton had to eject quickly by parachute out of their crippled aircraft. Several A-1E Sky Raider escort aircraft and Two HH-43 rescue helicopters were dispatched toward the area where Aman and Houghton were expected to land.

Pilot Bob Houghton suffered a very painful compression fracture of a vertebra due to high-G (acceleration of gravity) ejection and floated directly toward a Laotian village. As the pilot was dropping, guerrillas came running, shouting, and shooting. He landed in a small tree and quickly unbuckled his parachute harness. In spite of his terrible back pain, his self-preservation ignited the speed in his feet and legs as he ran through the tall elephant grass to a small stream and began going up the hill. After climbing for 20 minutes, Lieutenant Houghton lay hidden and hurting in the brush near the top of the hill with his radio in one hand and his .38 caliber pistol in the other. He was expectantly waiting and hoping the helicopters would come in time.

As the dogs found his scent and armed guerrillas came nearer, he again ran with excruciating pain up the hill where he stopped exhausted and hiding quietly in a thicket and waiting to fight the oncoming gang of guerillas and their vicious dogs. Quickly, he radioed his and Aman's location to the rescue planes and that the Laotian guerillas were nearby.

Captain Aman's parachute had landed him below a slippery cliff in a helpless quandary. Each time he tried to climb up the rock with his slick soled boots, Aman kept slipping down with his sore back reminding him of his hard landing. Luckily, the armed and rampaging Laotians could not see him. Aircraft Commander Pardo and pilot Wayne headed south as fast as their one engine could go for about a minute. Then they turned back northwest toward a U.S. Special forces camp in Laos to avoid crash landing near the North Vietnamese Army headquarter camp in Laos. Their fuel lasted them about two more minutes, then flamed out. Steve Wayne ejected, fortunately landing northwest of Aman and Houghton. He hid in the brush with his handgun and radio, alertly awaiting a desperate fight with the enemy or rescue by the Air Force helicopter. Houghton radioed his location and told the fighters that armed Laotians were hunting him along the hillside.

Soon, the rescue team came roaring down near Houghton's position, scaring the Laotians away from the U.S. Air Force aviators. The excited Laotian gangs and their dogs raced back toward their village as the threatening planes frightened them without firing, forcing them to run away in retreat. Bob Houghton signaled the planes, and soon one of the helicopters came in and rescued him by extending a 100-yard cable line and winching him up. Then they flew up to the cliff and rescued Earl Aman the same way. A little further northwest, they located Steve Wayne and rescued him. Bob Pardo had glided their crippled plane a little further northwest before ejecting. As he landed, he was knocked unconscious with two fractured vertebrae in his neck. When he became conscious, he heard shouting and wild gunfire coming after him. He radioed to the fighter planes to strafe the hillside as he painfully ran about a half mile up the mountainside. Suddenly, the planes came zooming through the sky over the mountains, strafing to protect the downed Americans. The second helicopter finally located Pardo on the hillside 45 minutes later, picked him up and flew northwest to a remote outpost in Laos to refuel with the others. There, Pardo, Aman, Wayne, and Houghton were placed on one helicopter. These four courageous Air Force men were then taken to Udorn, Thailand, for hospital physicals and medical treatment. Later, they were safely returned to their base in Ubon, Thailand and reunited with their U.S. Air Force 433rd Tactical Squadron. Each of them was later awarded a richly deserved Silver Star Medal for Gallantry in Action during Combat.

Taken from Garth Seegmiller, "Courage in the Sky with Pardo's Push," unpublished manuscript, 1998, Bob Houghton file, Saints at War Archive, L. Tom Perry Special Collections Library, Harold B. Lee Library, Brigham Young University, Provo, Utah.

MICHAEL HUFF

From 1969–1972, Vietnam veteran Michael Huff served in the Army's 101st Airborne Division. His assignments included that of squad leader, platoon sergeant in an infantry rifle company. He is currently a produce manager and store supervisor in Utah. Presently, he serves as a high priest assistant.

Before I left for basic training my bishop and father gave me a special priesthood blessing. In that blessing I was told that I should accept this calling with a positive attitude and serve well. Also, that this was an opportunity to make contact with those the missionaries were unable to contact at this time. It also said that through my example and influence, I would influence others towards accepting the gospel. I was promised that through my faithfulness, the Spirit of our Father in Heaven would direct and protect me and that I would return home safely at the completion of my time in the Army.

During my tour in Vietnam I was guided and directed literally where to step and where to be to stay alive. I did my best to live the gospel to its fullest while serving in the Army. We had small Books of Mormon given to us by a Mormon chaplain. I gave seven or eight to different soldiers I had had a chance to talk to about religion. I lived with a prayer in my heart at all times. There was a fellow soldier in my company who was a Baptist and I had church services whenever we were in a place we could meet together. We usually had a prayer and a scripture reading, a song and a closing prayer. All we had was a Bible to read from. Usually there were four or five of us, but the Spirit was there and made us feel better.

Michael L. Huff served in the U.S. Army from September 1969–March 1972 as squad leader-Platoon Sgt. in the Infantry Rifle Company.

ROBERT HUGHES

As a Utah resident, Robert served as a Marine in Vietnam from 1968–1969.

Being a member of the Church gave me more stability and more confidence when it came to my position in the event of death or something else. It also gave me a better, firmer position in being there in Vietnam. I of course had the fear of the unknown, such as not knowing if a guy was going to jump out from behind the bush or whatever.

Out in the field we couldn't do too much with church, but back in the rear there was a branch of the Church that was held every Sunday. There was a group leader, and every Sunday that I was able to attend, I did. There was a different group of fellows there every time because people were coming and going all the time. There was a kind of nondenominational chapel that we could use for our Mormon services every Sunday.

The meetings were different in that they were very short. The group leader would conduct the services and we would have an opening hymn and prayer. The main purpose was taking the sacrament and then the group leader would share a little lesson or message concerning a topic of the gospel.

From the experiences I had and also from reading the Book of Mormon, and other scriptures that we have, I believe firmly that the only time a person can be offensive in battle is when he is guarding their families and their possessions. I feel that it is a sin to be aggressive in fighting when the only purpose is to fight to try and gain control of something else. I completely feel good in fighting for a cause when it is motivated by righteousness—to defend your property, to protect your family and your rights. That is my philosophy when it comes to war.

JIM IDLE

While living in California, Jim enlisted in the Air Force. Assigned to support flight operations in Vietnam, he experienced the challenges of war. Currently he is involved in construction and is a member of his ward's high priest group leadership.

I was attached to the 377th Civil Engineering Squadron, and we had just built a bunker around the corner of the paint shop. This particular night I had gone to see a movie. I don't remember the movie, just that I was thinking about getting up and leaving. In a split second this very strange noise, a kind of whistle with a kind of airy sound came from what seemed like overhead and then a huge explosion, similar to the sound of thunder right over you. Immediately, almost instinctively, everyone in the theater was down on the ground between the seats. I

remember a couple of women behind me saying, "We are being hit." In those minutes that followed everything seemed like slow motion, as if in a dream.

I remember thinking, what did I do to these people? I didn't do anything to them. Why are they attacking me? I guess I took it like a personal attack. After a short time all of us in the theater started to leave. The sirens began to sound warning of an attack. All I could think of was getting back to the bunker in our compound. I started walking along the edge of the ditch thinking that I could lie on the inside edge lower than the surface in case of another hit. Sure enough, there was another hit and I jumped to the inside of the ditch, but not down in the mud. I got to the compound, met with the other guys there, and I began talking about what had happened. The attack stopped, but it was difficult to sleep that night and many nights after as well.

Jim Idle in Saigon, 1971.

DAN JAMES

Dan served in the Navy during the Vietnam War. His assignments as Lieutenant included being involved in towing different materials into Saigon and up and down the coast of Vietnam. He was also assigned as a senior advisor to the Vietnamese Navy.

I think one experience I remember more than any was when I was with a bunch of the Vietnamese and we had this small boat and patrol boats that patrol the rivers. We had come to a Vietnamese Army outpost on the river where we stopped to spend the night because it was safer there than on the river.

They had nothing but a barbwire parameter and a few bunkers. Some time during the night I woke up and Vietcong were overrunning us. They had gotten into the compound. We had one bunker where I was. It was myself and two or three Vietnamese in there. We had all the communications for where I could talk to the Americans and receive support. I finally got a hold of some Air Force planes that managed to come in and was in our bunkers when they were bombing. At daylight, there was more noise outside and we finally got out of the bunker and the Vietcong were all over our outpost. We had lost all but about ten of the people we had. There were probably a hundred and twenty Vietnamese there with us. I was kind of frightened to come out of the bunker and see the bodies lying all over and know that they were that close to me. Some of the Vietnamese were right around our bunker. They had satchels of charges they had tried to throw into the bunker. That was the closest I had come to them. The worst experience I had there was that night.

LAWRENCE W. JENKINS

Larry was an air force officer in Vietnam from 1966 to 1967. He graduated from Brigham Young University in 1962 and received a commission in the United States Air Force after having finished the ROTC program there. He also attended Stanford University in 1963 before entering active duty in Vietnam.

I had been called as a counselor in the Southern District Presidency in the Vietnam Zone in late September of 1966. As a district presidency, we had difficulty in getting flights to visit our servicemen's groups throughout the southern part of Vietnam, which was our district. We decided to make it a matter of prayer and fasting. On fast Sunday in January of 1967, we fasted and prayed for the Lord to help us solve our transportation problem. After the fast we continued to struggle to catch flights to bases each Sunday during January.

On the first Sunday in February, I was greeting members as they came into the Saigon Branch Sacrament Meeting when a tall, handsome fellow came up to me and introduced himself as an Army Captain and a helicopter pilot. As a District presidency, we got quite excited and told him of our problem in getting around the district on Sundays. He then told us that he had already talked to his commander and that his helicopter, would be available for our use. You can imagine how excited we became. Captain Tim Bowering told us he had been in Vietnam on a previous duty assignment and had rotated back to Fort Rucker in the U.S. as a helicopter instructor pilot. He had been in the states long enough to receive new orders to go to Thailand in February of 1967. As mentioned earlier, we had fasted on the first Sunday in January and on the day after our fast, the first Monday of January 1967, Captain Bowering

Captain Lawrence (Larry) W. Jenkins, August 1967.

received a call from Army Personnel telling him that his orders had been changed and that he would be reassigned to Tan Son Nhut, Air base in Saigon. We knew that the Lord intervened in his assignment and had it changed so that Capt. Bowering could help us travel to our groups.

For the next seven and a half months, we traveled in his helicopter, appropriately named "Hereafter 727," three to four Sundays a month. It was through the use of that helicopter and being able to fly wherever we needed to go that we were able to increase the number of Servicemen's Groups in our District from 7, when we were called, to the 19 that had been organized.

We had another experience that happened shortly after Captain Bowering started flying us. We were going from Saigon to Dau Tieng Army Base north of Saigon. That part of Vietnam was very flat, with no hills to speak of, except for a mountain just to the east of the Dau Tieng named Nui Ba

1st Lt. Larry Jenkins flying in a UHIB-Huey Helicopter over Vietnam. 1967.

Dinh. Generally speaking when we would take off and head in that direction we would go to a flying level of 1000-3000 feet so we could see the mountain and fly in that direction. This particular day there was haze and smog. There was so much haze, which consisted of water droplets and particles in the air: kind of a semi fog. We headed in the direction that he thought was the right direction.

I liked to sit on the jump seat because I could draw pictures. We usually had the door open and I was looking out there and all of the sudden I noticed a very dramatic change in the terrain. Immediately I got on the intercom and I asked the pilot, "Do you know where we are?" He said, "To be honest with you, I don't." He said, "My compass has gone out on me and I was headed in the direction that I thought was the right direction." I said, "I hate to tell you this, but we're over Cambodia." And sure enough, we had entered Cambodian air space at a time when relationships between the United States and Cambodia were very cold.

Captain Larry Jenkins receiving bronze star for meritorious service from Brig. Gen Jamie Philpott, DI, 7th air force, Tan Sin Nhut. AB, Republic of Vietnam. August 1967.

A couple of interesting side bars here: First, an Associated Press writer had heard about the "Mormons" that traveled on Hereafter 727 to visit its LDS Servicemen. He had asked if he could travel with us one day. We welcomed him aboard, but it just happened to be that day. Second, My roommate, Lt. Larry Atkinson, also a Counselor in the District Presidency, and I were both Air Force Intelligence Officers. With a major operation happening along the Cambodian border, if we were forced down in Cambodia, it would not be a happy situation for any of us.

Cambodia had Russian-built MIG aircraft at an air base near Phnom Phen, the capital of Cambodia. We kept expecting these MIGs to intercept us at any time, but fortunately for us, that didn't happen.

Captain Bowery wasn't quite sure what to do when we realized that we were over Cambodia. His radio started malfunctioning, so he couldn't call for help. Finally, his last resort and the only thing he could decide to was to beam an emergency signal to see if we could be picked up by our side and see if some communication came back to us. We had a prayer and asked the Lord to guide us to get out of this situation.

After the prayer, Captain Bowery said, "I feel impressed that I should head off in this direction" and he actually made a right turn and flew for about 20 minutes which gives you an indication about how far into Cambodia we were. We crossed back into Vietnamese air space, which was very evident by two things. Number one, we saw the activity down below us and the bomb craters, but the most surprising thing that happened was just after we came back into Vietnamese air space. And, I'll never forget this--on our right was a Forward Air Controller (FAC) in an O-1 aircraft. As I looked at that 01 pilot, and he looked at us, his eyes were as big as saucers. I'm sure he couldn't believe that here was this helicopter flying back into Vietnamese air space.

A few minutes later the air kind of cleared up and our radio started working again. We got a hold of a tower and the controller there was so surprised that "where did you come from? You all of a sudden appeared on my radar screen out of no where." We said, "didn't you track us coming in?" We told him we'd been lost, but we didn't tell him where we'd been. He said, "all of a sudden you popped up on my radar screen. I had not seen you before then." Anyway, he directed us into the base and we landed.

It was very evident to all of us that even though we had been lost over enemy air space the reason the MIG's never scrambled and the reason the F102's out of Bien Hoa Air Base never scrambled is that no one saw us on their radars! The lord had literally hidden us from all radar during that period of time, until he guided us out. However, we also believed it was necessary for us to ask him for help. He immediately came to our assistance.

LARRY RICHARD JOHNSON

During his tour of duty in Vietnam, Larry flew as a technical observer in an Army OV-1A Mohawk aircraft. His plane was shot down April 1966, and he was declared missing in action (MIA). Larry currently works in a city engineering department and has served as a member of the high council in his stake.

Approximately two hours of flight time had passed in the area around Moung Nong, south of Sepone, Laos when we began a second traverse from one valley to another from west to east through a shallow pass. Captain Duensing and I were in the lead Mohawk and had just reached the apex, when we heard a loud "snap" directly beneath us. A small puff of smoke curls up between us and a second or two later the aircraft began to shudder, and vibrate slightly. Captain Duensing radioed our sister ship and said, "We're hit," followed by Captain Gates's response, "Ya, Harry, you're on fire, and we're hit!"

We had taken two rounds, presumably from a .30- or .50-caliber machine gun. A second round had hit our left engine causing the fire and vibration. After feathering the engine and extinguishing the fire, we took immediate action to compensate for the power loss. Maximum power was applied to the right engine. It seemed to throb and pulsate. Next, the drop tanks were jettisoned. I happened to glance out the window just as the right tank peeled away from the wing. In the OV-1A there is a stick on the observer side. It had been drawn full back and to the right, and was vibrating against my right leg. All trim, aileron, and rudder controls had been adjusted which resulted in a temporary smooth and level flight altitude. Even so, I began mentally and physically to prepare for a certain command word that I felt would soon be given. It must have been an aileron cable or rod severed by the fire or other hits that caused us to experience a gradual roll to the left. "Mayday, Mayday," yelled the captain on the radio. He then gave the command, "Go." Without hesitation, I raised both arms and pulled a large plastic ring, located above the headrest, forward and then down. Suddenly the light went out! Now you may think that the time lapse between the "snap" and the "go" was of considerable duration, but I doubt it was much more than sixty seconds, if even that long. I have always felt that the difference between rescue and capture was that precious minute or so of flight time which allowed us to put some distance between us and the enemy.

The cool air blowing in my face ended the blackout caused by the jolt and the acceleration force of the ejection. Just how my strapped-on helmet came off without my head still in it, I'll never know. Awake, but in a stunned, semiconscious state, I glanced to the left and saw a large column of black smoke ascending from the crash site. The mountains in

Larry R. Johnson was a Technical Observer in the 131st Aviation Company during the Vietnam War.

the distance appeared to be rising, giving me the first awareness of descent. Better think about landing, I thought. When I looked down all I could see was the tops of some trees coming up at me. I am not sure whether I blacked out again or simply closed my eyes to avoid the danger or distress. There was no awareness of any contact with tree limbs or a sudden stop. Upon opening my eyes, I found myself suspended from a tree. I reached up, released the two clips holding the parachute to the harness, and turned around to see Captain Duensing about thirty or forty feet away doing the same.

Flying as a technical observer in these Army OV-1A (Mohawk) aircrafts was Larry Johnson's specialty during his tour of duty in Vietnam. His plane was shot down April 1966 and he was declared missing in action (MIA).

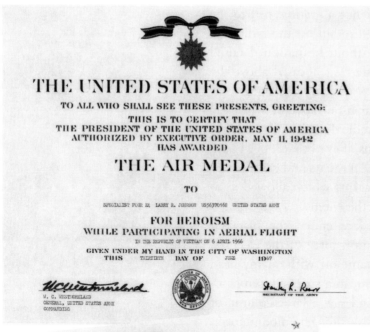

Larry Johnson received the Air Medal and Purple Heart for his heroism and the wounds he received while participating in aerial flight on April 6, 1966.

Our, "Well, now what do we do?" conference was quickly ended by two or three shots in the distance followed by the shouting of a couple of one syllable words sounding like, "Ho, Ho!" If fantasy had existed momentarily, it was certainly replaced by reality. I chambered a round in my .45, which I had never fired and hoped it would not be necessary to do so. We proceeded in a northeasterly direction, opposite to the sounds, as fast as we could, which didn't exactly break any land speed records due to an extremely dense growth of shrubs, trees, and worst of all, tangling vines. At the same time, caution, quietness, and frequent stops to rest and listen were necessary due to an almost certain pursuit by the enemy who would have no difficulty in locating our parachutes. After a few minutes I suggested that we discard our flak vests because of their weight, the heat, and the poor maneuverability through the vegetation. We buried the vests and leg straps under some leaves to conceal our trail. I doubt we had gone more than a quarter of a mile when we happened to stumble into a small clearing perhaps thirty feet in diameter with a small shrub or two in the center. At least it was an area where we could see more than a few feet in any direction. Thirst, fatigue, and pain must have convinced us that this was the place to call home and so it was for the duration.

Suddenly, there was absolutely nothing to do but wait and listen. Tension, apprehension, biting flies, and perhaps worst of all, the heavy weight of silence became unwelcome guests. By now the effects of the ejection began to set in. Namely dull aches in our backs, necks, and legs.

"Well, at least Captain Gates knows where we are," I said, desperately seeking something positive.

"Well, they're down too," was the totally unexpected response. Obviously some of the radio traffic had not registered. Contrary to our situation, their ejection occurred right after being hit which was like going from the frying pan to the fire, from a disabled aircraft to right in the laps of those who did the disabling.

At this point a realistic assessment of the situation made things look bleak. We were some sixty to seventy miles from the nearest friendly forces in rugged, densely vegetated terrain. We had no food, no water, and were in the middle of an area that was well known as a hotbed of enemy activity. We were also suffering from severe compression sprains, and had little or no survival training. To walk out and avoid capture would have been highly improbable. Terribly alone, I sought the only source of comfort and power that I knew could possibly deliver us from almost certain destruction. I lay down by the small bush and offered a short, humble, and sincere prayer. "Father in Heaven, if I have ever needed you in my life, I need you now. Please help us!"

No less beautiful than an angel from heaven was the sight and sound of that little O-1E forward air controller (Hound Dog). He circled a few times very low until finally he passed close enough to our little clearing to see my waving arms. Can you imagine the feeling of seeing him smile and wave back?

The tempo of key events quickly increased, starting with the arrival of additional aircraft types included Jolly Green Giant helicopters, prop-driven Sky Raiders, and at least one Phantom jet fighter. With Jolly Green 54 now in the vicinity, Hound Dog returned to our clearing, opened his window, and threw out a smoke grenade to mark out location. "Oh boy, now everybody knows where we are, they had better get to us soon," commented Captain Duensing. Jolly Green made a pass to the side of us but stopped too far away to be able to see us. About that time one of the Sky Raiders made a dive at a nearby enemy position. He dropped what looked like napalm canisters. I couldn't see them hit, but I heard them explode. Shortly after this a jet fighter made a low level pass, in the same general area as the Sky Raider, and cut loose with a high-speed minigun or cannon.

"If you don't get us on the next pass forget it because they are all around us!" Captain Duensing reported hearing this radio communication from Captain Gates and Captain Lafayette probably to Jolly Green 55, the second of the two rescue helicopters.

Once again, Hound Dog returned and dropped a second smoke grenade marker out of his window. Jolly Green again passed to one side and overshot us. We then heard a 3- or 4-round burst from probably an AK-47. Whoever fired that weapon couldn't have been more than a hundred meters from us. The two of us aimed our .45s in the direction of the shots, thinking, "Well, this is it." The dense growth was now our best friend and defense.

Dusk was just beginning to set when Jolly Green returned a third time to our area. Again, they were off course and overshot us by one, maybe two hundred meters; however, this time they stopped in the only position, which, because of a break in the tree line permitted a direct line of sight between us. Four frantically waving arms and voices silently yelling, "Over here, over here," finally caught their attention and soon that beautiful machine was hovering about twenty-five feet directly overhead. They lowered a pod or rather a tree penetrated by cable. I ran a few feet, grabbed the cable, returned to the center of the clearing, and wrapped both legs around the pod. Rather than calling it panic, call it a case of overwhelming desire to get the hell out of there! We did open the pod and found a collapsible seat with a mess of straps. Again, with a, "To hell with this" attitude, and this time with the captain's directive, I repeated the initial action of wrapping my legs around the seat which, now deployed, was at least easier to hang on to.

Slow, by this time, could be defined as a twenty-five-foot cable ride. With safety so visibly close, tension for me reached a climax. Again the mental self-defense mechanisms were induced. The clenched teeth and little or no breathing surely created a bulletproof barrier. As I neared the open door, four arms yanked me aboard. The floor was slick with hydraulic fluid, which was still leaking from a severed line. "Oh no, not this one too," I thought. This was the target of that burst! As soon as Captain Duensing was pulled aboard, we started to gain altitude. One of the crewmen stuck his M16 out a window and emptied a clip at the ground to keep heads down. For nearly two hours emotions and tensions had been held in check. Release of said tensions occurred, only after safety had been assured, in the form of deep sighs and some tears.

TERRY M. JORGENSEN

In the Vietnam War, Terry served in the Army's Headquarters Company, 9th Infantry Division from 1968–1970. He received the rank of sergeant, E-5. Upon returning from the war, he worked as a locomotive engineer for thirty years for Southern Pacific Railroad.

Dear Mom and Dad,

Yesterday we were assigned to fly support missions for some of the outlying firebases. While there I learned that my good friend Jay had gone out on patrol with his platoon three days ago, was overdue and was presumed missing. I asked our pilot Captain Holloway if there was any way we could help in the search for my friend and still complete our missions for that day. Captain Holloway is a kind and good man and he understood my concern. He said he would do whatever he could. It was not until later that day and with some effort on his behalf that we felt that we had found them.

As we flew over I could see bodies everywhere, my heart cried out as we made an attempt to land. As we did so we came under ground fire and were forced to land a short distance away. I pleaded with Captain Holloway to let me go out myself and try to bring back my friend and anyone else who might still be alive. Reluctantly, he said that he would cover for me and that I could go; he knew he would do the same thing. "We'll pick you up here at 0600 tomorrow, but I don't think it will be worth it," he said. "Your friend and everyone else are probably already dead and you'll just be throwing your life away." As the chopper flew away, Mom, my heart cried out with so much fear, and I began to cry.

I crawled on my belly half the night and somehow, I managed to reach their position. One by one I searched for Jay until I found him. It took me all night to drag him back and at times I would carry him on my shoulders until I could no longer walk. Finally, somehow, we made it back to where the chopper was waiting. Captain Holloway with tears in his eyes, looked at me so tenderly; and he then said, "I told you it wouldn't be worth it, your friend is dead and now you are wounded."

I said, "It was worth it, Sir."

He said, "Listen to me, I am telling you that your friend is dead."

"Yes sir, I understand, but it was still worth it."

"How do you mean it was worth it, son?"

"It was worth it, Sir, because when I got to him, he looked at me and said, 'I knew you would come.'"

* * * * *

Saigon may sound like it was a bed of roses, especially after having been in the jungle for six months. In a way it was, but there was still a lot to do. Camp Davies was a supply depot and responsible for supplying the outlying units. One of the problems I encountered was a shortage of drivers. One of the

units we were responsible for was the 82nd Airborne, about twenty-five miles outside of Saigon. For some reason the 82nd wanted their fuel (gasoline) delivered on Sundays. On week-days the drivers would hang around the motor pool like flies, I couldn't get them to leave. On Sundays it was a different story, we were always short one driver and no one wanted to drive the fuel truck. So guess who drove the truck? You

Terry M. Jorgensen after only one month in Vietnam. The background is Dong Tam, 9th Infantry Division with a view of the helicopter pads.

Terry M. Jorgensen in front of his bunk, six months into his tour in Vietnam. This was one of the few times that he had a soft place to sleep.

guessed it: Yours truly.

Driving in Saigon traffic was like driving on L.A.'s freeways at peak rush hours. Everyone and his uncle had these Honda scooters and they all drove them at the

Above: While on patrol in Vietnam, Terry Jorgensen took this picture of a village in the Jungle.

Right: After landing near a village were he was going to give medical aid, Terry Jorgensen saw a very typical scene of children from the surrounding area coming to beg for food. He explains that it was a "difficult experience to bear; even today it hurts to the very soul."

same time. Maybe that's why I don't have any hair today. I have always loved flying, so after making it out of Saigon alive, I would park the truck at the end of the Tan Son Nhut Air Base runway. The F-4 Phantom jets would taxi to the end of the runway and wait to take off. With their afterburners wide open, down the runway they would go. Their bomb racks were always full and as they would take off, the jet would almost settle back to earth. For that brief moment it looked as if they would not make it.

Each Sunday at 1200 hours the armed forces radio would broadcast the Mormon Tabernacle Choir and the *Spoken Word*. Like clockwork, each Sunday I would watch the F-4s

take off and then listen to the choir sing the most beautiful songs. For that brief half hour I was no longer in Vietnam. When the program was over I would bow my head in prayer. Then put the truck in gear and head down this long narrow road to the 82nd Airborne.

★
★
★

JOHN THOMAS KALLUNKI

John was born in Oregon. During the Vietnam War he served as a lieutenant colonel in the Army's special forces and air cavalry from 1961–1983. Currently he lives in Utah and is a retired assistant dean of students and professor of military science. He has served in many Church positions including that of president of the Ivory Coast Mission.

I frankly had read a lot of books about war and seen a lot of movies and enjoyed them, especially the World War II movies. There is no glory in war, not a bit. Yes, I got some ribbons and all of that kind of stuff that they give you in the military. Yes, I like parades and I love my country. But there is absolutely no glory at all in war. In Vietnam, there was no glory in it at all.

You narrow down your perspective to the things that are really important in life. I probably did the most meaningful scripture reading and praying during that period of time because my life was very uncomplicated, and I was just worried about basic survival.

My second tour in Vietnam, I was the servicemen's group leader for a good part of my tour. I talked to a lot of people about their feelings.

In retrospect, would I do it again? Probably, with the same circumstances, I would probably do everything that I did again.

I am a voice crying in the wilderness it seems at times when I listen to people who didn't think the U.S. involvement in Vietnam was justified. Everybody wants to unload that one because they see it as one of our major failures in our history. Yet, history ought to give you some more perspective than saying we withdrew so it was a failure. History, and our allies ought to realize that we spent an enormous amount in lives and money to protect an ally. Also, our allies ought to realize that we were and we still are willing to do those kinds of things. The short answer is yes; I do believe we should have been there. That is why I say that if I had to do it all over again, I would do it. The question is do I want to do it? No. If I had to do it over again, I would do it even knowing what I know now.

Taken from comments from "Hillam's War Project" interview, March 26, 1985.

PAUL H. KELLY

Paul served as an Air Force Captain during the Vietnam War. His assignment was in the Philippines, the supply base for the war. He traveled throughout the Asian rim as the Chief of the Armed Forces Courier Station. In this capacity he was responsible for many of the classified documents that traveled between Vietnam and Washington. Paul currently lives in Idaho and is the author of a successful book on the experiences of LDS veterans of World War II.

Leaving my family to go to the Philippines was the most difficult thing I have ever done. I suppose it is the same for everyone. This may be the way it feels to die, I thought, as I kissed them all and went on my way. Reporting at the boarding area at Travis Air Force Base in California, I found that our departure time had been delayed. We were bussed to a motel in nearby Vacaville. Aboard the bus were twenty-two sailors just out of nine weeks of intensive training preparatory to sending them to patrol boats in the Mekong River Delta, a very dangerous assignment. They appeared to be about nineteen years old, just out of high school. These men were tightly wound, very anxious and apprehensive about the task ahead. They jibed at each other and began singing marching songs. One of these went, "We've had our training and made our wills, now all we've got to do is kill." I thought about my younger brother and wept as I listened to them.

I had the privilege of being present as the Philippines Mission was organized on August 20, 1967. We met in the Buendia Chapel, near Manila, under the direction of President Keith Garner. He read a letter from the First Presidency outlining the area to be included in the new mission, and authorizing its establishment by division from the Southern Far East Mission. Paul S. Rose, from Salt Lake City, was sustained as Mission President.

There were then about 2,000 members in all of the Philippines, a large continent of which were LDS Servicemen supporting the US military buildup in South East Asia. It was interesting to me to not that even in time of war, the seeds of the gospel are planted and the gospel introduced in yet another nation of the earth. The LDS servicemen were the instruments by

Paul H. Kelly in the Philippines, 1969.

which the Church was established in the Philippines.

On November 21, 1968, President Bruce R. McConkie and his wife visited our District. I was at the Base chapel at Subic Bay when they arrived with President and Sister Rose. He took me by the hand, and in that wonderful big voice said, "I am Bruce McConkie." I told him I knew who he was, that I had been listening to him all my life. His visit was a delight. He had a wonderful sense of humor, and when he was not speaking from the pulpit, he was relaxed, and we laughed with him often. At the District Conference meeting at Capas, Tarlac, I spoke just before he did. When I finished my talk, I moved the pulpit so that he would not bump his head on the light fixture above it. When he arose, he stood up under the light and put his head up into it. The Saints loved it. After the meeting, he and Sister McConkie were very gracious as they met with the Saints. We then drove them to Clark Air Base where he had an aircraft standing by to take them to Manila to meet with the members there. I went to Manila to hear him speak and was amazed to watch as he kept the meeting a full half-hour past the appointed hour. The people sat and listened quietly. In the three days we spent with President and Sister McConkie, I heard him speak four times, all without notes, quoting extensively from the scriptures, from memory, and in those talks he never repeated himself.

✫
✫ ✫
✫

JUDY BLACKMAN KIGIN

Judy was a physical therapist in the Army from 1965 to 1969. She continues to work as a physical therapist and serves on the board of the Washington D.C. Physical Therapy Association. She is a temple ordinance worker and is the nursery leader in her ward. She and her husband, Mike, have exchanged their army uniforms for Boy Scout uniforms and enjoy their involvement in Church scouting activities.

Voltaire is credited with the following profound statement: "The art of medicine consists of amusing the patient while nature cures the disease." Soldiers who had been seriously injured in Vietnam were generally medevacked to hospitals in the Far East before being sent to the medical facility nearest their homes in the States. The military hospitals in Japan, the Philippines, Okinawa, and Hawaii must have seemed almost like oases to these wounded men, and perhaps they did provide that place of amusement spoken of by Voltaire. Of course, the main reason the injured weren't sent directly to the States was because the rate of physical recovery was faster if a wounded man had a few weeks to psychologically recover from the time he was dragged, bloody and frightened from the horrific scene of his injury, to the time he was safely back in "the world" with friends and family.

As a physical therapist, my job was to help these wounded men start using their injured body parts again, so they would have a better chance at a full recovery in a hospital back home. Some, of course, were not quite so seriously injured, and they would be rehabilitated in Japan. When their recovery was complete, they would then be sent back to finish their tour in Vietnam. I worked with the patients both in the PT [physical therapy] clinic and at bedside (many were in traction or were too injured or ill to get out of bed). They came to us with amputated arms and/or legs, multiple fragment wounds, gunshot wounds, fractures from various causes, burns, head injuries, and unusual diseases. Some arrived from Nam with open wounds, which were crawling with maggots, deliberately placed there by the doctors in the field hospitals! The doctors knew the maggots would only eat the dead tissue, and leave the living flesh to heal, better preparing the wound site for subsequent surgery. There were lots of guys who were paralyzed or comatose, and yet many more who were on the road to recovery and were just as much fun to be with as my friends from college.

A lot of the patients had been injured by gunshot wounds; many had stepped on land mines or had tripped booby traps. There were fellows who had survived chopper crashes, explosions, and intense rocket attacks. The nurses who were stationed in Vietnam would see the guys arrive with much more immediate injuries than we saw, and many of their patients never lived to make it out of country. However, for those of us who worked in the hospitals outside of Vietnam, it was a different story: the patients stayed for a much longer time, and we became attached to them. As we worked with them, they became our friends. That was hard too . . . especially if they had to go back to Vietnam. Most of us (nurses, therapists, dietitians and Red Cross workers) were so young, and I'm amazed that we were able to cope so well with what we were seeing, day in and day out . . . but we just did our jobs, I guess mainly because the men really needed us.

I was luckier than most because I had a built-in Church family from the moment I arrived in Japan. The branch members welcomed me into their homes, and these visits helped ease the heavy burden of what I had to face at work every day. To escape from the stress, my friends at the hospital and I would go off base as often as we could, and we did a lot of in-country sight-

seeing, as well as much travel to other parts of the Far East. We needed each other's support in dealing with the painful things we witnessed during the war. The tight bonds of friendship formed with the branch members and my closest friends who worked at the hospital have lasted through the years, and the many exciting adventures we experienced are among my fondest memories.

In addition to my work as a physical therapist, I also worked as the LDS liaison with the chaplain's office. I visited every LDS patient who came through the hospital and tried to

Top: Physical therapist Judy Blackman Kigin at the 106th General Hospital in Yokohama, Japan.

The Japanese people were intrigued by Caucasian women. A Japanese photography student in Nikko, Japan, saw Lieutenant Judy Blackman (Kigin), and asked if he could photograph her in October 1967. Judy was a photography and clothing model for a Japanese modeling agency after she got out of the Army.

make sure each was visited by a priesthood leader from the branch. If the LDS guys were allowed off base, I would take them to church on Sundays and to MIA activities during the week. I had an unforgettable experience with some incredibly devoted LDS parents who had flown to Japan to be with their son who was dying from wounds he received in the war. They had such strong testimonies, and they built our spirits up because they wanted to be with us at church only hours after their son died. I met many wonderful men and boys (some were only eighteen or nineteen years old), and was privileged to see a number of patients (as well as one hospital staff member) who previously had been inactive in the Church regain their testimonies, and return to Vietnam or to the States as much stronger Latter-day Saints. I felt that my work as a 'spiritual therapist' was of equal importance to what I did as a physical therapist.

In April 1968, at the Far East Servicemen's Conference held annually at the base of Mt. Fuji, I had the opportunity to meet Elder Gordon B. Hinckley, the current prophet and president of The Church of Jesus Christ of Latter-day Saints. I invited Elder and Sister Hinckley to come to Yokohama, Japan, to visit the wounded at the 106th General Hospital (also known as Kishine Barracks). They accepted my invitation, and a few weeks after their visit, Elder Hinckley gave the baccalaureate address at the Dixie College commencement in St. George, Utah. The following excerpt is taken from his address, which was published in the *Church News,* June 15, 1968:

> Four or five weeks ago my wife and I walked through the wards of a great American Army hospital in Yokohama, Japan. Row on row, floor on floor, stood the beds of Vietnam War casualties.
>
> Our escort was a captain, a physiotherapist, a lovely girl from Maryland, with dark hair and dark eyes, she was beautiful in her white nurse's uniform. Every man lifted his eyes as she passed. There was always a smile for her, but never a leer. I talked with one of the men about her.
>
> "She's different," he said. "She has class. There's something about her that's almost spiritual. She does something for this drab place. She's better than medicine."

Although I was honored and humbled by what was written, I realize the patient's comment to Elder Hinckley could easily have applied to any number of women who served in the military hospitals. In addition to what we actually did in our jobs, what's suggested here is that because of the spiritual and other attributes of women, we were able to bring comfort to the wounded men—perhaps as much as their medications and treatments did. I remember trying to always be friendly, encouraging them and cheering them up, trying to appear happy even when I wasn't, wiping their tears, being a sister to some and a mother to others, writing letters home for guys who couldn't use their hands or couldn't see, caring so much that it sometimes hurt so badly, playing my guitar and singing with the patients on the wards, getting off base with those who could leave, and praying with those who asked me to do so. Working with the wounded GIs in Japan was a life-changing experience for me. Right after the Tet Offensive and also following other intense battles in Vietnam, my friends and I would sometimes work twelve-hour shifts, six days a week, but it didn't seem like much of a hardship to us. Those brave young men, our patients who had sacrificed so much, were the true heroes of our day. We as caregivers considered it an honor and a privilege to be able to share a bit of ourselves with them as we helped them to recover physically, emotionally, and spiritually from their wounds. We did what we could to help build them up so they could go on and face whatever lay ahead, to help them forget, to help them laugh and appreciate life again. Yes, I do believe Voltaire was right . . . "amusing the patient" is "the art of medicine."

MICHAEL J. KIGIN

Mike graduated from Saint John's University as a distinguished military graduate. During the Vietnam War he served as an Army finance officer in Japan. He is now an Associate Chief Accountant for the U.S. Securities and Exchange Commission, where he has worked for over twenty-seven years. Mike is currently serving as the Scoutmaster in his ward. He and Judy have five children and reside in Arlington, Virginia.

June 9, 1969 Tachikawa Air Force Base, Captain Judy Blackman and 1st Lt. Mike Kigin, on the day that Judy left to go to Europe. She returned to Japan on August 20, 1969.

Opposite: 1st Lt. Mike Kigin and Captain Judy Blackman were legally married on September 16 (Mike had been baptized only three days before the wedding) and then married in a church service on the base on September 27th, 1969.

I thought it strange that a confirmed Catholic from Minnesota would be halfway around the world on a Japanese train listening to a pretty Mormon girl bear her testimony to me. My conversation with Judy was strange in that I had taken a Protestant theology course as part of my required curriculum in college and all that I remembered about the Mormon Church were a few disconnected ideas: polygamy, Joseph Smith, Salt Lake City, non-drinkers. So I thought, here was a chance to continue my education on a personal basis. Saying I was "a confirmed Catholic" is an exaggeration. I had run the gamut in college from doubts, to unbelief, to atheism, to belief in a Supreme Being who was to be worshipped, not in an organized religion but on a personal, man-to-God, basis. I was a non-committed believer in God, who thought that if there was a true church it was the Catholic Church, but I had no evidence that it was. There Judy was, on the train, bearing her testimony to me, although at the time I didn't have the slightest idea what a testimony was. She was just telling me what she believed about her religion and her God. Of course, that is exactly what a testimony is.

Judy's was the first personal testimony I had ever heard. It left a lasting impression on me, and aroused a great deal of curiosity. The second testimony witnessed by me was merely in the personal conduct of all of Judy's Mormon friends in the Yokohama Servicemen's Branch to which she brought me on later Sundays. They were above reproach and impressed me greatly. The next testimony that impressed me was when Judy finally got up enough nerve to ask me to come to a fast and testimony meeting. There a man sang "I Have a Testimony," which brought tears to my eyes. I continued to attend church with her, and was impressed by the actions of the people I met there, but my testimony had not yet grown strong enough.

Judy got out of the Army in June 1969 and left Japan. She had planned to tour Europe for six months and then settle in Salt Lake City. I asked her to stay and marry me but she said she didn't want to marry anyone who was not a Mormon. I wasn't ready for conversion, so Judy left and I stopped going to church. I could only stay away about three weeks before I missed it terribly. I resumed the missionary lessons, taught by members of the branch, and I began to pray diligently to know the truth. I also began following the Word of Wisdom. In mid-July, I climbed Mt. Fuji with friends, and arriving near the summit during the middle of the night, I was overcome by the beauty of the heavens and went off by myself to pray. I needed to know whether or not the Church was true, and fervently asked for an answer. I received a strong witness that I should be baptized. When I got back to Camp Drake, I wrote to Judy in Europe, telling her that I was going to join the Church, whether or not she came back to Japan. But at the same time, Judy wrote to me and said she would come back to Japan whether or not I joined the Church. Our letters crossed in the mail. You can imagine the joy each of us felt upon receiving the other's letter. After two transoceanic phone calls, we decided to get married in Japan and that Judy would come back to Japan as soon as possible. Two weeks after she returned I was baptized a member of the Church. Three days later we were married, and the day before our first anniversary we were sealed in

the London Temple. It has been a long journey from that Japanese train ride when two young Army officers first became acquainted, but it's only the beginning of our eternal journey together.

VIRGIL N. KOVALENKO

As a native of Arizona, Virgil served in both the Korean and the Vietnam Wars. During his Vietnam tour he was the political warfare advisor and community relations advisor assigned to the Political Warfare Division, Vietnamese Air Force Logistics Command. At that time he was also the group leader of the Bien Hoa LDS Servicemen's Group. Currently he is a Spanish professor and resides in Utah. He was a founding member of VASAA (Veterans' Association for Service Activities Abroad), the LDS veterans' association from 1982–2000. VASAA officially terminated all humanitarian projects and programs in a formal ceremony at Fort Douglass on June 6, 1998. Two years later, all legal activities ended and the organization was disbanded, having accomplished its major objectives.

A beautiful day for the most part, it is bright and hot. As I make my usual routine, I checked out the air force bus from the motor pool. We've taken to calling it the Mormon Battalion Bus Line on Sundays. It is kind of funny, in a way, because when I am driving, the other LDS men provide a buffer from the catcalls and comments of soldiers we pick up during our rounds. When those men complain and want to know why they can't smoke or swear on the bus, our fellows tell them it's a chapel bus for the day. "Oh," say some, "is this the God Squad?"

Priesthood had seventeen present. Warren Soong conducted. As we were starting, Charles Merill, the district mission president and Wayne Heffords, a Seventy and district counselor drove up. They both addressed us and left some pamphlets with us along with more copies of the Book of Mormon. Sunday school saw twenty-two present including Phuong and Ky, our investigators. We had some kind of hassle with the Vietnamese gate guards, again, to get Phuong onto the base. This is not unusual, but it does bother us somewhat. I guess they think she's a prostitute and don't understand her desire to attend religious services with the Americans. Our sacrament meeting speakers were John Walton and Paul Simkins. John spoke of what the words of "Come, Come Ye Saints" mean to him, and Paul spoke of the meaning of Christmas to him, and he related the story of the Lord's birth to his understanding. The singing tonight was rousing and wonderful. It really must have been something because there were quite a number of Vietnamese airmen standing outside the windows and doorways listening and watching. With Brothers Chuck Lindquist and Nicholas North in the music department, we surely have some good singing going on now.

We had to adjourn quickly because of artillery activity. While driving on the army side of this big base complex and making the rounds of the smaller camps, we heard and saw some rockets explode on the air force base. The sirens began screaming and people were running everywhere. What a heck of a position to be in, driving a big bus—a great big target, friends, and full of the Saints. Peter Bell was standing behind me and calling out the names of the camps. When a man would stand up, Peter yelled, "Stand in the door," and when I came skidding into the area, Peter put his foot on the man's rear and pushed as he hollered, "Airborne!" I drove fast and with the lights off because of the sirens and rockets. I quickly got everyone back to his hooch or unit, in a driving rain, no less with lots of lightning. I made a run for the guard shack or gate leading from the army to the air force side of the base. The guard stopped me there, one corporal with his M16 at port arms. I yelled at him to get out of the way but he told me in no uncertain terms and with much profanity to move my blankety-blank bus off from his road. I protested again, and he leveled his gun at the bus and me. Nothing to do but to drive off the pavement, down a gully, and into plain sight in a field, which I was certain was mined. So there we were, in the rain, with lightning, rockets exploding, and artillery blasting, and flare guns

going off near us. The guys at the guard shack set up a mortar and were firing from that position, which was interesting for us because of the concussion effect, especially in the rain.

I don't think I was frightened for my safety or of Merwin Ruesh who was on the bus with me. Peter is a seasoned Green Beret so there was no worry about him. I was concerned, however, about getting the bus back to the motor pool. What was amazing to me was the calm which came over me. When Merwin asked me what we were going to do, I told him, "Well, we can't go anywhere for now, so just start compiling the group reports for the district." About that time, I sensed something extraordinary happening. It seemed that from behind the rear of the bus a giant, transparent bubble came over the top of the bus and closed in directly in front of us. We could hear and see everything that was going on. I watched a VC [Viet Cong] rocket explode inside one of the revetments where the F-5 aircraft are sheltered. Our side of the base was taking a pounding. About twenty minutes later, the all clear sounded and we took off in a hurry. I backed the bus up onto

Virgil Kovalenko and later John Parr, from the Bien Hoa group, would check out a chapel bus each Sunday morning, afternoon, and evening in order to drive and pick up anyone in the outlying camps who wanted to attend Church services. The word spread quickly that if you wanted to go to church you should be on the road when a large, blue air force bus came by. Pictured is the "Mormon Battalion" bus line (June 1971) with the Nguyen Ngoc Thach family on the right. Virgil Kovalenko is in the bus doorway. Nguyen Ngoc Thach and three of his children, Huong, Nga and Vu are pictured. On Vu's eighth birthday, his father had just been ordained a priest and given permission to baptize his son, which was done at the base swimming pool.

the road, not daring to attempt turning around. Just as I fired up the engine, the bubble I saw retreated back over the bus and disappeared. I even looked in the rear and side view mirrors to see if I could watch it. It just disappeared! During that time we had waited, I had given Merwin the minutes of our firebase trip, which I instructed him should be entered in the group's history. The time in the bubble was well spent, if a little on edge.

A few thoughts reflecting on that experience. After I dropped off the two Green Berets at their camp, I drove the bus back to the motor pool. I discovered that the one rocket we saw hit and blow something up, actually hit one of the buildings in the motor pool and damaged a bunch of equipment. Later, I heard that other rockets landed in the perimeter somewhere. What was startling to me was that if I had driven immediately to the motor pool, that rocket would have hit the bus because of where I had to park it. I haven't heard of any casualties as yet from all that. But, with all the scare and noise, I can't recall feeling fear of injury or death, only concern for the

safety of those on the bus and the property entrusted to me. I wonder whether that would be the case if I were directly involved in a bombardment. I know that those mortars that hit us Friday night, came very close within seventy-five yards or so. That is like the old saying, "A miss is as good as a mile." Well, at least my history will show I was here during a bunch of this nonsense, which men have dreamed up against each other. This can be the crucible in which a man discovers where his treasures lie. And though I am here, I feel the Lord's comfort. I am not too worthy of much, but I am confident that He will look after us since we are doing His work. That's why I didn't fear too much tonight for our safety. Foolhardy, ye critics? I say no, because His power does exist. How else can I explain our Bus in the Bubble?"

* * * * *

December 9—Steve and I were driving in my jeep to the army side when another jeep passed us going the other way . . . toward the air force base. One the front of the jeep was written the name "Mahonri Moriancumr." I yelled at Steve that we ought to follow that one since it was obviously Mormon. After dropping him off and heading back to my side, I passed that jeep again, only this time it was caught in the lineup waiting to be checked through the gate. I quickly pulled off the road and ran over to the driver (who was smoking a cancer stick) and asked who the jeep was assigned to. I guess they are used to weird people asking about that name, so he smiled and gave me the name of Major Schultz or something like that at Long Binh and his phone number. I shall have to call him, I thought to myself. And today I did just that . . . he laughed and said he surely does get some questions but always draws out the Mormons who recognize the name as that of the Brother of Jared. Crazy business, this Mormonism. I remember that Tad Derreck's F-100 aircraft had "The Mormon Meteor" painted on its nose.

* * * * *

John Parr was an American Air Force captain, aeronautical engineer. His wife had joined the Church in Ohio and had sent a missionary referral card for her husband. That card was sent up to our group. It sat in my desk drawer for several weeks and every time I'd open the desk as I was working, that card would yell at me, "You have to do something, you have to contact him." Well, I finally did and his story is one of the fun experiences in Vietnam. After having Thanksgiving dinner in 1971 together, we had a discussion about the Church. The first two hours were spent in his response to my asking him, "How come your wife came to join the Mormon Church?" The second two hours were spent with him answering my question, "Well, what's your hangup with the Mormons?" He started telling me it was all centered on his worry about a living prophet and on how Joseph Smith could have been called as a prophet. I responded, "Well, what does it say in Amos 3:7 about prophets?" without being able to remember the scripture. I was shocked that he knew it immediately, and then I found out that his father was a Methodist chaplain, a full colonel in the Army. This kid had grown up with the scriptures and so those two hours were spent going through the scriptures to show that the Lord can call and does call prophets in every age and then. Yesterday, today, and forever, why can't we have a prophet today? At the end of that particular phrase he stopped and

✯ Left: 1970 Vietnam District Conference with Mission President, Don Carlos Smith.

Below: Typical street scene outside the Bien Hoa base. The man is riding a cyclo, which is a combination of a rickshaw and a bicycle body loaded down with bamboo cages and other merchandise he is taking to the marketplace (or corner of one of the intersections). Behind him is a very typical view of any street in Vietnam, clogged with every conceivable kind of vehicle you can imagine.

Bottom: LDS servicemen's group.

looked at me and said, "That's the most eloquent thing I've ever heard."

It was about midnight and time to go home. I had to go across the base which was very dangerous. Once the sun went down in Vietnam it was black, and Americans were counseled to say in their bunkers, to not be out roaming around because that is usually when the Viet Cong would start throwing rockets at us. We had to go clear across the base, and he said he's walk with me. I didn't want him to because I didn't want to put him at risk, but he still had questions so we walked across the base over to my place. As we went inside the Spirit told me, "You need to close this day with prayer." So I said, "John would you mind if we end the day with prayer?"

He said, "No I think that's appropriate."

We knelt down on the cold concrete floor in my room and I asked him if he would mind saying the prayer, which he did. At the end of that prayer, I put my arm around his shoulders and said, "John, that's the most eloquent thing I've ever heard." So we shook hands and embraced. And just as he was going out I said, "Well John, you've heard the truth tonight. Your spirit has heard the testimony of the Holy Ghost."

He looked me right in the eye and said, "Yes. I know."

I said, "Well that means then that you're responsible for what you've heard and you have to make a decision, don't you?"

He said, "Yep. I'll let you know."

He had to go off on TDY [temporary duty] and go up country to do some evaluations of aircraft that had been shot. About a week later, he called me from somewhere in the country. Because the phone lines in Vietnam were cross-circuited, so you could hear six or seven conversations going on from everywhere, he simply said, "Virgil, this is John. Let's do it."

I said, "Okay, Saturday morning at the swimming pool."

He came back to the base and I put the word out to the group.

Top: Bien Hoa VNAFAB 31 July 1971 at a promotion Party for Col. William Comstock. Left to Right Col. Roy B. Skipper, Chief, AFAT-6; Virgil Kovalenko; Maj Nguyen Ba Thao, Chief POLWAR ALC.

Bottom: Virgil Kovalenko.

Several of us went to the swimming pool at six o'clock in the morning, and we baptized him.

Our district president felt that anybody who was baptized could be given the priesthood, but he had to come up through the different offices so he could learn what the different offices were. I complained and asked, "Why can't we just ordain him a priest for heaven's sakes."

"No, he has to learn." So after the baptism we went over to the little chapel and we confirmed him. We gave him the Aaronic Priesthood and ordained him a deacon. The next day was Sunday so he passed the sacrament. The next week, we ordained him a teacher so that he could prepare the sacrament. The week after that we ordained him a priest so he could bless the sacrament.

We asked John if he had told his family that he had joined the Church. He said no, that he said he was going to tell them when he went home for R&R [rest and recuperation] to see his family for a week. On the Sunday that John arrived, his wife heard noises in the kitchen and went out to see her husband dressed in a suit and tie, banging pots and pans and fixing himself some breakfast. She was used to him sleeping in on Sunday and then watching football all day while she took the children to LDS services. She asked him where he was going. He replied, "Where else should I go on a Sunday morning? I'm going to priesthood."

Her mouth hit the floor and she said, "What?"

He said, "Well, yeah, didn't you know? I was baptized in Vietnam."

Their little five-year-old boy who was in the kitchen blurted out, "Oh goody, daddy, does that mean we can be a forever family now?" To me that is one of those joyous missionary things that came out of Vietnam. This is the brotherhood of the priesthood.

Top: Virgil Kovalenko and John Parr eating Thanksgiving dinner (1971) during which they talked about the gospel and John received his witness of the truth of it.

Bottom: Typical firebase out in the weeds and the standard way in which they lived in the bunkers dug into the ground and covered with sandbags.

Taken from Virgil Nicholas Kovalenko, (1934), *Vietnam Journal and Group Leader's Desk Calendar, 1971 May–1972 February,* MS 17326, Historical Department Archives, The Church of Jesus Christ of Latter-day Saints; and also some excerpts taken from an interview with Dennis Wright.

PAUL B. LARSON

During the Vietnam War, Paul was a corporal in the Marine Corps' 1st Marine Air Wing from 1968–1970. His assignments included that of rifleman and squad leader. Currently he works as a coal miner in Utah and serves in the Church in his ward's elders quorum presidency.

On September 9, 1968, the day before I left, I received my patriarchal blessing. In the blessing the patriarch asked the Lord to bless and protect me from combat that I might perform my duties and return home. I was ready to leave for Vietnam when all of the infantry's private first class Marines were called and told we would not be going yet. Instead I was delayed at Camp Pendleton [California] for seven more weeks. While at the tank battalion I met a Sergeant Gaylor from Salt Lake [City, Utah]. He had already been to Vietnam and was experienced in the way of the corps. I always remember the compassion and empathy he had for me. He gave me good advice and helped me get home for five more days, which allowed me to spend the weekend at home.

When I went to Vietnam, my time was made easier because of Kathy's letters and support. I witnessed many things that I wish I had not during this time and was shot at and shelled on several occasions. I witnessed enough death and destruction to make me appreciate life like I never had before. One night I was trying to sleep inside a bunker where it was safe. That night it was so hot and humid I moved outside. We received mortar fire and the first shell hit about twenty-five yards from me. The mortar hit the other side of a truck that protected me from the explosion and shrapnel. I received a new marine award, the Combat Action ribbon for my duty in Vietnam.

CALVIN (CAL) W. LATHEN

Cal served as a Marine Officer in Vietnam from 1965–1966. He was the commander of a mortar platoon that saw considerable action during the war. Following the war he completed his education and is now a college administrator with the University of Idaho. He has served many positions in the Church including that of a counselor in a stake presidency.

On 24 May 1965, about one week after the first combat forces (U.S. Marines) landed in Vietnam, my unit, the 1st Battalion 7th Marines, left San Diego on a ship for the Orient. I was a 1st Lt. and the Platoon Commander of the 81 M.M. Mortar Platoon with over 80 men in my platoon. After a layover in Okinawa, we landed at Chu Lai, Republic of Vietnam, which is about 50 miles south of Da Nang. On the fifteen of June 1966, my tour of duty was complete and I flew out of Vietnam to Travis Air Force Base in California.

In May of 1961, I received my patriarchal blessing. In that blessing I was told, "you will be called into the armed services. Accept the call freely and without complaints . . .

I promise you that if you observe the laws of health, you will not be cut down in untimely death but will live out the full years which have been allotted to you." This blessing provided great comfort to me that if I were righteous, I would return from the war and live out a full life.

It was hard to have friends and fellow Marines killed. One casualty was an officer and a close friend of mine. He was the first black person I had ever been close to. His memory is still sharp in my mind and I seek out his name when I visit the Vietnam War Memorial in Washington D.C. He was a wonderful man who had a daughter born while he was

serving in the war. He was never able to see her.

I learned the value and price of freedom and felt privileged to be able to serve my country. That service opened up great avenues for me, as an individual, and for my family. Freedom truly comes at a great price. Spending nearly a year in a combat zone in a Marine Corps Infantry Battalion, one experiences numerous combat situations. I participated in seven different combat operations. The first of these was Operation Starlite, which was the first successful major kill operation of the war. With these combat operations and the defense of the Chu Lai onclave, created the condition for war related casualties. I can remember several times when small arms fire, shrapnel, or potential accident situations occurred which could have easily been fatal for me. On one occasion, I was injured from the

Top: Platoon GYSgt. W. Nash of the 81st MM Platoon, and Platoon Commander 1st Lt. Calvin W. Lathen working with a map and plotting board and drinking soda. November 1965, Chu Lai, Vietnam.

Bottom: Calvin W. Lathen issuing jungle boots to his troops. November 1965, at Chu Lai, Vietnam.

explosion of one of our own rounds. After that, I spent about a week in the division field hospital. Probably my most frightful close call was on a chopper, which took on enemy fire. There was nothing one could do except sit over the thin sheet of metal, separating me from the rounds. On that occasion, I fully understood why chopper crews sat over steel plates and flak jackets.

As I have reflected upon my experience in Vietnam, I realize that I could have lost my life on many occasions. Without a doubt, my patriarchal blessing provided a shield of protection, which allowed me to return to my wife, two sons, and a daughter who was born five months after I left for Vietnam.

BOYD R. LEMON

As a career master sergeant in the Air Force, Boyd served during both the Korean and Vietnam Wars. During the Vietnam War, Boyd was stationed at Clark Air Base in the Philippines. Here he served as a communications supervisor involved with missions that supported the combat effort in Vietnam.

We usually went down on Saturdays, which nearly everyone had off. We took sack lunches with us and carried as many people as we could crowd in our station wagon. Later we had to lease a bus from the base motor pool because our car couldn't carry everyone.

We took our three oldest boys and our oldest daughter with us. We'd have our district meetings, then spend the rest of the afternoon working on the chapel. Sometimes Sister Grimm even had us over to her house in Manila for a picnic after we finished our labors.

In building a house of the Lord there is no work that is not important. Most of the men helped with heavy work like laying brick or tamping the heavy, sticky clay soil. The kids chinked wet cement in the cracks around the doors and the windows even though the cement ate the skin off their hands. They picked up and salvaged scraps of wood and lumber. They picked up and hauled off rocks. We all did anything and everything we could to help. Having spent my career in the Air Force and moving frequently, my family and I had helped raise money for many building funds and build many chapels, but this was the first one where we were able to attend the dedication. President Hinckley and Elder Hugh B. Brown dedicated it in April 1967.

TESS G. LEMON

As the wife of a career airman, Tess lived in the Philippine Islands during the Vietnam War with her husband and eight children. During that time she worked for twenty-eight months as a volunteer in the Clark Air Base Hospital. This base was the major medical center for the Vietnam War. Through her service, she experienced firsthand the price war requires of so many. While being a full-time mother and volunteer, she also served as the local branch Relief Society president.

Clark Air Base Hospital had approximately 1100 members of the staff, military and civilian. They provided 24 out of 26 medical specialties at Clark.

To supplement these services there was an army of wives, mother and daughters—Red Cross volunteers who were guided by full-time Red Cross career personnel. They did everything from baking birthday cakes for injured soldiers to furnishing nursing care for them. There were registered nurses, laboratory, X-ray, EKG technicians, dieticians, as well as many more who had only a love of people, a desire to help, and a willingness to learn what was necessary to be able to meet the personal needs of approximately 1,000 patients each month, as well as to assist the professional staff of the hospital in accomplishing their mission.

I worked some on the bloodmobile where we did much the same thing that would have been done here at home. We drew blood from volunteers and then the blood was typed, processed, and stored for use in the blood bank in the Clark Hospital.

I worked one day a week in the clinical laboratory, which was the center of all activity in the hospital. The clinical laboratory was where all tests were performed which ultimately confirmed diagnoses made in the hospital, and often meant the difference between life and death.

I spent time in the hospital field director's office, at the nurses' station, in the medical clinic, in the specialty clinics, in the steno pool, in the records station, and in the autopsy suite. [I] shopped for patients, baked cakes for patients, and [worked] at the information desk, but over 1200 hours of my volunteer time was spent in the intensive care wards and in the air evacuation wards, working directly with surgical patients and casualties from Vietnam. I had had two years of college in nursing, so I worked on the floor as a nurse's aide. Those months spent there will never be forgotten. The wonderful feelings you got when you did something for others that they could not do for themselves. Those feelings you got when you saw someone get well. And to know that you, also, had convictions about the war, that you didn't like it either, in fact you abhor war, and you saw almost daily the results of this terrible carnage, but you knew that at least you were doing something about it. Something besides adding more violence and destruction on top of what already existed.

You talked to the fellows and asked them what they thought about over there. They told you they think mostly about staying alive. They told you they knew what they were fighting for: to preserve the rights of free Americans to continue to live as free Americans.

When there would be a big battle going on, or extra heavy fighting, the number of casualties we would receive would also be heavy. At times like these we would often receive patients directly off the battlefield, still in their muddy, bloody, torn battle fatigues. You worked, fast and hard. You talked to those who wanted to talk, and also to those who had to talk because they couldn't believe that they were actually still alive.

You gave only a comforting hand to those who could not talk, those who had glazed eyes, who could not believe the horror they had just experienced.

You tried to reassure the seventeen-year-old boy who had gunshot wounds in the chest who begged, "Please don't let me die. I don't want to die."

After the work was done, you sat down to write a letter for a patient who had just lost both eyes, from a gunshot wound directly behind the eyes. You knew it was a miracle that he was even alive. He did too. He writes to his wife and family, reassures them that he is alright, that he will soon be home, and that nothing is going to change. You let the tears spill over a little because you knew he could not see.

You learned to be objective when you heard them recount the tales of the battles and how they were wounded, how they lived while their buddy next to them was blown to bits. They didn't understand this and neither did you. It was just a fact of war.

You worked hard, you worked overtime. There never seemed to be enough people to do the work that needed to be done. You stayed late, thinking that maybe you could help get caught up and tomorrow it wouldn't be so bad, then you returned tomorrow and found it was always the same.

You prayed fervently, every day of your life, that sometime this will all end, but you knew that we couldn't just quit; we had a job to do, and it had to be done.

Life without freedom would be intolerable at best, but to accept life without freedom after giving so much would be a sacrifice that we cannot afford to make, for then all those who died would truly have died in vain.

FRANK P. LEUCK

Frank joined the U.S. Air Force as an aviation cadet in August of 1959 and completed aviation and officer training during a one-year course. His aviation experience included bombers, trainers, air-to-ground operations, and strategic reconnaissance aircraft. He is currently a cofounder and chief operating officer of a small business in Olympia, Washington. He and his wife Judith have eight children and fourteen grandchildren.

About one year prior to going to Vietnam, my wife and I decided it was my duty to serve in combat, so we took one year to "put our house in order." We attempted to live worthily of every blessing the Lord could promise to us. I had volunteered for a particularly hazardous flight duty as a forward air controller [FAC] and wanted the assurance that I (we) had done all in our power to warrant the Lord's choicest blessings—for me in combat and for the family at home. The FAC was the first on the combat scene, directed the ground-to-air battle and was the last to leave the scene.

Most of my care packages came from my immediate family. The most popular of all were the ones with Kool-Aid and pizza mixes. Because my unit knew I didn't drink, they made special labels for bottles and put them on the shelf of our unit bar. They were for the "Commander Only" and were labeled with the flavor names, such as Choo-Choo Cherry and Goofy Grape. Most of my correspondence was from family. As you can expect, a letter of any kind was a real boost to morale.

My faith remained solid during the duration of the war. I had several experiences that increased my faith and testimony. On one occasion, I was scheduled to fly several missions on fast Sunday. I knew the effects of fasting could alter my physiological condition and put me in a dangerous position. My missions called for engaging the enemy in such a way that I'd have to perform many high G maneuvers for a sustained period of time. Fasting would lower my blood sugar and thin my blood. Under a high G maneuver, my thin blood would pool in my lower extremities causing me to black out. As I repeatedly attacked the target I could tell that my tolerance for high G maneuvers was waning. On one pass at the target, I pressed too close to the ground and knew I'd have to pull more Gs than before to avoid crashing. As I did, I passed out in the cockpit and while I was vaguely conscious, my sight was gone and I didn't know what altitude my aircraft was in. As the aircraft stalled, I regained my sight and recovered from the maneuver and continued the mission. The fighters that I was directing to the proper target thought I had just pulled off a great maneuver which had taken me into new airspace avoiding a huge flak-trap the enemy had set up just for that rocket pass. Had I not passed out due to fasting, I'd have run right into that flak-trap.

An A4 single-seat lightweight attack Skyhawk prepares for takeoff from the flight deck of the attack aircraft carrier USS Kitty Hawk.

After flying several missions, I decided to get the kinks out of my system by running around the compound, about three miles. At the conclusion of the run I decided to lay on top of one of the gun emplacement bunkers and get a headstart on my suntan, since I was going home in a couple of weeks. I was just about to fall asleep when the Spirit urged me to roll off and under the bunker which was covered by sandbags about two feet thick. I had no preconceived reason as to why I had been urged to move to safer ground until a moment later when a rocket hit exactly where I had been suntanning. The Holy Ghost had not spoken, but every fiber in my being was compelled to do as commanded. I had had no choice but to move. I have since had many times when I've been urged by the Spirit to take some sort of action. I've learned to not doubt the feeling when it comes. It has saved my life on several occasions.

JOHN ROBERT MALLERNEE

John was baptized on May 6, 1967. He served in the U.S. Army from 1967 to 1976, in the 501st Signal Battalion, 101st Airborne Division "Screaming Eagles," as a radio relay repairman. He now lives in the Armed Forces Retirement Home in Washington, D. C.

Quang Tri LDS Servicemen's Group. The brother not wearing a cap is Bob, the group leader, and he was a Specialist Five (E-5), and a combat medic assigned to the First Brigade, Fifth Infantry Division (Mechanized) "Red Devils." The tall man wearing a pistol is Captain Johnny Rutherford, of Oklahoma, who commanded an artillery battery at Dong Ha.

Because the war was so controversial, it was difficult not to be adversely affected by all the negative feedback coming from America, questioning whether we were doing the right thing. Once, after sacrament service, while riding in his jeep back to Dong Ha, John Robert Mallernee expressed some of these doubts to Brother Rutherford, who became very angry, and chewed him out for being so susceptible to all the negative publicity and peer pressure. He strongly believed in what we were doing, and after he finished, I did too.

Left: Eagle LDS Servicemen's Group, at the 101st Airborne Division (Airmobile) "Screaming Eagles" chapel, Camp Eagle, near Hue and Phu Bai, Republic of Vietnam.

Opposite: Quarterly District Conference of the Church of Jesus Christ of Latter-day Saints for Northern I Corps Region. 19 October 1970 at a Navy Seabee base, Camp Tien Shau in Da Nang, Republic of Vietnam. The brethren wearing white shirts and neckties are President Harding of the Hong Kong Mission and President G. Carlos Smith of the Southeast Asia Mission. The men wearing military uniforms are their counselors.

When John Robert Mallernee was at Dong Ha, he posted this notice, seeking other Latter-day Saints, hoping to start their own group, and hold services on Dong Ha. At the time, he had to hitch-hike to Quang Tri to attend church services. Thanks to this notice being posted, he met Lieutenant James Mack Richards, who today is president of the Saint Louis, Missouri mission, and they eventually did organize a small group meeting on Wednesday nights.

※ Right: Official United States Army
※ photograph of John Robert
※ Mallernee during his Basic Combat Training in Company "D," Third Battalion, First Brigade, at Fort Lewis, Washington, during the Winter of 1968.

Above: After attending District Conference in Da Nang, John Robert Mallernee is hitch-hiking back to his unit, on Vietnam's highway QL-1, just north of the Hai Vanh Pass. He looks happy, but he is really scared, because this is a very dangerous area, he is alone, on foot, and it will soon be dark. Fortunately, he made it back without incident.

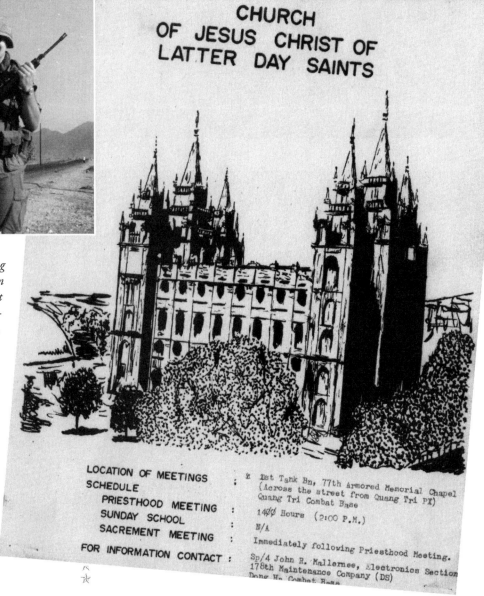

ROBERT T. MARKS

Robert enlisted in the Army in 1968. After completing his basic training at Fort Campbell, Kentucky, he obtained advanced training at Fort Sill, Oklahoma. In September 1968 he arrived in Vietnam and was assigned to an artillery unit near Chu Lai. There he served for a year.

I was off duty the night before I was to leave "the hill" (his artillery post) to go back to the "the world" and get married to Mary Frances Nelson. "Off duty" means no guard duty in the perimeter guard house bunker, no middle of the night artillery; I had nothing to do but pack and sleep. Heavenly Father sure watched over us that night. I slept right through a six-man sapper attack. I had been subjected to mortar fire, incoming rockets, and constant twenty-four hour vigilance was always needed, but never a sapper attack . . . In the dictionary a "sapper" is a person or thing that saps or weakens. In Nam a "sapper" is a kamikaze infantryman. A sapper spends all night sneaking up "the hill" for a chance to try to get through the Constantia wire and guard house bunker perimeter. His equipment may consist of just a loin cloth and two grenades, one in each hand. If he gets through the perimeter he does as much damage as he can. He can be very effective if he places a grenade down the barrel of a howitzer or into an ammo storage bunker or even worse if he lobs his grenade into a personnel bunker where you are sleeping. If he gets away in the confusion, fine for him. If he doesn't that's fine with him too. Like I said, Heavenly Father was watching over us that night. Not one, but six sappers attacked, but none of them made it through the perimeter. Thanks to the alertness of the guards on duty in the bunkers, all six "sappers" died outside our defenses. And I slept through everything, dreaming of my coming marriage the next week.

STEVEN MARSHALL

Steve went through basic training at Ft. Leonard Wood, Missouri. He served in Vietnam from April 1965–April 1967 as a maintenance clerk and a prop/rotor mechanic for the 220th aviation company and the 14th Aviation Battalion in the U.S. Army.

I was stationed at Hue Phu-Bai for the entire 13 months (November 1965 thru December 1966) that I served in Vietnam. Hue Phu-Bai was a small civilian airfield that was used extensively by the US to support the military effort in the North. The airfield was located 30 miles north of Da Nang, approximately 60 miles south of North Vietnam, 10 miles inland from the South China Sea, and 10 miles from the city of Hue. The city was the old capitol of Vietnam before the division took place.

The airfield at Hue Phu-Bai was secured by a battalion of marines on both the outer and the inner perimeters and served as a loading and dropping-off point for the troops. The troops were shuttled back and forth by helicopter to various battlefield locations and heavy gun emplacements. The airfield was also used by large C123s and C130s to move the troops from city to city. My first experience as I arrived in my company area in Hue Phu-Bai was being surprised and almost jumping off the ground or flinching every time one of the large howitzers went off. Those large guns were located in the marine encampment located just across the ravine. No matter what I was doing I would jump or flinch because these large guns were firing over our heads every 20 minutes 24 hours a day. It took me several nights before I could finally sleep through the night. After a while it actually became quite a secure

Equipment stacked in rolls near the Hue Phu Bai airfield in 1966. The equipment belonged to a company of soldiers that were preparing to go out on assignment.

feeling to know that they were there and ready to protect us from the enemy.

I had been in Vietnam for just a little over a month and was preparing to spend my first Christmas away from home. An opportunity was given to some of the members of the 220th to be involved in helping some young orphans celebrate Christmas at a military base about five miles from Hue Phu-Bai. There were ten of us volunteered to go on this special activity. Each one of us was assigned a boy or girl, and

Top Left: Steven Marshall standing near the aircraft maintenance hanger at the Hue Phu Bai airfield in the spring of 1966.

Top Center: Steven Marshall in his assigned bunker on the outer perimeter of the 220th Company area at Hue Phu Bai with the 50-caliber machine gun he was assigned to man in case of attack (spring of 1966).

Top Right: An Army Mohawk aircraft on the Hue Phu Bai airfield in the summer of 1966. The person on the left is Major William O. Schmale, the 220th Company commander. Also pictured are two Mohawk Pilots on the right, and the crew chief and maintenance personnel working under the aircraft. The Mohawk is both an observation and an attack aircraft that is equipped with infrared so it can observe at night.

Bottom Left: Company of Vietnamese soldiers standing near the maintenance hanger of the 220th Aviation Company at Hue Phu Bai. The unit was waiting to board helicopters to take them out on an assignment in 1966.

Bottom Center: A few Vietnamese dignitaries and reporters in front of the Vietnamese air terminal at Hue Phu Bai as they greeted Secretary of Agriculture Freeman and other American visitors in 1966. Secretary Freeman is the man in the dark suit and wearing glasses.

we were their companions for the afternoon. The children were ages four through ten. I was assigned a little boy about six years old and his name was Ty. We first took the children through a lunch line and made sure they had plenty to eat. We then took them to a small theater to see some cartoons. After that, Santa Clause arrived and gave them presents and clothes. The children were thrilled and had a good time. I had a wonderful time as well. It was a special opportunity for me to feel the spirit of Christmas so far away from home.

Bottom Right: Marine helicopter that had engine failure and dropped from the sky while hovering near the Hue Phu Bai airfield in 1966. Unfortunately, the pilot and crew were all killed in the crash.

Several Vietnamese women doing their laundry on the banks of the river that flows through the city of Hue (1966).

Inset: Children and other family members in a village near the City of Hue (1966).

It became evident almost every day that the men in 220th respected me because of my values and work ethic. Most of the time I was complimented on my values, and I did find a few that had the same values even though they were not LDS. I was given responsibilities and trusted with certain tasks because of my values. Honors and promotions came my way because of the way I lived. I had a good relationship with both officers and enlisted men alike. I feel it was the values that I stood for that helped foster those good relationships.

ROGER McLAUGHIN

Roger McLaughin served in Vietnam as an air force medic. In 1971, following his tour of duty, he wrote the article below for the New Era *magazine. Following the war he became a student in hospital administration at the University of Colorado and an early morning seminary teacher.*

The sun cascaded down in soft, warm waves of delight against my hardened muscles. The light and warmth gently massaged me from the lazy slumber by bringing to mind this morning's inner glow—this morning's miracle.

It was a conference Sunday. Don, Tracy, and I were the only Mormons left on base. We were on call and couldn't get the day off to go to Nha Trang to conference. Since we were all in the same unit, we met after breakfast and had our own sacrament and testimony meeting. It had been a simple service, with two of us to bless and one to pass to the two who had blessed. It was solemn and very special to us.

After our little meeting, Tracy left to go to the squadron post, and Don and I spent the next hour and a half at the Base Exchange, visiting and drinking thin, powdered milk malts. They weren't good, but the longer we were in Vietnam, the better they tasted. Then Don and I decided to go over to MACV (Military Assistance Command Vietnam) and see the Vietnamese tailors about making some poncho jackets to take home.

Don commented that Tracy wanted one, so we jumped in the cracker-box ambulance and drove down to the flight line to get him. Don went inside the rescue shack but soon returned with the news that Tracy had gone over to the morgue building to help with some KIAS (killed in action) that had just arrived.

We sat there for a few minutes trying to decide whether or not to go and get him; if we did, we might get put to work. We could simply go on over without him. We decided we wanted him along, even if it meant working for a while on our day off. We were going to relax, even if we had to work all day at it.

As we entered the building, the air conditioning felt like a tidal wave of relief from the smothering sun outdoors, which had soaked our fatigues with sweat. We stood there and enjoyed the cool breezes, joking about how if we got too cold, the sweat might turn to ice and then, of course, we wouldn't have to work.

An army master surgeon, who had come through the door that led to the back rooms, asked us politely what we wanted. Don answered that we wanted Tracy. He pointed a thumb over his shoulder and said he was "back there." We walked through the doorway to the huge back room where Tracy was working. A strong odor of medical cleansing chemicals permeated the coolness.

Tracy was standing over a nearly nude body lying on one of the cold metal tables. Corpses were on eight other steel tables. Some of the bodies were still clothed with muddy, blood-soaked fatigues. Others were nude except for a towel draped across them. The room was well-lighted, and there was no real feeling of being in a morgue, except for the presence of the bodies.

Tracy looked up and smiled. "Hey guys, what are you doing here?" We smiled back and told him about the jackets we were going to have made. He lit up like a diamond and assured us that he did want one, but he couldn't go with us until he finished cleaning the bodies.

We asked how he had got this duty. He told us how he had been helping Dustoff go after casualties down by Dok. He helped pick up a bunch of guys and had taken them to 71st

Evacuation Hospital (EVAC): when he had noticed these corpses in the emergency section, he volunteered to bring them here to the morgue and get them ready to be shipped stateside. The master surgeon appreciated the help, as his troops had left earlier that morning to go to Pleiku City.

We understood Tracy's desire to help, and we pitched in to help him with the four remaining bodies so we could go over to MACV compound together.

Don and I grabbed cleaning solution rags, and picked out the nearest casualty to work on. We talked about the way these guys had been killed and about the war in general.

First we took off their fatigues, then washed and scrubbed their bodies with a thin green disinfection solution, rinsed them in warm clean water and dried them off. With the three of us working and talking together it didn't take long to finish cleaning the bodies.

We were about ready to leave when Don asked, "Hey, Poco, is it true a person's system keeps on going in some respects after he has died?"

I looked up at him and replied, "Well, I've heard the hair keeps growing for a couple of hours but it really isn't really that noticeable. The brain can function a few minutes after the heart stops, but I guess that's about all. Why?"

"Well, what about the tear glands? Can they still work after death?"

"I've never heard of anything like that but I guess it's possible—why all the questions?"

"Well, I thought we might have left some of the rinse water in this guy's eyes, but I've wiped them twice now and he is getting water in the corners of the eyes again. I think he's tearing."

Tracy and I stood up and walked over to the body. As we looked into the face of the shrapnel-torn boy of about eighteen, a single tear crept and ran down the side of his face and into his ear.

"This man is alive," I breathed. The response was immediate, as if we had done this a hundred times. Don grabbed the keys to the cracker-box ambulance and opened the doors for us as Tracy and I carried the body out. We put him on the stretcher and Don headed the ambulance toward the 71st EVAC, the siren blaring our warning.

As we bounced along Tracy wiped another tear from the boy's face. I looked at his dog tag to get his name as I wanted to give him a blessing. It was then I noticed on the bottom of the tag three little letters—LDS. I placed my hands on his head and uttered an almost inaudible prayer: "By the authority of the Holy Melchizedek Priesthood which I hold and through the power of Jesus Christ, I command you to stay alive until we can get the proper medical attention to restore your life."

Tracy looked at me and wiped a tear from his own eyes, smiled a thankful smile, and bowed his head in a silent prayer.

The siren stopped and we cruised down the asphalt road to the open door of the 71st EVAC Hospital. Army medics helped lift the soldier out of the ambulance and carried him into the emergency room. Two doctors began asking us questions, and we told them all we could. Without a word, they disappeared through the doors of the emergency entrance and we sat on a long wooden bench for more than two hours.

We were discussing going over to get the jackets when one of the physicians came outside and walked toward us. We stood up.

"I'm glad you guys waited." He began, "I want to tell you of a miracle that has happened. That boy in there should by all medical standards be dead. He had been wounded in nine places. He had lost so much blood he wasn't bleeding anymore. His heart was so weak we couldn't hear a heartbeat or feel a pulse. He had become so weak his breathing was unnoticeable. He was legally dead. But in reality he was still alive.

"He was so weak he couldn't move or respond, and so he lay there on that cold table of the morgue and cried. He is mighty lucky you noticed the tears, because he could have died soon. As a matter of fact, he should have died even after you brought him here. Although we gave him four pints of blood and repaired his wounds as best we could, he still lacked the strength to recover, but he did."

He paused, then looked directly at us, "In the eight years I've practiced medicine and for the fifteen months I've been here in Vietnam I've never seen such a miracle." He looked at the

Propaganda leaflet, front and rear views. These leaflets were dropped out of aircraft asking the enemy to please not shoot down innocent U.S. Medical Evacuation helicopters, since the enemy might also need to be evacuated.

Medical Evacuation helicopters were called, "Dust Off" in the 101st Airborne and were choppers that flew into combat unarmed. The Army decided to paint the "Dust Off" helicopters completely white, with giant red crosses, making them even better targets.

ground as he spoke. "You know something, that young soldier looked at me a few minutes ago, smiled a very weak smile and said, 'Priesthood.' What do you suppose he meant by that?" Not waiting for an answer, the doctor slowly turned and walked back through the opened doors of the hospital.

Now as I lie here basking in the sun, I know I'll go back sometime and explain to the doctor. But right now I just want to rest and experience the joy of having participated in a modern-day miracle.

Taken from Roger McLaughlin, "A Vietnam Sunday," *New Era* (January 1971): 12–14.

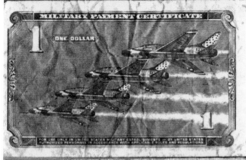

ROAN McCLURE

Roan was born in California. During the Vietnam War he served in the Army's B Company, 179th Airborne Brigade from 1969–1972. His assignments included that of mortar crewmen and team leader. He is currently living in Oregon where he serves as a consultant to the Brigham Young University Saints at War Project.

Wherever I went, the Church was there. The Church had a presence on all the posts. I had an intense desire to learn the Church hymns. I would sit and listen and I would get to Church early. In July of 1970, Carlos Smith was the mission president that covered that area and he was going to be there. He was the nephew of Joseph Fielding Smith. I interviewed with President Smith at the beginning of the conference. He had received a letter from my bishop, and the bishop had indicated that I was worthy to be advanced to the position of an Elder and ordained to the Melchizedek Priesthood. At the same time that President Smith indicated that I would be ordained to the Priesthood, he called me to be an assistant to the group leadership. There were five or six guys that would meet in our group in the 173rd airborne brigade. I explained to President Smith that I had just joined the church. I would be willing to do whatever, even though I had no Church knowledge, background or anything like that. He said, "Don't worry, this is a call made by the Lord and it is by the spirit

Two months later I get an in-country transfer. I was assigned a member of ground loudspeaker team; my team leader was Frank DeLong. That is when I became really associated with Church members who were so missionary-minded and so thoroughly involved in spreading the word of the Lord and making sure that every Latter-day Saint there in Vietnam could have some contact with the Church. Having not been in the Church very long, I didn't know anything about missionary work. My third week meeting was with Cordell Vail, and he said we have a lot of time together and if we get together I can teach you the missionary lessons and then you and I can go out and teach the lessons. I thought great.

Well, the blessing I had received from President Smith indicated I would have a number of experiences that would testify to me that events in Church history and events in my life would show me that this is the Church of Jesus Christ. And so when I received the blessing, I began to try and be sensitive enough to the Spirit so I would know what I was asked to do and be able to do it in as good a way as possible. We met for our first meeting and there was nobody else around. We would go over the missionary lessons

The camp where I had my hymn singing experience.

for about an hour and a half. We had the missionary discussions and he said, "Now I will say it and you just repeat it after me and we'll go through the missionary lessons." I said, "Okay," and he said the first sentence and I had a feeling come over me that terrified me. I was unable to speak. I couldn't say a thing and I felt as though something had a hold of me and I literally could not speak. For a moment I tried. I was so spiritually immature that I did not recognize what was happening. The feeling I had, had so overcome me in my ability to even try and speak, I ran out of there. I then got really sick. I was literally overcome and I know that the adversary was responsible for it. Back then I had no idea. I was unable to use my voice, couldn't utter a word, or a sound. I was terrified because of the feeling that I had. I got sick and the next night I knelt

Opposite: Military payment certificates (MPC) used by US Troops to keep the use of American greenbacks on the Vietnamese Black Market. 1-dollar certificate; 25-cent certificate; 5-cent certificate.

down and said, "Heavenly Father, I have a work to do. Whatever it is, I want to be able to do it. Please help me, because tomorrow morning at seven a.m., I have to start. And I literally fell into bed, I was so sick. The next morning I got up and went about my work and only after about an hour into the work and out in the field, I realized l was no longer sick. I learned that there is a difference between just praying and then praying with the knowledge that you will receive an answer. Knowing comes because of absolute faith.

Top: The LDS Conference 18-19 July 1970 held at Cam Ranh.

Bottom: The only Church material we had to hand out in the Vietnamese language was the Joseph Smith's Testimony pamphlet. These are my favorite pictures. I had been speaking with some of the girls at the school and handed two of them pamphlets. They continued reading them as we continued on our mission.

Left:4–6 Dec. 1970. Center: 4–6 Dec. 1970. Right: Personnel carriers preparing to take men to Camp Jones. 4 Dec. 1970.

Below: "I'm the God of Hell Fire" written on an APC with Flame Thrower M-50 and M-60 1/5th (Mech) 4–6 Dec. 1970.

RUSSELL MEACHAM

Russ Meacham completed his master's degree at the University of Wisconsin (Madison). He served in the U.S. Army through World War II and the Korean and Vietnam Wars. During Vietnam he was an information officer for NORAD (North American Aerospace Defense Command). He achieved the rank of colonel before retiring in 1970.

One of my treasured memories of Vietnam is the time I was able to spend with Elder Marion D Hanks. I've written and told many people of the tremendous respect I have for him and for what he did on his visits to Vietnam. He spent very little time around the relative comforts of higher head-quarters. He spent his time in the muddy fields, talking to the LDS "grunts" (to me, that's a term of deep respect, not of denigration) alone or in small groups. They were the ones who

During Elder Marion D. Hanks' visits to see LDS servicemen, he would make lists of the names and hometown addresses of everyone he met. He then spent countless hours, while traveling and elsewhere, dictating letters on a portable tape recorder to the loved ones back home. It was a privilege and a pleasure for a spouse, mother, or friend to get a letter from a General Authority, who had recently visited the loved one in the filed in Vietnam.

were shooting rifles and getting shot at, day and night. The thing that made his visits so much more meaningful was that Elder Hanks, with the help of those who were accompanying him, made lists of the names and hometown addresses of everyone he met. He then spent countless hours, while traveling and elsewhere, dictating letters on a portable tape recorder, to the loved one, "back home." I can tell you by experience in my own family that a letter from a General Authority, who has recently visited your "loved one," in the field in Vietnam is a real morale-builder.

I don't doubt for a minute that I was shot at many times during the 288 sorties I flew during the year that I was there. I credit a much greater power than man's for my safety during these travels and duties. I know that God was on my side when I got out of Vietnam less than forty-eight hours before the beginning of the Tet Offensive of February 1968. That deadly battle began with the VC [Viet Cong] blowing up the Long Binh ammunition dump less than a mile from my office and quarters.

Above account taken from the *Church News,* November 19, 1966.

Church leaders and servicemen confer in South Vietnam. Standing (l. to r.) by DC3 "Gooney Bird": Larry Atkinson, 2nd Counselor District Presidency; Lawrence Jenkins, 1st Counselor District Presidency; Robert J. Lewis; President Keith E. Garner, Southern Far East Mission; Elder Gordon B. Hinckley, Council of the Twelve; Major Allen C. Rozsa, Pres. Vietnam Zone of Church; Elder Marion D. Hanks, First Council of the Seventy; Ray Cox, 2nd counselor Zone Presidency; Capt. Herman Twede, Southern District President; Theodore Okiishi, District Clerk.

Formal dedication of the lands South Vietnam and Thailand for the preaching of the Gospel and the dedication of six chapels marked a six-week tour of the Far East be Elder Gordon B Hinckley of the Council of the Twelve and Elder Marion D. Hanks of the First Council of the Seventy.

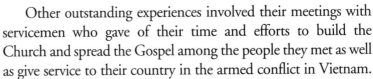

Other outstanding experiences involved their meetings with servicemen who gave of their time and efforts to build the Church and spread the Gospel among the people they met as well as give service to their country in the armed conflict in Vietnam.

Elder Hinckley was impressed with the work of the Church there. He said: "I cannot say too much for the faith and goodness of our church members who are involved in this difficult conflict. Nor will I ever forget meetings held with these wonderful servicemen. The church is well organized and functioning with three districts and 30 branches and groups. We met and visited with hundreds of our servicemen and had one of the richest experiences of our lives in doing so. Their morale is high. Their attitude is excellent. No more faithful members are found anywhere in the world than among our servicemen."

The Air Force made a DC3 "Gooney Bird" available to Elder Hinckley and Elder Hanks, which made it possible for them to hold the district conferences. At their meeting in Saigon, with 205 members present, Elder Hinckley dedicated the land of South Vietnam for preaching of the restored Gospel. About 25 native Vietnamese have joined the Church through the example and teaching of LDS servicemen.

"That Sunday evening," Elder Hinckley said, "we held a testimony meeting. The words of those who spoke were punctuated by the sound

Colonel Russ Meacham, Information Officer, United States Army, Vietnam, 1967–1968, wearing a flack jacket that he was requireed to wear during his 288 helicopter sorties.

of artillery and mortar fire on the outskirts of the city. I have never heard more inspiring testimonies. We bring to their loved ones at home the appreciation of these wonderful young men who are involved in the struggle of a deadly war."

Elder Hinckley brought a briefcase filled with special messages sent by servicemen to their folks. Typical of such notes was this message:

"I would appreciate it very much if you would contact my lovely wife and assure her of my well being here. I am presently serving in the Diam group presidency."

"I would like to give the parents of the servicemen in Vietnam assurance that the Church is available to all our boys there. Local servicemen leaders will not spare effort or avoid danger to find those who desire to have contact with the church."

The church leaders expressed deep appreciation for the help given by the air force officers that made it possible to get around the country in the three days and hold meetings with the servicemen.

Colonel Russ Meacham receiving Oak Leaf Cluster to legion of merit from Lt. Gen. G. B. Underwood, Commanding General, Army Air Defense Command, upon his retirement from 30 years of active duty. June 30, 1970, Colorado Springs, Colorado.

Dan Mecham in uniform November 1966, Basic Training.

DAN MECHAM

Dan volunteered for induction in the U.S. Army when he was eighteen years old. During the Vietnam War he was assigned to the Long Binh Ammo Supply Depot, where he had several close encounters with the Viet Cong. As a result of his experience in Vietnam, his desire to gain more knowledge of the teachings of the gospel increased, and his faith became stronger.

Top Right: Foxhole—Long Binh Ammo Depot, 1968.

Above: Officers barracks after rocket attack. Long Binh Ammo Depot, April 1, 1968.

HENRY L. MEYER

Born in Illinois, Henry served as a second lieutenant in the Army's 101st Airborne Division and 10th Chemical Platoon from 1969–1971. His assignments included that of a platoon leader. Before his Vietnam tour Henry received an ROTC [Reserve Officer Training Corps] commission from John Hopkins University in Baltimore, Maryland. Currently he works as a biologist in Utah.

I was a nonmember at the time I received my orders to go to Vietnam. I had always been a religious person. I had read the Bible completely through and always felt that there was a higher being—a Heavenly Father that looked over me. Right after I got to Vietnam, my search for religion became more pronounced because of the death and destruction that was going on around me. I really had a desire at that time to know if there was in fact a true church on the earth and what church it might be. I began to pray to my Heavenly Father about wanting to know about a church and after being in Vietnam for about six weeks, I was assigned to the 101st Airborne Division, the 10th Chemical Platoon.

After going through two weeks of training on how to be a soldier in Vietnam and how to stay alive, I was assigned to the division in Camp Eagle. About six weeks after arriving there I received a packet of mail from home. I decided that because this was a special occasion, I would go to the division chapel and read these letters. I sat down and started to read; I was there for about ten minutes, and then a soldier came in. He asked me if I would like to come to a fireside and since he seemed a congenial enough guy, I decided to do just that. I went with him for about half a mile and when we got there the fireside ended up being the first [missionary] discussion of the Church. What's interesting about this is that the young man who stopped in to see me in the division chapel knew that the firesides took place in the division artillery chapel which was about a half mile down the road. He claims that he absent-mindedly walked into the division chapel and just so happened to see me sitting there. I believe it was the influence of the Holy Ghost that caused him to come in there. He had never come into the chapel before, and he walked in there thinking that he was going to the right place, knowing that in reality the other place was about a half a mile away. I felt like there was divine intervention getting him in to see me.

Over the next six weeks I went to the firesides and received the six discussions about the Church. I decided that I would wait until I got back to the United States to see what the Church was really like before I joined it. I got back to the States and then in April, Elders Kelly Whiting and Lennard were the missionaries there. Lennard was the football player of the pair, and he finally got through to me and helped me to feel the Spirit and know that the Church was true. One day he was talking to me and basically said, "Hal, I know the Church is true and I know one day you are going to be a member of the Church and I would like to challenge you to be baptized." At that point I decided it was time to be baptized. I did have a testimony of the Church and that in fact I had it when I was in Vietnam.

ROY MILLER

Roy returned home from his mission and was working in California when drafted into the U.S. Army. He became a part of the Fire Direction Control for a 105 howitzer in the jungles of South Vietnam. He felt that his life was blessed and spared as he kept the Word of Wisdom and strived to maintain a missionary spirit.

When we were waiting to be shipped to Vietnam from the Travis Air force base. We were in a large barrack facility and every morning we would go out for role call. On one occasion we had been there for about 4 days and we were on about the second day. Every morning if your name was called then you shipped out to Vietnam that day. One afternoon a gentleman came into our barracks and hollered my name out and gave me an assignment to be at a warehouse to pull guard duty at night, of which I didn't get back to the barracks till about noon the next day. Well, early that day in role call my name was called out. That particular shipment of troops went out to the northern VMZ where most of the action was at that time. Three of the firebases that most of those gentlemen were assigned were eventually overrun so if I would have been on that particular flight there was a good chance that I would've been in those bases that were overrun. The next day we met out in role call and my name was called and that particular flight of troops went to the Southern end of Vietnam into Benwall where there wasn't as much conflict. That was a neat spiritual experience that got me thinking that someone of a higher power was watching out. Because I was pulled to do guard duty that particular night, it exempted me from that flight into an area that was extremely dangerous.

CLAUDE D. NEWBY

Claude Newby accepted a commission in the Army as a chaplain. He first learned of his appointment from Elder Boyd K. Packer, one of the Twelve Apostles. He served two tours of duty in Vietnam with the 1st Calvary Division. He is the only chaplain to have received the Combat Infantry Badge during the Vietnam War.

Upon returning home from our June trip to Tennessee, we solidified plans for the move to Alaska and readied ourselves to receive the packers. That's when the telephone rang. We received the call on a wall telephone in our small kitchen. Helga came close when she heard me say, "Elder Packer." Standing face to face with her, I heard him say, "I regret to inform you, you've been selected to be a chaplain in the Army. Do you accept?" With barely controlled emotions and feigned dignity, I accepted. . . . The main business attended to, Elder Packer instructed me to attend an orientation meeting at Church headquarters where I would receive further instructions.

December 20 was a rare sunny day during the rainy season on LZ [landing zone] Santa. Around the perimeter grunts struggled and sweated to sink foxholes into very rocky soil. A trooper with his back to me as I approached cursed the rocks, the sun, his entrenching tool, and sergeants and so forth with generous use of God's title. Upon looking up and recognizing me as a chaplain…he mumbled a weak apology for his language. Seriously, but with a touch of tactful humor, I said, "You've got to quit talking like that, else you may die and go to hell."

He said, "Promises, promises, I never get promoted." He left no doubt about his opinion of what and where he was.

* * * *

Combat Infantry Badge

Army Regulation 600-8-22 (Military Awards)

DESCRIPTION: A silver and enamel badge 1 inch in height and 3 inches in width, consisting of an infantry musket on a light blue bar with a silver border, on and over an elliptical oak wreath. Stars are added at the top of the wreath to indicate subsequent awards; one star for the second award, two stars for the third award and three stars for the fourth award.

SYMBOLISM: The bar is blue, the color associated with the Infantry branch. The musket is adapted from the Infantry insignia of branch and represents the first official U.S. shoulder arm, the 1795 model Springfield Arsenal musket. It was adopted as the official Infantry branch insignia in 1924. The oak symbolizes steadfastness, strength and loyalty.

AWARD ELIGIBILITY: Awarded to personnel in the grade of Colonel or below with an infantry military occupational specialty who have satisfactorily performed duty while assigned as a member of an infantry unit.

I attended an LDS conference at Nha Trang, along with fifteen troopers from the 1st Calvary. I spoke during the conference as did Sp4 Paul Moody, a grunt from a 7th Calvary battalion. We received inspiring talks and counsel by Keith Garner, head of the Southern Far East Mission, and Colonel Rojsa, the leader of LDS personnel in the III Corps area of Vietnam. Master Sergeant Fanoimoana, with whom I had served briefly at Fort Ord, California, led the music.

My pleasure in the conference was lessened when Fanoimoana informed me that Captain Stephen A. Childers of Alton, IL a friend from the recent Fort Ord days, had been killed when he hesitated to fire on a VC [Viet Cong] who shielded himself behind a child. More sad news awaited me the next day back at Camp Radcliff. Pfc. Gerald W. Gannon, of Poughkeepsie, NY had been killed during my absence.

Taken from Claude D. Newby, *It Took Heroes: A Chaplain's Tribute to Vietnam Veterans and Those who Waited for Them* (Springville, UT: Bonneville Books, 1998), 3, 61, 94.

Friday, May 30, nine Latter-day Saints infantrymen and artillerymen and I met on my side of a cramped bunker and shared the sacrament and testimonies. We'd finished the Sacrament and began to share testimonies when a young Jewish officer, the medical platoon leader as I recall, stuck his head in the door, "Chaplain Newby?" Upon realizing that a service was in process, he froze. I invited him, the lieutenant, to finish his message. "I'll wait." He said. Instead of withdrawing to return later, he remained for thirty minutes, standing bent over, just inside the bunker doorway. The service and testimonies completed, I thanked him for waiting and asked what I could do for him, to which he responded, "Chaplain Newby, that was the most meaningful religious service, I ever saw."

Taken from Claude D. Newby, *It Took Heroes,* vol. 2 (Bountiful, UT: Tribute Enterprises, 2000), 144.

LDS Chaplains Who Served in the Vietnam War

NAME	BRANCH	NAME	BRANCH
Anderson, D. Brent	Army	Hawkins, Richard J.	Air Force
Baker, Terry R.	Army	Hess, Don G.	Army
Boone, Joseph F.	Air Force	Holmes, Brent H.	Army
Breinholt, Mark F.	Army	Kearsley, Preston N.	Navy
Bright, Barry H.	Air Force	Kuehne, Wayne E.	Army
Brown, Adam S.	Air Force	Kunz, Calvin S.	Army
Bryner, Norman K.	Army	Larkin, J. Kent	Air Force
Campbell, Cline G.	Army	Madsen, Spencer D.	Army
Cardon, Earl L.	Navy	McKonkie, Joseph F.	Army
Carver, Dale R.	Air Force	Millington, J. Kent	Air Force
Christensen, Douglas C.	Army	Nelson, Jan H.	Air Force
Christensen, Marius A.	Army	Neuenswander, Val J.	Air Force
Christiansen, Robert L.	Air Force	Newby, Claude D.	Army
Cluff, Merlin H.	Navy	Nielsen, G. Barry	Air Force
Cooper, John H.	Army	Nielsen, Ralph R.	Air Force
Cordner, Robert R.	Air Force	Osmund, Russell L.	Air Force
Curzon, Michael G.	Army	Palmer, James R.	Air Force
Ellsworth, Arnold T.	Army	Parker, Morris W.	Air Force
Eyring, Philliph M.	Air Force	Peterson, Frederic G.	Army
Fitzgerald, Crozier K.	Air Force	Pocock, Thomas R.	Navy
Fletcher, Joel R.	Navy	Probst, John B.	Air Force
Galbraith, Lynn H.	Army	Rast, Lawrence R.	Army
Goates, Leo W.	Air Force	Richardson, Frank D.	Army
Goff, David E.	Air Force	Roberts, Alexander	Air Force
Green, Garry B.	Army	Sirles, James W.	Air Force
Griffeth, Vernon N.	Navy	Smith, David E.	Navy
Hall, Blaine D.	Army	Smith, Ferrell M.	Air Force
Hanchett, Donald G.	Army	Smith, Kenneth S.	Army
Hansen, Peter M.	Air Force	Taggart, Lloyd M.	Navy
Harper, Darrel A.	Air Force	Whaley, Richard H.	Army
Hatch, Howard F.	Air Force	Wood, Richard F.	Navy
		Young, George B.	Army

NGUYEN VAN THE

At the age of twenty-three, Tay, as he was known by the U.S. servicemen, met Airman Roy Moore who introduced him to the Church. On September 3, 1966, he joined the Church as one of the first Vietnamese converts. Two years later he was drafted into the army of South Vietnam. At the time of the fall of Saigon in 1975, he was serving as branch president. He played a critical role during these difficult times for the Vietnamese Saints.

In the midst of all the political activity in America and the intense fighting in Vietnam, I received my draft notice. I knew it was coming, but I was no less devastated. It seemed I had no sooner found warmth, comfort, and fellowship among the Latter-day Saints, and the light of the gospel began to glow within me, than I was plucked from my Saigon haven. One day I was wearing a suit and carrying the scriptures and then the next day I was wearing army fatigues and carrying an M16 rifle. I was twenty-five years old when I was drafted into military service by the Army of the Republic of Vietnam. Because I was older than most draftees and had more education, I was selected to be an officer. After a nine-month training period at officers school in Thu Duc, I was graduated as a warrant officer, a rank between master sergeant and second lieutenant, and immediately assigned to a combat unit in Bien Hoa province about thirty miles from Saigon. The contrast in lifestyle was drastic and complete. My surroundings had been transformed in a few short months from love and brotherhood among the Saints, to one of intense hatred and continual carnage in the battles of war. Even so, it could have been worse. I was assigned to the Regional Militia with responsibility to defend a small area and drive out any North Vietnamese that entered our region. I was not subject to being transferred to other areas where the regular army was involved in heavy fighting. We rarely even saw the enemy face to face. We always sought them out, and they hid from us until they could devise an ambush or hit and strike. Just knowing they were there and then suffering the effects of their presence was sufficient to keep our nerves frayed and our lives miserable.

Occasionally, I was granted leave to go to Saigon and there I renewed my fellowship with the Saints and especially my beloved Lien. Although I had little to offer and life was uncertain, my love for Lien had grown to the point that I felt compelled to seek her hand in marriage. She had not fully accepted the gospel, partly out of respect for her family. I knew she was a choice woman and the one I wanted to marry. I was selfish to ask her to marry me under the circumstances, but her love was such that she accepted my proposal. We were married during one of my trips to Saigon.

Almost immediately after our marriage, I returned to my combat unit. Because of my new responsibilities, I was more concerned than ever about my situation. I had a keen desire to escape the horrors of combat and to return to my home. Endless torment to me became the war itself. When you are fighting, the war is not the big war going on all over the country; it is within you and around you. The war is behind every tree, around every bend of the river, across every rice paddy. War is remembering what has happened before and anticipating what might happen next. It is in the shadows; it is in your mind. It is in every waking moment for you never know when an enemy will strike or from where. It is in every sleeping moment when you place your life in the hands of your sentry and hope he gives you sufficient warning if an attack comes. It fills your thoughts by day and your dreams by night. It is your cold food, your wet feet, and your insect-infested bed.

The war takes over your life and tempts you with death as a means of relief. Some men die instantly as they are blown apart by incoming mortar shells. Others die painfully slow with infected wounds from booby-traps or disease or mental torment. Others harden into nonhumans and live to fight another day. The war, real and imagined, is nothing short of hell. In fact, hell is probably better. My future seemed like a giant black space, void of light and value. I continually prayed for a way out.

The Lord watched over me well during my combat experiences. I had been sick frequently because of exposure to the elements, but was never wounded or seriously injured. Often, when we were sent in search of the enemy, we were met by ambush or mine traps. Some of my comrades lost their lives as they fought beside me. I was protected by Heavenly Father,

Inset: This picture gives an idea of the thick brush in Vietnam. Soldiers could not get far without using machetes to cut trails.

Below: Nguyen Van The (left) and Tran Hoang Nghia (right) set apart Nguyen Cao Minh in Saigon Branch, circa 1973. Saigon, Republic of Vietnam.

and my life was preserved in spite of the many dangers I was called on to face in my army assignments. Still I could not expect such favored treatment to last forever. I began to realize that in a combat unit such as mine, there was not a time placed on my services. Here, you fought until you won or until you died. It was common knowledge that those who were drafted such as I, were eventually either killed or wounded. With no end to the hostilities in sight, it was unlikely that I would be spared the fate of so many of my comrades. When Lien became pregnant, I began to worry mightily about our future as a family. I began to worry that I would never see my baby. I began to picture another little boy without a father. I began to pray mightily for the Lord to save me.

Finally, a door was opened for me to leave my perilous situation. After more than two years of combat duty, I learned that language teachers were needed in the Armed Forces Language School in Saigon. My heart rate doubled when I contemplated the possibilities. I immediately applied to teach English and took the examinations. How I prayed that the Lord would assist me in being reassigned to teach English at that school! My hopes were raised so greatly by the opening of this door; I would be crushed beyond recovery if that door slammed in my face. After some weeks of nerve-wracking suspense, I received my new orders. I was ecstatic. I was accepted as a teacher and permanently reassigned to Saigon. In the same month, my first child, our son Vu, was born. My son would have a father and I would have a son! Words cannot express the terrible conditions and happening of war, nor can they express my extreme happiness when I was reassigned to a noncombat position that allowed me to be with my family again. It was a miracle to me. My life was transformed again back to the peace and brotherhood among the Saints that I had so cherished and dreamed of when I was walking terrified through the jungles and fields of Bien Hoa. As I attended Church services regularly at the Saigon branch, I was soon called as a counselor in the branch presidency. Native Vietnamese members numbered about eighty and the Church was just beginning to grow in Vietnam.

JAY NIELSEN

Jay Nielsen was a medic in the infantry platoon in Vietnam during 1971. After arriving in Vietnam, he was assigned as a combat field medic with the First Cavalry Division. Jay taught at Brigham Young University for twelve years and then started his own business. He has served in many Church positions that have included financial clerk, young men advisor, and teacher.

I was having a really hard time with all the things that were happening around me. I thought with tears streaming down my face, "Jay, this is not what you thought it was going to be." The tears stopped, but I thought. "I have ten months of this and I just don't know how this is going to go." As I walked toward the bunker a man at the firebase stopped me. He said, "Are you Jay Nielsen?"

I said, "Yes."

He said, "My name is Joe Hansen and I am from Logan, Utah. Jay, I would really like to have a sacrament meeting tonight. I have another person from Utah. Why don't you come to my bunker tonight?" It was Sunday and I showed up. We had this stale bread and we had the water. We had the sacrament meeting and basically the sacrament meeting was kind of the saving…it was what I needed. For that time it was exactly what I needed to make it. There were only the three of us at this meeting. There was no moon and it was absolutely pitch black. There was a presence there in that bunker that I cannot deny. There were more than the three of us in that bunker. It was a feeling that I even have to this day. As an LDS person in Vietnam, that was a very powerful meeting and it was just what I needed. I was happy that Joe did that for me. I think he was quite inspired to look me up and invite me to that meeting.

* * * * *

When asked about how he felt when he returned home from Vietnam, Jay related the following:

By the time the ten hours were up at the airport, I had the feeling something was wrong. Because of my uniform and medals all the people at the airport knew I had returned from Vietnam. All the civilians walked by me and looked at me like I had the plague or something.

POW/MIA Bracelets

Above is a MIA/POW bracelet for 1st Lt. Morgan J. Donahue. Morgan was baptized at the USAF Academy, and was a navigator aboard a USAF C123K aircraft when it was hit midair by a British B57B over Laos on 13 Dec 1968. Despite reports which indicated he survived the collision, Morgan never returned.

The idea for the bracelets was started in the 1970s by college students Carol Bates and Kay Hunter in Los Angeles, California as a way to remember American prisoners of war suffering in captivity in Southeast Asia. Miss Bates became the National Chairman of the POW/MIA (Prisoner of War/Missing In Action) Bracelet Campaign for VIVA (Voices In Vital America), the Los Angeles based student organization that produced and distributed the bracelets during the Vietnam War. The two friends met the wives of American pilots who were listed as missing in Vietnam. A leading local television personality, who was later elected to Congress, introduced the girls to the wives. They thought the student group could assist them in drawing public attention to the prisoners and missing in Vietnam. Carol Bates wrote of this beginning, "The idea of circulating petitions and letters to Hanoi demanding humane treatment for the POWs was appealing, as we were looking for ways college students could become involved in positive programs to support US soldiers without becoming embroiled in the controversy of the war itself."

From that beginning, the idea caught on, especially through various organizations of veterans and families of POW/MIAs. Millions of bracelets, bumper stickers, and other items were sold through many associations. The students who began the project never intended it to be a profit-making enterprise. Although the VIVA organization closed its door in 1976 with a waning interest in Vietnam, the idea grew into a broader concept through subsequent wars in Desert Storm to Iraq. Books have been written with the stories of the American warriors whose names appear on the bracelets. Quite often, bracelets are left at the Vietnam Memorial Wall in Washington, D.C. and many other sites throughout the country.

If you have a bracelet and would like to get information on the man whose name is on the bracelet, send a letter to:

> Defense POW/Missing Persons Office
> ATTN: Public Affairs
> 2400 Defense, Pentagon
> Washington, DC 20301 -2400

Give them the information off the bracelet and you will receive an answer. Be certain to ask them for the current status of the individual.

Written by Virgil Kovalenko. Source: Carol Bates Brown's article "The Origin of the POW/MIA Bracelets."

Right: This "Code of Conduct" pamphlet was given to each American serviceman. It contained instructions in the event that they were captured by the enemy.

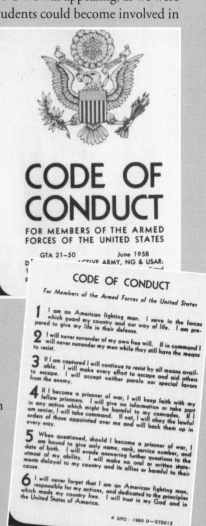

I realized at that time that there would be no thanks from anyone about my Vietnam service. When I was young, my father told me when he returned home from World War II everyone wanted to buy him a drink and wanted to talk to him. On my return home from war it seemed to me that everyone wanted to ignore me and I got the feeling I owed everyone a drink. No bands, no speeches, no parades, and nothing else for any returning Vietnam veteran. Even the real war heroes like Randy Mace and all the others received nothing. The worst part was not to even receive a thank you or to be looked upon with respect. Even my small hometown paper did not bother writing one item about me or most other Vietnam veterans.

RICK NYE

Rick served in Vietnam from May 1966 to 1968 as a sergeant in the Army's 25th Infantry Division. His assignment was that of a rifleman. Rick explained years later how he felt about the war.

PBS had a feature on the war last night. I saw the final fifteen minutes of it. There was a young boy, about eleven, who visited the Wall [Vietnam Veterans Memorial Wall] for the first time with his parents. His uncle, whom he had never met, was MIA [missing in action], and was listed on the wall as such. He was a bomber pilot, and his mother had launched a massive campaign demanding that Washington account for his remains. The emotion the little boy showed was so real and honest, and he hadn't even known the man. It was like invisible hands reached out from the Wall and tugged at his heart.

Tears came as I watched him react to the name on the Wall. It has been twenty-six years, why do I still react? I was glad I was alone, but there have been times I wish I could more deeply share those emotions. But even when someone is there, I know his or her comprehension is minimal. I recall the final episode of *China Beach* about two years ago. I had to leave the room during the final scene shot by the Wall. I later replayed the videotape copy when I was alone. I am constantly coming across articles on the war, from generalities to personal acts of heroism; all seem to have the little tug. I both look forward to, and fear my visit to the Wall. I will go there with someone, probably my family and Jay. I have played that visit over in my mind many times, trying to ease what I know will be the mother of all emotion.

There will be so many names . . .

GORDON R. ORME

During the Vietnam War Gordon served in the USAF's 556th Recon Sq as a pilot. His assignments included flying reconnaissance missions off the coasts of Russia, Korea, and China.

LDS servicemen in Vietnam felt a need to gather together for moral support and meet to partake of the sacrament on Sundays as often as was possible. At DaNang we met in a small chapel located just outside the Air Force compound every Sunday. These were very spiritual experiences. Combat has a way of making servicemen feel a reliance on a Supreme Being. The saying, "There are no atheists in foxholes", proved to be quite accurate while I was in Vietnam.

One particular fast and testimony meeting still remains very vivid in my memory. As the

A non-denominational chapel located on the DaNang airbase. The LDS group held regular meetings here. As part of their tour of Church units in Vietnam, Elder Gordon B. Hinckley and Elder Marion D. Hanks visited here in December, 1966. They convened a servicemen's conference for the LDS servicemen in the area. Thirty soldiers were able to attend, many still in their combat gear with rifles in hand. Those in attendance remember this meeting for the strength and encouragement it provided.

servicemen from all branches of the service entered the chapel, they would take off their weapons and lay them on the benches in the back of the chapel. Indeed, it felt as if they were taking off the armor of war and putting on the armor of God for the period we were in the Sacrament Meeting service. About twenty servicemen were in attendance and we all felt the strong need to bear our testimonies. We were all enriched by this experience, and at the end of the meeting, the arms were again put on and the men went back into the field of combat. Some of them would not return again and their names were placed on the Vietnam Veterans monument in Washington D.C. It was indeed a very sobering experience.

During December of 1966, Apostle Gordon B. Hinckley and Seventy President Marion D. Hanks visited Vietnam and spent an evening with the servicemen at DaNang. I volunteered my crew for three successive night missions so I would be able to attend these special services. It was a special moment in my life and I still remember it vividly. Brother Hinckley offered to write a letter or make a phone call to each of our parents if we would supply him the information needed. This he did, and my Dad remembered the phone call.

MEL PALMER

As an Arizona native, Mel served during the Vietnam War as a company clerk for the Army's 101st Airborne from 1969–1970. Currently he lives in Arizona where he teaches for the Church Educational System.

During the late 60s, as the Vietnam War was in full force, many of us compared our patriarchal blessings. Some of my friend's blessings indicated that they would "Serve their country." Mine didn't say anything about that. I figured that I wouldn't get drafted. My patriarchal blessing did say I would "preach the gospel to the nations of the earth." Having been on a mission to New Zealand, and then being called as a stake missionary in Flagstaff, Arizona, I figured that I had already preached the gospel to the "nations" of the earth. The Lord had other things in mind. I was drafted, and eventually sent to Vietnam. I had an assignment as a clerk typist. I was spared many of the ugly encounters that those in other assignments had to endure. I was, however, able to be a small part of a wonderful little branch of the Church in Bien Hoa.

Mel Palmer in Vietnam, 1970.

I was called to be a district missionary. Shortly after I received that assignment, I was able to start teaching the Nguyen Van Thach family—along with Brother Wayne Allen. Brother Thach had been baptized earlier, but we were able to start teaching his wonderful wife, and seven beautiful children. He could understand and speak English fairly well. We would teach him in English. He would turn to his wife and children and relay the messages in Vietnamese. It was fascinating. There was a wonderful spirit in their home. They were so humble, and so receptive. After a short time, we were able to go to a local swimming pool and baptize Sister Thach and all of the children who were of baptismal age. What a wonderful, wonderful association we had with this very special family! Every LDS serviceman in Bien Hoa came to know and love the Thach family.

When the communists took over South Vietnam, the Thach family was not able to escape. The love of the gospel continued to burn in their hearts. Through the loving efforts of people like Virgil Kovalenko, contact was eventually made with the Thach family. Some family members were able to get out of the country. And, about twenty-five years after I left Vietnam, Brother and Sister Thach were able to come to America. In 1995, Brother Allen and I had the wonderful opportunity of attending the temple sealing of the Thach family in the Jordan River Temple. Marion D. Hanks, who had come to know the Thachs also, performed the sealing. It was a wonderful, wonderful day! It is interesting to see

Wayne Allen, Virgil Kovalenko (in back) and Mel Palmer with members of the Thach family that were sealed in the Jordan River Temple in West Jordan, Utah.

how, through "grafting of the tame olive tree," I was able to become a small part of this beautiful story, and preach the gospel to another nation of the earth! The Thach family now lives in Salt Lake City, [Utah].

MICHAEL K. PARSON

After serving a mission to Canada, Mike attended El Camino Jr. College until he was drafted into the Army. While in the service he was a platoon radio operator in the 1st Air Calvary Combat Infantry. Mike currently lives in California where he works for the Church Educational System.

I was riding in a large helicopter, which carried personnel (I think it was called a Chinook), and on the other side was a guy who had "BYU" written on his helmet. I was excited to have found another member of the Church, so when we got on the ground I asked him if he had gone to Brigham Young University. He replied, "No!" I asked if he was LDS. He replied once again, "No!" I asked why he had BYU on his helmet. He said his girlfriend was LDS and was a student there. I asked how much he knew about the Church and if he had read the Book of Mormon. He said, "Not much," but that his girlfriend was going to send him one. I had my small servicemen's copy and I gave it to him. We became friends, and at night after camp was set up I began teach him the missionary discussions. It was not long before he had gained a testimony and wanted to be baptized. By this time the entire 1st Air Cavalry Division had moved south to a location near the city of Tay Ninh. At Tay Ninh there was a swimming pool. After having an interview and receiving permission to be baptized, I baptized David Moss into the Church. We then went to a chapel nearby where he was confirmed and ordained to the priesthood. It was such a contrast to be participating in the ordinances of the kingdom of God amidst war and wickedness all around. I'm grateful to my Heavenly Father to have been given these experiences.

* * * * *

On the night of March 20, 1969, I retired as usual to a cot in the supply tent. I was awakened at about 4:00 A.M. by the sound of explosions and flying debris. The first thing I did was to get down on the ground. We were in the middle of a mortar attack! (A mortar is a small rocket that is dropped down a firing tube. At the bottom of the tube is a plate. When the rocket hits the plate, the firing pin, which is at the bottom of the rocket, fires, sending the rocket out of the tube. These tubes can be adjusted to aim in any direction with great accuracy.)

Within a minute I felt something hit my back, which I had supposed to be a fragment. Then I felt something hit my elbow. I was convinced that if I didn't move under cover I would soon be severely wounded or dead. I remembered that just outside the supply tent were some steel culverts. I crawled a few feet at a time towards the culverts. Each time a mortar would land I stopped and buried my head, and then would crawl another few inches. Once I got under the culverts I felt reasonably secure. As long as a mortar round didn't land at either end I would be okay! After a few minutes a round landed, filling the end of my tunnel with fragments and debris. When the fragments entered my legs the first thing I thought was that a round had landed on top of the culverts, causing two of them to turn sideways (against each other) and chopping off my legs! I was sure my legs had been chopped off. The pain was excruciating and I screamed and screamed. When the fragments from the mortar entered my flesh they were red hot from the explosion, so, much of the pain was from my flesh burning. After a moment or two I gained control of myself and looked down at my feet. I realized they had not been chopped off but that a round had landed near my feet, spray-

ing my lower legs with fragments. I called for a medic, not thinking that a medic wouldn't be dumb enough to run around in the middle of a mortar attack. I distinctly remember offering up a prayer at that moment. I asked the Lord to please not let me die in that land, but to please let me go home. Even if I had to lose my legs, I did not want to die in Vietnam. I asked Him to please spare my life and if He did I promised to always put the Church first in my life. The Lord heard my prayer and answered, as you will see.

Within moments, perhaps only seconds, I heard a sound that brought great relief to me. It was the sound of helicopters. It was the ARA (aerial rocket artillery). They were equipped with rockets and miniguns, which could spray a football field and not miss much. I knew that the attack was over because at night, when the mortars fired, there would be a flash from the tube, which could be seen from the air. As soon as the enemy heard the helicopters, they quit firing.

A helicopter flies above Highway 1, scene of many Viet Cong attacks on military convoys and civilian vehicles. Helicopters often escorted traffic on the road to prevent enemy ambush.

WILLIAM C. PETTY, M.D.

William served as an Army medical doctor (anesthesiologist) assigned to the 24th Evacuation Hospital in Long Binh, Vietnam from October 1969-1970. He recently returned home from his service as a couple missionary in Kenya, assigned to Tanzania.

"MASS CASUALTY!"

A shout that continues to strike terror into my heart. Mass casualty had a practical definition at the 24th Evacuation Hospital: The hospital holding area was full, casualties were coming out of helicopters faster than we could find places to put them, and the triage team had to start making life and death decisions, such as which soldiers to try and save and which soldiers were most likely to die with or without surgery. Many times the operating rooms never closed for five or six days. My longest stretch of continuous work without sleep was approximately 48 hours. I was eventually so exhausted, I went to my room and slept fourteen hours and then got up and went back to work. Mass casualties were so frequent they coalesced into a blur.

Decisions of life and death like this were a daily occurrence and were never taken lightly by anyone on the surgical team. In the intensive care unit the soldier had to be on a ventilator because of failing lung function. It was impossible to communicate with this young man. His vocal cords were blocked, he had no hands to hold, he could not hear, nor could he see, and we had no way to detect if he was experiencing pain, sorrow, or love. The nurses talked to him as though he could hear, touched him to let him know someone was there, and did their best to communicate to him that he was still alive and being cared for. After a few days, he was moved to a ward area but remained on the ventilator. It soon became apparent that he would not leave Vietnam alive. A difficult decision had to be made. He could be kept alive for an undetermined amount of time if we continued his ventilation and vital function support. However, such support would deprive other wounded soldiers of the ventilator he was using. The soldier's surgeon refused to turn off the ventilator because of religious reasons and asked me for an opinion since I was managing the ventilator care. I seriously thought and pondered about what was best for the soldier under the circumstances.

There is simply not a yes or no ethical or religious answer in such situations. Each dilemma must be faced on a one on one basis. Complex events make it impossible for anyone to look back and analyze the final decision from the classroom, the pages of a book, or the niceties of a structured ethical debate. The soldier's vital functions were rapidly deteriorating, his connections with the outside world were severed, and his wounds were totally incapacitating. I made the decision to disconnect him from the ventilator. As the plug was pulled out of the socket, the spirit of the soldier ascended to God. For me a moment of duality, sad to see him die but happy to relieve his burdens; a soul searching decision I have never regretted

Opposite top: Awareness was accepted as a necessary element of the anesthetic technique. Since the doctors had no way to evaluate awareness it was assumed the soldier was awake. Doctors like William Clayton Petty (pictured) talked to the patients throughout the surgery, assuring them he was doing everything possible to save their life. It was a very personal experience of Petty's that made him grateful for the medical skills accumulated prior to arriving in Vietnam. He personally felt blessed to be in Vietnam to share his skills with the wounded soldiers.

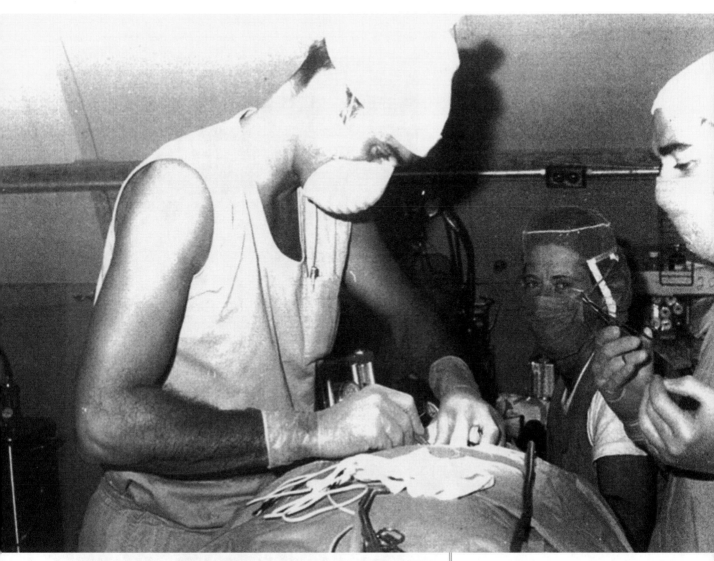

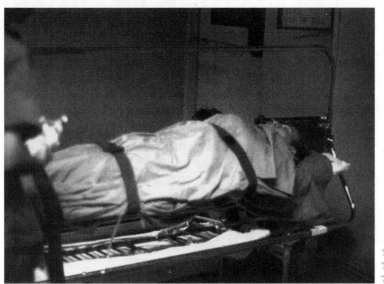

Left: A soldier on a Stryker frame following repair of a gunshot wound to the back. The Stryker frame allows him to be turned over easily and makes his hospital care easier. He will be kept on this frame until he is stable enough to be air evacuated to Japan and, eventually, to a Veterans Hospital near his hometown.

⋆
⋆
⋆

Top: Petty's Hooch: Large 50-gallon drums were filled with sand and topped off with bags of sand to serve as deterrents to a bomb or mortar attack. The sand bags were starting to leak because of the humid weather. Petty had a window with drapes no less and a window air conditioner. The air conditioner actually serviced 2 rooms, but he was lucky and the controls were on his side of the partition.

Bottom: One of the Vietnamese children brought in for elective surgery during a lull in the war. William Clayton Petty often did orphans who required either an eye surgery or plastic surgery. According to Dr. Petty, "Operating on these children was a pleasure and provided great satisfaction."

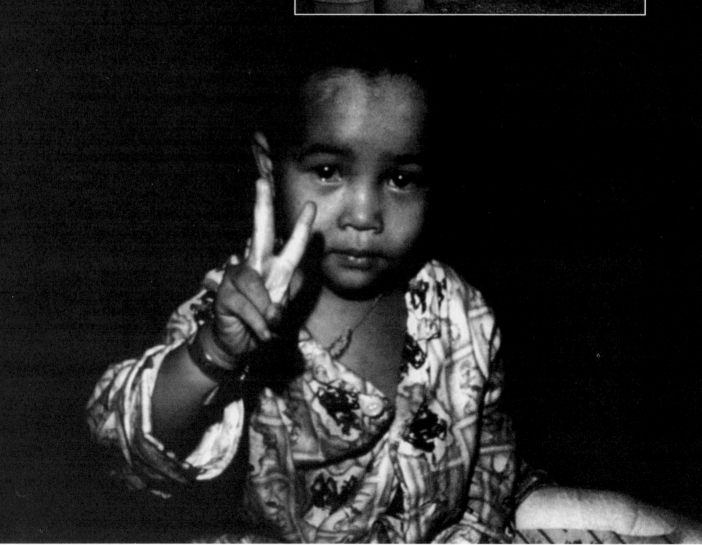

Below: William Clayton Petty's office in the Quonset hut used for surgery. Although he did not spend a great deal of time in the office, it was a nice place to go to write letters home and cool off during an exceptionally hot, humid day. Note the rug on the floor and the padded chair he scrounged from who knows where. They wore their combat boots, fatigue pants, and surgical tops a lot. If they were in the surgical area they usually put on a pair of surgical pants.

Top Inset: In the Triage area wounded soldiers came in on stretchers from the helicopters. The nurses and doctors immediately evaluated the status of the wounded soldier and began the initial resuscitation. A triage surgeon determined the priority of the injury and how soon the soldier would go to the operating room. Oxygen was in cylinders along the wall and stethoscopes were hung from a pipe connected to the ceiling.

Bottom Inset: John Powell, M.D., general surgeon, suturing a soldier in the Triage area. The soldier is on a stretcher laid on a simple wooden frame.

Above: A typical "dust-off" medical evacuation helicopter used in the Vietnam War. The dual fire extinguishers were present just in case there was a crash. Helicopter evacuation saved many lives in Vietnam. The helicopter pilots were brave, tenacious, and devoted to their jobs. The doctors had great respect for the sacrifices they made to get critically wounded soldiers to them in time to save their lives. The exceptional record of the 24th Evacuation Hospital was made because of the cooperation between the helicopter pilots, the medics, and the hospital staff.

Right: Military Religious Retreat at the Tan Son Nhut Air Force Base Chapel. Those who could came to Tan Son Nhut for the day to be uplifted and inspired. It was a wonderful day to be in the middle of the war with blood and gore left behind for just a few hours. The chapel was well built, had good solid benches, and even hymn books.

or had second thoughts about. In fact, the same decision had to be made for other severely wounded soldiers with no hope for recovery in Vietnam and who would never have survived an attempt to transport them from Vietnam to the United States.

ALLAN G. PIXTON

Allan served in both World War II and the Vietnam War. During his Vietnam tour he served as a commanding officer as the Chief of Research and Development. His assignment included responsibility for combat equipment used in Vietnam. Currently he lives in Texas and is a retired Brigadier General in the U.S. Army. Allan has served as a branch president and high priests leader for sixteen years.

In mid-October the third Marine Division made a sweep through our side of the DMZ, and uncovered a North Vietnamese artillery position on our side of the Ben Hai River. I flew in there to see what the enemy was up to and recovered several items that were forwarded to our intelligence technicians in Saigon. A few days later the marines discovered another position inside the DMZ. I flew to Firebase Rock pile for some business, and then planned to go into the newly discovered DMZ position. With a map, I pointed out to the helicopter pilot where I wanted to go. I indicated that it was sensitive because the landing zone was within the DMZ. The copilot of the helicopter said he had flown there previously and knew precisely where it was. I guess it was intuition that caused me to direct them to fly at 3,500 feet, rather than at treetop level or at a few hundred feet that we normally flew.

Allan Pixton is a Brigadier General of the U.S. Army and participated in both WWII and the Vietnam War.

We took off and for some unknown reason I did not follow exactly where we were going. Out the open door of the helicopter I become involved in looking at all the craters on the ground and identifying whether they were made by my 105 mm, 155 mm, 175 mm, or eight inch howitzer artillery, B-52 bomber flights, or others. After an unknown amount of time, my aid, Lt. Mark Hamilton, who was the only other passenger in the helicopter, came onto the intercom and said: "General, what is this well-traveled road over on my side?" I looked at the road and realized that there was no such road on our side of the DMZ. I looked up ahead, on my side of the helicopter, and saw the Finger Lakes. We were five miles inside North Vietnam, enemy territory. I changed intercom channels to talk to the pilot, telling him that we were five miles inside North Vietnam, and to get out of there in the fastest way possible. We turned around and headed back for South Vietnam.

While we were flying north into North Vietnam there had been no shooting from the ground, as the enemy was willing to let us go north as far as we wanted to. The moment we did an abrupt turn and headed back south toward the U.S. side of the DMZ, the ground erupted with enemy fire trying to prevent us from returning home. We could hear the bullets and the shells going by us, and we could see the tracers from those various weapons shooting at us. We could also identify the 37 mm and 57 mm shells as they went by because their tracers were bigger and more intense. Also, I remember that the tracers we saw were only one out of every five bullets being fired at us. Until that time I had never realized how much a Huey helicopter tilts forward when it is flying at its maximum speed, as I had never ridden in one at such velocity. It is a miracle that we did not get hit with any enemy bullets during that escape flight. It was probably due to the unexpected speed with which we were traveling and the troops on the ground not aiming far enough in advance of our helicopter to intercept and hit us. Whatever the reason, we made it back safely, landing at Dong Ha. There the pilot was given a royal chewing out by me. He was never permitted to fly me again. The helicopter had to be grounded and given rigid maintenance and testing as it had far exceeded all its normal range of engine RPMs and chopper speed. Once again the good Lord protected me.

CHARLES A. REITZE

During the Vietnam War Charles served as the Combat Engineer, Multi Weapons Specialist, Infantry support and backup in the Army's Company A, 62nd Engineer Battalion. He served in Vietnam during 1968–1969.

A rocket had exploded somewhere close by.

The concussion from the explosion slammed my face down onto the ground. I reached down and felt my knees. They hurt, throbbed, and were bloody, but I was alive, at least. I was alive. I shook, trembled, and trembled beyond control. Terror is a horrible thing, and I now knew terror. How long had I been there? I did not know.

I tried to rise but had no strength, and wondered if I was hurt worse than I knew. Terrified, I suddenly began to pray. I had been brought up to believe in God and in Jesus Christ, but I didn't know them, I didn't know how to pray. So I did all I knew how to do. "Heavenly Father," I thought lying there, "if you let me live through this night, through Vietnam, I promise I will go to church the rest of my life." Then before my eyes, like a video movie, I saw my entire life on vivid display. I saw the good, the bad, and the indifferent. I saw all my friends, family, and as each of them paraded before my eyes I said, named them. "Please,

Crossing the Saigon River in a convoy. The hood of the 10-ton truck Charles was in can be seen in the foreground.

Charles Reitze in front of one of the gun ships (before he became a member of The Church of Jesus Christ of Latter-day Saints.)

Heavenly Father let me see them one more time. Let me see my mother, my father, my brother Ray, my sisters, Kathy, Mary-Lou, Susie, and Judy. Let me see my school friends, Carroll, Owen, and Jerry." Almost as soon as it came, the vision of my life had passed by. It took only seconds. It was like my life was on fast forward. But it was there, all of it. And some of it I didn't like very much.

As soon as the vision passed, I felt strength ebbing back into my frame. It was as through I was being injected with a vile of strength. Rockets were still exploding, but I didn't care anymore. It was like I was beyond these explosions of death. There was a peace about me. Oh, I was still shook, and I was shook hard, but I knew I would be okay. I didn't know how I knew. I just did. Soon I found my way to a bunker. We built the bunkers out of sand bags, with wooden planked sides on some. They were about two feet thick. We had double rows of sand bags on both the roof and the walls. No sooner had I made it to the safety of the bunker, but First Sergeant Fitzgerald, stuck his head through the entryway. He said, "We have been overrun. The VC has penetrated the compound."

The only thing that saved us that night was the chopper. They came with bursts of machine gun fire and exploding rockets. The sky lit up like ten Fourth of July's all wrapped in one. They pounded our perimeters with rockets and incessant machine gun fire, driving the VC back. Had they not come when they did, many of the men of the 62nd likely, would not have seen another day. It was a night of horror, a night of agonizing screams, a night of death. It was a night that would forever lie in the minds of the men who served their country on the blood stained soils of Vietnam.

I had no idea how the promise I made to my Heavenly Father would change the course of my life in an eternal way. I didn't understand the magnitude of the promise. But I soon found out that a kind, loving, Father in Heaven knew. And though I forgot that promise for a time, He didn't. From this day forward, He, in a very literal, unmistakable way, watched over me, protected me, led me by the hand and carried me with one set of footsteps across the sand, until I humbled myself and listened to the gospel of Jesus Christ. For, He led me to it in a way that no man can deny.

Top: One of many bunkers built out of sandbags and wooden-planked sides that soldiers used for protection. Charles was able to make his way to a bunker like this after a life-changing experience while under fire.

Bottom: Three South Vietnamese boys. Their village can be seen in the background.

SAM RICHARDSON

Sam was drafted as a young man of twenty-four. He served his tour of duty with a combat infantry unit.

The first part of my tour was without garments. In this part of the combat zones, it was required that all GIs wear green underwear, for helping with the camouflage. Meanwhile, my mother asked her priesthood authorities if she could die my garments green so I could wear them. They considered it and then finally told her it was okay. Later, when my dyed garments came, I felt calm under their protection. My garments, along with my religious behavior provided many an opportunity to discuss and preach the gospel over in Vietnam. It didn't take long after I first got there to be offered marijuana. I politely declined, whereupon the soldier offering it gave me an understanding smile. He said, "I guarantee you that within a month you'll be using it, and smoking and drinking, too, even though you've never had that habit before. This type of war is too nerve-wracking. You don't know if the enemy is in front of you, or behind you, or if he's going to attack in the next five minutes, or day after tomorrow." My continued abstinence, yet calm behavior surprised them, and provided even more opportunities to discuss religious issues. When you come close to death, like seeing a buddy die, or having a mortar land near you, you begin to contemplate the things of the next life. I started to become the authority over these matters.

At the same time, I learned a new lesson about peer pressure. I fully expected them to continue to make fun of me for resisting such opportunities for an occasional escape. But when they saw that I was sticking to my morals, even in the face of death, they began to show respect for me. They now expected that behavior from me. Now, when a new soldier came into the company, the introductions were like this: "Over there, that's Cuts. Next is Biggs, over there, Fukes. And this is Richardson; he doesn't smoke or drink."

REED K. RICHENS

During the Vietnam War, Reed served as an army staff sergeant in an armored cavalry regiment from 1967–1969. His assignments included track commander and lead vehicle. He currently works as a teacher in the Church Educational System in Utah.

A few days after my first ambush patrol we were moved from base camp to an area northwest of Saigon. We traveled through Saigon to arrive at our destination. I was able to take some pictures of Saigon because I got to ride on the back of the vehicle. What an experience for a little farm boy from Myron, Utah. I had never seen anything so sad in all of my life. I think that my family was pretty poor as I was growing up, but I was rich compared to what I saw among the poor Vietnamese people in Saigon. They lived in very poorly built homes, on stilts, in the rivers that flowed through the city. There were also many people living in well-to-do circumstances in very nice homes with high walls around the property. The walls had barbed wire and broken glass on the top to keep people from climbing over them.

We traveled for about fifty to seventy-five miles northwest of Saigon where we would search through the villages for the enemy during the day and set up ambush patrols at night. During one of the day patrols we made contact with the enemy in an area where there had been a rubber tree plantation, but because of the war, all the rubber trees had been cut down but were still on the ground. We moved into an "on line" formation. This means we were all side by side, with about twenty-five meters between vehicles, going in the same direction, and trying to keep each vehicle in a line with out getting ahead or behind. This was very difficult because there were so many trees lying on the ground that we could not go over, so we were not traveling in a very straight line. Our vehicle was on the left side ,and we were getting out farther and farther because of the broken trees.

It was getting close to sun down time, which meant that things would get dark quickly when the sun was gone. We were trying to hurry and make the sweep before it was dark, because we did not want to lose the enemy because of darkness. All of a sudden there was a horrendous explosion on our left side, not more than five feet from the vehicle. I was on the left side. I looked out to the left front and saw standing there one of the enemy. I pulled the trigger of the M60 machine gun; it fired one round and jammed. I grabbed my M16 rifle and fired. It fired about two rounds and jammed, also. I looked at the enemy soldier and he was loading a rocket on his launcher. I grabbed a hand grenade and pulled the pin, and threw with all my might. From then till the explosion, it was as though everything was in slow motion. The grenade was in the air and was on target. The enemy soldier finished putting his rocket on the launcher. He brought the launcher to its firing position and looked up. As his eyes came to the forward position, he saw the grenade. I will never forget seeing him watch the grenade fall to its destination between his feet. The moment before it hit the ground there was a ball of fire and a deafening explosion. The enemy soldier was gone. I was so struck with fear that I could not think of what to do, I only reacted to what I had been trained to do. It then dawned on me that I had killed my first enemy soldier. I was able to see him and it dawned on me that he was a human being. There have been times when I think about the people I killed. What kind of men were they? Were they married? Did they have families? Did they have a little girl like me? Did they have religious beliefs? I guess most of all, Why did they have to die? Yes, war is hell!

I'm asked, often, by my students if it bothers me that I killed the men that I did. It isn't an easy thing to answer, because the answer is yes and no. I feel or maybe better stated, I felt a deep sorrow for their deaths. I do not feel responsible for their deaths. I believe that those wicked persons who caused and controlled the war may have to be responsible for their deaths. Those soldiers that were doing their duty to country will not be accountable for their deaths.

ROBERT H. RIDING JR.

Robert was born in Tennessee. During the Vietnam War he served as an Infantry Platoon Commander in the Marine Corps from 1967–1971. His assignments included forward observer. Currently he lives in California and is an oral surgeon. He has served in various Church callings such as branch president and Gospel Doctrine teacher.

I had served in the New England Mission from 1964–1966 and had President Elder Boyd K. Packer as my mission president. I got to know him well as mission secretary and later as a zone leader, so before going to Vietnam in June of 1969 I drove to Salt Lake City to visit with him and perhaps be comforted. He was very cordial and warm and we talked a bit about our time since the mission field. I then told him of my immediate deployment to Vietnam and my concerns with my physical safety. President Packer then went on to say that he could

A marine demolition team prepares to destroy 102-mm rockets discovered north of Cam Lo, Vietnam.

understand my concern but that losing my spiritual life was a more important issue. He said he was saddened because the Church was losing many young people to the "wages of sin" as they went on R and R from the war. His advice to me was to continue to live the Gospel and all would be well with me. It gave me a new perspective and helped me to focus on what was truly important. President Packer's words were sadly accurate as I associated with many young LDS servicemen who lost their virtue and personal values while in Vietnam.

Right: 1st Lt. Robert Riding.

Below: BBQ India Battery, 3rd BN, 11th Marines, FSB Ryder, October 1969.

Opposite top: 1st Lt. Riding filling Sandbags. October 1969.

Opposite center: Elder McConkie teaching at a meeting in Danang, Vietnam.

Opposite bottom: LDS servicemen choir singing at the meeting with Elder McKonkie in Danang, Vietnam.

I remember attending Sunday School/Sacrament meeting at the base chapel at Camp San Onofre, Camp Pendleton when all we had was some unleavened bread wafers as our bread and we used it. But one of the Sacrament meetings I remember most vividly was in Vietnam in October of 1969 with three other young members of the Church as we met in a little hut on LZ Ross, southern I Corps. All we had for the sacrament were some stale C-ration crackers that we passed around in the original tin container. We did not have any cups or any containers to put individual water samples in so we blessed a canteen of water treated with halogen and passed it around, each taking a drink. I had my triple combination that my fiancée had given me before coming to Vietnam, and from it we read the sacrament prayers. I always felt good over there as long as I had a toothbrush, some C-rations, dry socks, and my triple combination.

DENNIS A. ROBISON

Dennis served in the United States Army during the Vietnam War. He was newly married to Peggy Jo Beckstrom when his orders to ship out came. As an air traffic controller he assisted in many bombing missions flown throughout the war. As a member of the 1985th Comm. Squadron he achieved the rank of staff sergeant.

Dennis A. Robison USAF Class A Uniform.

On the SAC [strategic air command] base, when the bombers got ready to leave for a mission and they flew from there over to Vietnam they had certain times that they were supposed to leave. In the control tower every morning we would get all of the departure times from the SAC. There was also a control tower that colonels sat in across the field from us. They would send us the departure times and a half hour before departure times we would have to close the airport for no take-offs or landings, and we would have to broadcast in the blind the weather conditions every few minutes. The B-52s were usually two flights of three and they would listen at certain times to the broadcasts so they would know which runway to go to and then at a certain time they would start taxiing out of their bunkers to the end of the runway. It was all done in radio silence so that no one listening to the radios would hear them departing and know the arrival times of the targets. One day as they taxied out and got to the end of the runway to depart, I looked down and I saw a little puff of smoke come out from underneath one of the B-52s. It wasn't anything big; it was just a little puff. We were not supposed to broadcast at all on the radios, but the Spirit told me that there was something wrong and after thinking about it for a minute the as airplane started down the runway, I got on the radio and I called and told them to abort. They came to a stop at the end of the runway and pulled off. In the meantime, that was such a no-no that the SAC colonels were on the phone chewing me out like crazy. I really caught a lot of crap from it. They not only had the crew chief and the tower on the phone, they had our squadron commander on the phone and they wanted blood for doing this. The B-52 that was pulled off the runway was loaded with bombs and they checked it out and it had broken a hydraulic line. They had just barely got it stopped at the end of the runway when all of the hydraulic fluid was gone out of the whole airplane. The pilots showed up about an hour later and all the guys on the plane brought me two cases of beer to thank me for calling that abort. They said if the plane would have gotten off the ground, they would have never got it back on the ground and they would have had to bail out or crash. After all of that, the SAC colonels backed off from chewing me out anymore, and there was nothing else said about it. I was credited in our paperwork for an aircraft save because of that. And then I think, it was just because the Spirit said, "There's something wrong." You see stuff like that all the time and let it go, and let it go, and let it go.

JOHN G. SALDIVAR

John joined the Church in 1963 while stationed in Japan. Six years later he became a servicemen's group leader while serving in Vietnam. He gained the rank of captain.

In February 1969, the ammunition dump on our side of the landing strip caught fire. A large series of explosions totally collapsed the chapel that we had used to meet in. The group was broken down into smaller groups, and I was called to be the new group leader for the Wing Headquarters Group. I was wondering why I was the one called to lead the group. I was the newest member of the Church in the group. I had joined the Church five years almost to the date when I got to Da Nang. I then remembered the part of the blessing I had received at my confirmation (and later repeated in my patriarchal blessing). "Thou shalt be called to offices of responsibility and as thou shalt magnify thy calling in these offices, the Lord shall magnify thee before thy brethren and thou shalt find real joy and strength in this association."

We averaged eight to ten members attending in our group. Our problem was trying to find a place to meet on Sundays. The schedule for the wing chapel was totally filled. At first, Major Beason and I used to go visit all the members, but we knew that we had to find or build a place in which to meet.

Major Beason was the ground safety officer and had many other collateral duties. Thanks to his resourcefulness, he was able to get the materials from the Army to build us an elongated structure, which was used as a dojo for his newly formed karate club during the week and as our Church meeting place on Sundays. All our members and the members of the karate club helped build it, so it didn't take us long to do. It was built on the south side of the enlisted club. We borrowed chairs from there on Sundays for our meetings. Our closing song was always, "God Be With You Till We Meet Again." If someone was absent, we held a short meeting and then we would all go to his bedside and hold a meeting there. We usually only visited an absent member once. He would rather come to our meetings after that. We usually held a one-hour meeting, a combination of priesthood, Sunday School, and sacrament meeting. The sacrament was blessed and passed, followed by a lesson from our small military scriptures, and the singing of three hymns.

In April 1969 I met Elder Ezra Taft Benson in person as he came to Da Nang to hold an LDS area servicemen conference. Perhaps the highlight of this visit to the Orient was meeting with LDS servicemen. Elder Benson traveled to Vietnam, where he met with more than eight hundred soldiers in the south central and northern districts. Some of the gatherings were held just a few miles from the front lines, with guns stacked in the corners of makeshift Quonset-hut chapels.

Danger didn't particularly bother Elder Benson. He was confident that if he exercised reasonable care, the Lord would protect him. Even when artillery shells exploded nearby, he paused just long enough for the sound to dissipate and then began again. After shaking hands with hundreds of men, his hand ached and his heart was so filled with compassion that he couldn't always restrain the tears. I felt the compassion and the love of this great man, an Apostle of the Lord that wasn't afraid to shed a tear. His concern was for all the members of the Church, and he asked the group leaders to look out for all of our brethren.

Once Major Beason and I were walking along when a Marine approached us with a note for the major. The handwritten note seemed to have been authored by a very feeble individual with a shaky hand. It simply stated, "I'm sick, administer to me." We went right over and blessed him. He had been sick for three or four days, he could hardly talk or move, he hadn't eaten or consumed much liquid for that period of time. A very short time later, we could hardly believe our eyes; the Marine that looked like he was on his deathbed a short time before was running all over the compound.

1st Lt. and later Captain John G. Saldivar was the officer in charge of aircraft maintenance and material management systems analyst.

Major Beason taught the gospel to a fellow Marine and converted him. I only helped once; for even though I was a Seventy, I had never been involved in missionary work up to then. I had been the ward clerk since my ordination, doing everything by myself. When I got orders to Vietnam, I trained three brethren to do the different jobs involved with being a ward clerk (the job was just too much for one person). We went to China Beach for the baptism of the new convert, stopping on the way to pick up Chaplain David Smith, as he did the final interview and filled out the proper forms. The beach was deserted as Major Beason and the new member-to-be went in the water, waist deep. The life guard came over, running, screaming and yelling at the top of his lungs not to go in the water because it was full of poisonous snakes, and the beach was closed because of that danger. I gently calmed him down, explaining to him that a religious ceremony was taking place, that this was not a frivolous excursion, and that as soon as the baptism was over, they would come out. I ordered him to clean up his language, as the other officer witnessing the ceremony was a chaplain! Furthermore, I informed him that the officer doing the baptism was not only an ordained minister, but also a black belt in karate!! Everything went well, without any problems after that. The life guard apologized to the chaplain for the use of offensive language.

BRIGHAM SHULER

Brigham served in Vietnam in 1965. He was assigned as an officer in an infantry division. Later he became the company commander.

He was the enemy; he stood in the way of something that we deemed important. I guess as part of my naiveté, my job was to destroy the enemy by means of firing maneuvers or hand-to-hand combat. That's kind of the way I approached it at the time. I might look at it quite differently now. I always had a healthy respect for the caliber of soldier that the North Vietnamese had. It is amazing to me that they could get anybody to be so dedicated to a cause when they were treated so radically poor. We had found people, bodies literally chained to machine-gun positions with the machine guns chained in the ground by stakes, and the people chained to the machine guns to make sure they couldn't abandon the position. Still, they continued to fight.

I guess the best and the worst thing came all in the same afternoon and the same event. In my first tour in Vietnam I was seriously wounded. We had engaged a numerically superior enemy. We didn't know at the time that they were numerically superior to us, or we might not have engaged them. One of our units had been pinned down by hostile fire, and I had been ordered in to aid them and to extricate them from their circumstance. Once I got in there and found out that things weren't as they had been reported to us, I made a different report to my battalion commander. He ordered me to go through and clear the woods from which the fire had been coming. I wandered into the woods with my company, and that's where we met a main force Viet Cong guerilla battalion.

We were outnumbered almost four to one. The fight lasted about an hour and a half, and I was hit seven times in the fight. The bad part of that is that I lost my left ankle and the right side of my right foot. The good part of that is that I did a lot of growing up, and I gained a new testimony of the divinity of Jesus Christ. When the first round hit me, I had the presence of mind to say a quick prayer. As I said amen to that pray, I knew that my life wouldn't be taken that day. Although I knew that I'd been hit, I did not realize that I had been hurt badly. I stayed in full command of my company and I was fully conscious. When the fight ended, even though by that time I had lost my left ankle and the right side of my right foot, I walked unassisted out of the jungle to a clearing. I put my company into position and evacuated my wounded before I began to get woozy and lapsed into nearly unconsciousness because of the tremendous loss of blood that I had sustained. I'd say that was the best and worst thing that had happened to me. The doctors had told me that I could look forward to as many as eighteen months of hospitalization before they could get me up and moving around and teach me to walk again. A young elder came in and gave me a blessing of the priesthood, promised me a swift and speedy healing. Six months later, I walked out of the hospital and went back to work. That has stood with me.

STANLEY SHULTZ

Stanley Shultz, an officer in Vietnam, received a jeep for his use. Dismayed over the graffiti that decorated it, he cleaned it up and gave the jeep its own distinctive LDS identity by painting "Mahonri Moriancumer" across the front.

JAY R. SIMMONS

During the Vietnam War, Jay served as a pilot and commander of an AC-119-G fixed-wing gunship, with the 17th Special Operations Squadron. During his tour of duty from 1970–1971 he was assigned to various bases in South Vietnam.

The Tan Son Nhut LDS servicemen's branch and the Saigon branch celebrated Pioneer day by getting together to go from Saigon to Vung Tau, for a combined branch outing and baptismal service. We all went down on an army bus. It was great to get to know some of the local members. There were five people baptized, two U.S. Army guys and three Vietnamese persons, two men and a young lady. After the baptisms, all those present had a picnic and played football and volleyball on the beach. All had a great time. It was a welcome and wonderful break from the war. Servicemen, except those specifically called, were discouraged from participating with

This cargo aircraft was first used during World War II. Known as the "Flying Boxcar," it served multiple purposes. It also proved useful in the Korean War, and later in Vietnam. In Vietnam it was equipped for ground troop support. Side-mounted weapons capable of firing up to 6,000 rounds a minute made the aircraft most formidable.

the local branch, except for special activities because Church leaders wanted to lessen the American influence and increase local leadership opportunities.

Above: LDS servicemen's Church group, at Tan Son Nhut AFB in Saigon Vietnam, January 1971. Front (l–r): Bro. Thompson, Bruce Judd, Steve Hokenson, Jay R. Simmons, Norm White (group leader), unidentified, Lyle Norris, Don Smith. Back (l–r): Bro. Phillips, unidentified, unidentified, Martin Sorge, Bro. Clay, unidentified, Allen Meservy, Jim Snelby, unidentified, Wendell Moody, unidentified, unidentified, Larry Kelly, Jay Sylvester, unidentified. "The LDS Servicemen's group was a real strength while in Vietnam. Church services were always different than in the States—no white shirts or ties, lots of uniforms, and more than occasional weapons at sacrament meeting. I often went straight from the flight line, after completing a night flight, to church, with a stinky uniform and in need of a shave. The brotherhood was much needed, and a savior in many cases. After church, no one was in a rush to leave. Usually [the] group just relocated elsewhere to enjoy the sociality and association with others of like interests, habits, and morals.

Right: Baptism in the South China Sea, South Vietnam, July 24, 1971. Witness on the left: Dr. Myrn Riley, District President. Witness on the right: AF Capt Gary Carter from Salt Lake City, one of the Americans called to work with the local Vietnamese branch.

DAVID SMITH

Official Marine Corps photo of LDS Chaplain David Smith, April 14, 1969.

FARRELL SMITH

Farrell Smith graduated from BYU and took a commission in the Air Force ROTC upon graduation and initially planned to be a pilot. This changed when Elder Harold B. Lee called him to become a chaplain. He explained that Church leaders were concerned about the recruits and the draftees and wanted them to have access to LDS direction once they were in boot camps and training camps.

We had not had chaplains in the military for some time with a few exceptions, and the chaplaincy, the chief of chaplains, had declined the request of the Church to endorse chaplains that did not have doctorate degrees commensurate with the other professional ministers. It turns out that President Johnson had made a presidential courtesy call to President David O. McKay and asked if there was anything he could do

Presidency and some council members, 11 August, 1968. Back: Farrell Smith, Maj. Johnson, Col. Payne, Mission Pres. Hardy, Major Young. Front: Dr. Anderson, Joseph McConkie, Nguyen Cao Minh (only Vietnamese Elder in the Church at that time), Bro. Wakefield, and Maj. Klippel.

for the Church. President McKay said, "Yes, there really is. We have this concern, we need to have chaplain," and President Johnson says, "Well, you send a representative to me in Washington and I will look at it." So apparently Elder Harold B. Lee was sent along with Boyd K. Packer. But Brother Lee told me this story as he interviewed me in Houston. He said

Top: Blackhorse LDS Servicemen's group. Names of such groups often related to places they served or units they served in, and the group names were not permanent as the names of our wards or branches. They tended to be whatever fit at the time, and changed as the situation changed. The groups were not considered official Church units, but rather informal gatherings wherever two or more LDS servicemen were gathered.

Bottom: Cuchi LDS servicemen's group. (L–R): Lt. Marvin Hardy (Group President); Brother Larry Marriott (1st Counselor); Dr. Desmond Anderson (District Counselor), high-ranking U.S. head of Vietnamese General College. Former Dean of U.S.C.'s college of Political Science); Brother Tom Raymont (District Counselor and chopper pilot); Farrell Smith.

that he sat in the oval office with President Johnson explaining the church's program of seminary and institute and missions etc, and that we felt that young men could serve as military chaplains if they qualified as military officers. After that explanation, President Johnson got on the phone with the chief of chaplains at the Pentagon and Elder Lee said he heard only the one side of the conversation, but it went something like this, "I don't care what you preachers think, I have never met a bad Mormon. You get 'em in there!" And Brother Lee said a week later the chief of chaplains and some of his associates were in Salt Lake spending time with the military committee and the Brethren understanding our system.

I do remember a funny experience where we visited what we had been calling the "Mormon Battalion" which was an activated Idaho National Guard unit in a place up in the highlands of Vietnam. A typical army assigned a black southern Baptist chaplain to be the chaplain of mostly Mormons, probably more than half of the returned missionaries. This chaplain was telling Brother McConkie that he sure found it frustrating because he had nothing to do. They were so well organized, and took care of themselves etc.

Top: New Air Force chapel where Chaplain Captain Farrell Smith was stationed on Tan Song Nuht Air Force Base in Saigon. It looked this way for only 11 days after his arrival in February, 1968.

Center: The night of February 18, 1968. Chapel took a direct hit from a 122-mm rocket, launched by Viet Cong from outskirts of Saigon.

Bottom: February 19, 1968—the morning after the rocket hit.

Normally the officers were assigned to live on the economy off base in Saigon. I had no place to stay except in my office in this nice chaplain complex that had recently been built and so I drug a mattress in at night and would put it in front of my desk in my office, and there I would sleep. I was there just a little over a week. The Tet offensive was still running pretty hot and heavy, and we could not get off base and go into Saigon, but other than that, and hearing some explosions from time to time, it seemed a fairly secure place. On the evening of February 17th, 1968, just before I was dragging my mattress in, in front of my bed I noticed a great big rat going across the rafters in our cultural hall gymnasium and was a little concerned that one of those might crawl over me while I was lying on my mattress, so I went and borrowed another mattress and had two layers of mattresses, thinking that might at least keep the rat from crawling over me, maybe go around me. That turned out to probably save my life.

While asleep that night, a 122 millimeter rocket aimed for our seventh air force headquarters across the street impacted the chapel, landed in front of the desk that I was sleeping by, and blew the building apart starting a tremendous fire. First thing I remember was the explosion and the fire and wondering where I was. It turned out that apparently the shrapnel from that rocket, the way it had exploded, had I been one mattress layer lower, it would have severed my spinal cord and probably killed me instantly. But being that one mattress higher, I received shrapnel wounds in my leg and through the front of my stomach, but it missed my vital organs, and as a result, I was able to get out of the chapel before it collapsed under the fire, and saved my life. I've always considered that a very interesting experience, and one that I've been grateful to the Lord for preserving my life.

GARY W. SMITH

Gary was born in Arkansas. During the Vietnam War his assignment in the Army included that of radar maintenance. He joined the Church during his tour of duty.

The infirmary was a small, long room with a few medical supplies and a gurney in it. I got up on the gurney to take a nap, and I noticed some pamphlets lying on the counter next to it. One of these was the Joseph Smith story in his own words. I read this and was unable to sleep. It touched my heart with a feeling that somehow, if this were true, it would be the most wonderful thing that had happened in our time. I had a two-week leave during the summer and used part of it to hike up into the woods of Oregon by myself and to think and contemplate on the things I had read and had heard from Lee. I tried praying there, but felt no closeness to God. The only thing I felt was that I should join this weird church, a feeling that kind of scared me.

I went back to the missile base, and Lee and I moved out of the barracks and got an apartment in the nearby small town of Damascus. My period of being taught the gospel was a little unorthodox. I sat on a couch while they sat in front of me on two antique chairs and read the discussion and asked the questions out of a loose-leaf binder. This seemed fine to me, and I found nothing odd about it. After the introductory discussion, they invited me to come back in two weeks. That was

Top: 2nd Counselor Keith Knighton, Farrell Smith as district president in the southern district, and 1st Counselor Joseph McConkie, 12 May, 1968.

Center: Phan Rang Air Base, Vietnam 21 September, 1968. (L–R): Joseph McConkie, Bishop Victor Brown, President Keith Hardy, Farrell Smith.

Bottom: Living conditions were less than luxurious.

the way they all went. I came over, they would read, and then make an appointment for weeks later. I did this for twelve weeks, or three months. They challenged me to read selected passages from the Book of Mormon, and I instead read the entire book and the entire triple combination. I was tired; I knelt down and said a prayer to know the truth. If ever I wanted something to happen to me spiritually, it was at this time, but nothing happened. I knelt down again and prayed to my Heavenly Father and a rush of pure knowledge went through me; lifting my heart and my mind to a level I had never before known. The room was infused with a clear, yellow light that I cannot describe, because I had never seen it before and have never seen it since, at least not in the intensity that I saw and felt it at this time. And I knew without a doubt that Jesus was the Christ, that Joseph Smith was a prophet, and that the Book of Mormon was true.

I was baptized on October 2, 1971. If I had not been in the Army, if I had not been sent to D.C. instead of Washington state, if Lee had not been so obnoxiously insistent, and if I had not been taught by exactly the right people to keep me going, none of this might ever have happened. But it was all arranged in the wisdom of Him who knows all things and for that I will be eternally grateful.

HYDE TAYLOR

During the Vietnam War, Hyde served as Sergeant Major in the Army's Airborne Infantry from 1970–1971. Currently works in construction management in Utah. He has served in many Church positions such as Scout Master and priesthood advisor.

In one patrol in enemy territory they came upon a VC [Viet Cong] camp that held several POWs. The VC had recently departed as their fires were still going, but they left the starved POWs behind. Hyde and his patrol tried to carry the POWs back to friend's forces. They put them on their backs and when they stopped to rest and tried to let the POWs down their skin stuck to their packs. Needless to say, not many survived.

There was never a time that I ask the Lord why I was in the situation I was in. It had become evident early on that I was much needed where I was and that I was doing what I was supposed to be doing.

CALVIN DOUGLAS TEBBS

From 1970–1971 Calvin served in the Vietnam War as a navy radio operator. His assignments included patrolling rivers in the Mekong Delta. He now lives in Utah where he works as a business consultant. The following excerpts are from his journal, accompanied by his memories of these experiences as a 46-year-old man looking back on his youth.

April 14, 1970, the day is Tuesday.

Today for me was very full. I didn't do much work but we had two church meetings. Our family home evening was at 6:00 P.M. I gave the prayer and Brother Nay talked about the Joe Hari Square. This family home evening was wonderful; it did much for me spiritually. We went to a meeting at 7:30 P.M. and discussed class courses to take. I'm signing up for

"Introduction to the Book of Mormon and its Teachings," 121 x for $9.00. I got to give the closing prayer. I'm sure getting some practice at praying, which I need badly. At 9:27 P.M. I talked with Mother in Salt Lake City, [Utah] for three minutes through the MARS station on the hill. It was so wonderful to hear her voice. For a while I was thinking of joining the river patrol boats (PBRs), but after hearing Mom all I wanted to do was make it back home. Somehow, Dale isn't getting any letters from Mom. I don't know how to get a hold of him to get things straight. Tonight I'm going to pray for the Lord's guidance in this coming year and to help me in my endeavors to try to make a more righteous person of me. That's it for tonight.

Spent the afternoon washing and ironing my greens. In the short time I've been here I've come to gather up four to five sets of greens. I'm only issued two sets but people leave the country and leave their greens for anyone who wants them. I'm fasting dinner and breakfast in preparation for a blessing to be given to me later. I need the Lord's help in my future here in Vietnam. I'll never forget tonight. Scott and I went to the home evening meeting at the servicemen's chapel. It started out good. Then just as the lesson started all of the base lights went out. A candle was lit and we proceeded with the lesson. The Spirit of the Lord was there amongst us. We were close. Our lesson was about the Atonement of Christ. I was asked to give the prayer. I gave a prayer that was different than my other ones. It was deeper, as though God was helping me along. Words concerning our following Christ and praying, living the gospel and He'll always be with us if we do these things. After the prayer came my blessing in the dark. Hands were laid upon my head by Brother Donaldson, CYM2; Brother Downey, medical corpsman second class; Brother Wilinson, photoman second class; and our visiting LDS chaplain (I called him Lieutenant Chaplain). Lieutenant Chaplain spoke. A feeling came over me beyond any description. I knew the Holy Ghost was with me. I feel safe now. No one is going to harm me. It was good it was in the dark because I was crying because I was so happy. Scott and I said our goodbyes to the others and left for our barracks. No sooner had we started walking that the lights came back on. I somehow can't help feeling that the lights going off were no coincidence. It was raining on our way back to the annex, but stopped as soon as we go out of the truck at the gate. I'm going to pray some more for help and guidance from the Lord. Good night and God bless America for it is truly a land of the blessed.

August 12–14, 1970, Wednesday–Friday

My orders came. I can't believe it, I'm actually leaving. During the evening all of the men gathered together to give me a going away party. They didn't serve alcohol, only soda pop, all in my honor. It was a pleasant goodbye considering how our relationship got started. I was given a plaque making me an honorary Green Beret. I can honestly say that I will miss many of these men.

My last night on watch was filled with activity. At 2:00 A.M., while I was standing my last watch, ten people were spotted moving by our compound at five hundred meters. They stopped behind some trees and continued to survey our camp. Two APCs [armored personnel carrier] were started up and sent out to check the situation. From the tower, I guided them

In fighting near Thakhek in central Laos in mid-November, Lao forces captured 15 North Vietnamese soldiers and large supplies of equipment from communist countries. Prisoners and equipment were presented to the public and international press. Prisoners can be seen in the background.

to the target. From the tower we could see everything using the starlight scope, which allows us to see in the dark. I guided the halftracks through the claymore mine defenses toward the people when a heavy firefight suddenly broke loose. A big enemy contact was established. The APCs got most of them.

In the morning, with no sleep, I prepared to leave Chi Lang on the next chopper. I couldn't help but reflect on my experience at Chi Lang: from being an outcast to becoming a friend to many of the men while still preserving my values; experiencing frequent challenges until they knew I wouldn't give in; being able to learn for myself why the commandments are so important and that they are rules given by a loving Father that knows following such rules will bring us the greatest happiness; having many hours to study the gospel and then apply it to my experiences. I can say that my testimony has grown immensely as a result of my struggles at Chi Lang. The adversity truly helped me grow whereas being in a safer place may have resulted in slower growth. After saying my goodbyes I climbed aboard a chopper for Binh Thuy and hopefully a safer tour of duty.

CURTIS L. TRACY

During his time in Vietnam Curtis served as an Army procurement officer. Following the war he was assigned as a legal officer in the Judge Advocate General Corp, where he served for 26 years, achieving the rank of Colonel.

Major Curtis L. Tracy standing in front of Hong Kong Bachelor Officers Quarters in Cholon (Saigon) Vietnam, about December 1969.

There was a very special conference that was held sometime in November 1969. It was held in the Bien Hoa post chapel. The Tan Son Nhut Servicemen's Group arranged for bus transportation. Elder Bruce McConkie was the visiting General Authority. Three things stick out in my memory. First: The troops filing into the chapel, apparently from places near and far, including areas of combat. It evoked a strange feeling to see many with mud on their combat fatigues and a rifle in their hands as they entered the door of a building dedicated to the Lord. They stashed their weapons under a bench or in a corner and their faces seemed to soften as they did so. Secondly, the fervent testimony of the Lord Jesus Christ, which was born by Elder McConkie is never to be a forgotten experience. The last memory of all, but the most indelibly etched is the sound of the congregation, GI's, civilian employees, and Vietnamese members, singing the hymn, "Come, Come Ye Saints." The tears flowed freely as the words, "And

should we die before out journey's through", reverberated through the chapel from throats choked with emotion and from souls touched by the silent promptings of the Spirit.

Major Curtis Larry Tracy in the General Counsel's Office, United States Army Procurement Agency (USAPAV), Plantation Road, Saigon, Vietnam. About December 1969.

THOMAS LEE TYLER

As a California native, Thomas served as a Public Information and Broadcast Specialist in the Army's II Field Force Headquarters Information Office from 1966–1967. He is currently living in Utah and has retired from his administrative position with the Church Educational System. He has served as both a former stake and mission president.

My new assignment permitted me to be active in the LDS servicemen's group at the Bien Hoa airbase during my entire time in Vietnam. The group met in a roughly constructed wood and corrugated tin-roofed chapel. I heard that the Church owned the small plot and the building. Oh, how we enjoyed being together in worship, fellowship, and service projects. That chapel and the association of those devoted men in our group were an oasis from the war and the world. Early in my stay there, one of the group was able to secure sufficient quarter-inch plain pine plywood to panel the unfinished interior of the chapel. In that project, we also built a group leader's office where he could conduct confidential interviews. A second small classroom was also built next to the office so two classes could be taught at the same time. There was enough lumber left over to construct a separate sacrament table, which added a touch of dignity.

The chapel was a short distance from the runway. When fighter jets took off the noise was so loud, whoever was speaking paused until the noise had passed. If we were singing, we just continued to sing with more gusto.

There was a remarkable miracle of physical protection of that humble dedicated building. One Saturday night the Viet Cong attacked the airbase with a heavy mortar barrage. Several planes and nearby military buildings were destroyed or damaged. When we came for church meetings the next morning several of us carefully went around the building expecting to find damage on the chapel. One shell had hit directly into the sewer drain on the street corner at the front east end of the chapel. The drain had absorbed the explosion. Another mortar shell hit at the opposite west end, about 5 feet from the corner of the building. We were amazed to see a several foot crater. But the explosion blew in a direction away from the chapel. We found no shrapnel damage on the building.

Early in my experience in Vietnam, I felt I was floundering in a cesspool of decadence, filth, and ugly language. Everywhere I turned sensuality was displayed or rolling off the tongues of men. But I learned quickly the Lord's protection and help was equally powerful in our preservation from spiritual dangers as it was from physical threats. About every three weeks we took our turn in pairs at all night guard duty in the sandbag bunkers around the perimeter of our camp. While one stood watch for a two-hour period, looking out the narrow opening of the bunker, the other soldier would sleep on a cot to his side. One night, as I stood watching the darkened jungle countryside, my heart was pleading for divine help in resisting the overwhelming and ever present evil of carnality. In a moment, a calm, sweet peace quietly came to me. In my mind I was within the hallowed walls of a temple. The words of the endowment began to flow freely, word for word. And with it came an energizing of my spirit. I felt clean again. I felt fortified in my resolve to resist evil. That sacred review continued to flow until it was time to awaken the other guard. When I awoke and began my second block, the sweetness of spirit returned and the sacred portrayal in my mind picked up exactly where it had left off two hours earlier. Words cannot describe the strength I felt. I knew I was clothed in a spiritual armor, and felt renewed and confident to go forward.

There was another occasion of obvious divine intervention protecting me from evil, as my father's blessing had promised. I had "choppered out" to a jungle artillery camp to do hometown releases, we called them. The officer in charge told me they would have me use the non-commissioned officers club to conduct the interviews. They would send interested men over to it. He then escorted me to the little building made from shipping crates and whatever materials could be found. As we walked inside, my heart sank. The walls, floor to ceiling, were lined and "wall-papered" with gross pornography. And I had to spend eight hours recording

Opposite top: L.D.S. (Mormon) chapel map. Priesthood Meeting at 1300 Hours, Sundays; Sacrament Meeting at 1400 Hours, Sundays; Size 500.

Opposite bottom: Our little grey chapel. Some of the junk at the side is material we are using in fixing up the interior. Later we want to repaint the outside in a more appealing color than grey, possibly white for the most part and another color on trim and wood around the bottom. April 1967.

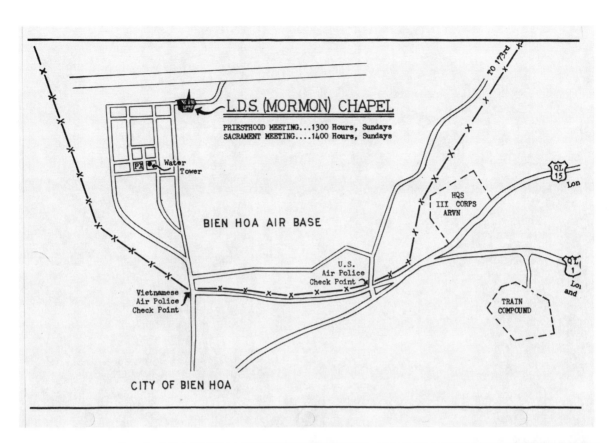

Left: American soldiers clearing a road through the jungle.

Below top: Helicopter in flight.

Below bottom: Tank of the 2nd Battalion, 34th Armor moves down a suspected VC supply route parallel to Highway 1 during recent road-clearing and securing operations. Republic of Vietnam, 18 Dec 1965. Photographer Sp5 Ted Phelps 16th Sig Det.

in this atmosphere! As soon as the officer left, I knelt and prayed with all my heart for deliverance. Was there another place? Would the officer be impressed to change locations? As I prayed, that special peace came again. As I stood from my prayer, in some indescribable way I was oblivious to the walls and the pornography. It was as though they were painted white. I felt no impulse to look at it. I worked the entire day doing interviews without so much as a consciousness of the environment. To this day I can see in my memory the makeup of the little building, the bar, the bar stools, and the tables. I can see the sunlight coming through the only window by the door. But I cannot recall anything on the walls! Over the years I have thought about that experience and the promise of the Lord, in the words of Paul to the Corinthian saints, "There is no temptation taken you but such as is common to man: but God is faithful, who will not suffer you to be tempted above that ye are able; but will with the temptation also make a way to escape, that ye may be able to bear it" (1 Corinthians 10:13). I know that when we "pray always," as the Lord directs, he "pours out his spirit upon you, and great will be thy blessing." He does "give you the victory." (See D&C 10:5; 19:38; 104:82)

Left: Gentle friendship.

Opposite top: American soldiers cautiously checking for enemy mines with a mine-detecting device.

Opposite bottom: Evacuation of civilians from VC controlled area. Notice the load the fragile woman carried—a young calf as well as personal effects balanced on a shoulder stick.

Below: Guard Bunkers on the camp perimeter. The sandbag walls are about 3 feet thick. Sept. 1967.

Vietnamese refugees on the move.

LDS Missionaries in the Southern Vietnamese District

Taken from CHURCH NEWS *February 25, 1967 (Pg. 9 & 15)*
Contributed by Thomas Lee Tyler

Above: Republic of Vietnam, Long Thanh, 2 Jan 1967. Members of Bien Hoa LDS Servicemen's Group at special baptismal service of Harold C. Lynch. (L–R) SP4 Thomas L. Tyler, Major James B. Fisher, Capt. Stuart Slingerland, 1st Lt. Harold C. Lynch, TSGT Ronald E. Moore, Capt. Robert Sweetwood. Photographer WO1 Jimmie W. Bynum.

"This is a most unusual baptism—going by helicopter under armed guard." So stated Capt. Robert Sweetwood, first counselor, to Maj. James B. Fisher and LDS Bien Hoa Servicemen's group president in Vietnam, as group officers took off to hold a baptismal service in a countryside stream. Maj. Fisher piloted the helicopter.

The convert who had applied for baptism was 1st Lt. Harold C. Lynch, 23, of New Brunswick, N.J. He is one of many servicemen who are studying the Gospel through the activities of LDS missionaries.

The Southern Vietnamese District Mission has 15 part-time missionaries in the Saigon area. But greater in scope are the informal discussions by many other members about the Church, its teachings and way of life as they meet in barracks, foxholes, office or tents. Fellow servicemen are invited to LDS services. Fireside groups are organized where Church books and pamphlets are circulated among non-member buddies.

Vietnamese citizens as well as servicemen are being taught the Gospel. In the Saigon Branch alone there are now 45 Vietnamese members. A Relief Society also has been organized for Vietnamese members.

The conversion and baptism of Lt. Lynch is representative of LDS servicemen's missionary work. He was on board a ship bound for Vietnam last fall when impressed by quotations from Capt. Stuart Slingerland, an Army doctor from Salt Lake City.

After the orientation Lt. Lynch asked for more information about the Mormons. He accepted an invitation to attend an LDS group meeting on board the ship. He accepted a copy of the Book of

Mormon and by the time they reached Vietnam he was converted and requested baptism.

Once in Vietnam it became difficult to arrange a suitable time and place convenient with military duties. Finally, during a job assignment in the area of Long Thanh, a town some 20 miles east of Saigon, Lt. Lynch noticed a neighborhood "swimming pool" in a small stream. The semi-jungle location was suggested to Maj. Fisher and details were arranged.

The next day several members of the Bien Hoa LDS group flew to Long Thanh by helicopter piloted by Pres. Fisher. Meeting Lt. Lynch on the outskirts of the town, the group drove by jeep to the stream, only to find a number of Vietnamese children having the time of their lives swimming. The children courteously got out of the pool as preparations were made for the baptismal service.

Despite light rain, baptismal services were held on a point of land jutting over the stream. Capt. Slingerland and Lt. Lynch then waded into the stream and the baptism was performed.

After baptism, the group hiked back to their jeeps, crossed over barbed wire entanglements and drove to the village dispensary where, in a quiet room, Lt. Lynch was confirmed a member of the Church.

Pres. Fisher's non-member copilot accompanied the group during the service.

Because the baptism was held near the

Top: Captain Stuart Slingerland (right) baptizes 1st Lt. Harold C. Lynch. Photographer SP4 Thomas L. Tyler.

Bottom: Members of Bien Hoa LDS Servicemen's Group stand beside helicopter in which they flew to area to conduct baptismal service. (Left to right) 1st Lt. Harold C. Lynch, Capt. Robert Sweetwood, TSGT Ronald E. Moore, Capt. Stuart Slingerland, Major James B. Fisher (pilot), and SP4 Thomas L. Tyler. Photographer WO1 Jimmie W. Bynum.

scene of Viet Cong activity, members of the group carried weapons to the service. All members of the group were in different types of military work uniforms of the Army and Air Force. Raised eyebrows of towns people indicated the group looked different from most military groups as they drove by.

A breakdown of those who participated in the service show the unusual composition of the group who had gathered in Vietnam to baptize one of their fellows: Maj. James B. Fisher, Army, of 4311 Monoco Dr., San Antonio, TX, president of the Bien Hoa LDS Servicemen's group and a member of the San Antonio 2nd Ward, San Antonio Stake; Capt. Robert Sweetwood, Air Force, of 4717 Dragon Dr., San Diego, CA, first counselor in the group presidency and a member of the San Diego 8th Ward, San Diego Stake; Capt. Stuart Slingerland, Army, of 533-11th Ave., Salt Lake City, UT, second counselor in the group presidency and a member of 24th Ward, Salt Lake Stake; First Lt. Harold C. L3aloh, Army, New Brunswick. N.J.; T. Sgt. Ronald E Moore. Air Force, of 3812 Elrod Ave, Tampa, FL, group clerk and a member of the Tampa Ward, Tampa Stake; SP4 Thomas L. Tyler, Army, of 5647 Orizaba Ave., Long Beach, CA, group Priesthood instructor and a member of Long Beach 7th Ward, Long Beach Stake, CA.

Top: Republic of Vietnam, 23 Oct, 1966. A recovered UH-1D Huey that had been shot down during an infantry extraction near Phu Cuong, South Vietnam, is brought into Phy Loi Airfield for repairs by a CH-47 Chinook recovery ship of the 178th Assault Support Helicopter Co., 11th Combat avn.Bn. Photographer SP4 John C. Grove 16 Sig Det.

Bottom: Helicopter dropping off soldiers in combat zone in Vietnam.

EUGENE CORDELL VAIL, SR.

Cordell served in the Army as an Infantry platoon leader, and a brigade signal officer. During the war he was involved in LDS group leadership and was the editor of the Soldier Saint Magazine for LDS soldiers in his division. He currently works as a computer-software testing specialist.

We were not allowed to get closer than one mile to the Cambodian border. One day my sister platoon got too close to the border, and the enemy started to shoot mortars at them and they were pinned down. My company commander called me on the radio and told me to wake up all of my men and get them into battle gear and move out to the border to help defend our sister platoon in trouble. The battle that was raging was a couple of miles across open rice paddies and through bamboo hedgerows. We could not see them because we were behind several other hedgerows of bamboo from where they were pinned down. We could only see the smoke rising from the mortars that were being fired at them. We did not even know if they were still alive.

We all put on our heavy battle gear and started marching in a long horizontal column towards the hedgerow. I told my men to spread out about 20 feet apart shoulder to shoulder so if we took fire ourselves we would not all be hit. We walked for about fifteen or twenty minutes and could hear the mortar fire picking up in front of us. We were about halfway to the hedgerow walking across open rice paddies when my company commander called me on the radio and told me to start running.

The Army had devised a small radio speaker that fit into the helmet of each soldier so that all the men in the platoon could hear what was being said on the radio to the platoon leader. That way he did not have to shout the orders to them, and we all knew what we were supposed to do at the same time. The soldiers could not talk; they could only listen. When the company commander called me on the radio and said that we had to run not just walk, they all heard him say that. It was not easy to run with all that battle gear on, and we all had a heavy steel helmet, lots of gear and our weapon. Each of us had to help carry the machine gun ammunition, so that we would have enough to last. We all heard what the company commander said on the radio. I gave them the order to start a dogtrot, which was similar to a slow jog.

Just as we started to do that I heard a very clear impression in my mind to stop. I knew that if I stopped I could be court marshaled. The company commander had just ordered me to run not walk and all my men heard the order on their radios. However, I recognized the source of that impression. It was not a loud voice; it was just a feeling inside me. It was just a small feeling inside to do this or don't do that. When I felt that impression, I immediately gave the signal to all my men to hit the dirt. Having been with me for a few weeks already, I can assure you that when I told them to get down they had learned to get down, no matter what they heard on their radios from the company commander.

We all hit the dirt, causing a huge cloud of dust to fly up as we literally dove into the ground. Then we heard this strange sound from far behind us. It was a boom, boom, boom, boom, and then silence for a second. I realized that they had just fired 155 artillery from Jackson Fire Base behind us.

Within seconds, the rice paddy about 100 feet in front of us went up in a brilliant plumb of white phosphorus smoke and fire. The artillery people use a marker round made of white phosphorus as their first shot each time so they can see where the gun is aimed. They then

Group Leadership meetings held each Tuesday night in Cuchi, Vietnam. Group Leadership in October 1970. (L-R) Cordell Vail (counselor), Don Glover (counselor), Peter Cooksen (group leader), Brother Taylor (secretary).

Inset: Lt. Cordell Vail studying the scriptures in his hooch at night. Cuchi, Vietnam.

make adjustments, from smoke that is visible for miles, to where they want that shot to be on the enemy target. If white phosphorus gets on the human body, it does not just burn you, it burns right through you.

If we had kept jogging, we would have been exactly at the location of the marker round when it went off. Because we stopped when we did, all of the white phosphorus went in the air and came down about 20 or 30 feet in front of us and no one was hurt.

We all lay there in the dirt stunned at what had just happened. Then I heard an emotionally, shaky voice on the radio. It was my company commander's voice. You could tell from his voice that he was terrified. The voice said, "Lt. Vail! Lt. Vail! Where are you?" I stood up, took my radio headset in hand and said, "I am here. We are alright." He then explained that they had a new artillery officer and he had just put that first marker round 1000 yards off the mark. He said from where they shot it, it should have landed right on top of us. I told him we had stopped and that we were okay. Then he said to me in a relieved voice, "Well then get going again."

We all stood up to start going again. Before we started, my Platoon Sergeant came walking over to me. He was a really good kid. He was a very religious young man from Chicago. He looked at me and said, "Lt. Vail, how did you know that? How did you know to stop?"

I said, "God told me".

He then smiled and said to me, "Well keep it up." We got up and moved out and no more was said about it, but everyone knew. They knew that only by the grace of God and his still small promptings that we were still alive.

Right: 1st Lt. Cordell Vail 25th infantry division, 3rd Brigade, Brigade signal officer convoy heading out of Cuchi, Vietnam, with signal equipment on board.

Below: Cuchi group leadership in Saigon at district conference. (L-R) Lt Cordell Vail (counselor), PFC4 Peter Cooksen (group leader), Lt. Don Glover (counselor).

P. DOUG WALTERS

Doug was born in Connecticut. During the Vietnam War he served as a major in army intelligence from 1965–1969. He was involved in the follow-up to the Tet Offensive. While serving in Vietnam, Doug was baptized. Currently he lives in Utah where he has served as the bishop of his ward.

P. Doug Walters in his expert marksman pose.

In Vietnam I had much more time to myself during guard duty in foxholes or bunkers. It was in these mostly quiet times that I really began to think and ponder the meaning of life. I would hear the huge 155-millimeter howitzer shells tearing through the sky almost as if a train were going by, and I would ask myself questions about where I came from, why I was on a ball of mud (earth) stuck near the border of some galaxy, and where I would go after this life. I wasn't asking questions about the war or the controversy about the war at home. I wasn't sophisticated enough for that. I was trying to keep my head down and serve my time.

One day it was a beautiful sunny morning, although I didn't appreciate it enough as I had been pulling kitchen police duty since 3:00 A.M. It was about 8:00 A.M., and I was walking back from the kitchen tent to my tent to get some sleep.

Three soldiers were walking towards me and as they got close a voice whispered to my brain, "Ask them where they are going?" I looked around as if to find the speaker, and seeing no one I looked at the three men who by now had passed me by. Either my own mind or the voice of the adversary quickly filled my consciousness and distinctly said, "Wait! You are from the East Coast, we don't go up to strangers and ask them where they are going, and it is none of your business." As I look back I thought the use of the words "you," "our," and "we" was interesting.

Before I could follow up or get any more promptings, I was transferred from the middle of the jungle to the edge of the jungle otherwise known as Bien Hoa Air Base. From a small detachment of about 400, I was now in a unit of 1500. There was one LDS person in the unit, and I got assigned to pull guard duty with him. We spent many hours talking about all kinds of stuff, and we finally got around to religion. He said he was a Mormon. I immediately thought Amish and the idea of living a secluded life in some kind of caring family organization appealed to me. He quickly shattered the dream of seclusion, but the caring family organization was still true.

Top: P. Doug Walters.

Bottom: Moving out on search and destroy convoy.

It wasn't long before he gave me a Book of Mormon and I began reading it. It was fine and I didn't have a problem with it. What impressed me more at the time was when I went to my first meeting. A low-ranking guy was teaching the class and some high-ranking enlisted and officers were the students. Seems he was a returned missionary and also called to be the teacher. Also, all the questions I had about the here and there were answered. Soon I was sitting in front of a branch president being interviewed for baptism and the protocol was for the duty chaplain assistances to provide the cover anyway. So in a swimming pool in the middle of Vietnam the wonderful, simple baptismal prayer was said and I began my Church service.

DANIEL LEE WEBSTER

Daniel was born in Cedar City, Utah. While attending college in Cedar City, he was drafted into the U.S. Army. He served in light weapons infantry, spending most of his time in the jungles on reconnaissance and search and destroy missions. Daniel achieved the rank of E-5 sergeant.

I got shot up.

We were on a reconnaissance patrol. We weren't supposed to make contact; we were supposed to find. There was a whole division of [Viet Cong] infantry that they figured was coming out of Cambodia and hitting our LZs [landing zone], so our mission was to locate them and find out as much as we could and not make contact, just call in artillery and have at them. But the particular day that we got shot up, the company had split up into three platoons that were operating a couple of miles apart so that we could cover more area. We'd have the German shepherd dog teams out. With any luck they'd come out three days at a time. It was about all they could take in the humidity and the heat and then the dogs would get fired and they'd bring out a new bunch. We just couldn't seem to find these guys. We'd run into small groups. We'd have firefights not every day, but two or three or half a dozen, but we never could find this whole division. I was walking point and then we came to an area where there was just elephant grass and then an L-shaped tree line. Coming out of that elephant grass, which was just on the Cambodian border, was a well-used trail. The Vietnamese used trails to haul their supplies and ammunition. They'd pull it on bicycles and use our C-ration cans. They'd wire them to the front of their bikes. Then they'd put a candle in the front of them and they would wheel them down those trails at night and we'd ambush them.

Well, where this trail came right out of Cambodia it intersected with another trail that headed off in the direction of the Ho Chi Minh Trail trail, so we figured this was a highly used route and probably where this division was coming from. The sun was about to set and we decided that it was a good opportunity to set up an ambush so we dug foxholes, and we set the gun up right where those two trails intersected. Then we put up our trick flairs and our claymores. We were watching to the front thinking that if any of the VC were coming they'd come out of the tree line and come down along there.

So we were sitting eating some C-rations for supper and all of a sudden there were two NVA [North Vietnamese Army] regulars that walked right in on the back of us. There they were and there we were and I don't know who was more surprised, them or us. They took off and ran right in the middle of us. We didn't dare shoot them because we thought they were probably a point team for this division that we were looking for, so we threw grenades at them and we killed one of them outright. I don't know who threw the strike, but it hit him and killed him instantly. The other one was wounded really bad, leaving a pretty nasty blood trail through the elephant grass. We had a second lieutenant that had been with us for about three weeks who'd just come from OCS [Officer Candidate School] and he said we would hold up until morning, then we'll send out a patrol. Myself, Chief from New Mexico, and David Oleah from Maui had been walking point for about a week. We were 100 percent alert, had the safeties off the clamors and our hands on the detonators, waiting for the trick flares to pop and we'd set off the ambush.

Nothing happened, so the next morning the lieutenant says, "Okay, we'll go single file and when we hit the tree line we'll spread out and see if we can find this guy."

I looked at Chief and looked at Dave and said, "There is
no way I am going to walk up that trail single file in elephant
grass—that's suicide. We'll be killed. If there are any VC
around, they'll be waiting and they'll kill us." So we told the
lieutenant that we were burned out, and we wanted to walk
rear security, which meant the three of us would walk backward, one facing dead center and the others facing out to
either side. So he picked a new point team and just as the
point team got to the tree line they opened up on us with mortars and automatic weapons, and we were flaky. We had nothing to hide behind but elephant grass and anthills. They cut us

Dan Webster's platoon heading out on a patrol.

Dan Webster standing outside a culvert at an LZ.

to pieces. I imagine that the initial firefight must have lasted five to ten minutes. It was hard to say. I took an AK round through the tibia in my left leg, almost breaking it in two. The other two guys were hit too. It was evident that there was no fire coming from our side except from the three of us. Of course we didn't have the radio, and we could hear artillery in the distance. Pretty soon the rounds started going off almost right on top of us. We had VC within ten or twelve feet of us several times. We had climbed under some bamboo, giving ourselves shots of morphine trying to bandage each other up and just praying that somehow we were gonna get out of there.

And about forty-five minutes to an hour later the other two platoons from our company got to our position. They pushed the VC back into the tree line and then they got the Phantom jets in there with the napalm and finally got it secure enough that they could get some medevacs into us. They flew in a medivac and they put me and Doc, and Chief and Dave in the chopper. Chief had been hit three times in the chest now. Last I'd seen him he had picked up a 60-millimeter and was charging the tree behind him. I went down and I had figured he was dead, but when they put him on the floor of the chopper he didn't even look like he was breathing. I can still remember the blood running off the floor of the chopper and out those open doors. As soon as we cleared the tree line, the VC opened up on the helicopter, filling it full of bullets. According to the Geneva Convention they were not supposed to shoot planes with red crosses, but it didn't seem to matter. They were going take us out anyway. We got to Cu Chi where there was a field hospital. We were operated on and that was the last we saw of each other for 11 years. I went to Japan and had surgery again. After spending two weeks there, they flew me the states to Fort Carson, Colorado, where I spent eleven months the hospital having nine more surgeries, including a skin graft.

GORDON H. WEED

From 1971–1972 Gordon served in Vietnam as a Colonel in the Air Force's 8th Special Operations Squadron stationed at the Bien Hoa Air Base. His assignments included command pilot of an A-37 Fighter Bomber.

In addition to my Air Force assignment, which to say the least, was very demanding, I was called by Major Montie Keller to serve a part-time mission for the LDS church. Montie had been called as the Saigon District President and was our former Bishop at the Scott Air Force Base in Illinois. I told him I thought I was too busy to accept the calling. I was flying two to three combat missions a day besides my commander's responsibilities, and I didn't see how I would have time to do missionary work. He wouldn't take no for an answer, and in spite of my objections, he came over to the Bien Hoa Air Base in a helicopter to set me apart. He introduced me to my companion who was an Army enlisted servicemen who was stationed at Long Bin Army Base across from the Bien Hoa Air Base. I complained that it would be very uncomfortable for me to be involved with an Army

Lt/Colonel Gordon H. Weed and his LDS Crew Chief Airman Kelly Siple. Summer of 1972, Bien Hoa Air Base Vietnam.

Above: Sacrament Meeting of LDS Members, Bien Hoa Air Base, Vietnam, 1972. Lt/Colonel Weed is second from the left.

Right: Major Montie Keller and Lt/Colonel Gordon H. Weed in front of the 8th Special Operations building, Bien Hoa Air Base, Vietnam; October 1971. Montie came over from Tan Son Nut Air Base in Saigon to set Weed apart as an LDS Missionary in the Hong Kong Mission.

★
★
★

enlisted soldier as a missionary. I was Lt. Col. at the time and due to military protocol of that era, I did not fraternize with my own enlisted personnel and it certainly would not be appropriate for me to be involved with an Army enlisted man under those circumstances. Montie reminded me that there was no rank in the Priesthood and if I didn't stop complaining, he would make me junior companion. We were set apart to do missionary work and surprisingly there was ample time to serve and we had many faith inspiring experiences together. Montie promised in my blessing, when he set me apart, that if I would serve an LDS mission as well as could be expected under those difficult circumstances, that I would be blessed in my other responsibilities. He also said that I would be protected in combat and return with honor, unharmed, to my home and family; a promise that was literally fulfilled. My

This photograph was taken from an A-37 Fighter Bomber in 1972 over Anloc, Vietnam. Lt/Colonel Gordon H. Weed was getting ready to roll in on a dive bombing run in support of friendly troops being overrun by the enemy.

aircraft was hit many times, but never shot down. Since I was the Squadron Commander, I was able to select my Aircraft Crew Chief. His name was Kelly Siple and he was from Idaho. I knew he was LDS from his records. When he reported to me at the aircraft for the first time, I said, "You are from Idaho aren't you? He replied, "Yes Sir." I said, "Aren't there a lot of Mormons in Idaho." He replied, "Yes Sir." I said, "Do you happen to be one of them?" He gulped and said, "Yes, Sir, I am." "Good, so am I, we should get along very well together." He took excellent care of my aircraft, which performed flawlessly.

WERNER GLEN WEEKS

Before Vietnam, Werner began his military training in the ROTC [Reserve Officer Training Corps] program at Brigham Young University. Upon graduation he joined the army helicopter-training program. He served in Vietnam from 1964–1966.

When I first arrived in Vietnam in my aviation company, I looked around to try and find someone who seemed to fit the role of a good Mormon, someone who had the appearance that would suggest an excellent MIA leader and who just looked like he ought to be a leader. I found a fellow from the adjoining company, a scout dog company commander by the name of Eugene Amberson, who seemed to fit the role. Gene was a very friendly fellow who used to eat with his company in our mess hall. He was a first lieutenant and I was a lowly warrant officer, so by rank we would not have been associating except that we ate in the same section of the mess hall with each other. I asked Gene the golden questions one day, only to be politely refused. A couple of days later I asked again, "Don't you think you'd like to know something about the Church?" His response was even more negative. Finally a week or two later, trying not to be a pest, I asked him a third time, only to be flatly refused. I was completely burned out with Gene Amberson and now he began to avoid me.

Just at that time, Ray Hales was assigned to Gene's company. Upon arrival in Vietnam, a scout dog handler would require a certain amount of time to train a new animal. The dogs were kept in the country, and the handlers rotated in and out, and Ray had to learn to relate well to the animal to which he was assigned. The process normally required about two weeks. In that two-week period, this magnetic man had won the respect of all of the members of his scout dog company. Ray was magnetic, very mature—well beyond his years. Recently married, he had left his three-month pregnant wife to enter combat knowing some terrible things that none of us ever suspected. Ray's power and magnetism were so manifest to everyone that they nicknamed him "Noah." The men further named their company "Hale's Angels."

As a new group leader, I had been fasting and praying for the Lord to reveal to me who I should call as counselors; Ray was a shoe in for the job. I prayed about him, but my mind remained confused, and therefore I did not call him to the position. I had made him a priesthood instructor, which I felt was one of the most important positions of responsibility in the branch. In the three weeks that Ray was in Vietnam, in his patient, peaceful, loving, powerful way he had won over every one of his contemporaries as a quiet, humble example of the gospel.

The night of July 19, 1969, the Lord had me assigned as company staff duty officer. My duties required me to remain awake all night long and monitor the operations in the company area at our base camp. About 8:15 P.M. in through the door of operations walked

Lieutenant Gene Amberson bearing the news with deep regret that Raymond Draper Hales had been killed that afternoon. The once antagonistic Amberson was now coming to me to ask me what it was that made Raymond Hales so different from the other men that he had known in his life. I was so grateful now to have the opportunity to spend as many hours in the evening as Gene desired to tell him about the gospel that had made Ray so magnetic, and after seven hours of discussion, I sent him back to his company with a *Meet the Mormons* book and the Joseph Smith Story tract. Over the course of the next two weeks, I was able to teach him the discussions, and August 17, Eugene Roger Amberson and I entered the swimming pool of the officers' club in Phy Bai, Vietnam, in our jungle fatigues, and I baptized him into the Church. But Ray's story certainly should not end here. I came to learn later that Ray had spent an afternoon one Sunday comparing patriarchal blessings with those of his brothers. He had made the statement after reading his blessing that after a mission, marriage, and a family, that would be the end of his life; his sojourn on earth would be of a very short duration. When he kissed his wife and family good-bye at the airport on his way to Vietnam, he looked at them and bid farewell, promising to see them in the eternities. The spiritual strength of his family had dispelled much of the gloom of that departing. When the message came from the Department of the Army, it was not at all a surprise. It was a certainty, had Ray Hales not come to Vietnam, Gene Amberson would not have become a member of the Church. Ray's stewardship was not complete until Gene was safe in the fold.

* * * * *

This was to be one of those days my bishop had referred to as being a day when I would seemingly find no escape from a critical situation and yet would return to my unit safely. As we strung out our longer formation through the sky to allow time for each aircraft to descend, drop their load, climb, then back out, the first aircraft reported short final, they had a major malfunction. An oil line in the engine had ruptured, their gauges had dropped to zero, and they were going to land as quickly as they could at the nearest firebase. As the second aircraft of the formation, we now became lead and the first ones to test the flight conditions of our landing zone.

The hazards of the combat job always required us to fly our helicopters close to the upper limits of their performance capabilities. Our weights were always near maximum, and we were constantly required to monitor atmospheric conditions to ensure that there was sufficient life to keep us flying. As we approached our hover hole in the trees, I monitored the gauges while the other pilot flew. Hovering out of ground effect above the trees, we seemed to have enough power to make the two-hundred foot vertical descent to drop off our packs. As we fell below the effects of the slight breeze blowing across the top of the trees, we subsequently lost that bit of life that the wind had provided us, and at maximum power available we found ourselves short of sufficient power to remain airborne. In short, we began to fall out of the sky as the RPMs began to bleed on our main rotor system. Our operating RPM normally would be 6600. As we fell through 5600 RPM, I knew we were incapable of sustaining flight. My final emergency procedure in reading the gauges was to leave the inside of the aircraft and look outside to find a place to crash softly and hope to preserve all lives on board.

At that moment, when I knew death was possible, the voice of the Lord came to me in my mind. I could hear Him very audibly say, "Glen, let your heart be at ease and watch." My terrified heart was suddenly calm as warm hands wrapped around it. My spirit became very meek again, and with both feet on the floor of the aircraft and releasing my grip on the

A marine helicopter on its way to recover a downed Ch-46 helicopter on a hillside near the demilitarized zone.

seat, I folded my hands and watched. There was nothing I could do to aid the other pilot, whose hands were full in trying to maintain control, but, not only did we stabilize, a miracle in itself, we climbed and were coming up out of the hole. The Spirit then testified to me that the man who had been at the controls on the other side knew that there had been a greater hand than his manifesting its power to maintain our flight, and I knew he knew the extent of the divine help we had received to get out. We relayed by radio the condition we had encountered to the other aircraft, warning them of the possibility of severe danger, but the seasoned veterans who followed us went into the same landing zone, and all three remaining aircraft suffered battle damage for their decision. That day my aircraft was the only one that came back untouched. Word was out that Weeks had defied the law of averages again.

ROBERT C. WESTPHAL

Robert was born in Oregon. During the Vietnam War, Robert served as a Specialist in the Army's 1st Air Cavalry Division from 1963–1967. His assignment was as a Chinook helicopter mechanic and temporary crew chief. Currently he lives in Washington as a retired mechanic. He has served in many Church callings and is currently the executive secretary to the bishop in his ward.

Having served in Vietnam, luckily for only a year, I too have an association with some of those whose names appear on the memorial [Vietnam Veterans Memorial]. I often think of some of my friends and coworkers that were killed while they were serving their country in Vietnam. I wonder if the young husband and father we all called "Sloopy" (after a then popular song named "Sloopy Hang On") was lying in his bunk the night the recoilless rifle round landed in my replacement's bunk. The very bunk I had slept in for almost a year! Our bunks were side by side! If he was there as usual, his name is on the memorial along with my replacement's.

I also have an association for some of those whose names don't appear there. I speak of some of the people of Vietnam we called Viet Cong. Were they evil people? Definitely not! I knew some of these people personally. They were husbands and fathers just like Sloopy! They loved their family and country just like Sloopy! They also loved freedom. Many of them didn't want to be Viet Cong. Don't be shocked! Many of the Viet Cong were just like you and me, husbands, fathers, wives, children, butchers, bakers, candlestick makers and on and on. They wanted no part of the political struggle that was raging in their homeland! Most Viet Cong were forced to serve in a war they wanted no part of! During the Vietnam conflict in America, there were many war protesters as well as draft dodgers. The American draft dodger, when caught, went to prison or was given some lesser punishment. In Vietnam, if you were to be drafted into the Viet Cong army, you weren't treated so lightly. The leaders of the Viet Cong had other

Robert Westphal in front of the Chinook he crewed on.

The barber of Ankhe.

methods to assure your service. An example is the "barber of Ankhe."

The barber was a very amiable, kind, generous, and likeable fellow. He loved his wife and children, his neighbors and his country. He also loved to be left alone, to do for himself and his family and friends. I know because he cut my hair and cleaned my ears (if you were in Vietnam you know about that) many times. I had many pleasant conversations with him and his lovely wife. I really liked this guy! One day while he was cutting my hair, a boy about six years of age came running through the hooch he used as his shop. He was a lively little guy and full of fun like most six year olds. As he came through from another direction, I noticed his left cheek had a large hole in it, a little larger than a quarter. It took a little while for me to get enough courage to ask the barber if this young man was his son. The answer was, "Yes. Me VC." He then related how the Viet Cong leaders had visited him many times attempting to recruit him to serve in their army. He always refused. Then one night they came by again. They said this was the last time they would come because tonight he would join them! The leader stuck the business end of his rifle in the barber's son's mouth and said to the barber, "Sign here!" He refused again, thinking that they surely wouldn't shoot his son. The leader pulled the trigger. The boy jerked to one side just as the rifle went off. The bullet went through the boy's left cheek instead of the back of his head. Thus the boy was alive but now had a large hole in his cheek. The barber immediately signed the enlistment papers, as I'm sure you or I would! Several weeks later the American military base at Ankhe was attacked by the VC. During the cleanup after the attack, we found the body of the barber of Ankhe! I never knew what happened to his family, and I'm certain his name doesn't appear on the Vietnam Memorial. Who will build a memorial for all of the people who die in political wars no matter what side they are on? Thankfully Heavenly Father knows each of us and is aware of our sufferings.

RICHARD WHALEY

Richard was born in Illinois. During the Vietnam War he served as Lt. Colonel iwith the Army's 7th Combat Engineers. His assignments included that of Company Commander and Chaplain. His Church assignment in Vietnam was as a District Mission President. He is working in the Church's Military Relations department.

I was assigned as the group S4 (supply and logistics) when I got to Vietnam. I had never been an S4 and I knew little about it; but I knew where to learn about it (more four-inch think binders to read). After I had been there two months, the Colonel took a seven-day R&R and the XO took over. He was an infantry Officer and expected everyone to obey him instantly, which was OK with me. But, then, he did something that presented a serious problem. The day after the Colonel left, the XO called me on the radio and told me to meet him at a certain location. I immediately met him. He showed me the area, the terrain and then told me to do something that was illegal and wrong. I pointed out to him, politely, that the mission could be accomplished in a different manner; but he insisted I do it the way he ordered. When I explained that I couldn't do it that way; he relieved me on the spot.

In the combat zone, to get relieved of duty is the kiss of death. I knew my career was over. That's just the way it is; I was sick at heart. I left and went to my little hootch and bemoaned my fate. The days passed very slowly and I feared what the Colonel was going to do to me when he got back. The day arrived and he returned. Apparently, the S1 explained to the Colonel what had happened to me because the next thing I knew, I was ordered to report to him. I did so. As I walked into his office, he walked over to me, stuck out his hand and said, "What happened, Rich?" He had never called me by my first name so I figured I was really in for it. I told him. He thanked me and said, "You did the right thing and I'll take care of the situation. Not to worry." Then he informed me that I was to become a company commander the following week when that command slot became vacant.

When I got promoted to captain, the tradition was for the newly promoted to buy a round at the club for everyone. Now, I don't drink and I am not willing to buy someone else alcohol. But, what to do? I spoke to the Club manager and told him that when I came in that night he was to provide soft drinks for all in attendance. I got to the club and for the first time

Capt. E. T. Farrell (left) discusses a possible trouble area that may require an air strike with Lt. Col. Jackson, commanding officer of the battalion, and Maj. J.L. Cooper, executive officer.

probably in history the Club was packed. I had never seen it like that! As soon as I walked in, everybody stopped talking and watched me. Now everyone new I was LDS. I was the only LDS officer in the command and everyone knew I didn't drink and everyone was watching to see what I'd do. I turned to the bartender and said in a loud voice, "The drinks are on me!" There was literally a gasp from the crowd, but when he started putting cases of soft drinks on the bar the guys stood and cheered. Now, suppose I had not served soft drinks? It would have been easy to do and go with the traditions; but you maintain your standards and your honor and the Church's honor, too. Like many things in life, it takes prior planning and decision-making in order to achieve the desired results.

Remember: Duty and Honor are crucial.

ELDER LANCE B. WICKMAN

Elder Wickman served in the army from 1964–1969. During that time he completed two tours of duty in Vietnam as an Army Ranger officer assigned first as an infantry platoon leader and next as an advisor to the South Vietnamese Army. For his service he was awarded the Bronze Star and Purple Heart medals. He currently serves as a member of the First Quorum of the Seventy.

It is difficult to describe the emotions associated with service in the infantry in the jungles and rice paddies. Potential danger lurked in every tree line and stand of bamboo and around every turn in a jungle trail. These dangers were exacerbated by the heat, humidity, snakes, insects, and the green tapestry that enveloped and entangled us. Although the standard tour of duty was twelve months, the infantry soldier quickly learned that it might just as well have been forever. He learned rather quickly that for the infantryman the only time that matters is here and now. Even tomorrow often seems far distant.

It was early November 1966. I had been in country for nearly ten months. Our battalion had spent several weeks in the field and had just returned to our base camp for a period of rest and relaxation. It was a Saturday night and having just taken our first shower in many days, we were sitting on our bunks cleaning our weapons and listening to music on the Armed Forces Radio Network. Suddenly, an urgent message was received at our battalion headquarters. A large enemy force was overrunning another battalion in our brigade that was still out in the jungle. Our battalion was needed to go to the rescue immediately.

In my case, that feeling of anxiety that is more or less one's constant companion in the combat zone ripened into a dark sense of foreboding. However, there was no time for reflection or a kneeling prayer. We had to grab our weapons and equipment and go. As we moved out through the entrance to our base camp, I uttered a silent prayer in my heart. As I did so, there came to my mind—literally—a still small voice. It was as clear as crystal, and it spoke the words to a passage of scripture that I had first memorized as a seminary student and then later as a full-time missionary. It is found in Proverbs 3: 5–6: "Trust in the Lord with all thine heart; and lean not unto thine own understanding. In all thy ways acknowledge him, and he shall direct thy paths." No sooner did that voice come into my mind than the sense of foreboding vanished. In its place was a warm reassurance of peace.

Our battalion's night rescue mission lengthened into another extended operation that took us far from our base camp, almost to the Cambodian border in Tay Ninh Province. As the days and weeks went by, that experience with the Spirit was crowded to the back of my mind. Finally, it was the day of Thanksgiving 1966—the last day that we were to be in the field on that particular operation. I was riding in an armored personal carrier through a lightly forested area of jungle. Suddenly, there was a tremendous explosion beneath the vehicle that seemed to lift it into the air. We had rolled over an enormous enemy land mine! I believe it was a command-detonated mine because several other personnel carriers had passed over the same spot only moments before. Moreover, this was no ordinary land mine. I believe it was a dud artillery shell that the enemy had found and then rigged as a mine.

The force of the explosion was so great that it blew the engine apart. It blew the tracks and all of the road wheels off both sides of the vehicle. The driver was blasted from the vehicle, landing some fifteen or twenty feet in front of it. Everyone inside was wounded, including me, but no one was killed.

44th Co, RANGER CLASS # 7, 11 FEB to 15 APR 65 FORT BENNING, GEORGIA

Lance B. Wickman's class at the U.S. Army Ranger School. Wickman is standing on the second row from the front, eighth from the left.

No sooner did that land mine explode, than there again came to my mind that same voice and that same passage of scripture: "Trust in the Lord with all thine heart and lean not unto thine own understanding. In all they ways acknowledge him, and he shall direct thy paths."

There is no question that my life was spared that day by divine intervention. More than that, this experience serves as one of the most profound in my life in testifying of the reality of God and His Beloved Son, Jesus Christ. Now, as a Seventy and a General Authority, I stand as an "especial witness" (D&C 107:25). I testify that I received an essential element of that witness on a jungle battlefield far from home on that November day in 1966.

Less than two months before the jungle epiphany just described, I had another profound spiritual experience of a different kind. Our unit was out in the field on another combat operation when I learned that Elder Gordon B. Hinckley of the Quorum of the Twelve Apostles was coming to Vietnam. He was going to hold a meeting of Latter-day Saint servicemen and women at the Caravelle Hotel in Saigon. How I wanted to attend!

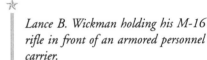

Lance B. Wickman holding his M-16 rifle in front of an armored personnel carrier.

There were three of us in our battalion who were Latter-day Saints—two enlisted men and me. I approached our battalion commander, explained the significance of the upcoming meeting and asked if we might be excused from duty in the field long enough to attend this special meeting. Almost miraculously (it seemed at the time), he gave his consent.

So, on the day appointed for the meeting (it was in the afternoon), we caught a hop on a helicopter returning to our base camp. Quickly showering and changing into clean uniforms, we boarded another helicopter headed to Tan Son Nhut Air Base in Saigon. Upon arrival, we made our way as quickly as we could to the Carvelle Hotel, arriving just as the meeting was about to begin.

It seems now that there may have been as many as two hundred Latter-day Saints in this meeting atop the hotel. Most were servicemen dressed in khaki and olive drab. There were also a few nurses and Red Cross workers and a sprinkling of Vietnamese. Seated in the front behind the podium were President W. Brent Hardy, the president of the Southern Far East Mission, Elder Marion D. Hanks, and Elder Gordon B. Hinckley. It was almost surreal! I could not believe that he was there in that war-torn land! I was almost overwhelmed in my emotions.

Lance B. Wickman with good friend and fellow officer, Captain Carlton L. Eck.

The meeting proceeded and was most inspiring. Elder Hinckley was the last speaker. Upon concluding his remarks, he told us that before leaving Salt Lake City, [Utah]he had met with President David O. McKay. President McKay, he said, had authorized him—if he felt so inspired—to dedicate the land of South Vietnam to the preaching of the gospel. "I feel so inspired," he said. And so, as we bowed our heads, this great Apostle of the Lord dedicated that land to the work of the Lord with simple yet profound eloquence.

Words cannot describe the spirit that settled over that small congregation. As the apostolic words of blessing and dedication flowed, I marveled. I marveled that in the midst of that terrible war, where Satan was having his heyday with every evil known to man, the Lord of the universe, had found a way to advance His work.

The better part of four decades has now passed since that singular experience. Over those years, I have visited in numbers of congregations where wonderful Vietnamese Saints—refugees from the land of their nativity—have been present. Each time, as I have looked into their faces, in my mind's eye I have seen myself in that assemblage atop that hotel in a bustling city far away. I see a prophet once again and hear his words of dedication. In the moment, I see the beginning of the fulfillment of the divine promises expressed that day. I am reminded that more than a land and a people were dedicated that special day. I too was dedicated.

JOHN W. WILCOX

John was born in California. During the Vietnam War, he served in the Army's 17th Cavalry as an instructor pilot assigned to the 18th Combat Aviation Company. It was his responsibility to check out all aviators in the Company, and insure that they knew their helicopters, and were able to perform their flight duties. Currently, John lives in Washington and serves as a seminary teacher.

CW3 John William Wilcox.

The war was winding down and combat units and men were being sent back to the states and home. Because of my flight ability and experience with combat flying I was reassigned to the Joint Military Commission Region VII. I was now assigned to the Embassy in Saigon. For me the war was still going on. My flight unit was small, and as such we became close. I was still performing my IP duties and training those men to fly with increased skills and ability. As I flew with those men, I would share the gospel whenever they would listen. Some would listen and some would not.

It was Sunday, another hot and humid day in Vietnam. I was playing with the Automatic Direction Finder radio and "BOOM" there it was, the *Spoken Word* from Salt Lake City.

Every Sunday morning thereafter I would tune in the ADF and listen to words of wisdom contained in the *Spoken Word* message. My weeks now revolved around Sunday, and the *Spoken Word* message. It was great!

There was political unrest back in the States. Every evening on the news my family would watch with horror as they showed helicopters and the missions they were flying. They knew that was my job and they worried and prayed for me. The war was coming to a close. Peace documents were being signed in Paris. We hoped we would be leaving too, but no such luck! The enemy were attacking and trying to take as much territory as possible before the cease-fire went into effect. It seemed that my bird and crew came under enemy fire every day. The damage was always superficial. No one was hurt while they flew in my Helicopter. I was humbled by the Priesthood blessings and how my life was being spared.

It was Saturday. I took my crew and we flew out towards the border of Cambodia. We were assigned to support a small detachment of Army personnel who were assigned to help with the peace keeping. The compound came under heavy enemy fire. Rockets and mortars began to fall all around. One

Orphaned children near the border of Cambodia who lost their lives when a 122-mm rocket landed in their school play yard.

large 122mm rocket landed in a school play yard. It was a school and home for orphaned children. When that rocket exploded the results were devastating. Dead and wounded children were everywhere.

As I evacuated the wounded and dead children, my heart went home to my young son and prayers that he would never have to see and live this nightmare. So much hurt, and now anger started to grow inside me . . . It wasn't fair . . . they were little innocent children. They were not part of this war. Now they were hurt, crying, and dying.

We finished the mission and headed back to base camp. In route back we learned by radio that one of our other Helicopters had been hit and there were casualties. Anthony was my roommate, and was reported dead. I hated this day! I hated this war! I was starting to develop hatred for everything.

LDS Servicemen's Group in front of Lane Army Helicopter. J. W. Wilcox is pictured fifth from the left.

Saturday Sunshine in Vietnam

Linda (Tami) Kurtz, an enthusiastic blonde from Walnut Creek, California, was born in Portland, Oregon. Tami has studied practically all types of dance: tap, ballet, modern jazz and even acrobatics. A graduate from BYU in speech and dramatic arts, her education also includes a semester's work in France. Her future plans include continuing for a Master's Degree in oral interpretation and broadcasting.

The girls of "Saturday Sunshine" aboard the USS Enterprise *entertain sailors on Thanksgiving just off the coast of Vietnam.*

Linda Williams served with the U.S.O. (United Services Organization) Tour group "Saturday Sunshine." Her group members were all LDS including three returned missionaries. The group served two tours traveling though Japan, Korea, the Philippines, Guam, Vietnam and Thailand.

The group always let people know they were LDS, so the LDS soldiers would come and talk to them. Linda writes, "As we traveled to firebases, we always carried a can of bread and a canteen of water so if we met any LDS soldiers we would be able to hold a sacrament meeting with them. I will never forget one sacrament meeting in the back of a building on the base at Pleiku, Vietnam with two very young-looking soldiers. As the boys blessed the Sacrament using our canned bread and water, I will never forget the beautiful, warm feeling as the spirit encompassed our little group in the middle of a hostile war and gave us a beautiful feeling of peace.

Each of us took a few copies of the Book of Mormon with us. We had written our testimony in the front of each book and we would give them to soldiers who appeared interested. I have always wondered if the books had an effect on the soldiers lives.

There is a line in my patriarchal blessing that says, "You will bring relief of body and spirit to those in need." I believe that our wonderful U.S.O. Tours fulfilled part of that statement. I felt it was a great privilege to serve our country and our soldiers in a small way by using talents with which we had been blessed."

Tami sitting in their USO truck in Pleiku, Vietnam.

We landed and I gave orders to my crew chief and co-pilot, turned in my reports, went to my hooch, and threw myself on my bunk. I sobbed tears of bitterness. I was so angry! It wasn't fair! Father where are you? Why them? Why now? They were little children! Anthony was my friend! He would help me, and I him when we were down and lonely. That night sleep came "hard"! The anger in my heart was "overwhelming".

Another day, another mission! I took my crew and we flew back to the Cambodian Border. We were flying re-supply missions, when the sounds of the *Spoken Word* came over the ADF radio. I was still carrying anger and hurt from the day before. I was not interested in listening this day. However "I had made a commitment!" so I listened. The message given that day was okay, but the closing song, "changed my life forever". It was, "God Be With You 'Till we meet again".

My heart softened that day. There was a peace and stillness. My anger and hate were gone, replaced by those sweet words, "God be with you till we meet again."

"Oh, Father In Heaven, please forgive me. They are with You." With a humble heart and tearful eyes I said good-bye. "I know they are in Your care. 'God be with you, till we meet again.'"

BOYD D. WILLIAMSON

Boyd served in World War II, the Korean War, and the Vietnam War. He was a lieutenant colonel in the Air Force during his Vietnam tour. While in Vietnam, he flew 344 combat missions and helped in the organization of a gunship unit based at Phan Rang. He flew many mercy missions, where they prevented the Viet Cong from overtaking villages. He retired from the military in 1971 and is now employed as a high school instructor.

Since the very early days of my boyhood, I had always wanted to become a pilot. This was motivated when a flyer landed his open cockpit, cloth-covered airplane on the nearby farm. Running to where he brought his airplane to a halt, I had countless questions to ask. The pilot gracefully answered them. I was hooked. Someday I had to be like him. This ambition was realized many years later when I was able to enter the aviation cadet program of the newly created U.S. Air Force.

One day in 1967 orders were received that would send me to Vietnam after some intermediate combat training in an airplane which was new to me. The AC-47 gunship was also known as "Spooky." Jungle survival training was also required. I have long-lasting memories of my departure from the U.S. on this particular assignment. On December 1, my mother and sister drove me to the Travis Air Force Base [California] passenger terminal where I boarded a civilian contract aircraft for the 16-hour flight to Saigon. Looking out the small round window of this airline airplane, I watched us fly over the Golden Gate Bridge and then watched the California coast gradually fade from sight. The flight attendant then put on a tape of Christmas music. That one tape played constantly for the entire flight. Imagine heading for Vietnam to engage in combat duties, with Christmas music playing such as "I'll Be Home For Christmas," "Here Comes Santa Claus," "I'm Dreaming of a White Christmas," and others. That music would be more appropriate for those who would be returning home from their combat tours aboard this airplane the following day.

I have many and varied memories of year 1968 in Vietnam. Two experiences remain indelible in my mind. One was having a non-G.I. dinner aboard a floating restaurant near Saigon. At my dinner table I was able to watch fighter planes make bombing and strafing runs just across the river, hardly a mile away. Then there was the attending of LDS chapel services at Bien Hoa Air Base. The chapel had been constructed earlier by some LDS members from large, wooden shipping crates. There was no glass in the window openings. Attendees sat on rough wooden planks with no backrests.

Years later when discussing this time period in my life, I have often been asked if I ever sought help from my Heavenly Father. The answer is always an emphatic "Yes." During the 344 combat missions flown, there were numerous cockpit conferences with my Creator seeking His help and guidance.

1968 Boyd Williamson in front of his unit's plane. In Vietnam, his unit was known as "Spooky." Note the Spooky ghost below the pilot's window.

1968 Boyd Williamson in front of the aft section of his "Spooky" gunship.

I prayed not only for myself, but also for the crews of my airplanes and the mission to which we had been assigned, plus others.

Other questions have sought out my opinion concerning the U.S. involvement in that South Vietnam conflict. My feelings are different than many others I have heard expressed. I believe in honoring commitments. The United States had made commitments to the South Vietnamese. Whether our involvement was right or wrong, we had obligations to the people in South Vietnam. I am proud to have been able to render my assistance. To me, such a commitment should be taken just as seriously as one made to a friend, or one taken in the pledging of allegiance at such events as flag ceremonies.

✳ ✳ ✳

GEORGE WILLMORE

Below: As Civil Affairs Officer, George Willmore was responsible for directing the civic activities of two villages, which allowed him to initiate humanitarian programs that won the minds and hearts of the Vietnamese.

Below right: George Willmore is carrying a Vietnamese child to the showers that the soldiers have just built as part of the personal hygiene program Willmore initiated as the 11th Aviation Group's Civil Affairs Officer for the An Khe area. This will be the young girl's first shower. Willmore's hygiene program reduced sick-call patients by 62 percent within the first two weeks. In addition, he distributed soap and toothpaste to villagers and increased medical supplies.

Above: Politics was an important part of Captain George Willmore's entire life. He would have resigned from the Army in order to fight for his country as a congressman instead of as a soldier if he had received 521 additional votes in Idaho's Democratic primary election of 1966. Captain George A. Willmore, army helicopter pilot, received a medal of valor while piloting a partially disabled aircraft damaged by Viet Cong ground fire that also wounded a crew member.

PHILIP W. WINKLER

Philip was drafted into the Army on December 4th, 1968. While in Vietnam he was assigned to the 199th Light Infantry Brigade. His responsibilities included that of squad leader and Platoon Sergeant. As an infantryman, most of his time was spent in the field. His platoon would go into the rain forest for a week to two weeks at a time, and then come into a fire support base for a few days and then go back out again. He currently lives in Colorado and works as a Lead Programmer Analyst. He serves as secretary of his high priests group.

Near the end of my thirty-day leave just before leaving for Vietnam, my father gave me a Priesthood blessing. He promised me that if I were faithful, I would return home safely. My patriarchal blessing also promised things that had not happened yet. I clung to these blessings; they gave me hope.

* * * * *

On March 21st, our platoon was by itself—we had been since the first or second day of this mission. At this time, Sgt. Lyle was training me to take over as squad leader. That day, our squad had point. Adams was on point; I was walking second and had the compass. It was my job to navigate, and to direct the point man where to go.

We had not gone far, not more than a couple of hundred yards, when we came under fire. Adams and I hit the ground immediately. As we lay there on the side of a hill, I saw the weeds move, apparently because of the rounds that went by, within eight to twelve inches of my head. After some return fire, the enemy eventually seemed to leave. We could not see anyone. There was dense undergrowth up there—a real tangle.

After a while the platoon began to move again, Adams and I still walking point and compass respectively. We came to a rocky area, and passed between two large rocks, about four to five feet high. The ground sloped down in front of us, and we could see only more jungle. Adams noticed on the ground in front of us, indications that someone may have gone through that spot ahead of us. Just then word came from behind us to hold up. For a few seconds we stood there: open, standing, stationary targets.

From not more than twenty or thirty yards away came the crack of automatic weapons. At that distance, with that kind of target, there was no reason to miss. In the first instant I thought I was a dead man. I had a heavy rucksack on my back, so the easiest way to go down was backward. In that first second I went down backward, but it was not a conscious decision. I had the odd but very distinct impression that I was pushed. As I went back I could feel chips of rock hitting my face, from where the rounds were striking the rock behind me.

I remember looking at Adams lying on the ground and thinking he was dead. But he was also unhurt. I quickly got behind a tree, and discovering that Adams was alive, helped him get behind it also. From that moment I never doubted that I would return. I know that the Lord intervened and saved my life. I think I came as close to living the counsel of Amulek in Alma 34:27 to continually have a prayer in your heart, as at any time in my life.

ROBERT JOHN WREN

Robert John Wren served as a Green Beret in Vietnam. As a member of a handpicked special forces team he experienced firsthand the combat realities of war.

The situation in Plei Me was much more desperate than we had anticipated. There were stacks of dead men at the front gate. We were all sickened by the smell of over a hundred bodies that had been lying, for days, in the heat of the sun. Before the siege was lifted, there would be many more dead men in those stacks. We discovered that an enemy battalion of over a thousand men had moved into position, and was poised for an attack. Even with the air support we were getting, it was clear to all of us that our small force could not repel a full attack by the enemy without sustaining very heavy casualties. Mortar rounds had been falling day and night for weeks, and continued to explode in camp, killing and maiming, while we were there. We were still hoping for the arrival of the armored battalion that had started into Plei Me four days before us, but which was still trying to get through the enemy encirclement.
Finding retreat likely, Wren's company received orders to make a wide sweep on the area in an attempt to clear an escape route if needed. He describes what happened next.

We left the relative safety of the camp and began moving across the empty field. I was patrolling near Captain Pusser as we got about halfway through the field. Suddenly a hidden enemy machine gun at the edge of the clearing began firing at us. Our men were being shot and were dropping all around me . . . everyone was in retreat, with the dead and dying lying all over the field. I felt the sting of an enemy bullet in my right hip.

Wren was then able to locate the source of the attack and return fire. As a result of his efforts and those of others the attack ended.

When the guns were all quiet, I turned to witness the scene of death spread before me. Why was I spared? The dead and dying were scattered around the field the way twigs lay under an old tree. Now that the fighting was over, the day seemed like any other day, except for the blood and sorrow lying before me, the silence of the countryside being broken by the moans of the dying.

A doctor at the camp removed the bullet in the hip and finding no bone damage, he simply stitched me up.
Then, while a platoon was sent out to retrieve the wounded and the bodies from the field, I found a C-ration meal and ate it under the protection of a sheet of metal that was leaned against a short wall. The moans of the wounded, the smell of the dead and the explosions of mortars were my only dinner companions. I thought of Barbara and the boys.

Taken from Michael S. Wren, *Faith under Fire: A True Story of Love, War, Faith and Miracles* (Orem, UT: Granite Publishing and Distribution, 2000), 66–68.

SOURCE CITATIONS

The name of each individual quoted in the book is listed below with a citation of the original source of the account. While most of the material in this book will be preserved in the Saints at War archive located in the L. Tom Perry Special Collections of the Harold B. Lee Library at Brigham Young University, some items have been previously published in other sources. For these special cases, a specific reference is provided. The accounts that were not previously published are identified as "SAW," indicating that the original source is in the Saints at War archive; the page numbers that follow refer to the manuscript of the veteran's account. When sources do not have page numbers, the citation reads n.p.

The book contains only a few of the many veteran accounts contained in the Saints at War archive. The collection is open to the public, and all are invited to examine the many other wonderful accounts of faith and courage placed in the archive by veterans and their families.

KOREAN WAR

Allan, Dean S.	SAW, n.p.
Anderson, Charles V.	SAW, n.p.
Anderson, Ruel E.	SAW, n.p.
Baldwin, Richard	Baldwin History, 7–10. L. Tom Perry Special Collections, Brigham Young University, Provo, Utah
Ball, Val Lyman	SAW, n.p.
Barnes, Richard M.	SAW, n.p.
Bleak, David B.	No source indicated.
Bowers-Irons, Timothy Hoyt	SAW, 67–67. L. Tom Perry Special Collections, Brigham Young University, Provo, Utah
Bradshaw, Howard W.	Letter to Chaplain Covington
Brimhall, Don S.	SAW, 22–26
Bunkall, Thomas Merlin	SAW, n.p.
Bunker, B. Allen	SAW, n.p.
Bush, Douglas P.	SAW, n.p., letter
Carlson, Ralph J.	SAW, n.p.
Carpenter, Carl H.	SAW, 9–10
Christensen, Joe J.	SAW, 11–13
Christensen, Thomas R.	Letter to SAW
Dailey, Joseph W.	SAW, n.p.
Dumas, William J.	SAW, 12–15, 19, 27–28
Fullmer, Ben C.	SAW, n.p.
Gailey, Ferrel S.	SAW, n.p.
George, Don A.	SAW, 5–6, 12–15
Gividen, Bert	SAW, 140–141, 161–162
Hansen, Homer K.	*Legend in Flight,* 50–54
Harrington, Phil C.	SAW, 7, letter
Head, Harry P.	SAW, 4–6
Heaton, H. Grant	SAW, n.p.

Henstrom, Richard H.	SAW, 1–2, 21–22
Hinckley, Eldon D.	Letter to SAW
Hickman, Don Rue	SAW, 105–106
Hill, James K.	Letter to SAW
Hulen, Alberta Jean Owens	SAW, n.p.
Jenkins, Clifton W.	SAW, n.p.
Jensen, Keith A.	SAW, 44–45
Johnson, Blaine H.	SAW, n.p.
Jones, Jack R.	Letter from secretary of Navy
Jones, John Milton	SAW, 5–6
Lloyd, Ray D.	SAW, n.p.
Martin, James D.	SAW, n.p.
Middleton, Ward	SAW, n.p.
Money, Mark L.	SAW, n.p.
Morgan, Glen D.	Account in possession of Dennis Wright Family.
Mullican, Lloyd R.	SAW, n.p.
Nelson, Elder Russell M.	SAW, oral interview, June 2003
Noorlander, Daniel O.	SAW, 38–40
Oyler, Lester J.	SAW, n.p.
Palmer, Spencer J.	SAW, n.p.
Parsons, Robert E.	SAW, 128–131
Pendleton, Keith	SAW, n.p.
Poulton, Gail Wesley	SAW, 10, 128–129, 131
Rector, Hartman, Jr.,	SAW, n.p.
Redden, Boyd J.	SAW, n.p.
Rowley, Arden Allen	SAW, 36, 50, n.p.
Runyan, George Richard	SAW, 26–32
Russell, Kenneth F.	SAW, Letter to SAW
Sandberg, George Woodard	SAW, n.p.
Seegmiller, William Garth	SAW, n.p.
Sessions, Marc H.	SAW, n.p.
Slover, Robert Henry	SAW, n.p.
Smith, Dean Morris	SAW, n.p.
Stephenson, Merlin J.	Letter to SAW
Sudweeks, Dean Alan	SAW, n.p.
Terry, Victor LeMar	SAW, n.p.
Thomas, Thayne Llewelly	SAW, 79
Tietjen, Melvin E.	SAW, 2–3
Tovey, Terrel R.	Account in possession of Dennis Wright Family.
White, Quentin H.	Biography, 32–43
Willes, Frank J.	SAW, n.p.

Wilson, Richard D.	SAW, n.p.
Wimmer, Leland Kent	"Korea: My Ups and Downs," autobiography, 140–142
Workman, Wesley Harold	Autobiography, 28–32

VIETNAM WAR

Adams, David D.	SAW, n.p.
Anderson, D. Larry	SAW, 1, 2, 9, 10, 14, 15, 18, 19, 21
Anderson, Stephen	SAW, n.p.
Andrews, Donald G.	SAW, n.p.
Banz, Robert K.	SAW, n.p.
Beason, Richard W.	W. Richard Beason, "Our Prayers Took Flight," *Ensign,* August 1994, 56
Biddulph, Stephen G.	SAW, 3, 4, 8, 11–13
Billings, Ronald	SAW, 5–6, 10
Bitter, C. Eldon	SAW, n.p.
Bradford, Craig S.	SAW, Craig S. Bradford, "Nevermore," unpublished manuscript, 13–14
Braithwaite, Douglas Charles	SAW, 4
Cannon, Donald Q.	SAW, n.p.
Chesley, Larry	SAW, J. A. Moss, typescript of fireside video of Larry Chesley speaking on 30 September, 2000.
Childs, Terry E.	SAW, n.p.
Clark, Sid	SAW, n.p.
Clayton, Jerry	SAW, n.p.
Coleman, Gerald S.	SAW, n.p.
Cox, Gary E.	SAW, n.p.
Cox, Richard D.	SAW, n.p.
Day, Alma L.	SAW, 1, 42, 44, 57–59
Decker, John	SAW, n.p.
Derrick, Thales A.	SAW, 1–3
Dinkelman, John	SAW, n.p.
Essex, William	SAW, n.p.
Featherstone, Stephen E.	SAW, n.p.
Fisher, Bernard F.	Editor's note, "The Gathering of Eagles," *Guideposts,* September 1967, 17
Foote, Dan	Foote History, 9, 27, 28, 32. L. Tom Perry Special Collections, Brigham Young University, Provo, Utah
Gardner, David	Gardner History, 8. L. Tom Perry Special Collections, Brigham Young University, Provo, Utah
Geddes, Garth Lowe	SAW, n.p.
Gunnel, Earl Leroy	SAW, n.p.
Hall, Doug	Hall History, 15–17. L. Tom Perry Special Collections, Brigham Young University, Provo, Utah

Hansen, Kent	SAW, 8–10
Hansen, Scott	SAW, n.p.
Herbert, Dave	SAW, clipping from *Box Elder Journal,* n.d.; submitted by Dave Herbert Family
Houghton, Bob	SAW, Garth Seegmiller, *Courage in the Sky with Pardo's Push,* 4–17
Huff, Michael	SAW, n.p.
Hughes, Robert	SAW, n.p.
Idle, Jim	SAW, n.p.
James, Dan	SAW, n.p.
Jenkins, Lawrence	SAW, n.p.
Johnson, Larry Richard	SAW, n.p.
Jorgensen, Terry M.	SAW, n.p.
Kallunki, John T.	SAW, transcript, "Hillam's War Project," oral interviews, 26 March 1985
Kelly, Paul H.	SAW, n.p.
Kigin, Judy Blackman	SAW, n.p.
Kigin, Michael J.	SAW, n.p.
Kovalenko, Virgil N.	Church Archives, MS 17326; Virgil Nicholas Kovalenko, Vietnam journal and group leader's desk calendar, 1971; SAW, transcript of oral interview, February 2003, n.p.
Larson, Paul B.	SAW, n.p.
Lathen, Calvin W.	SAW, n.p.
Lemon, Boyd R.	SAW, n.p.
Lemon, Tess G.	SAW, n.p.
Leuck, Frank	SAW, n.p.
Mallernee, John Robert	SAW, n.p.
Marks, Robert Truman	SAW, 3–4
Marshall, Steven	SAW, 3–5, 8
McClure, Roan	SAW, transcript of oral interview with Robert Freeman, October 2002, 14, 16
McLaughin, Roger	McLaughin, Robert, "A Vietnam Sunday," *The New Era,* January 1971, 12–14.
Meacham, J. Russell	Scott, George L. "South Vietnam, Thailand Dedicated for Missionaries," *Church News,* 19 November 1966, 5
Mecham, Dan	SAW, n.p.
Meyer, Henry L.	SAW, n.p.
Miller, Roy	SAW, n.p.
Newby, Claude D.	Claude D. Newby, *It Took Heroes: A Chaplain's Tribute to Vietnam Veterans and Those Who Waited for Them* (Springville, Utah: Bonneville Books, 1998), 3, 61, 94; Claude D. Newby, *It Took Heroes,* vol. 2 (Bountiful, Utah: Tribute Enterprises, 2000), 144
Nguyen, Van The	SAW, D. L. Hughes, "The Saigon Shepherd and the Scattered Flock," unpublished manuscript, 49–50
Nielson, Jay	SAW, n.p.
Nye, Rick	SAW, n.p.

Orme, Gordon R.	SAW, n.p.
Palmer, Mel	SAW, n.p.
Parson, Michael K.	SAW, *A Journal of the Life of Michael Parson,* 13, 18
Petty, William Clayton	SAW, n.p.
Pixton, Allan	SAW, n.p.
Reitze, Charles	SAW, n.p.
Richardson, Sam	SAW, n.p.
Richens, Reed	SAW, n.p.
Riding, Robert H., Jr.,	SAW, n.p.
Robison, Dennis	SAW, n.p.
Robison, Jerry	SAW, n.p.
Saldivar, John G	Sheri Dew, *Ezra Taft Benson: A Biography* (Salt Lake City: Deseret Book, 1987), 2, 3, 5, 6
Shuler, Brigham	Shuler History, 8–10. L. Tom Perry Special Collections, Brigham Young University, Provo, Utah
Shultz, Stanley	SAW, n.p.
Simmons, Jay R.	SAW, n.p.
Smith, David	SAW, n.p.
Smith, Farrell	SAW, n.p.
Smith, Gary	SAW, n.p.
Taylor, Hyde	SAW, n.p.
Tebbs, Calvin Douglas	SAW, n.p.
Tracy, Curtis L.	SAW, 7
Tyler, Thomas Lee	SAW, n.p.; Thomas Tyler, *Church News,* 25 February 1967, 9, 15
Vail, Eugene Cordell, Sr.	SAW, n.p.
Walters, P. Doug	SAW, n.p.
Webster, Daniel Lee	SAW, n.p.
Weed, Gordon	SAW, n.p.
Weeks, Werner Glen	SAW, transcript of oral interview, 7 March 1985
Westphal, Robert C.	SAW, n.p.
Whaley, Richard	SAW, n.p.
Wickman, Elder Lance B.	SAW, 3–9
Wilcox, John W.	SAW, n.p.
Williamson, Boyd D.	SAW, 1–2
Willmore, George	SAW, n.p.
Winkler, Philip	SAW, n.p.
Wren, Robert John	Michael S. Wren, *Faith under Fire: A True Story of Love, War, Faith, and Miracles* (Orem, Utah: Granite Publishing, 2000), 66–68.

PHOTO CREDITS

FRONT MATTER:

p. vi   Courtesy of Val Lyman Ball.

THE KOREAN WAR:

p. 2–3   Courtesy of National Archives Still Pictures Branch.

p. 4   Photo © Hisham Ibrahim/Photov.com/Alamy.

p. 7   Courtesy of National Archives Still Pictures Branch.

p. 8   Courtesy of Mark L. Money.

p. 9   Courtesy of National Archives Still Pictures Branch.

p. 11   Courtesy of National Archives Still Pictures Branch.

p. 12   All images courtesy of National Archives Still Pictures Branch.

p. 13   Courtesy of National Archives Still Pictures Branch.

p. 14   Courtesy of National Archives Still Pictures Branch.

p. 16   Top photo courtesy of Ruel E. Anderson. Bottom photo courtesy of National Archives Still Pictures Branch.

p. 18   Courtesy of National Archives Still Pictures Branch.

THE CHURCH AND THE KOREAN WAR:

p. 23   Courtesy of Val Lyman Ball.

p. 24   Courtesy of Richard H. Henstrom.

p. 25   "Special Tags Available for LDS Soldiers" *Church News,* Wednesday, May 9, 1951, 10.

p. 26   Courtesy of *Church News.*

p. 27   Courtesy of *Church News,* February 28, 1953.

p. 28   "LDS Chaplain Irons Commended for his 'Devotion, Ability'," *Church News.* Bottom photo courtesy of Mark L. Money.

p. 29   Left photo courtesy of Richard H. Henstrom. Right photo appeared with article called "LDS Boys in Korea Attend Conference" by Chaplain Lawrence R. Rast, courtesy of *Church News.*

p. 31   All images courtesy of Mark L. Money.

p. 33   All images courtesy Mark L. Money.

p. 34   Top photo courtesy of Robert Parsons. "Dr. Kim Leads LDS Group in Worship" newsaper clipping and photo of Korean Testimony Meeting courtesy of *Church News.*

p. 35   Courtesy of Robert Parsons.

p. 36   All images courtesy of Robert Slover.

p. 37   Seoul Korea Temple at the time of its dedication, courtesy of *Church News,* Dec. 14, 1985.

p. 39   Courtesy of Richard H. Henstrom.

KOREAN VETERAN ACCOUNTS:

p. 40–41   All images courtesy of Dean S. Allen.

p. 42–43   All images courtesy of Charles V. Anderson.

p. 44–45   All images courtesy of Ruel E. Anderson.

p. 46–47   All images courtesy of Val Lyman Ball.

p. 49   "LDS Servicemen Hold Conference in Korea,"courtesy of *Church News.*

p. 51–53   All images courtesy of Howard W. Bradshaw.

p. 54   Top image courtesy of Ferrel S. Gailey. Bottom image courtesy of Don S. Brimhall.

p. 56   All images courtesy of Don S. Brimhall.

p. 57   Courtesy of Thomas Merlin Bunkhall.

p. 61–63   All images courtesy of Ralph J. Carlson.

p. 64–65   All images courtesy of Carl H. Carpenter.

p. 66	Top image courtesy of Carl H. Carpenter. Bottom image courtesy of Joe J. Christensen.
p. 68	Courtesy of Joe J. Christensen.
p. 68–69	All images courtesy of Thomas R. Christensen.
p. 70	Courtesy of Joseph W. Dailey.
p. 72	Courtesy of Emma Weber, widow of Louis E. Weber.
p. 73	*The Daily Herald,* courtesy of William J. Dumas.
p. 74	Courtesy of National Archives Still Pictures Branch.
p. 75–76	Courtesy of Ben C. Fullmer.
p. 77–79	All images courtesy of Ferrell S. Gailey.
p. 81–83	All images courtesy of Don A. George.
p. 84–86	All images courtesy of Bert Gividen.
p. 88–89	All images courtesy of Homer Hansen.
p. 90, 92	Courtesy of Phil C. Harrington.
p. 93	All images courtesy of Harry P. Head.
p. 95–97	All images courtesy of Richard H. Henstrom.
p. 98	All images courtesy of Don Rue Hickman.
p. 100	Courtesy of National Archives Still Pictures Branch.
p. 102	Courtesy of Alberta Jean Owens Hulen.
p. 103	Courtesy of Keith A. Jensen.
p. 105	Courtesy of *Church News.*
p. 106	Images courtesy of Don R. Alger.
p. 109	Top image courtesy of John Milton Jones.
p. 109	Courtesy of National Archives Still Pictures Branch.
p. 111	Courtesy of Tom Christensen.
p. 114	All images courtesy of Ward T. Middleton.
p. 116–17	All images courtesy of Mark L. Money.
p. 118	Ford Ord church, courtesy of Mark L. Money.
p. 118	Glen D. Morgan courtesy of Dennis Wright.
p. 119	Courtesy of Lloyd R. Mullican.
p. 121	Courtesy of National Archives Still Pictures Branch.
p. 122–26	All images courtesy of Daniel O. Noorlander.
p. 127	Courtesy of Lester J. Oyler.
p. 129	All images courtesy of Spencer J. Palmer.
p. 131–35`	All images courtesy of Robert E. Parsons.
p. 136–37	All images courtesy of Keith Pendleton.
p. 138–41	All images courtesy of Gail Wesley Poulton.
p. 143	Newspaper article from *Deseret News: Church Section,* Wed. July 2, 1952.
p. 143	LDS Serviceman's group aboard USS *Philippine Sea*, courtesy of Harry P. Head.
p. 144–45	All images courtesy of Hartman Rector, Jr.
p. 147–50	All images courtesy of Arden Allen Rowley.
p. 154	Newspaper article from *Deseret News: Church Section,* 1951.
p. 157	Drawing by Lt. Gray, 1952, courtesy of William Garth Seegmiller; photo courtesy of William Garth Seegmiller.
p. 159–61	All images courtesy of Robert Henry Slover.
p. 163	All images courtesy of Dean Morris Smith.
p. 164	Courtesy of Merlin J. Stephenson.
p. 165–67	All images courtesy of Dean Allen Sudweeks.
p. 168	Courtesy of Victor LeMar Terry.
p. 169	Courtesy of Thayne Llewelly Thomas.
p. 170	Newspaper clipping from *Deseret News: Church Section.*
p. 171–72	All images courtesy of Melvin E. Tietjen.

p. 173	All images courtesy of Terrel R. Tovey.
p. 174	Top two images courtesy of Ned Martell Vowles; Bottom image courtesy of Ballard T. White.
p. 176	All images courtesy of Ballard T. White.
p. 179	Courtesy of Dean Morris Smith.
p. 182	Courtesy of National Archives Still Pictures Branch.
p. 185–86	All images courtesy of Dick Wilson.

THE VIETNAM WAR:

p. 190–91	Courtesy of National Archives Still Pictures Branch.
p. 192	Brand X Pictures/Alamy.
p. 194	Ho Chi Minh photo by Vo An Ninh.
p. 195	Courtesy of National Archives Still Pictures Branch.
p. 197	Courtesy of National Archives Still Pictures Branch.
p. 199	Photo by Nguyen Ngoc Rao, © Bettmann/CORBIS.
p. 200	F-4 Fighter Bomber, courtesy of Hill Aerospace Museum, Hill AFB, UT 84056-5842; F-111 Fighter Bomber, courtesy of Hill Aerospace Museum, Hill AFB, UT 84056-5842; UH-1D helicopters courtesy of National Archives Still Pictures Branch.
p. 201	Top image courtesy of Terry M. Jorgensen; center image courtesy of National Archives Still Pictures Branch; bottom photo by Dick Wilson.
p. 202	Courtesy of National Archives Still Pictures Branch.
p. 203	Photo by Dick Wilson.
p. 204	Courtesy of National Archives Still Pictures Branch.
p. 205	Courtesy of National Archives Still Pictures Branch.
p. 206	Courtesy of National Archives Still Pictures Branch.
p. 207	Photo by Dick Wilson.
p. 209	Courtesy of National Archives Still Pictures Branch.
p. 210	Courtesy of National Archives Still Pictures Branch.
p. 211	Courtesy of National Archives Still Pictures Branch.
p. 212	Courtesy of National Archives Still Pictures Branch.
p. 214	Photo by Dick Wilson.
p. 215	Photo by Dick Wilson.
p. 217	Top image: Vietnam Wall dedication © Wally McNamee/CORBIS. Bottom photo by Gene Marshall.

THE INFLUENCE OF THE CHURCH DURING THE VIETNAM WAR:

p. 218–19	Courtesy of George Willmore.
p. 220	Courtesy of Farrell Smith.
p. 221	Courtesy of Robert K. Banz.
p. 222	Map appeared in *Deseret News: Church Section.*
p. 223	Courtesy of Farrell Smith.
p. 225	All images courtesy of Virgil Kovalenko.
p. 226	Top image courtesy of Terry Jorgensen. Bottom image courtesy of Robert K. Banz.
p. 227	Top image courtesy of Thomas L. Tyler. Bottom image courtesy of Farrell Smith.
p. 228	Top image courtesy of Virgil Kovalenko. Bottom image courtesy of Thomas L. Tyler.
p. 229	All images courtesy of Roan McClure.
p. 231	All images courtesy of Virgil Kovalenko.
p. 232	Top image courtesy of Steven Marshall. Bottom image courtesy of Judy Kigin.
p. 233	Top photo courtesy of John Mallernee. Bottom photo courtesy of Judy Kigin.
p. 234	Top photo courtesy of Judy Kigin. Bottom photo courtesy of Terry Jorgensen.
p. 235	Top photo courtesy of Virgil Kovalenko. Bottom photo courtesy of Farrell Smith.
p. 236	Courtesy of Virgil Kovalenko.

p. 238	Courtesy of National Archives Still Pictures Branch.
p. 239	Courtesy of Mel Palmer.
p. 241	Courtesy of Terry Jorgensen.

VIETNAM VETERAN ACCOUNTS:

p. 242–43	All images courtesy of David D. Adams.
p. 244–45	Photos by Douglas Murphy. All images courtesy of D. Larry Anderson.
p. 246	Photo by Dick Wilson.
p. 247	Top photo by Douglas Murphy. All images courtesy of D. Larry Anderson.
p. 249	Top photo by Douglas Murphy. All images courtesy of D. Larry Anderson.
p. 251	Photo by Dick Wilson.
p. 253	All images courtesy of Donald G. Andrews.
p. 254–56	All images courtesy of Robert K. Banz.
p. 257	Courtesy of Richard W. Beason.
p. 260	Photo by Dick Wilson.
p. 263	Photo by Dick Wilson.
p. 264	Courtesy of C. Eldon Bitter.
p. 267	Courtesy of Donald Q. Cannon.
p. 270–71	All images courtesy of Terry E. Childs.
p. 273	All images courtesy of Sid Clark.
p. 275–76	Photos by Dick Wilson.
p. 279	Photo by Dick Wilson.
p. 282	Photo by Dick Wilson.
p. 285	Photo by Dick Wilson.
p. 287–88	All images courtesy of Alma Day.
p. 291–92	All images courtesy of John Decker.
p. 293	Top image courtesy of Thales A. Derrick. Bottom image courtesy of Hill Aerospace Museum, Hill AFB, UT 84056-5842.
p. 294	All images courtesy of Thales A. Derrick.
p. 297	Courtesy of Bill Essex, Jr.
p. 299–301	All images courtesy of Stephen E. Featherstone.
p. 303	Courtesy of Bernard Francis Fisher.
p. 304–05	Photo by Dick Wilson.
p. 312, 314	All images courtesy of Kent Hansen.
p. 315–16	All images courtesy of Scott Hansen.
p. 318	Courtesy of Dave Herbert.
p. 321	Photo by Dick Wilson.
p. 232	Courtesy of Michael Huff.
p. 234	Courtesy of Jim Idle.
p. 326–27	All images courtesy of Lawrence W. Jenkins.
p. 329–30	All images courtesy of Larry Richard Johnson.
p. 333–35	All images courtesy of Terry M. Jorgensen.
p. 338	Courtesy of Paul H. Kelly.
p. 340	All images courtesy of Judy Kigin.
p. 342–43	All images courtesy of Judy Kigin.
p. 345–46	All images courtesy of Virgil Kovalenko.
p. 348–49	All images courtesy of Virgil Kovalenko.
p. 349	Top image courtesy of Virgil Kovalenko. Bottom image courtesy of Dale Clawson.
p. 350–51	All images courtesy of Virgil Kovalenko.
p. 353	All images courtesy of Cal Lathen.
p. 357	Photo by Dick Wilson.

p. 358–60	All images courtesy of John Robert Mallernee.
p. 362–64	All images courtesy of Steven Marshall.
p. 367	All images courtesy of John Robert Mallernee.
p. 368–71	All images courtesy of Roan McClure.
p. 372–375	All images courtesy of Russell Meacham.
p. 376	All images courtesy of Dan Mecham.
p. 382	Top photo by Dick Wilson. Bottom photo courtesy of Virgil Kovalenko.
p. 384	Bottom two images courtesy of John Robert Mallernee.
p. 386	Courtesy of Gordon R. Orme.
p. 387	All images courtesy of Mel Palmer.
p. 389	Photo by Dick Wilson.
p. 391–94	All images courtesy of William C. Petty, M.D.
p. 395	Courtesy of Allan G. Pixton.
p. 396–98	All images courtesy of Charles A. Reitz.
p. 401	Photo by Dick Wilson.
p. 402–03	All images courtesy of Robert H. Riding, Jr.
p. 404	Courtesy of Dennis A. Robison.
p. 406	Courtesy of John G. Saldivar.
p. 408	Courtesy of Stanley Schultz.
p. 409	Courtesy of Hill Aerospace Museum, Hill AFB, UT 84056-5842.
p. 410	All images courtesy of Jay R. Simmons.
p. 411	Courtesy of David Smith.
p. 412–15	All images courtesy of Farrell Smith.
p. 418–19	Photo by Dick Wilson.
p. 420–21	All images courtesy of Curtis L. Tracy.
p. 423	Bottom photo by Thomas Lee Tyler.
p. 424–26	All photos by Thomas Lee Tyler.
p. 427	Left photo by Thomas Lee Tyler. Right photo courtesy of Thomas Lee Tyler.
p. 428–29	All photos by Thomas Lee Tyler.
p. 430	Photo by Jimmie W. Bynum. Courtesy of Thomas Lee Tyler.
p. 431	Top photo by Thomas Lee Tyler. Bottom photo by Jimmie W. Bynum, courtesy of Thomas Lee Tyler.
p. 432	All photos by Thomas Lee Tyler.
p. 434–35	All images courtesy of Eugene Cordell Vail, Jr.
p. 436–37	All images courtesy of P. Doug Walters.
p. 439–40	All images courtesy of Daniel Lee Webster.
p. 441–43	All images courtesy of Gordon H. Weed.
p. 446	Photo by Dick Wilson.
p. 447–48	All images courtesy of Robert C. Westphal.
p. 450	Photo by Dick Wilson.
p. 452–54	All images courtesy of Lance B. Wickman.
p. 455–57	All images courtesy of John W. Wilcox.
p. 458	All images courtesy of Linda Williams.
p. 460–61	All images courtesy of Boyd D. Williamson.
p. 462–63	All images courtesy of George Willmore.

INDEX

Vietnam,
    after WWII 195
    dedication of 227, 373
    map 195
Vietnamization 208, 213
Vietnam District Conference
    349
Vietnam Service Medal 190
Vietnam Veterans Memorial
    194, 217
Vietnam Veterans Memorial
    Wall 383
Vietnam Veterans Women's
    Memorial 217
Vietnam War, casualties of 216
    LDS stance on 218
    media coverage of 211
    protests against 204
Vietnam Veterans' Memorial
    352
Vietnam Zone 325
Vietnam, dedication of 227
Vietnamese Air Force Logistics
    Command 344
Vietnamization 208, 209
Voices in Vital America (VIVA)
    383
Voltaire 339
Vowles, Harold 187
Vowles, Ned Martell 174
Vy, Cong Ton Nu Tuong 235

Wahlstrom, Elmer W. 29
Wakefield, Brother 412
Walker, Major LeRoy J. 32
Walker, Walton 12
Walter Reed Army Medical
    Center 120
Walters, P. Doug 436, 437
Walters, Richard 78
Walton, John 344
Warsaw Hill 185
Washington Ward 26
Washington, George 172
Watergate 214
Watergate Hotel 213
Waterman, (Arden Allen
    Rowley account) 151
WAVE 102
Wayne, Steve 321
Weathermen 204

Webb, Ron 242
Weber, Louis Edward 72
Webster, Daniel Lee 438–40
Weed, Gordon H. 441–44
Weeks, Werner Glen 444–46
Welfare Day 35
Wellard, Gordon 143
Westmoreland, General
    William C. 202, 203, 204,
    206
Westphal, Robert C. 447–49
Whaley, Richard 449, 450
Whaley, Richard H. 380
Wheat, Jerry 238
Wheeler, Homer 147
White Horse Hill 14
White, Ballard T. 174–76
White, Norm 410
White, Quentin H.177–81
Whiting, Kelly 377
Whitman, Ray 249
Whittington, Howie 225
Wickman, Elder Lance B.
    451–54
Widstoe, John A. 30
Wilcox, John W. 455–57, 459
Wilinson, Brother 417
Will, Elizabeth 91
Willes, Frank J.181–84
Williams, Linda 458
Williamson, Boyd D. 459–61
Willmore, George 462, 463
Willmore, Geroge A. 218
Willorial, Robert R. 148
Wilson, Richard D. 184–86
Wimmer, L. Kent 187, 188
Wing Lead Crew 42
Winkler, Philip W. 464
Witcomb, Richard B. 176
Wolfhounds 99
Wood, Louise 110
Wood, Richard F. 380
Woods, John 161
Woods, Richard V. 143
Word of Wisdom 58, 145, 147,
    168, 174, 258, 271, 272,
    275, 276, 300, 302, 343,
    378, 399, 417, 450
Workman, Wesley Harold 188,
    189
Wren, Barbara 465

Wren, Robert John 465
WWII F4U Corsair 114

Xuan, Tran Thi 228

Yakota Air Force Base 154
Yokohama Harbor 62
Yokohama Servicemen's Branch
    342
Yokota Air Force Base 40
Young, George B. 380
Young, Major 412

Zedong, Mao 7, 8
Zippo 201

Printed in Canada

VIETNAM WA

1500s: Portuguese traders arrive in Vietnam seeking trade relationships.

1600s: French missionaries and traders arrive in Vietnam.

1860s: French establish French colony in Vietnam.

1880s: French use military force to create French Indochina.

1900: Various factions rebel against French domination.

1930: Ho Chi Minh organizes the Communist Party in Vietnam.

1940: France falls to Germany; Japan assumes control of Vietnam.

1941: Ho Chi Minh organizes the Vietminh to oppose Japanese occupation.

1943: Ho Chi Minh appeals to President Roosevelt for military assistance; the American OSS (Office of Strategic Services) supplies Ho Chi Minh forces.

1945: Japan surrenders, and the Vietminh declares Vietnam's independence; France sends troops to Vietnam to reclaim colony.

1946: Ho Chi Minh writes President Harry S. Truman asking for support; Truman refuses to help based on his opposition to communist expansion; Vietminh begins war with France.

1950: United States enters the Korean War; United States sends first military aid and advisors to Vietnam.

1953: Korean War ends.

1954: French surrender to Vietminh; Ho Chi Minh declares Vietnam free; Geneva Accord ignores Vietminh and partition Vietnam into North and South Vietnam; SEATO (Southeast Asia Treaty Organization) founded to oppose communist influence.

1955: Presidential elections held in South Vietnam; civil war between pro- and anti-government forces in South Vietnam.

OCT: U.S. Pres. John F. Kennedy decides to provide South Vietnamese Pres. Diem more equipment and advisers. Top aides recommend combat troop intervention; Kennedy disagrees.

National Liberation Front established to oppose South Vietnam government.

JULY 8: Maj. Dale Buis and Sgt. Chester Ovnand killed by guerrillas at Bien Hoa, the first Americans to die in what would be called the Vietnam Era; U.S. Pres. Dwight D. Eisenhower provides 1000 military advisors and financial aid to South Vietnam.

NOV 2: South Vietnamese President Diem and Nhu are murdered following coup staged by VN generals. NOV 22: U.S. Pres. Kennedy assassinated; by year end, 15,000 American military advisers in Vietnam, and U.S. provided more than $500 million in aid.

FEB 6: American Military Assistance Command formed in Saigon. By mid-1962, American advisers increased from 700 to 12,000.

Lyndon B. Johnson elected U.S. president; Gulf of Tonkin incident prompts U.S. to approve direct military involvement in Vietnam; OCT: China explodes first atomic bomb.

AUG: Henry Kissinger and North Vietnamese negotiato Xuan Thuy meet secretly in Paris to start discussions of e ing war; U.S. military streng reaches 400,000 by year-end

Operation "Rolling Thunder" bombing campaign begins; first U.S. combat troops arrive in Vietnam; DEC: American military strength increases to 200,000; bombing of North Vietnam continues throughout year.

JAN 23: U
JAN: Battl
begins wit
attacking
troops in
talks begir
ends; Rich

Operatio
and "June
troop stre
listed at 5

1500s–1955 | 1959 | 1960 | 1961 | 1962 | 1963 | 1964 | 1965 | 1966

MID–LATE 1950S: A few LDS civilians, diplomats work in Vietnam.

First non-English-speaking stake organized in Netherlands.

Three Vietnamese sisters baptized (Ha sisters)—first of their population; Elder Gordon B. Hinckley's first visit to Vietnam.

Among American advisers in Saigon are several LDS members, including families of military members. (Maurice Lee and the Cecil Cavender family form the first LDS branch; perform first baptism of record: John Talbot Mulleneaux, USAF captain.) First official LDS Church service held in Vietnam; first LDS servicemen's group organized in Vietnam.

LDS servicemen's group organized at Bien Hoa Air Base in Vietnam; LDS chapel erected at Bien Hoa; Selective Service requirements limit each ward to one missionary every six months; Vietnam made one of the four zones of the Southern Far East Mission; 1,500 LDS servicemen in Vietnam.

First LDS chaplain assigned t Vietnam; Church provides se men's kits for distribution by and branch leaders; estimated 2,200 LDS servicemen in Vie Church authorizes green tem garments to comply with arm ulations; Nguyen Cao Minh becomes first Vietnamese bro to receive priesthood; OCT: E Marion D. Hanks and Gordo Hinckley hold conferences throughout Vietnam—in Saig Elder Hinckley dedicates land preaching of Gospel. By this South Vietnam is divided into major districts with more tha LDS servicemen's groups scat throughout the land.

Elder
make
visit
Thre
distri
ized

STATISTICS (1960-1972)

- 58,000 Americans died
- 300,000 Americans wounded
- 2,500 Americans listed as MIA or POW
- 1,500,000 Vietnamese killed in action
- 300,000 Vietnamese listed as MIA or POW

- Approx. 15,000 LDS members went through Vietnam during the span of the war. (Includes military in uniform, civilians at the embassy and consulate staffs, civilian aid workers and civil engineers, repairmen from many logistical bases in the U.S., as well as Australian, British, New Zealanders and Koreans who were members.)
- 63 LDS chaplains served in the war
- According to Saigon Branch records, there were approx. 200 Vietnamese members
- 23 LDS Vietnamese families were found by VASAA and elements of 16 of those families were extracted or assisted to leave Vietnam between 1983-1997.
- Church membership doubled (1.6 million to 3.2 million) during Vietnam War
- 85,000 full-time missionaries set apart during Vietnam War
- Three temples dedicated (Oakland, Ogden, Provo) during Vietnam War